D1245868

 INSIGHT GUIDES

GREAT GARDENS OF
BRITAIN & IRELAND

DISCOVERY CHANNEL

APA PUBLICATIONS
Part of the Langenscheidt Publishing Group

Editorial
Editor
Dorothy Stannard
Design
Tanvir Virdee
Picture Editor
Hilary Genin
Editorial Director
Brian Bell

Distribution

UK & Ireland
GeoCenter International Ltd
The Viables Centre, Harrow Way
Basingstoke, Hants RG22 4BJ
Fax: (44) 1256 817988
United States
Langenscheidt Publishers, Inc.
46–35 54th Road, Maspeth, NY 11378
Fax: 1 (718) 784 0640
Canada
Thomas Allen & Son Ltd
390 Steelcase Road East
Markham, Ontario L3R 1G2
Fax: (1) 905 475 6747
Australia
Universal Press
1 Waterloo Road
Macquarie Park, NSW 2113
Fax: (61) 2 9888 9074
New Zealand
Hema Maps New Zealand Ltd (HNZ)
Unit D, 24 Ra ORA Drive
East Tamaki, Auckland
Fax: (64) 9 273 6479
Worldwide
Apa Publications GmbH & Co.
Verlag KG (Singapore branch)
38 Joo Koon Road, Singapore 628990
Tel: (65) 6865 1600. Fax: (65) 6861 6438

Printing

Insight Print Services (Pte) Ltd
38 Joo Koon Road, Singapore 628990
Tel: (65) 6865 1600. Fax: (65) 6861 6438

©2003 Apa Publications GmbH & Co.
Verlag KG (Singapore branch)
All Rights Reserved
First Edition 2003

CONTACTING THE EDITORS
We would appreciate it if readers
would alert us to errors or outdated
information by writing to:
Insight Guides, P.O. Box 7910,
London SE1 1WE, England.
Fax: (44) 20 7403 0290.
insight@apaguide.co.uk

www.gardens-guide.com
www.insightguides.com

ABOUT THIS BOOK

This guidebook combines the interests and enthusi-
asms of two of the world's best-known information
providers: Insight Guides, whose titles have set the
standard for visual travel guides since 1970, and Discovery
Channel <*www.discovery.com*>, the world's premier
source of nonfiction television programming.

The book, the only fully illustrated guide to the gardens
of the British Isles, features more than 320 of the best
gardens open to the public. Those in England are organised
by region (sub-divided into counties) while the less
numerous gardens of Scotland, Wales and Ireland are
grouped by country. All gardens are plotted on the regional
maps. The yellow pages at the back of the book contain
useful addresses and websites, a glossary of garden terms
and a further reading list.

The editorial team

This book was put together by Insight editor **Dorothy
Stannard** in collaboration with the **Armchair Travel
Company**, whose website <*www.gardens-guide.com*>
was the source for the text and many of the photographs.
In addition, Insight Guides commissioned two highly
respected garden historians to provide introductory
essays. The first, **Candida Lycett-Green**, the author of
several books on the great gardens and houses of Britain
– including one on Highgrove, co-authored with the
Prince of Wales – traces the history of garden design from
the physic gardens of medieval monks through to the
grand projects of the great 18th- and 19th-century landscape designers. The second, **Maggie Campbell-Culver**,
author of the acclaimed *The Origin of Plants*, explains
why the British Isles have become one of the richest
regions in the world for horticulture.

The photographs are the work of many different people
(*see Art & Photo Credits, page 338*), including a number of
garden owners, but some of the most evocative images were
taken by the well-known specialist garden photographers
Andrew Lawson and **Jerry Harpur**.
Picture research was handled by
Hilary Genin. In addition, **Tanvir
Virdee** worked on the design,
Pam Barrett helped edit the
text, and the proof-reading
and indexing were completed by **Sylvia Suddes** and
Elizabeth Cook respectively.

COVER: topiary
at Levens
Hall,
Cumbria.

LEFT:
Knightshayes
Court, Devon.

BELOW: a trug
of onions.

INSIGHT GUIDE
GREAT GARDENS OF
BRITAIN & IRELAND

CONTENTS

Maps

Great Britain
and Ireland
Inside Front Cover

London and the
Northern Home
Counties **38**

The Southeast **62**

Dorset, Hampshire
and Wiltshire **94**

Gloucestershire
and Oxfordshire **126**

The Southwest **146**

East Anglia **184**

Central England **208–9**

The North **248–9**

Scotland **280**

Wales **304**

Ireland **320**

ABOVE RIGHT: Hidcote Manor,
Gloucestershire

Introduction

Insight's Top Ten
Gardens **8–9**
The History of
Garden Design.....**17**
A Wealth of Plants. **23**
Introduction to
Gardens listings **31**

Gardens

**LONDON AND THE
NORTHERN HOME
COUNTIES**

LONDON &
MIDDLESEX

Chelsea Physic
Garden **37**
Chiswick House **39**
Ham House **39**
Hampton Court
Palace **40**
Kew Gardens **41**
Myddleton House ..**42**
Syon Park **42**

BERKSHIRE

Frogmore **43**
Waltham Place **44**

BUCKINGHAMSHIRE

Ascott **45**
Chenies Manor **45**
Cliveden **46**
Stowe **47**
Turn End **47**
Waddesdon Manor **48**
West Wycombe
Park **49**

ESSEX

Amberden Hall **50**
Audley End **50**
Beth Chatto.......... **51**
The Gibberd **52**
Glen Chantry **52**
Saling Hall............ **53**

Leeds Castle 67
Mount Ephraim 68
Nettlestead Place.. 68
Penshurst Place.... 69
Scotney Castle...... 70
Sissinghurst
    Castle 70

SURREY
Claremont 72
Loseley Park 73
Painshill 73
Polesden Lacey 74
RHS Wisley 74
Savill Garden
    (Windsor Gt Park)..75
Valley Gardens
    (Windsor Gt Park) 76

EAST SUSSEX
Bateman's............ 77
Clinton Lodge 78
Great Dixter 78
Monk's House 79
Pashley Manor...... 79
Royal Pavilion,
    Brighton 80
Sheffield Park 81

WEST SUSSEX
Borde Hill 82
Denmans 82
High Beeches 83
Highdown 84
Leonardslee 84
Nymans 85
Parham House 86
Petworth House 87
Sculpture at
    Goodwood.......... 87
Wakehurst Place .. 88
West Dean 89

DORSET, HAMPSHIRE &
WILTSHIRE

DORSET
Abbotsbury 93
Athelhampton 94
Cranborne Manor ..95
Forde Abbey.......... 96
Kingston Lacy 97
Kingston
    Maurward 97
Knoll 98
Mapperton 98
Minterne 99
Sticky Wicket 100

HAMPSHIRE
Bramdean House 101
Brandy Mount 102
Exbury................ 103
Fairfield 103
Furzey 104
Gilbert White's.... 104
Heathlands 105
Hinton Ampner.... 106
Houghton Lodge.. 107
Longstock Park .. 108
Manor House...... 108
Mottisfont Abbey 109
Sir Harold Hiller
    Gardens &
    Arboretum 110
Spinners 111
West Green 112

WILTSHIRE
Bowood 113
Corsham 114
The Courts 114
Heale 116
Home Covert 117
Iford Manor 118
Longleat 118

Stourhead 119
Stourton House .. 120
Wilton House 121

GLOUCESTERSHIRE &
OXFORDSHIRE

GLOUCESTERSHIRE
Barnsley 125
Batsford 126
Bourton House .. 127
Dyrham Park 128
Hidcote Manor 128
Kiftsgate..............129
Painswick 130
Rodmarton Manor 131
Sezincote 131
Snowshill Manor 132
Stancombe Park.. 133
Westbury Court .. 134
Westonbirt 135

OXFORDSHIRE
Brook Cottage 135
Broughton Castle 136
Buscot Park 137
Greys Court 137
Pettifers 138
Rousham House 139
Skippet 139
Stansfield 140
Waterperry 141

THE SOUTHWEST
CORNWALL
Antony House 145
Bosvigo 147
Caerhays Castle.. 147
Chyverton 148
Cotehele 148
The Eden Project 149
Glendurgan 150

HERTFORDSHIRE
Benington Lordship 54
Gardens of the
    Rose 54
Hatfield House...... 55
Knebworth House 56
St Paul's Walden
    Bury 57

THE SOUTHEAST
KENT
Belmont 61
Chartwell 61
Church Hill Cottage 63
Emmetts 64
Godinton 64
Goodnestone Park 65
Great Comp.......... 66
Hever Castle 66

continued overleaf ▷

EXPLORE YOUR WORLD®

Map Legend

—··—	International Boundary
——	National Boundary
-----	County Boundary
✈ ✈	Airport: International/Regional
✳	Garden/Arboretum

All gardens are coordinated by number with a full-colour map (e.g. ❶), and a symbol at the top of every right-hand page tells you where to find the map.

Gardens /continued

Heligan 150
Lanhydrock 151
Mount Edgcumbe 152
Pencarrow 152
Pine Lodge 153
St Michael's
  Mount 154
Trebah 155
Trelissick 155
Trengwainton 156
Tresco
  (Isles of Scilly).. 157
Trevarno 157
Trewithen............ 158

DEVON
Arlington Court.... 159
Buckland Abbey .. 160
Burrow Farm 160
Castle Drogo 161
Coleton Fishacre 162
Dartington Hall .. 163
Killerton 164
Knightshayes 165
Marwood Hill 166
Overbecks 167
RHS Rosemoor .. 168
Saltram 169
Tapeley Park 170
University of Exeter
  Botanic Garden 170

SOMERSET
Barrington Court 171
Cothay Manor 172
Dunster Castle.... 172
East Lambrook
  Manor 173
Gaulden Manor .. 174
Greencombe 174

Hadspen 175
Hestercombe 175
Lady Farm............176
Lytes Cary Manor 177
Milton Lodge 177
Montacute House 178
Prior Park 179

EAST ANGLIA

CAMBRIDGESHIRE
Abbots Ripton
  Hall.................. 183
Anglesey Abbey .. 184
Crossing House .. 185
University Botanic
  Garden 186
Wimpole Hall 187

NORFOLK
Blickling Hall 189
Bradenham Hall .. 190
Courtyard 191
Dell, Bressingham 191
East Ruston Old
  Vicarage 192
Fairhaven 193
Felbrigg Hall........ 194
Houghton Hall 194
Mannington Hall.. 195
Oxburgh Hall 196
Sheringham Park 197

SUFFOLK
Euston Hall 198
Haughley Park 198
Helmingham Hall 199
Ickworth 200
North Cove Hall .. 201
Shrubland Park .. 201
Somerleyton Hall 202
Wyken Hall 203

CENTRAL ENGLAND

BIRMINGHAM AREA
Birmingham Botanical
  Gardens 207
Castle Bromwich
  Hall.................. 208
University Botanic
  Garden 210

CHESHIRE
Arley Hall............ 211
Hare Hill 212
Lyme Park 213
Ness Botanic 214
Norton Priory 214
Rode Hall 215
Tatton Park 216

DERBYSHIRE
Calke Abbey........ 217
Chatsworth 217
Dam Farm House 218
Elvaston Castle .. 219
Haddon Hall........ 219
Kedleston Hall 220
Melbourne Hall .. 220
Renishaw Hall 221

HEREFORDSHIRE &
WORCESTERSHIRE
Burford House 222
Eastgrove Cottage 223
Hergest Croft...... 224
Stone House
  Cottage 224

LEICESTERSHIRE
Long Close 225
Orchards 226

LINCOLNSHIRE
Belton House **226**
Grimsthorpe
  Castle **227**
Gunby Hall **228**

NORTHAMPTONSHIRE
Canons Ashby
  House **229**
Coton Manor
  Gardens **230**
Cottesbrooke Hall **230**
Holdenby House ..**231**
Kelmarsh Hall **232**
Sulgrave Manor .. **233**

NOTTINGHAMSHIRE
Clumber Park **234**
Felley Priory **235**
Newstead Abbey **235**

SHROPSHIRE
Hodnet Hall **237**

STAFFORDSHIRE
Biddulph Grange **238**
Dorothy Clive **239**
Shugborough **240**

WARWICKSHIRE
Farnborough Hall ..**241**
Packwood House **242**
Upton House **242**
Woodpeckers **243**

THE NORTH
CUMBRIA
Charney Well **247**
Holehird **249**
Holker Hall **250**
Levens Hall **250**

Muncaster Castle **251**
Sizergh Castle **252**

DURHAM
Eggleston Hall **253**

GREATER MANCHESTER
Dunham Massey **254**

LANCASHIRE
Gresgarth Hall **255**

MERSEYSIDE
Croxteth Hall &
  Country Park **256**

NORTHUMBERLAND
Alnwick **257**
Belsay Hall **258**
Bide-a-Wee
  Cottage **259**
Cragside **259**
Howick Hall **260**
Wallington **261**

N & E YORKSHIRE
Aldby Park **262**
Beningbrough
  Hall **263**
Castle Howard **263**
Duncombe Park .. **264**
Harlow Carr **265**
Newby Hall **266**
Parcevall Hall **267**
Rievaulx Terrace &
  Temples **268**
Ripley Castle **268**
Studley Royal and
  Fountains Abbey **269**
The Valley **270**

S & W YORKSHIRE
Bramham Park **271**
Brodsworth Hall .. **271**
Harewood House **272**
Wentworth Castle **273**

SCOTLAND
Arduaine **277**
Benmore Botanic **277**
Biggar Park **278**
Branklyn **279**
Brodick Castle **281**
Broughton Place.. **282**
Carnell **283**
Castle Kennedy .. **284**
Cawdor Castle **284**
Cluny House **285**
Crarae **286**
Culzean Castle.... **287**
Dawyck Botanic .. **288**
Drummond Castle **288**
Glenarn **289**
Glendoick **290**
Greenbank **290**
House of
  Pitmuies............**291**
Inverewe **292**
Kailzie **293**
Leith Hall........... **294**
Little Sparta **295**
Logan Botanic
  Garden **295**
Manderston **296**
Pitmedden **297**
Royal Botanic Garden,
  Edinburgh **298**
Threave Garden .. **299**

WALES
Bodnant **303**

Cae Hir **305**
Chirk Castle........ **306**
The Dingle **307**
Dolwen **307**
Erddig **308**
Hilton Court **309**
Pant-yr-Holiad **310**
Penrhyn Castle.... **310**
Plas Newydd **311**
Plas Penhelig...... **312**
Powis Castle **313**

IRELAND
NORTHERN IRELAND
Castlewellan........ **317**
Mount Stewart.... **318**
Rowallane **319**

REPUBLIC OF IRELAND
Ballymaloe **321**
Birr Castle **322**
Butterstream **322**
Derreen **323**
Dillon **324**
Earlscliffe **324**
Fota Arboretum .. **325**
Glenveagh Castle **326**
John F. Kennedy ......
  Arboretum **327**
Lakemount **328**
Mount Usher **329**
Powerscourt **330**
Primrose **331**
Talbot Botanic **331**

DIRECTORY
Useful
  Information........ **332**
Art & Photo
  Credits **338**
Index.................. **339**

Westonbirt Arboretum *Gloucestershire [p135]*. The national arboretum, Westonbirt contains some 18,000 specimen trees in 600 acres (240 hectares) of Cotswold countryside.

Royal Botanic Gardens Kew *London [p41]*. Kew is the world's first and greatest botanic garden. Its spectacular glasshouses are masterpieces of Victorian engineering.

Longstock Park Water Gardens *Hampshire [p108]*. Fed by the River Test, this is a languorous sequence of serene pools and lushly planted islands linked by bridges.

Stowe Landscape Gardens *Buckinghamshire [p47]*. The grandest of England's many 18th-century landscape gardens, Stowe contains more than 30 temples and monuments.

Great Dixter *East Sussex [p78]*. Inspiration for the plantsman is found in abundance at the home of the gardener and writer Christopher Lloyd.

Ballymaloe *Republic of Ireland [p321]*. The ultimate kitchen garden, this is a feast for all the senses, providing fruit, herbs and vegetables for the Ballymaloe Cookery School.

Alnwick Castle *Northumberland [p257]*. Audacious modern landscaping has made the Alnwick Garden the most talked-about garden design since the Eden Project.

Levens Hall *Cumbria [p250]*. The desire to tame nature is taken to extremes at Levens Hall. The huge topiary is breathtaking, but also disturbingly surreal.

RHS Wisley *Surrey [p74]*. A garden for all tastes and all seasons, RHS Wisley delights and educates its visitors at every turn.

The Eden Project *Cornwall [p149]*. More theme park than garden, the Eden Project is futuristic, fascinating and fun – and getting better year by year.

Aloe Africana humilis spinis inermibus & verrucosis obsita Com. prael.
Vintners Barge-house.
Tallow Chandlers Barge-house
Apothecarys Barge-house.

THE HISTORY OF GARDEN DESIGN

Garden historian Candida Lycett-Green traces the development of gardens in Britain and Ireland, from medieval physic gardens to the great landscapes of Humphry Repton and Capability Brown

Our relationship with the land springs from a primal instinct. Since time immemorial we have sought to contrive the landscape for a variety of reasons, and the legacies of our Neolithic forbears still serve to stir the soul. In Britain, the great earthwork of Maiden Castle in Dorset, its curvaceous contours flowing around the hilltop, the myriad stone circles in wild and lonely places up and down the land, and the abstract informality of the White Horse depicted on the chalk down above Uffington in Wiltshire are proof that art is a continuing process and testament to an underlying need for beauty in landscape.

The British Isles are among the most geologically complicated areas in the world. In consequence their gardens are as varied as the soils they bloom in, and their gardeners, constricted by conditions, have emerged as some of the most confident and best gardeners of all. Few countries can match the great contrasts that these islands provide, from hidden temples among the old, red, sandstone peaks of the Kaha mountains in Ireland to the sylvan elegance of the Palladian bridge over the lake at Stowe in Buckinghamshire, or from the stark simplicity of Little Sparta, Ian Hamilton Finlay's moorland garden in Scotland, to the tumultuous explosions of colour around the deep tiled roofs and tall chimneys of Great Dixter in Sussex.

PRECEDING PAGES: Gresgarth Hall, Lancashire; Great Dixter, East Sussex; Goodnestone Park, Kent.

LEFT: map of the Chelsea Physic Garden (1751).

Foreign influences

BELOW: *Lilium lancifolium* (tiger lily).

Though religion, defence and agriculture had been the primary shapers of the British landscape in prehistoric times, it was the Romans who introduced the concept of gardening for aesthetic purposes. They also brought almonds, sweet cherries, figs, peaches and grapes, and their villas often contained decorative gardens within their confines. When they began to leave our shores, however, their great gardens, such as Fishbourne in Sussex and the sweeping terraces in Swindon's hinterland, were lost in undergrowth. It wasn't until various monastic orders, from the 5th century onwards, began to make physic gardens using herbs for medicine and beds of flowers for holy festivals that the seed of plantsmanship was first sown.

It was the Crusades from the 11th century onwards which really set Britain's gardening ball rolling. The Holy Land was on the edge of both worlds. Islamic gardening was by then highly advanced compared to that of the West: water was used sparingly and elegantly, and flowers, sometimes grown in the patterns of a Persian carpet, were set in large courtyards. Western Europe was suddenly wakened to the riches of the Orient.

The crusaders returned with new ideas and new plants, most famously the red and white striped rose Rosamundi. Enclosed gardens became more fanciful as time went by, displaying wild flowers in their lawns, arbours of roses and flower bed divisions with lattice fencing. Medieval monarchs began to express their status through their gardens. Perhaps the most famous was Henry VIII's garden at Hampton Court Palace, which contained depictions of the royal coat of arms at every turn.

Above:
image from a
florilegium
by Van de
Passe
(1614–15).

The Renaissance garden

By the 1500s the Renaissance garden began to develop, not only around royal palaces but around the great houses of England. The Italians had taken the arts and sciences to new heights and as a result of the growth of commerce and the huge accumulation of wealth, art in all its forms flourished. Renaissance theologians thought that all God's handiwork should be gathered together in one place, and important botanical gardens sprang up in European seats of learning. The Oxford Botanical Garden, the oldest in Britain, was founded by Henry Danvers in 1621, inspired by physic gardens he had seen at Padua in Italy and Leiden in Germany. Its function was to promote learning and glorify the works of God. Gradually gardens became symbols of power but the basic structure of a walled enclosure containing a fountain and a flower bed, called Hortus Conclusus, remained. The 15th-century Italian Leon Battista Alberti produced books reiterating the site designs defined centuries before by Pliny, and a steady stream of garden literature provided inspiration for ever more elaborate knot gardens. The British began to enjoy creating different patterns within a framework, often inspired by the most glamorous gardens of all at the Villa D'Este and the Vatican Belvedere in Italy, as well as the Royal Gardens at Blois and Fontainebleau in France.

The most famous name to come from this period was Salomon de Caus, a Huguenot from Normandy who had studied Italian gardens at the end of the 16th century in detail. De Caus had a tremendous influence on England's Sir Thomas Vavasour, who created the famous Hortus Pembrochianus for the 4th Earl of Pembroke at Wilton House near Salisbury, a reflection of the ideals of the court of Charles I. Such was its glory that it gained European fame. The gardens of the aristocracy got ever larger – avenues and vistas radiated for miles from stately piles like the rays of the sun.

FORMALITY RULES THE 17TH CENTURY

It was the French who dominated 17th-century gardening in Europe. Andre Le Nôtre, who created the garden at Vaux-le-Vicomte with its terraces, manicured grass, broad gravel paths, statuary and perfectly trimmed evergreens, set the grand standard which the British then translated in their own gardens. The gardens at Audley End in Essex were on a stupendous scale.

Tulips and new and exotic plants were arriving from foreign parts and much the most celebrated plant collector of his time, John Tradescant, began the great British tradition of pioneering plant collecting, which continues to this day.

By 1700 the formal garden had reached its zenith, and William of Orange introduced a fashion for Dutch gardens in which exaggerated topiary hedges lined endless gravel walks. Nearly every great garden of any note was surrounded by complicated geometrical patterns. There was a rigidity and a formality about them which generally suited the symmetry of the new houses rising up during this golden age of building.

Few of these formal gardens remain today, for the 18th century heralded a radical new gardening movement that decreed, in the words of the garden designer William Kent, "nature abhors a straight line". The English Landscape Movement swept away many a formal garden and replaced it with a contrived informality. The Hortus Pembrochianus *(see above)* was razed to the ground in one fell swoop.

ABOVE
Badminton
House.

BELOW:
Capability
Brown.

Winding walks and looping lakes

The 18th-century English landscape garden is arguably one of Britain's great contributions to European art. Garden designers such as William Kent, Charles Bridgeman, Capability Brown, Sir William Chambers and Humphry Repton advised their clients to replace their formal gardens with winding walks, looping lakes and natural-looking plantings of trees. This romantic approach went hand in hand with the paintings of such artists as Claude Lorrain and Nicholas Poussin, which told of mythology and the appreciation of classic art and architecture, and Edmund Burke's book *The Beautiful and the Sublime*. By the end of the 18th century false rock formations simulating England's Lake District, and grottos of tufa stone resembling stalactited coastal caves abounded in gardens and parks and some style-conscious aristocrats even employed hermits to inhabit the hermitages they had built in groves of trees.

William Kent's fashioning of the garden at Rousham near Oxford *(see page 139)* remains one of the greatest legacies of this 18th-century landscape ideal, and the classical serenity of the park at Stowe in Buckinghamshire displays the idea on a grander scale. Not everything, however, suggested a natural arcadia or a Greek grove. Many inventive designers came out of this century, such as Thomas Wright, an astronomer and philosopher who created arbours and summerhouses in rustic, Gothic, Palladian and castellated styles at Shugborough in Staffordshire and Badminton in Gloucestershire. Batty Langley produced pattern books of garden lodges and an eclectic range of garden ornamentation began to proliferate. The smaller manor houses and rectories retained their flower gardens, but not in such rigid forms as had gone before.

The Victorian art of bedding

The 19th century witnessed ever more fanciful flower gardens and a burgeoning of brave and different ideas. At Sezincote in Gloucestershire, for instance *(see page 131)*, a Moghul garden unfurled across an unsuspecting Cotswold landscape, displaying Indian temples, onion-shaped domes and the flaunting of its owners' long service in the East India Company. A gardening hero of the early Victorian period was the Scotsman John Claudius Loudon, who was a follower of the Scottish philosopher Archibald Alison. He believed that a garden should be seen to be a work of art. To this end he believed in artifice and in planting trees in isolation

ABOVE:
Joseph
Paxton's
Chatsworth.

from each other and composing a garden of non-native species. He was against deceiving the eye by pretending nature had created the garden. The art of bedding out was born and proliferated around the many new villas that were springing up on the edges of cities. The architect Charles Barry, assisted by William Nesfield, laid out terraces in a style adapted from the Italians around the garden at Trentham in Staffordshire. By the middle of the century many practitioners, notably Joseph Paxton at Chatsworth *(see page 217)* and George Kennedy at Bowood *(see page 113),* were creating strong architectural gardens to be seen from the windows of the house. Another favourite of the new rich was Harold Peto, who designed a series of waterfalls at Buscot House in Oxfordshire *(see page 137).*

The Industrial Revolution created untold wealth and the building of ornate Victorian houses with lavish gardens. Perhaps the most startling of all was Waddesdon Manor, the home of Baron Ferdinand de Rothschild in Buckinghamshire *(see page 48).* The gardens today are maintained to the same high standard and are awash with carpet bedding and three-dimensional flower sculptures, epitomising the high Victorian style of gardening. Rockeries and ferneries were also popular and gardens were filled with exciting plants, which Victorian plant collectors were bringing back from places such as the Himalayas and New Zealand.

Sweet disorder

As at the end of the 18th century there was a move among artists and poets to return to an age of romanticism. John Ruskin and William Morris set a precedent by eschewing opulence and seeking a pre-Raphaelite simplicity. The architects and garden designers who followed this natural, organic school, such as William Robinson, who wrote *The English Flower Garden,* and Gertrude Jekyll, became influential. It was a return to the "sweet disorder" of a cottage garden and was adapted for much larger houses like Hestercombe in Somerset *(see page 175).* The framework was designed by Jekyll's favourite collaborator, the architect Edwin Lutyens. The style featured shallow brick steps, wisteria-clad pergolas, simple rills of water edged with flag irises and borders of lavender, lilies and lupins allowed to grow without stricture.

The 20th century witnessed the disappearance of many of the more lavish gardens and the radical reduction in size of others, not least as a result of two world wars. A mechanical revolution rendered lawns like billiard tables, and the clouds of daisies, speedwell and clover flowers were mown out of the picture. Odd interspersions of Hollywood glamour

"LADY" GARDENERS

It seems strange to realise that the phenomenon of female gardeners was almost unknown up until the early part of the 20th century. Though from the 14th century women had a reputation for being careful "weeders", and "…good huswifes who attends the garden", it was not until 300 years later, in 1617, that a gardening book appeared written for women. Called The *Countrie House-wife's Garden,* it was a wholly practical treatise by William Lawson and thus differed from the later (1707) book by Charles Evelyn, *The Ladies' Recreation,* which concentrated on floral beauty. By the end of the 18th century the first volume written by a woman, *The Florists' Manual,* by Marie Jackson, had appeared. This was followed by two more businesslike books, *The British Garden* by Lady Charlotte Murray (1754–1808) and, by Mrs Henrietta Moriarty, *Viridarium-Fifty Plates of Greenhouse Plants* (1806).

There were two notable women gardeners of the early 19th century, Jane Loudon (1808–58), whose books *Gardening for Ladies* and *The Ladies Country Companion* encouraged many ladies to take an interest in their garden, and Louisa Lawrence (1803–55). At her home in Middlesex, Mrs Lawrence developed a passion for garden design, winning prizes at the RHS shows and hosting visits by Queen Victoria and Prince Albert.

Lawrence and Loudon paved the way for the gardening and writing of Gertrude Jekyll (1843–1932), Ellen Willmott (1858–1934), Vita Sackville-West (1892–1962) and today's Penelope Hobhouse and the late Rosemary Verey.

While it was recognised in the horticultural world that "lady" gardeners had a contribution to make, it was another matter when it came to taking on the role of journeymen-gardeners. In the manly world of the Royal Botanic Gardens at Kew it was reluctantly decided to begin admitting women trainees from 1896. Just three doughty women, dressed in a uniform specially designed not to inflame the opposite sex, enrolled for the first year. The view of the establishment was one of disgust that female gardeners were "not ladies in any sense of the word".

Maggie Campbell-Culver

cropped up in the 1920s with the introduction of the swimming pool as a garden feature.

Rhododendrons and azaleas were popular, as, once planted, they required little maintenance. The Savill Gardens in Windsor Great Park *(see page 75)* and those at Exbury in Hampshire *(see page 103)* set precedents for gardens all over Britain. Women began to play a part in garden design. Vita Sackville-West created a series of garden rooms at Sissinghust, including a white garden displaying her advocacy of "good taste": not a red hot poker to be seen.

Geoffrey Jellicoe's and Russell Page's use of simple water features, paving and flowers in blocks of colour looked cool and streamlined compared with what had gone before, but still retained echoes of the past: 2,000 years ago the Romans created simple pools in their gardens and used fruit trees ornamentally. Over the centuries and through all the many influences the gardens of Britain and Ireland have emerged as something unique. ❏

BELOW: woman in a Surrey garden, from *Our Sentimental Garden* (1914) by A & E Castle.

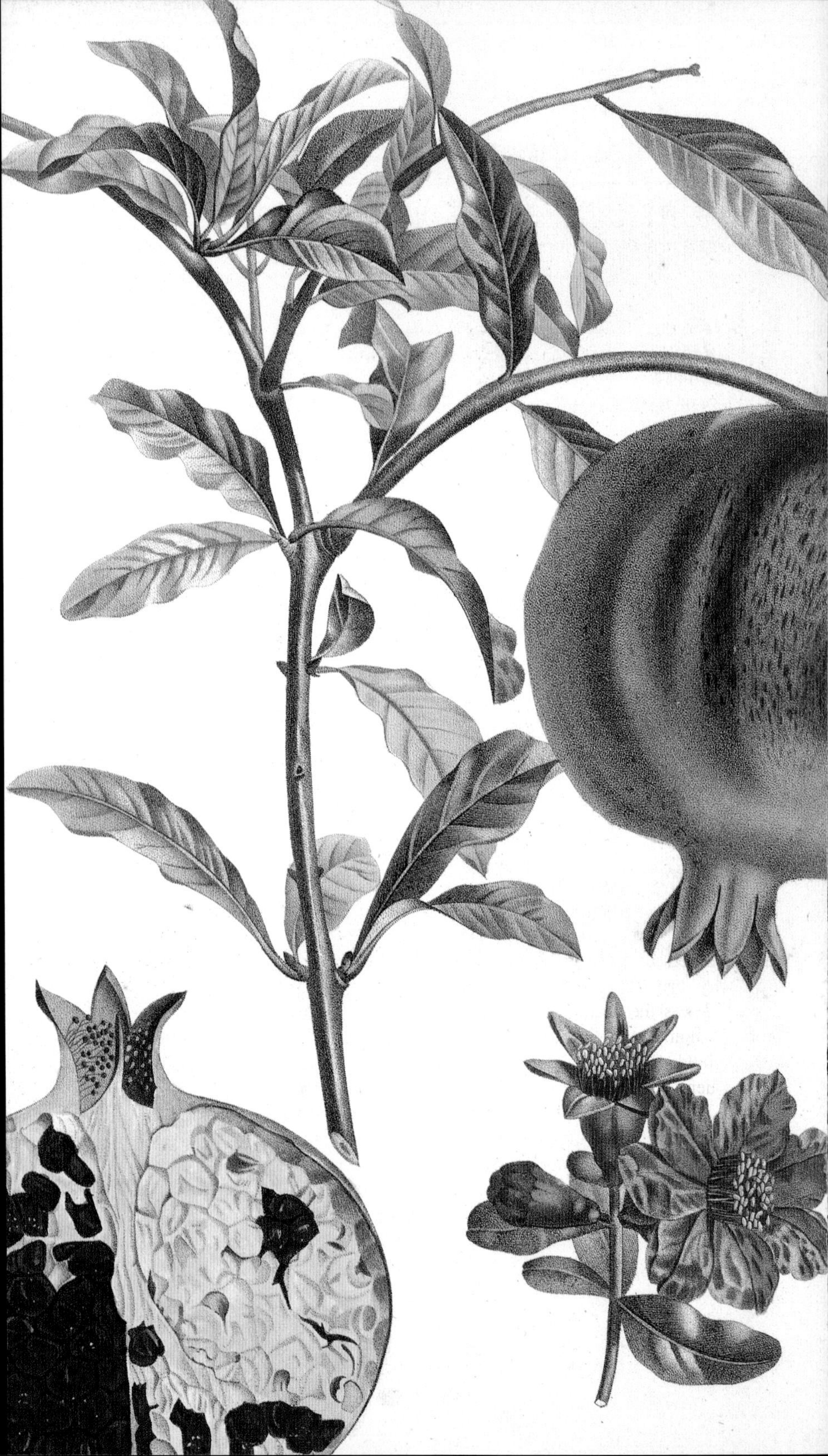

A WEALTH OF PLANTS

Maggie Campbell-Culver tracks the transformation of the British Isles from denuded, isolated islands into an immensely rich horticultural area hosting plants from all over the globe

Writing about the British climate in AD 77, Tacitus observed, "The climate is unpleasant, with frequent rain and mist, but it does not suffer from extreme cold." Quite unknowingly, Tacitus had put his finger on the reason why Britain, and indeed Ireland, have blossomed with a world-wide selection of plants. Previous to that, at the end of the last great Ice Age some 8,000–10,000 years ago, the region had emerged denuded of almost every living plant. All that remained were a few ferns, reeds, algae, and abundant swampland.

However, when we visit a garden or nursery there is always some floral *bonbouche* to tempt us, be it something for the garden's darkest, driest corner, the fullest sun or the damp ground by a pool. Plants have accepted Britain as a home from home since Roman times. With the arrival of the Imperial purple in AD 43, vegetables, fruit and herbs were not only imported from the European mainland but grown in the new territories as well. Botanists believe that about 600 different plants were introduced into Britain at this time, almost all of them indigenous to Europe and particularly to southern Europe around the Mediterranean. A selection includes the radish, onion, cucumber, garlic, medlar, almond, apricot, sweet chestnut, pot marigold, walnut and bay tree.

LEFT: *Punica granatum* or pomegranate, by Pierre J.F. Turpin.

BELOW: the cover of Dixon's seed catalogue, 1885. Seed companies flourished in the 19th century.

Medieval herbalists

From about 800 the building of monasteries and convents with their well-kept herbers and gardens brought a further influence to bear on what could be grown and eaten in the British Isles. In 995 Abbot Aelfric, a Benedictine monk and teacher, compiled what seems to be the earliest dictionary, *The Glossary to Grammatica Latino-Saxonica*. His pupils were so lax in learning their Latin that he made a list of familiar Anglo-Saxon words with the Latin equivalent, and scattered among the list are some 200 plant names, most of which are familiar to us today. Their use may not have been purely decorative: the medicinal qualities of plants was highly important and recorded in great detail in the herbals which every monastery had. One of the first recorded incomers to be described was the Madonna lily, *Lilium candidum*, from its probable homeland of Turkey, but even this perfection of beauty could be used to help alleviate colic.

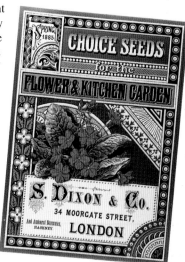

The alien baggage of the Norman invasion may well have been enhanced with the arrival of a pink from southern Europe, *Dianthus caryophyllus*, and a wallflower from the same area, *Erysimum cheiri*. Supposedly, the seeds of both were in the dust of the Caen stone which was imported to build William the Conqueror's castles. The former was used to flavour wine, and the latter pounded into a paste to relieve gout.

The moving of people around the globe, whether because of war, trade or tourism, exploration or invasion, has nearly always resulted in some plants being transferred from their native environment to a host country. Evidence of this is particularly clear in Britain because of its denuded botanical

beginnings and its island status. In the Middle Ages a number of plants indigenous to the eastern Mediterranean and beyond were introduced by crusaders and pilgrims on their return from the Holy Land. These include the evocatively named "Blood Drops of Christ", *Anemone coronaria*, and the hollyhock *Althaea rosea,* which is associated with Eleanor of Castile, Queen of Edward I. Two plants known respectively as the Jerusalem Cross and the rose campion (*Lychnis chalcedonica* and *L. coronaria*) are also associated with the crusades.

Medieval trade with the Arab world and the Iberian peninsula also had botanical repercussions. The quince, *Cydonia oblonga* (the fruit of which made the first "mermelada") arrived from Asia during this period, as did the garden stock *Matthiola incana* (from which the Brompton stock is descended), which is a native of Egypt and the Arabian peninsula. *Ocimum basilicum*, sweet basil, was a 14th-century introduction from the same area, as was *Crocus sativus*, the saffron crocus, and the pomegranate, *Punica granatum*, although these last two may have been reintroductions.

Collectors and hunters

The expansion of Europe's horizons during the 16th and 17th centuries brought botanical rewards, particularly when John Tradescant the Younger (1608–62) made three collecting trips to Virginia between 1637 and 1654. He and his father have a high profile in plant history in the British Isles, as just like Abbot Aelfric some 650 years early, they recorded what they collected and grew in their garden at Lambeth. The herbalist and gardener John Gerard (1545–1612) was also an enthusiastic collector and recorder of "exotic" plants, as was John Parkinson (1567–1650), the apothecary to James I, whose book *Paradisi in Sole Paradisus Terrestris*, published in 1629, describes some 1,000 plants worth cultivating in

THE CLASSIFICATION OF PLANTS

The naming of plants must have begun thousands of years ago, but it was not until Carl Linneaus (1707–78) invented the binomial system in 1753 that a true order was brought to the chaos of botany. The system was adopted world-wide and is in use today.

Two words, shown in italics, are used to identify a plant, the first being its genus name (a group of similar plants) and the second describing the individual plant, the species (these share the same characteristics and can freely interbreed). Similar *genera* are grouped in some 350–500 families.

Taxonomy is finding the correct botanical name for each plant according to the rules of nomenclature, and the classification of a plant is the placing of it in its correct relationship to the family, genus,

and species. Another name, in brackets and also in italics, is sometimes written alongside the plant name. This is its synonym, and it shows that the plant was known by an earlier name that has been altered (usually for botanical reasons).

After the two Latin names of the plant, the name of a person or place is often shown in single quotation marks, indicating that the plant is either a cultivar – a cultivated variety, propagated vegetatively – or a hybrid (shown without quotation marks), which is the result of a cross between two species or cultivars. Such a plant is very rarely the result of breeding between different genera.

Knowing the meaning of the plant's Latin names helps in understanding its character, and even where to place it in the garden.

British gardens, including an early arrival from America, the Virginia Creeper *Parthenocissus quinquefolia*. Tradescant brought to Britain the first Michaelmas Daisy *Aster tradescantia* and the first Rudbeckia (coneflower), *Rudbeckia laciniata*. There is also the Tradescantia species or spiderwort, believed to cure the poisonous bite of the Phalangium arachnid. As it turned out, the spider was quite harmless, but the vernacular name of the plant has remained.

The 1700s saw one of the greatest periods of change in gardening as Capability Brown (1716–83) altered the face of Britain *(see The History of Garden Design, page 21)*, and Carl Linnaeus (1707–78), the Swedish naturalist, created a system of codifying plants which is still in use today. The Chelsea Physic Garden was established in London, headed by Philip Miller (1691–1771). Miller's botanical learning, his keenness in growing and sharing the new plants which were sent to him, particularly from America, laid the foundations of our knowledge about the plant world. Miller's *The Gardener's Dictionary* still has a direct influence on today's garden and plant encyclopaedias.

Philip Miller died in the same year as another great botanical event was drawing to a conclusion, the voyage of the *Endeavour* under Captain Cook (1728–79) and Joseph Banks (1743–1820), who when they docked at Chatham in Kent in 1771 had some 1,500 plants from the newly discovered lands of Australia and New Zealand. Within a year the first Antipodean plants were on offer commercially, the tea tree *Leptospermum scoparium* and the New Zealand laburnum *Sophora tetraptera,* both widely available today. There soon followed the olearias, grevillia and pittosporum, and the tree fern *Dicksonia antarctica*.

The Cape of Good Hope and southern Africa became part of the botanical bonanza of the late 1700s when Francis Masson (1741–1806), the first person to be invited by the Royal Botanic Gardens Kew to collect plants on its behalf, journeyed to the Cape in 1772. Although some plants from southern Africa had arrived earlier, like the *Amaryllis belladonna* and the Arum lily, *Zantedeschia aethiopica.* Masson's plant-gathering let loose a flood of gorgeous bulbs and corms into Britain, including several gladiolus species, ixias (corn lilies), as well as heathers, geraniums, aloes, the spectacular *Strelitzia reginae,* and the extraordinary *Protea cynaiodes,* later to be adopted as the South African national flower. Masson duly sent a specimen of the latter to Sir Joseph Banks at Kew in 1774: it grew in the Temperate House for 50 years before flowering in 1826, and it was another 160 years (1986) before it flowered for a second time.

BELOW: Captain Cook's ship *Endeavour* brought back plants from Australia and New Zealand.

The Royal Horticultural Society

An indication that the 19th century was to become a great horticultural period began in 1804 when the foundations were laid of what was to become the Royal Horticultural Society. In addition, British imperialism combined with the vision of Sir Joseph Banks and, later, Sir Joseph Hooker (1817–1911) at Kew created conditions that could change the economic potential of landscapes on any continent. The

possibility of moving trees, crops and plants from one part of the globe to another was an attractive proposition untrammelled by thoughts of conservation or biodiversity. It also involved setting up a number of botanic gardens throughout the British Empire, usually with Kew-trained employees.

Transport problems

However, the successful transportation of plants was still problematic. In the *Garden Book*, written in 1659 by Sir Thomas Hanmer, there is a practical paragraph on "How to Packe up Rootes and Send them to Remote Places". John Evelyn two decades later was also interested in the minutiae of the sea-going survival of plants, when he was waiting for the arrival of trees and seeds – the former (as he instructed the captain) put "in Barills their rootes wraped about mosse" and the latter sensibly packed in paper, labelled and placed in a box.

Long-distance journeys of saplings and shrubs were the most hazardous (as it still is) and nearly all recommendations were for barrels tightly packed with the collected material surrounded with damp moss. The transportation of seeds, bulbs, corms and cones was more convenient, although weird and wonderful ways of preserving them were tried, such as pressing seeds into warm wax, smothering them in honey, then sealing them in ox bladders or gourd husks, even burying them in sugar barrels. Mostly it was agreed that seeds should be packed in paper and carefully labelled.

The movement of plants around the world was helped by the invention of what became known as the Wardian Case, named after its inventor Nathaniel Bagshaw Ward (1791–1868). It consisted of a sealed wooden box with windows to let in light. It was found that plants transported in such a way usually survived their travels by making their own atmosphere. Kew embraced its novelty wholeheartedly and Wardian Cases became part of every overseas expedition right up until 1962 when it was used for the last time to deliver plants to Fiji.

ABOVE:
Dianthus
from Fillipo
Arena's
La Natura e
Coltura de'
Fiori,
1767–8.

Spotlight on China

Two countries, China and Japan, remained closed to all foreigners for much of the 19th century. Although in the 17th and 18th centuries French Jesuits had managed to establish a presence in China and had described and drawn some of the natural habitat, little plant material had found its way into the wider world. In China and Japan plant hunting was quite different from elsewhere in the world, as horticultural knowledge and practice had begun long before the European tradition of gardening. Consequently it was cultivated garden plants that first made the long voyage to Europe.

The East India Company held a toe-hold on the tiny island of Macao (Aomen) and its officials were infrequently allowed onto the mainland to visit Canton (Guangzhou) when the merchant fleet docked. However, such was the interest shown in the plants of the Far East that in 1803 an intrepid Kew-trained gardener, William Kerr (d.1814), stayed on Macao for eight years. Almost immediately he began sending plants back home. Kerr had a good "garden eye", and several of his introductions are firm favourites today, including the shrub Jew's mantle, *Kerria japonica*, the tuberous fragrant begonia, *Begonia grandis*, and the tiger lily, *Lilium lancifolium*. In the same year another of William Kerr's introductions was the beautiful *Rosa banksiae* "Alba-plena", named in honour of Lady Banks.

Among those employed by the East India Company during this period was John Livingstone (d.1829), a surgeon who showed interest in the vegetables of China (he is reputed to have introduced the Chinese cabbage *Brassica pekinensis*), and John Reeves (1774–1856), the Assistant Inspector of Tea, who like his son (also John) spent almost his whole working life in China. On a trip to England in 1816 Reeves senior brought with him a number of well-established plants, including the climber *Wisteria sinensis* and a camellia, *Camellia welbankiana*, named to honour Captain Wellbank of the *East Indiaman*, which brought them to England. Eventually in 1842, following the Treaty of Nanking (Nanjing), travel restrictions in China eased and the Horticultural Society (later the RHS) decided to take advantage of the situation. Robert Fortune (1812–80), who trained at the Royal Botanic Gardens Edinburgh and then at the Horticultural Society's own garden at Chiswick, was appointed to investigate the country. He spent three years travelling, collecting and observing, and returned again in 1853. Between 1860 and 1862 he made a third journey, this time principally to Japan. Fortune was entranced by the plant material he found and his introductions such as *Anemone japonica*, the winter jasmine, the first forsythia, and the lovely winter-flowering honeysuckle *Lonicera fragrantissima* still grace the gardens of the British Isles. He was the first plant-collector to use the Wardian Case.

BELOW: the Wardian Case made transporting plants easier and more successful.

Commercial considerations

Nurseries were beginning to be aware of the commercial advantages of introducing newly collected plants and offering them for sale, and it was this enterprise which drove much of the collecting from 1850 for the next 100 years. The two great nurseries of the Veitch family in Exeter and London flourished up until the time of World War I, sending out some 50 or so plant collectors during that period. Other nurseries followed suit, as did the RHS. The Society was responsible in 1823 for inviting David Douglas (1799–1834) to collect suitable material from the newly explored western shores of the American continent. Little did its members realise what a cornucopia of garden-worthy plants and conifers were

to be collected by him before his untimely death in Hawaii, gored by a wild bull. In Britain there is only one native pine, *Pinus sylvestris*, the Scots pine, so the collection of conifers made by Douglas (and others) has had an immense impact on the British landscape.

From gentians to rhododendrons

In the latter part of the 19th century the spotlight again fell on the Far East and remained so until after World War I. There is no doubt that in every garden in the land there is at least one plant under cultivation which was first collected from this area by one of the four key plant collectors. Ernest Wilson (1876–1930), George Forrest (1873–1932), Reginald Farrer (1880–1920) and Frank Kingdon Ward (1885–1958) were responsible for thousands of new introductions into the European gardening world.

If one were to choose only one plant from each of the Sino-botanists it would probably have to be the regal lily, *Lillium regale*, from Wilson; *Rhododendron sinogrande,* the largest-leaved rhododendron of all, from George Forrest; and from Reginald Farrer, who is best remembered for alpine plants, the gentian *Gentiana farreri*. Kingdon Ward, who travelled in China, Tibet and Burma from the 1920s to the 1950s, collected innumerable and now familiar shrubs including species of berberis, honeysuckle, acers and cornus, but his introduction of the startling Himalayan blue poppy, *Meconopsis betonicifolia*, was perhaps his greatest contribution. All four men, however, were overwhelmed by the number of rhododendron species they found, and collectively introduced.

Who would have realised that 2,000 years ago, when the British Isles began to receive and grow "foreign" plants, that its gardens would eventually become a microcosm of the world? Gardening and growing seem so fundamental to the well-being of the people here that it is no wonder that John Ruskin in the 19th century wrote "Flowers seem intended for the solace of ordinary humans," or, put another way (by W.C. Sellar and R.J. Yeatman) in the 1930s, "It is utterly forbidden to be half-hearted about Gardening. You have got to LOVE your garden whether you like it or not." ❑

BELOW: back to basics in Fillipo Arena's *La Natura e Coltura de' Fiori*, 1767–8. RIGHT: Nicholas Culpeper.

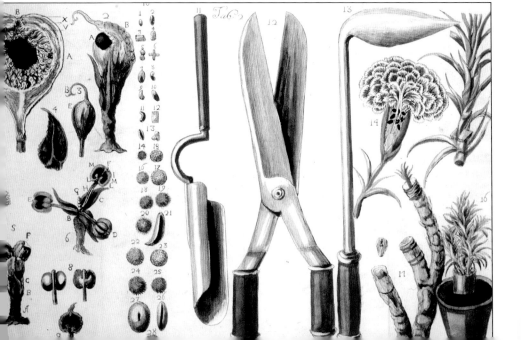

HEALING PLANTS

NICHOLAS CULPEPER
View in this face, whom Heaven snatcht from hence,
Our Phisicall and Starrie Influence;
Had not Great Culpeper such order tooke,
In spight of Fate to Live still in this Booke.

Plants that are known for their healing qualities are an underrated asset of modern gardening. For thousands of years the essence distilled from plants was the only remedy available to help improve the health of mankind. Embedded in plant tissue is what is called the active principle, one of a small number of chemical substances which have been divided into six categories. Between them they have helped keep many of our ills at bay. Today, cutting-edge medical research is being carried out on plant material in an effort to eliminate some of man's worst diseases.

Plants with medicinal properties have been known about since pre-history. At a 60,000 year-old site in Iraq, for example, a number of medicinal plants were discovered in the same place. The earliest civilisations all had their pharmacopoeia, and discovered through trial and error that various plants prepared in special ways could help alleviate illnesses and fevers.

In Britain and throughout Europe by the 16th century a rather peculiar code of practice had evolved to assist in the identification of plants for their medical efficacy. Called the Doctrine of Signatures, its defining principle was how closely the external shape of a particular plant resembled a part of the human body. Thus the walnut, which resembles the brain, became associated with the healing of head wounds.

Lungwort *(Pulmonaria)* tells its own tale. A native of the Near East, its original name was "Jerusalem cowsloppus", but it soon became known as a plant that was able to alleviate breathing problems. One only has to examine the spotted hairy leaves to be reminded of the human lung.

During this period more scientific reasoning about the classification of the flora developed in the newly founded botanic gardens (the earliest were established in Pisa in 1543 and in Padua in 1545. In Britain, Oxford Botanic Garden was founded in 1621, Edinburgh in 1670, and in 1673 the London Chelsea Physic Garden was founded. Today there are more than 400 botanic gardens world-wide. All these institutions carry their own archive of pressed plant specimens in a herbarium, where the plant type species is mounted on paper, described, classified and named. Field notes are added, along with other relevant information discovered at the time. These vast numbers of desiccated plants are vital for researchers scouring the world's resources for potential medicines.

Many flowers which we nurture in our gardens belong to this huge band of healing plants. Some of them are surprising, such as lady's mantle, Alchemilla, known by herbalists for its astringent and sedative qualities. The gorgeously scented lily-of-the-valley *(Convallaria majalis)* secretes within its character powerful poisonous elements which, when used correctly, help in the treatment of heart disease. We all know that a certain amount of garlic, *Allium sativum*, is good for us, but cabbage too *(Brassica oleracea)* can aid our good health: the Greeks and the Romans used it both medically and as a food.

The whole of the plant world contributes to our well-being, whether they inspire us with their beauty, feed or clothe us, or make us feel better. They should never be ignored.

GREAT GARDENS

A region by region guide to more than 320 of
the top gardens open to the public
in the British Isles

Britain and Ireland have thousands of gardens open to the public, ranging from the great estates created for the aristocracy by the foremost landscape architects of the 18th and 19th-centuries to tiny cottage gardens that may be the result of a lifetime's labour of love by one man or woman. Some are open every day of the year, excluding Christmas; others are open just one or two days a year for charity under the National Garden Scheme. The best of them, whether great or small, whether comprising a series of sublime prospects or brimming with colourful cabbage roses and hollyhocks, are described and illustrated in the following pages.

The English gardens are organised by region (the Southwest, the Southeast, East Anglia, etc), which are sub-divided into counties, while the less numerous gardens of Scotland, Wales and Ireland are grouped by country (the latter split into Northern Ireland and the Republic of Ireland). All gardens are numbered in the text and can be easily located on the regional maps; an overview of the regions can be found on the map on the inside front cover. Every description of a garden includes details of opening hours, admission charges, facilities and any national collections that the garden contains. Where relevant, its grade according to English Heritage, which lists all historic gardens, is also provided (for an explanation of these grades, *see page 334*). Any unfamiliar terminology relating to garden features can be looked up in the glossary on page 337.

At the end of each entry we have listed any nearby hotels and pubs serving food that have been recommended by the garden's owners. A garden visitor's calendar, detailing what to see when, is on the inside back cover.

The bold text at the beginning of each entry also indicates any gardens belonging to English Heritage or the National Trust, both of which offer free entry to their members. The National Trust took many historic properties in the aftermath of the two world wars, when death duties and soaring running costs often made their upkeep unfeasible for private individuals. However, some of the great country estates remain in private hands, including a good number of those belonging to the highest echelons of the aristocracy – such as Chatsworth (the Duke of Devonshire), Longleat (the Marquess of Bath) and Alnwick (the Duke of Northumberland) – who have ensured their survival by turning them into major tourist attractions, often with high admission charges.

Though we have felt it useful to provide admission charges, these can change at short notice, as can opening hours. For the latest information, consult the website *<www.gardens-guide.com>*, which is continually updated by the Armchair Travel Company. ❑

● The price bands shown for hotels (based on a double room) are as follows: **UK:** £ = under £60; ££ = £60–100; £££ = £100–150; ££££ = over £150. **Republic of Ireland:** € = under €100; €€ = €100–150; €€€ = €150–225; €€€€ = over €225.

LEFT: a profusion of roses at Goodnestone Park, Kent.

FOLLOWING PAGES: *Zantedeschia aethiopica*, the Pool Garden, Wisley, Surrey; the formal gardens at Ascott.

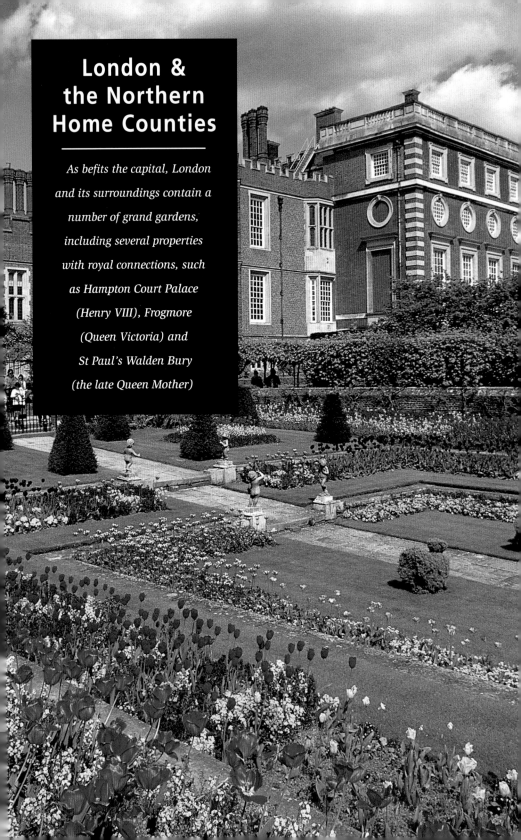

London &
the Northern
Home Counties

*As befits the capital, London
and its surroundings contain a
number of grand gardens,
including several properties
with royal connections, such
as Hampton Court Palace
(Henry VIII), Frogmore
(Queen Victoria) and
St Paul's Walden Bury
(the late Queen Mother)*

Map: page 38

LONDON AND MIDDLESEX

London is famous for its public parks and garden squares, but it also has many historic gardens, including the Chelsea Physic Garden, founded in 1673, and the famous Royal Botanic Garden Kew, built during the golden age of plant-collecting and discovery. London also hosts the UK's leading celebrations of horticulture, the Chelsea Flower Show in May and the Hampton Court Flower Show in July.

Chelsea Physic Garden

Famous botanic garden. English Heritage Grade I. Map reference ❶

66 Royal Hospital Road, Chelsea, London SW3 4HS; tel: 020 7352 5646; fax: 020 7376 3910.
< www.chelseaphysicgarden.co.uk >.
National Collection: *Cistus.*
Opening times: *Apr–Oct Wed noon– 5pm, Sun 2–6pm; special snowdrop opening Feb.*
Admission prices: *adults £5, children £3.*
Facilities: *parking, disabled access, shop, plants for sale, refreshments. Picnics permitted. No dogs except guide dogs. Guided tours may be booked in advance for groups.*

This garden, 3½ acres (1.5 hectares) in all, plots the history of medicinal plants. It has world medicine beds and the oldest rock garden in Europe (dating from 1773), two ponds, glasshouses, rare and tender plants and the largest olive tree to be grown indoors in Britain. A historical walk takes in a succession of plant species introduced by the garden's many well-known curators. The micro-climate created by the garden enables many rare plants to flourish.

History: The garden was founded in 1673 by the Society of Apothecaries. It is one of the oldest botanic gardens and the only one to retain the title "Physic" after the old name for the healing arts.

Accommodation: The Gallery, Queensberry Place, South Kensington (tel: 020 7915 0000: £££).
Local pubs: The Phene Arms, Phene Street; Kings Head & Eight Bells, Chelsea Embankment.

OPPOSITE: the magnificent Pond Garden at Hampton Court Palace.

ABOVE: West Wycombe Park in autumn.

LEFT: Chelsea Physic Garden.

The Pharmaceutical Garden

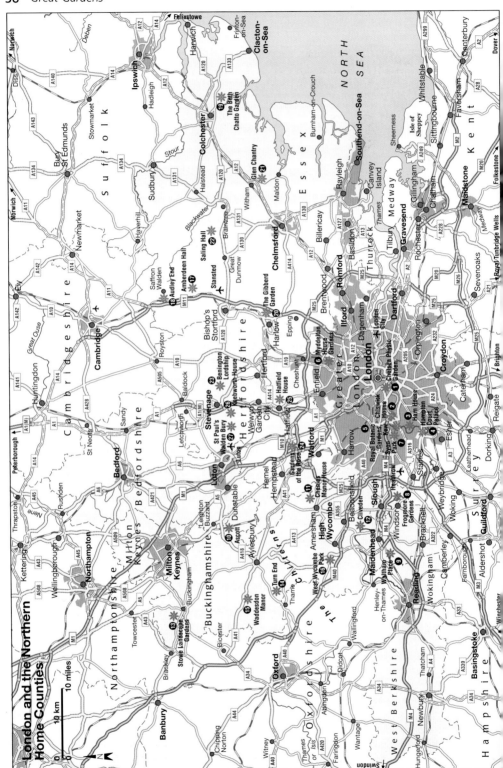

London and the Northern
Home Counties

10 miles

10 km

Chiswick House

Fine Palladian house and baroque garden. English Heritage Grade I. Map reference ➋

Burlington Lane, Chiswick, London W4 2RP; tel: 020 8742 1225.
Opening times: *daily 8.30am–dusk. Coaches/parties welcome but no viewing by appointment. House also open.*
Admission prices: *free.*
Facilities: *parking, disabled access, shop, plants for sale, refreshments. Picnics permitted. Dogs allowed on leads.*

The garden dates from the early 18th century and surrounds a perfect Palladian villa designed by the influential architect William Kent. Features include a rustic cascade and a serpentine canal. Classical busts, sphinxes, columns and an exedra help to recreate the landscapes of antiquity. The garden, which is being restored, evolved in stages, changing from a nobleman's country estate to an urban park. Much of the original design is still evident and features avenues leading to spectacular cedars of Lebanon, a canal, topiary, lawns and an attractive orangery.

History: In the early 18th century, the owner and chief designer Lord Burlington, with help from Charles Bridgeman and William Kent, built an Augustan villa modelled on Palladio's Villa Rotunda of 1550. The maze, built in 1730 between the house and canal, was the first in Britain.

Accommodation: Richmond Hill Hotel (tel: 020 8940 2247, ££–£££). **Local pub:** *George & Devonshire, 8 Burlington Lane.*

Ham House

Seventeenth-century riverside house and garden. English Heritage Grade II. National Trust. Map reference ➌

Ham Street, Richmond TW10 7RS, Middlesex; tel: 020 8940 1950.
< www.nationaltrust.org.uk >
Opening times: *garden: all year Sat–Wed 11am–6pm, closed 25–26 Dec and 1 Jan; house: last week in Mar–end Oct/beginning Nov Sat–Wed 1–5 pm. Parties/coaches may view by appointment.*
Admission prices: *house & garden: adults £6, children £3, family £15; garden: adults £2, children £1.*
Facilities: *parking, disabled access, shop, plants for sale, refreshments. Picnics permitted. No dogs.*

Ham House is one of the few formal gardens to survive the English Landscape Movement of the 18th century. The layout and feel of the gardens are strongly architectural, with gravel paths, parterres of lavender and borders planted in repeated patterns, which were based on 17th-century inventories. The Wilderness is a rare and important original feature; future development will be based on a painting by Dankerts of the south elevation of the house and gardens in 1675.

The garden restoration, begun in 1973, has influenced recent restorations of some of the great gardens in Europe.

ABOVE: cones of clipped yew at Ham House.

LEFT: classical buildings and statuary feature at Chiswick House.

History: Ham House was built in 1610 and enlarged in the 1670s when it was at the heart of Restoration court life and intrigue.

Accommodation: Richmond Hill Hotel (tel: 020 8940 2247, ££–£££).

Hampton Court Palace

Historic royal palace with famous garden and maze. English Heritage Grade I. Map reference ❹

East Molesey KT8 9AU, Surrey; tel: 020 8781 9500. < www.hrp.org.uk >

Opening times: park all year dawn–dusk; King's Privy Garden: 9.30am–6pm (4.30pm Oct–Mar), opens at 10.15am on Mondays. Parties/coaches accepted. Viewing by appointment.
Admission prices: Privy Garden: adults £2.80, children £1.90; maze: adults £2.80, children £1.90.
Facilities: parking, disabled access, shop, plants for sale, refreshments. Picnics permitted. Dogs allowed on leads.
Events: Hampton Court Flower Show.

ABOVE: the King's Privy Garden at Hampton Court Palace.

Laid out by William III (king 1689–1702) in the fashionable scheme of the time, the gardens of Hampton Court Palace are divided by avenues radiating from the house, with extensive parterres on the south and east sides. A plan of 1702 has been reproduced in order to restore exactly the great Privy Garden on the south side of the palace, with widely spaced roses and other plants in slightly raised beds. Next to it is the small Pond Garden, and further on is the Great Vine ("Black Hamburgh"), the world's oldest known vine. Planted in 1768 on the advice of Capability Brown, it produces 500–700lbs (220–320kg) of grapes each year.

On the other side of the Privy Garden is the huge formal East Garden with the Long Water cutting through the deer park. William III laid out the garden at the palace end of the Long Water as a parterre with 12 marble fountains. Later, in 1710, Queen Anne added the semi-circular canals. On the other side of the palace are the wilderness gardens, spread with naturalised daffodils in spring.

Also here is the Hampton Court Maze. Laid out in 1691, it covers ⅓ acre (0.12 hectares) and has yew hedges totalling nearly ½ mile (1km) in length.

Other areas in the wilderness also have considerable horticultural interest, including the rose garden, a herbaceous garden and walls covered with climbing plants.

History: The palace dates from about 1514 and was built by Thomas Wolsey, Henry VIII's Chancellor, who acquired it from the Knights Hospitallers of St John of Jerusalem. The Renaissance palace, the first in England, was so magnificent that when Wolsey fell from grace in 1525 he was forced to surrender it to the king, who reconstructed it. The palace continued in royal usage until the execution of Charles I (who was imprisoned there for three months in 1647), after which Cromwell used it on Sundays. After the Restoration, it was returned to the Crown, but royal visits ceased by 1737. Nonetheless, the palace and gardens were well looked after – the latter by Capability Brown. In 1838 Queen Victoria opened the palace and gardens to the public.

Accommodation: Carlton Mitre Hotel, opposite the palace (tel: 020 8979 9988; £££). Local pub: Kings Arms, Hampton Court Road.

Map: page 38

Royal Botanic Gardens Kew

**The world's first botanic garden.
English Heritage Grade I.
Map reference ❺**

*Kew, Richmond TW9 3AB, Surrey;
tel: 020 8940 1171. < www.kew.org.uk >*
Opening times: *Apr–Aug Mon–Fri
9.30am–6.30pm (last admission 30 minutes before closing), weekends & BHs
9.30am–7.30pm; Sep–Oct 9.30am–6pm;
Nov–1st week Feb 9.30am–4.15pm; 2nd
week Feb–Mar 9.30am–5.30pm.
Parties/coaches may also view by
appointment (tel: 020 8332 5648; email:
groups@kew.org). House closed.*
Admission prices: *adults £6.50, children
under 18 free (must be accompanied by
adult), concessions £4.50.*
Facilities: *parking, disabled access,
shop, plants for sale, refreshments.
Picnics permitted. No dogs.*

The world's first and greatest botanic garden, the Royal Botanic Gardens Kew occupies a 300-acre (120-hectare) site bordering the River Thames. It can be enjoyed as much by the casual visitor as by the keen gardener wanting to see prime specimens of particular interest. It includes many buildings of architectural and historic interest, not least the extraordinary Palm House and the Temperate House, as well as the recent high-tech addition of the Princess of Wales Conservatory.

The landscape was fashioned by many of the leading garden designers of their day, including Charles Bridgeman, Capability Brown and W.A. Nesfield. Among its features are an ice house, a cottage built for Queen Charlotte, a royal palace, a Japanese gate and garden, follies, sculpture, parterres, quiet – almost private – gardens, wide sweeping lawns, lakes, ponds and a rockery. Kew's superb collection of trees is surmounted by the tallest flagstaff in the world.

In the same vein the profusion of plants, shrubs and bamboos is astonishing. New plantings are constantly appearing while older features are redesigned and replanted.

History: Kew dates from 1678, when it was owned by the Earl of Essex's brother, Sir Henry Capel, and was described as having "the choicest fruit of any garden in England". It came into royal ownership in 1718 and was much visited by George II and George III.

The latter appointed Sir Joseph Banks, the botanist on Captain James Cook's voyage around the world, to take charge of the gardens at Kew. Banks encouraged plant hunters such as F. Masson to send back species from

ABOVE: the Palm House, one of several magnificent ornamental glasshouses at Kew.

the West Indies, Africa, Australasia, China and India. The cycad in the Palm House labelled "the oldest pot plant in the world" was brought back from Africa in 1775.

At the beginning of the 19th century the gardens suffered a period of decline, but in 1827 they were placed in the hands of W.T. Aiton, appointed Director-General of His Majesty's Gardens, and later in those of William Hooker and his son Joseph Hooker, both noted plant hunters. All played a major part in reinvigorating the gardens.

In the 20th century the emphasis on science and conservation continued with the rebuilding of the Jodrell Laboratory, the new Economic House, and the development of the Library and Herbarium.

Local pub: City Barge, Strand on the Green, W4 (just over Kew Bridge).

Myddelton House Gardens

Features thousands of naturalised bulbs. English Heritage Grade II. Map reference ⑥

Lee Valley Regional Park Authority, Bulls Cross, Enfield EN2 9HG, Middlesex; tel: 01992 717711.
< www.leevalleypark.com >
Opening times: Apr–Sep Mon–Fri 10am–4.30pm, Oct–Mar Mon–Fri 10am–3pm, Sun & BHs and National Garden Scheme days noon–4pm.

B<small>ELOW</small>: a dahlia in perfect bloom.

Parties/coaches accepted. House closed.
National Collection: *Bearded Iris.*
Admission prices: *adults £2.10, children £1.50, over-60s £1.50.*
Facilities: *parking, disabled access, plants for sale occasionally, refreshments Sundays only. No dogs or picnics.*

Born of one man's passionate interest in plants, Myddelton House Gardens were created by E.A. Bowles, an expert botanist, author, artist and Fellow of the RHS. They contain the National Collection of Bearded Iris and thousands of naturalised bulbs. Don't miss the Lunatic Asylum (home to unusual plants), Tom Tiddlers Ground and the Tulip Terrace. The gardens also have a carp lake, conservatory and a rock garden.

Accommodation: *Cheshunt Marriott (tel: 01992 451245; £££).* **Local pub:** *the Pied Bull, Bullsmoor Lane, Enfield; King's Head, Market Place, Enfield.*

Syon Park

18th-century garden with Victorian and modern plantings. English Heritage Grade I. Map reference ⑦

Brentford TW8 8JF, Middlesex; tel: 020 8560 0881.
Opening times: grounds: all year 10am–5pm or dusk if earlier; house: end Mar–beginning Nov Wed, Thur, Sun and BH 11am–5pm. Parties/coaches may also view by appointment.
Admission prices: *garden: adults £3.50, children; £2.50; house and garden: adults £6.95, £5.95.*
Facilities: *parking, disabled access, shop, plants for sale, refreshments. Picnics permitted. Dogs allowed on leads.*

With the River Thames meandering through its grounds, Syon Park is the essence of the graceful English landscape garden. It uses the river to great effect, and water features such as a Capability Brown lake, are in keeping.

Map: page 38

In the Wilderness Garden there is a lakeside walk in the shade of some of Syon's 3,000 trees. The 200 different species on show include the wing nut, Turkish hazel, a medlar and a quince. In spring and summer, the trees are complemented by grape hyacinths, snowdrops, anemone blanda and aconites.

History: Syon Abbey was founded in 1415 for the Bridgettine Order, endowed by Henry V. However, it wasn't until it became a private home in the 16th century that the gardens became important. Henry, the 9th Earl of Northumberland (1584–1632), was given the royal grant of Syon in 1603 and employed a Mr Styckles to give "direction for garden work". In the 18th century the 10th Earl's continental garden was replaced by informality under Capability Brown.

Among the highlights, the magnificent Great Conservatory (designed by Charles Fowler, the architect of the covered market at Covent Garden) houses sub-tropical plants in one heated wing and bedding plants, such as pelargoniums and geraniums in the other. The Rose Garden features old-fashioned rose varieties, such as the Damask, Moss, Gallicus and Albus roses.

Accommodation: Richmond Hill Hotel (tel: 020 8940 2247, ££–£££).

BERKSHIRE

Several of Berkshire's best gardens are not open to the public. The most significant one that is open is Frogmore, which was a favourite residence of Queen Victoria, whose mausoleum is in the grounds. It should be noted that Savill Garden and the Valley Garden, important woodland gardens in Windsor Great Park, are actually just over the border in Surrey and not in Berkshire as is sometimes supposed.

Frogmore Gardens

Landscaped grounds of former royal residence containing the mausoleum of Queen Victoria and her husband, Prince Albert. Map reference ❽

Windsor SL4 2JG, Berks; tel: 0207 799 23318; fax: 020 7930 9625.
< www.royalresidences.com >
***Opening times:** May BH weekend 10am–6pm (last admissions 5pm), Aug BH weekend 10am–5.30pm (last admissions 4pm). National Garden Scheme days. Coaches/parties accepted. Viewing by appointment. House also open.*

***Admission prices:** May: adults £3.60, children £1.30, over-60s £2.50; Aug: adults £5.20, children £3.20, over-60s £4.20.*
***Facilities:** parking, disabled access in garden only, shop (May only), refreshments (May only). Picnics permitted. No Dogs.*

The sweeping lawns, serpentine water course and mature exotic trees of Frogmore are a legacy of works carried out in the 18th and 19th centuries, primarily under royal patronage. The house has had royal residents since Queen Charlotte lived here from the 1790s, and

ABOVE: some of Syon Park's 3,000 trees.

House. Following the death of the Duchess no work of any substance was undertaken until the residency of Queen Mary, when a good deal of clearance was undertaken and many new plantings made. The structure of the garden we see today dates from this time.

*Accommodation: Oakley Court, Windsor (tel: 01753 609988; ££££), Castle Hotel, Windsor (tel: 01753 830244; £££–££££); Sir Christopher Wren's Hotel, Windsor (tel: 01753 861354; ££££). **Local pub:** Ye Harte & Garter Hotel, Windsor.*

ABOVE: the gardens at Frogmore.

the gardens have always reflected the prevailing tastes of the day.

Recent plantings have concentrated on adding spring interest to coincide with the Easter Court at Windsor. Japanese cherries strongly feature, along with daffodils. Sympathetic management of the less formal grass areas have allowed spring wild flowers, such as primroses, to prosper.

Statuesque forest trees are one of Frogmore's splendours. Among the more notable are giant specimens of Wallich pine, redwood, incense cedar and tulip tree. Careful planting continues today with the purpose of conserving the characteristic treescape.

History: The present house was developed, at the behest of Queen Charlotte, by James Wyatt from a building first raised by William Aldworth Price in the late 17th century. Queen Charlotte also took an interest in the gardens and commissioned William Price to add water features. He constructed the lake, using spoil from the excavations to form the banks.

The house was occupied in turn by Queen Charlotte's daughter, Princess Augusta and the Duchess of Kent, the mother of Queen Victoria. It was during Victorian times that the majority of the exotic trees were planted and many of the ornamental buildings were added, including the Indian Kiosk and Tea

Waltham Place

Organic gardens with 17th-century walled gardens and a lake. Map reference ❾

White Waltham, Maidenhead SL6 3JH, Berkshire; tel: 01628 824605.
***Opening times:** Apr–Sep (telephone for times). National Garden Scheme days. Parties/coaches may also view by appointment. House open.*
***Admission prices:** adults £3.50, children £1.*
***Facilities:** parking, disabled access, shop, plants for sale, refreshments. Picnics permitted. Dogs allowed on leads.*

Waltham Place is an organic garden of around 40 acres (16 hectares), with walled gardens dating from the 17th century. Newly planted in interesting patterns, the latter are best seen from the wooden eyrie in one corner. There is a Butterfly Garden, a Japanese Garden and a potager, as well as spectacular double borders leading from the house towards the lake and a grove of fine specimen trees.

*Accommodation: Fredrick's, Maidenhead (tel: 01628 581000; £££–££££); Red Lion, Henley-on-Thames (01491 572161; £££). **Local pubs:** Bell, Waltham St Lawrence; Crown, Burchett's Green.*

BUCKINGHAMSHIRE

**Map:
page 38**

Buckinghamshire has more than its fair share of very grand gardens, including the magnificent 18th-century landscape garden at Stowe. Several of the county's leading estates were developed by spectacularly wealthy tycoons, including the banker Baron de Rothschild (Ascott and Waddesdon) and the American Lord Astor (Cliveden).

Ascott

Victorian-style garden with herbaceous walk and a lily pond.English Heritage Grade II. National Trust. Map reference ⑩

Wing, Leighton Buzzard LU7 0PS, Bucks; tel: 01296 688242; fax: 01296 681904. < www.ascottestate.co.uk >
Opening times: *house & garden: Apr and early Aug–mid-Sep 2–6pm, closed Mon. Garden: also May–Aug Wed and last Sunday in month, plus one week in March (same opening times). Parties/coaches accepted. Viewing by appointment.*
Admission prices: *house & garden: adults £5.60, children £2.80; garden: adults £4, children £2.*
Facilities: *parking, disabled access. No refreshments. No picnics. Dogs on leads in car-park only.*

A former home of the Rothschild family, Ascott is famous for its superb Victorian gardens which include wide lawns, spectacular trees and topiary, in particular the toparian sundial with its gnomon in yew and Roman numerals in box. Lovely views over the Vale of Aylesbury present themselves between the cedars. Formal beds, the Long Walk, new statuary and a wild garden complement the design.

History: The original farmhouse was built in 1606 and enlarged by Leopold de Rothschild after he acquired it from his brother, Baron Nathan Meyer, in 1876. In recent years it has been redesigned and planted by Arabella Lennox-Boyd.

Accommodation: Hartwell House, Aylesbury (tel: 01296; ££££); Local pub: Cock, Wing.

Chenies Manor House

Tudor-style garden known for its blooms, bulbs and tulips. English Heritage Grade II*. Map reference ⑪

Chenies, Rickmansworth, WD3 6ER, Bucks; tel: 01494 762888.
Opening times: *Apr–end Oct Wed & Thur, BH Mons 2–5pm. Parties/coaches*

BELOW: views over the Vale of Aylesbury complement the gardens at Ascott.

accepted. *Viewing by appointment. House open.*
Admission prices: *adults £3, children £1.50.*
Facilities: *parking, disabled access, shop, plants for sale, refreshments. Picnics permitted. No dogs.*

Dating from the 15th/16th century, Chenies Manor House is surrounded by lawns, walls and garden recreated in the Tudor style. There are herbaceous borders, a white garden with interesting topiary, a Tudor bulb garden and a physic garden. A yew maze, a fountain court, a parterre and a productive potager make it a garden worth visiting from spring through to autumn.

Accommodation: *The George Hotel, Beaconsfield (tel: 01494 673086; ££).* **Local pub:** *Royal Standard of England, Forty Green.*

Cliveden

Historic estate overlooking the River Thames. English Heritage Grade I. National Trust. Map reference ⑫

Taplow, Maidenhead SL6 0JA, Bucks; tel: 01628 668561.
< www.nationaltrust.org.uk >

RIGHT: pagoda at Cliveden.

National Collection: *Catalpa.*
Opening times: *estate and garden: mid-Mar–Dec (except Apr and Oct) daily 11am–6pm (closes at 4pm after 1 Nov); Apr and Oct Thur and Sun 3–5.30pm. Woodlands open all year 11am–5.30pm (closes at 4pm Nov–Feb). Parties/coaches may also view by appointment. House: Apr–Oct Thur and Sun, though it is also open as a luxury hotel year-round.*
Admission prices: *grounds: adults £6, children £3, family £15 (house £1 extra, children 50p extra), group rate £5.50 pp. Woodlands car park £3 per adult, £1.50 per child, £7.50 family. Mooring charge on Cliveden Reach (£2 up to 4 hrs, £6 per 24 hrs, season ticket £30.*
Facilities: *parking, disabled access (wheelchairs and Braille guides available), shop, plants for sale, refreshments. Picnics permitted. Dogs allowed on leads in specified areas.*

A spectacular estate of over 180 acres (73 hectares) overlooking the Thames, Cliveden has a series of gardens, each with its own character, featuring roses, topiary, statuary, water gardens, formal parterres, woodland and riverside walks and informal vistas.

The famous balustrade which graces the terrace was acquired by Lord Astor from the Villa Borghese in Rome. Astor also obtained some ancient Roman sarcophagi, urns and statuary which are scattered amongst the formal gardens. It was in front of the dramatic "Fountain of Love", in 1963, at a party thrown by a later Lord Astor, that the then Minister of War, John Profumo, began his infamous affair with Christine Keeler, who was also involved with a Russian naval attaché. Profumo's denial of the affair in the House of Commons led to his downfall and disgrace, almost brought down the Conservative government and paved the way for a Labour victory in 1964.

History: The original house was built for the Duke of Buckingham, the favourite of Charles II in 1666, but the current house, the

This is one of the finest Georgian landscape gardens in Britain, extending over 400 acres (160 hectares), with valleys and vistas, lakes and rivers and more than 30 temples and monuments designed by many of the leading architects of the 18th century, such as Sir John Vanbrugh, Charles Bridgeman, William Kent and Capability Brown. It became one of the most influential landscapes anywhere in Britain.

Map: page 38

Much conservation work has been carried out over the past few years. The 1½-mile (2.4-km) avenue leading from the Buckingham entrance to the triumphal Corinthian arch gives a taste of the many fine features that can be explored.

History: The gardens were the concept of the first owner, Viscount Cobham, but were continually extended and enhanced, not least by Capability Brown, who was the head gardener from 1741. The vast mansion has been a public school since 1923 and the gardens have been in the hands of the National Trust since 1989, when a major programme of restoration and reconstitution began, with spectacular results.

Accommodation: Different Drummer, Milton Keynes (tel: 01908 564733; £–££). Local pubs: Queen's Head, Chackmore; Wheatsheaf, Maids Moreton.

third on the site, was built by Sir Charles Barry in 1850 and subsequently bought by the first Viscount Astor in 1893. The gardens have been worked on by many famous garden designers, including Geoffrey Jellicoe in 1959. The house is now a luxury hotel.

Accommodation: Cliveden House (tel: 01628 605069; ££££). Local pub: Stag & Huntsman, Hambledon.

Stowe Landscape Gardens

Outstanding classical landscape garden. English Heritage Grade I. National Trust. Map reference ⑬

Buckingham MK18 5EH, Bucks; tel: 01280 822850.
< www.nationaltrust.org.uk >
***Opening times:** garden: Mar–3rd week in Dec Wed–Sun and BH Mons 10am–5.30pm (closes at 4pm Nov–Dec); house (not NT) also open for selected periods. Parties/coaches accepted.*
***Admission prices:** garden: adults £4.80, children £2.40, family £12; house: £3*
***Facilities:** parking, disabled access, shop, refreshments. Dogs allowed on leads. No picnics.*

Turn End

A plantsman's garden surrounding a modern house within the village of Haddenham. Map reference ⑭

Townside, Haddenham, Aylesbury HP17 8BG, Bucks; tel: 01844 291383 or 01844 291817.
***Opening times:** National Garden Scheme*

ABOVE: Stowe Landscape Gardens have many architectural features, including the Palladian Bridge.

Waddesdon Manor

Grand Victorian gardens surrounding French-style chateau. English Heritage Grade II. National Trust. Map reference ⑮

Waddesdon, Aylesbury HP18 0JH, Bucks; tel: 01296 653211, info: 01296 653226. < www.waddesdon.org.uk >
Opening times: *garden: Mar–third week in Dec Wed–Sun and BH Mons 10am–5pm; house: Apr–Nov. Parties/coaches may also view by appointment.*
Admission prices: *house and grounds: adults £7, children (5–16) £6; grounds*

only: adults £4, children £2.
Facilities: *parking, disabled access (Braille guides available), shop, plants for sale, refreshments. Picnics permitted. Guide dogs only in grounds.*

days. Parties/coaches may also view by appointment. House open once per year (date is announced in the architectural press).
Admission prices: *adults £2, children 50p, parties £3 pp including talk and tour.*
Facilities: *disabled access, shop, plants for sale, refreshments. Picnics permitted. Dogs allowed on leads. No parking.*

Turn End is a post-war listed house closely integrated with garden rooms of differing character that have evolved over the past 30 years. The sequence of individual spaces, which cover about 1 acre (0.4 hectares), offers focal points and vistas at every turn, and sunken or raised beds, formal box-edging or climbers and unusual plants are displayed against a framework of old walls and mature trees.

History: In the early 1970s the architect, Peter Aldington, demonstrated how it is possible, against local opposition, to add three modern houses to an ancient village whilst complementing and enhancing it. He lives in the largest of the houses.

ABOVE: a quiet courtyard at Turn End.

RIGHT: Waddesdon Manor.

*Accommodation: Hartwell House, Aylesbury (tel: 01296 747444; ££–£££); Five Arrows Hotel, Waddesdon (01296 651727;££). **Local pubs:** Bell Inn, Beachampton; Bottle & Glass (A418 between Stone and Thame).*

Designed for the Rothschild's family in the late 19th century, Waddesdon Manor is a fantastical Loire-style chateau. Its sweeping grounds contain belts of beech, lime, horse chestnut and many other species, imported in a semi-mature state from Normandy. The garden is renowned for its seasonal displays of colourful shrubs and mature trees, much favoured by the Victorians. Spectacular carpet bedding displays on the parterre are created each year using thousands of plants.

From the parterre there is a panoramic view across the Vale of Aylesbury to a Rothschild pavilion at Eythorpe. Rock works near the avenue of double oaks were created from the excavations needed to level the site for the house, and a gulley carved out for a railway track to transport materials for the house is now a beautiful rock garden. Other highlights include a rococo aviary and a large wildflower garden.

History: Waddesdon was begun by Ferdinand de Rothschild and enhanced by Alice de Rothschild after his death in 1898. It was partly designed by Lanning Roper.

Accommodation: Hartwell House, Aylesbury (tel: 01296 747444; ££££); Five Arrows Hotel, Waddesdon (01296 651 727; ££). **Local pub:** *Bell Inn, Beachampton.*

West Wycombe Park

Eighteenth-century rococo landscape garden. English Heritage Grade I. National Trust. Map reference ⑯.

West Wycombe HP14 3AJ, Bucks; tel: 01628 488675.
< www.nationaltrust.org.uk >
Opening times: *garden: Apr–Aug Sun–Thur 2–6pm; house: Jun–Aug.*

Parties/coaches accepted. Viewing by appointment.
Admission prices: *house and grounds: adults £5, children £2.50, family £12.60; grounds only: adults £2.60, children £1.30.*
Facilities: *parking, Braille guide available, refreshments available at West Wycombe Garden Centre. Limited disabled access. No lavatories in grounds. No dogs.*

Map: page 38

West Wycombe Park is a perfectly preserved rococo landscape garden of 46 acres (18 hectares) created in the 18th century by the famous occultist Sir Francis Dashwood. Numerous temples, including the Temple of Venus, a cascade, a lake with several islands and another temple, fine trees and lawns provide a continuous series of interesting views.

History: The garden was created by Dashwood over a period of 45 years from 1735, with the first phase complete by 1752. The new impetus for less formal and more natural landscapes led to the employment in 1770 of Thomas Cook, a pupil of Capability Brown. Cook softened the appearance of the formal elements whilst retaining most of the earlier features.

Accommodation: The Inn on the Green, Cookham Dean, Berkshire (tel: 01628 482638; ££). **Local inn (with accommodation):** *George & Dragon, West Wycombe (tel: 01494 464414; ££).* **Local pub:** *Stag & Huntsman, Hambledon.*

LEFT: the idyllic lake at West Wycombe Park.

ESSEX

Audley End is the county's great historic garden, but Essex has several intriguing modern gardens, such as the Beth Chatto garden, created on wasteland over the past 40 years, the architectural Gibberd Garden, which serves as a setting for sculpture, and Glen Chantry, a plantman's garden. Essex is a relatively dry county, and its gardens tend to reflect this with plants that survive well in such conditions.

Amberden Hall

New garden developed around an old house. Map reference ⓱

Widdington, Saffron Walden, CB11 3ST, Essex; tel: 01799 540402; fax: 01799 542827.
Opening times: *by appointment only. House closed.*
Admission prices: *£2.50.*
Facilities: *disabled access, plants for sale. No parking, no picnics, no dogs.*

Amberden has recently been developed beyond its old climber-covered walls to include a secret garden, a moss garden, and a bog garden. It has cleverly planned walkways offering fresh views at every turn. Viburnum hedges with over-arching ivy extend the walled garden. In the vegetable garden there are labour-saving raised vegetable beds. A woodland walk has also been added.

BELOW: early autumn at Amberden Hall.

RIGHT: meandering walks at Audley End.

Accommodation: Cricketers, Clavering (01799 550442; ££); The Starr, Great Dunmow (01371 874321; £££). Local pub: Axe & Compasses, Arkesden.

Audley End

Jacobean house surrounded by grounds landscaped by Capability Brown. English Heritage Grade I. Owned by English Heritage. Map reference ⓲

Saffron Walden, Essex CB11 4JF; tel: 01799 522399.
Opening times: *Apr–Sep Wed–Sun & BHs: grounds 11am–6pm; house: noon–5pm (last admission 4pm); Oct weekends 11am–5pm (house until 4pm). Parties/coaches accepted. Viewing by appointment (pre-booked guided tours 10am–noon).*
Admission prices: *house & grounds: adults £8, children £4, concessions £5.20, family (2 adults and 3 children)*

£17.40; grounds: adults £4, children £2, concessions £3, family £10.
Facilities: *parking, disabled access, shop, plants for sale, refreshments. Picnics permitted. Dogs allowed on leads.*

A beautiful landscape garden designed by Capability Brown, Audley End includes a restored parterre, planted on the south side of the house in the 1830s. The River Cam, which winds through the grounds, is used to create a cascade and a pond garden and is crossed by a Robert Adam bridge. Other spectacular monuments include a Palladian Tea House, the Temple of Concord, which was built to celebrate George III's (temporary) recovery from madness, and several other follies, each designed to draw the eye down a particular vista.

The organic kitchen garden is supported by the Henry Doubleday Research Organisation, a body dedicated to researching and promoting organic gardening, farming and food. The Mound Garden, designed to allow guests to promenade in the garden, while viewing it from a height, is being restored.

History: Audley End lies on an ancient site which was originally part of a Benedictine Abbey. An enormous house, with formal gardens, it was built for Thomas Howard, commander of the British fleet against the Armada and later created Earl of Suffolk.

The property was acquired by Charles II in 1669, who described it as "too large for a King, but might do for a Lord Treasurer". Sir John Griffin Griffin (later the first Lord Braybrooke), who bought the property in the mid-18th century, tore down the wings of the house and favoured a more naturalistic approach in the garden, commissioning Capability Brown to discard the formal rectangular layout and landscape the gardens and park much as they appear today. The third Lord Braybrooke planted the parterre in the 1830s. The property was acquired by English Heritage after World War II.

Accommodation: *Cricketers, Clavering (01799 550442; ££).* **Local pub:** *Axe & Compasses, Arkesden.*

The Beth Chatto Garden

Imaginative modern garden offering year-round interest. Map reference ⓳

Beth Chatto, Elmstead Market, Colchester CO7 7DB, Essex; tel: 01206 822007; fax: 01206 825933.
< www.bethchatto.co.uk >
Opening times: *Mar–Oct Mon–Sat 9am–5pm, Nov–Feb Mon–Fri 9am–4pm. National Garden Scheme days. Parties/coaches accepted. Viewing by appointment. House open.*
Admission prices: *adults £3.50, children under 14 free, season double £15, single £10.*
Facilities: *parking, disabled access, plants for sale, refreshments. Picnics permitted. No dogs.*

T he site of the Beth Chatto Garden was originally wasteland consisting of several different problem areas. There was poor gravel soil 20 ft (6 metres) deep, dry shade beneath trees, and a sour boggy hollow. By selecting plants adapted to these different conditions, Beth Chatto created three contrasting gardens that have evolved over the past 40 years. The now famous Gravel Garden, cleverly planted to resemble a dried up river bed, is filled with drought-

BELOW: the Beth Chatto Garden with Emurus and Verbascum to the fore.

resisting plants. Shady areas make homes for woodland plants, while water gardens surround four large pools in the spring-fed hollow. The impact of the lush green growth is almost overpowering; huge upturned parasols of *Gunnera chilensis* tower above a hundred shades of green, creating a scene of harmony and tranquillity.

Accommodation: The Wivenhoe House Hotel, Wivenhoe (tel: 01206 863666; ££). **Local pub:** *The Kings Arms, Elmtead Market*

The Gibberd Garden

"Architectural" garden created in the mid-20th century, with sculpture collection. Map reference ⓴

Marsh Lane, Gilden Way, Harlow CM17 0NA, Essex; tel: 01279 442112.
Opening times: *Apr–Oct Wed, Sat, Sun, BH Mons 2–6pm. Parties accepted (small coaches only owing to narrow access). Viewing by appointment. National Garden Scheme days. House closed.*
Admission prices: *adults £4, children free when accompanied by an adult, over-60s £2.50, season single £15, family £25.*
Facilities: *parking, disabled access, shop, plants for sale, refreshments. Picnics permitted. Dogs allowed on leads.*

RIGHT: lime tree *allée* in the Gibberd Garden.

The Gibberd Garden is sited on the side of a small valley sloping down to a brook. Occupying some 7 acres (3 hectares), it was planned as a series of "rooms", each with its own character. The glades, pools and *allées* provide a setting for some 50 sculptures, large ceramic pots, architectural salvage, a gazebo and a children's moated castle with a drawbridge.

History: Sir Frederick Gibberd, the architect of Heathrow airport, Liverpool's Roman Catholic Cathedral, the Regent's Park Mosque and many other projects in Britain, acquired the property in Marsh Lane in 1956 and from then until his death in 1984 developed the site with commissioned sculptures and other works.

Accommodation: Cheshunt Marriott (tel: 01992 451245; £££). **Local pubs:** *Green Man, Toot Hill; Bee Hive, Epping Green.*

Glen Chantry

Highly acclaimed plantsman's garden created since the 1970s. Map reference ㉑

Wickham Bishops, Witham CM8 3LG, Essex; tel: 01621 891342.
Opening times: *Apr–Sep Fri–Sat 10am–4pm. Parties/coaches accepted. Viewing by appointment. House closed.*
Admission prices: *adults £2, children 50p.*
Facilities: *parking, plants for sale, refreshments. No disabled access. No picnics. No dogs.*

Glen Chantry has been developed since 1976. Most of the gently sloping, 3-acre (1.2-hectare) garden is laid out with large informally shaped, colour-themed mixed borders containing a wide selection of perennials, shrub roses and woody plants, underplanted with bulbs for early- and late-season interest.

Two ponds connected by a winding stream provide habitats for a wide range of

Map: page 38

shop, plants for sale, refreshments. Picnics permitted. Dogs allowed on leads.

Sixteenth-century Saling Hall lies in a 12-acre (5-hectare) garden and arboretum. Stretching mainly north and south of the house, these grounds offer surprisingly long parkland views, including, to the north, through a landscaped arboretum to a classical temple reflected in a serpentine lake. On the west side is a walled 17th-century garden with straight paths, apple trees and overflowing mixed borders. Throughout the garden there is a sense of discovery, as vistas of unusual planting succeed one another.

moisture-loving and woodland plants. Nearer the house, three substantial limestone rock gardens house a fascinating collection of alpine plants. The intimate White Garden with its central fountain and cruciform paths is luxuriantly planted in combinations of white, silver and green and enclosed by a rose-festooned trellis.

A formally shaped vegetable garden with central box parterre and surrounding borders of hot colours and grasses was created to mark the millennium.

Local pubs: Green Man, Little Braxted; Square & Compasses, Fuller Street.

History: The Elizabethan hall must have had a garden, but the only trace is the 100-yd/metre long moat to the east. The garden walls to the west were built in 1698 and the courtyard to the north with its old stables probably earlier. The present garden was started in 1936 by Lady Carlyle, who lived here until 1970. Since that date it has been extended by the present owners.

Accommodation: Whitehall, Broxted (tel: 01279 850603; £££–££££). *Local pubs:* White Hart, Great Saling; Green Man, Gosfield.

Saling Hall

Modern garden and arboretum with imaginative planting. English Heritage Grade II. Map reference ㉒

Great Saling, Braintree CM7 5DT, Essex; tel: 01371 850243; fax: 01371 850274.
Opening times: May–Jul Wed 2–5pm. Parties/coaches can also view by appointment (must be requested in writing) on weekdays. National Garden Scheme days. House closed.
Admission prices: adults £2.50, children free.
Facilities: parking, disabled access,

ABOVE: Glen Chantry is a plantsman's delight.

LEFT: around the pool at Saling Hall.

HERTFORDSHIRE

There are two great historic gardens open to the public, Hatfield House, with its splendid Jacobean gardens, and St Paul's Walden Bury, the childhood home of the late Queen Mother, which is a rare example of an early 18th-century garden in the French style. As far as plants are concerned, Benington Lordship is renowned for its snowdrops in February, while the Gardens of the Rose, belonging to the Royal National Rose Society, is glorious in June and July when its 30,000 roses are in full bloom.

L aid out on the site of a Norman castle, Benington Lordship overlooks Norman fishponds with views over countryside. Near the house is a formal garden entered by a magnificent folly – a neo-Norman gate house made of flint and Pulhamite. The old drive to the house leads to a rock/water garden with a good display of primulas in the spring. It backs on to double herbaceous borders, famous for their planting style. The wall behind the borders encloses a kitchen garden with raised beds. The garden is famous for its snowdrops in February.

History: The garden was designed in 1906 and restored by the present owner's wife, grandson and grand-daughter-in-law.

Local pubs: The Bell, Benington (tel: 01438 869270); Jolly Waggoner, Ardeley; George & Dragon, Watton-at-Stone.

Benington Lordship

Edwardian garden famous for its snowdrops and herbaceous borders. English Heritage Grade II. Map reference ㉓

Benington, Stevenage SG2 7BS, Herts; tel: 01438 869668; fax: 01438 869622. < www.beningtonlordship.co.uk >
Opening times: *Easter, spring and summer BH weekends pm only; snowdrop and winter flowers week in Feb (telephone end of Jan for times); herbaceous borders week in July (telephone for times). Parties/coaches (20 minimum) may also view by appointment. House closed.*
Admission prices: *adults £3.50, children free, season £10.*
Facilities: *parking, disabled access. Picnics permitted. No dogs.*

ABOVE: Benington Lordship in full bloom.

Gardens of the Rose

The leading rose garden in Britain. Map reference ㉔

Chiswell Green, St Albans AL2 3NR, Herts; tel: 01727 850461; fax: 01727 850360. < www.roses.co.uk/harkness/rnrs/ gardens.htm >
Opening times: *Jun–Sep Mon–Sat and BH Mon 10am–6pm. Coaches/parties accepted. Viewing by appointment. House closed.*
Admission prices: *adults £4, children (6–16) £1.50, disabled £3.50, parties £3.50 pp.*
Facilities: *parking, disabled access, shop, plants for sale, refreshments. Picnics permitted. Dogs allowed on leads.*

With some 30,000 rose bushes in 1,750 varieties together with 600 unnamed novelties in the trial grounds, the Gardens of the Rose contains the National Collection of roses. Emphasis is on the modern varieties but there is also a comprehensive collection of old-fashioned roses in The Queen Mother's garden, as well as shrub, rambling, climbing, miniature, ground cover and wild roses. The Peace Garden was opened in 1995 and a new Iris Garden in 1998.

For spring visitors there are also collections of bulbs and spring flowers. Among the highlights, look out for original varieties of what are believed to be the red rose of Lancaster and the white rose of York.

Accommodation: St Michael Manor, St Albans (tel: 01727 864444; ££££); Sopwell House, St Albans (tel: 01727 864477; ££££). Local pub: Black Lion Inn, St Albans (tel: 01727 851786; £–££)

Hatfield House

Historic garden originally laid out by John Tradescant the Elder. English Heritage Grade I. Map reference ㉕

The Curator's Office, Hatfield AL9 5NQ, Herts; tel: 01707 287010; fax: 01707 287033. < www.hatfield-house.co.uk >

Opening times: grounds: Easter Sat–Sep 11am–5.30pm; house noon–4pm. Parties/coaches (minimum 20) may also view by appointment. Note: on Fridays the gardens are intended specifically for connoisseurs (no concessions for children on Friday).
Admission prices: adults £4.50, Fri £6.50; children £3.50, Fri £6.50.
Facilities: parking, disabled access, shop, plants for sale, refreshments. Picnics permitted. Dogs allowed on leads.
Other attractions: national collection of model soldiers, a children's play area and 5 miles (8 km) of nature trails.

Map: page 38

The gardens cover some 42 acres (17 hectares) and include formal, knot, scented and wilderness areas, which reflect their Jacobean history. They are managed entirely organically and include a kitchen garden and Elizabethan fruit garden growing pomegranates. The formal parterres leading down to the lake to the east of the house are the outstanding feature.

History: Hatfield has a venerable history. John Tradescant the Elder, the celebrated plant hunter, was employed by Robert Cecil to plant and lay out the gardens after completion of the house in 1611. During the 18th century, when landscape gardening became fashionable, much of Tradescant's

LEFT: Gardens of the Rose contain the National Collection of roses.

Parties/coaches may also view by appointment.
Admission prices: house & garden: adults £7.50, children £7, family £19; season £25; grounds: adults & children £5.50.
Facilities: parking, shop, plants for sale, refreshments. Picnics permitted in park. Dogs allowed on leads in park. No disabled access.

K nebworth House and gardens are set in 250 acres (100 hectares) of parkland, grazed by deer, with the formal gardens and wilderness covering around 25 acres (10 hectares). Sir Edwin Lutyens designed the present layout between 1908 and 1911, and many of his features remain, including the Brick Garden and the pollarded lime avenues and sunken lawn.

A mixture of modern bush roses and older shrub roses, combined with herbaceous borders and two lily ponds, provide the cen-

work was swept away. Restoration started in the mid-19th century, a process that has been continued by the present Marchioness of Salisbury.

Accommodation: Bush Hall Hotel, Hatfield (tel: 01707 271251; ££–£££); Jarvis Comet Hotel, Hatfield (tel: 01707 265411; £–££); White Horse Hotel, Hertingfordbury (tel: 01992 586791; £).

Knebworth House

ABOVE: the superb Jacobean gardens of Hatfield House.

Right: the Jekyll Herb Garden, Knebworth.

Historic house, with formal gardens designed by Lutyens. English Heritage Grade II*. Map reference ㉖

Knebworth, Stevenage, SG3 6PY, Herts; tel: 01438 812661.
< www.knebworthhouse.com >
Opening times: selected periods between last week of Mar and end Sep: grounds 11am–5.30pm, house noon–5pm. National Garden Scheme days.

trepiece for the Rose Garden. The maze, reinstated in 1995, using box and yew, was created on the site of the Victorian maze. There are two ponds, one ornamental, the other more natural. The Horace Garden includes an evergreen oak, given by Queen Victoria to her godson, Victor, second Earl of Lytton, on his coming of age.

The Wilderness dates from Victorian

Map:
page 38

times and includes a 7-acre (3-hectare) area of ornamental trees, including Californian redwoods, the tallest cut-leafed silver birch in the UK, and a snowdrop tree.

The "quincunx" pattern and planting of the Jekyll Herb Garden was designed by Gertrude Jekyll in 1907 but was not laid out until 1982. The ornamental vegetable and culinary herb section in the Walled Garden was designed in 2000.

History: Knebworth has been the Lytton family home for more than 500 years. The structure and layout of its garden is mainly Edwardian, but it overlays an earlier elaborate Victorian design by Sir Edward Bulwer-Lytton, laid out from 1846 onwards.

Accommodation: Brocket Arms, Ayot St Lawrence (tel: 01438 820250; £–££). **Local pub:** *Lytton Arms, Park Lane, Old Knebworth.*

St Paul's Walden Bury

The childhood home of the late Queen Mother, with gardens in the 18th-century French style. English Heritage Grade I. Map reference ㉗

Whitwell, Hitchin SG4 8BP, Herts; tel: 01438 871218.
Opening times: *selected Sundays (National Garden Scheme days) in Apr &*

May, Jun 2–7pm. Parties/coaches also by appointment. House also open.
Admission prices: *adults £2.50, children 50p; £5 if by appointment.*
Facilities: *parking, disabled access, plants for sale, refreshments. Picnics permitted. Dogs allowed on leads.*

Laid out in the French style in about 1730, St Paul's Walden Bury covers 40 acres (16 hectares) and includes formal woodland garden composed of long hedge-lined avenues leading to classical temples, statues, lake and ponds, around an 18th-century house and a medieval church. Unusually, the original design remains intact, as the hedges and avenues have been replanted in their original positions. The woodland garden developed since 1950, has, amongst other plants, outstanding rhododendrons, azaleas and magnolia.

History: The gardens were designed by Edward Gilbert between 1720–30, in the formal French *patte d'oie* design. Gilbert's granddaughter, Mary Eleanor Bowes married John Lyon, Earl of Strathmore, and the house and garden still belong to the Bowes Lyon family. The late Queen Mother, Elizabeth Bowes Lyon, spent her childhood here.

Local pubs: Maiden's Head, Hitchin; Strathmore Arms, Hitchin.

Above: temple by a lake at St Paul's Walden Bury.

The Southeast

A mild climate, rich soil and a concentration of wealth all contribute to Southeast England having many of the finest gardens in the British Isles. Among its most famous gardens are Sissinghurst Castle, Sheffield Park, Great Dixter and RHS Wisley

Map: page 62

KENT

Kent is often described as the "Garden of England", not least because for centuries its market gardens supplied London with fresh fruit and veg. Outstanding ornamental gardens also flourish as the large number of English Heritage Grade I gardens testifies, and there are also interesting plantsman's gardens, such as Nettlestead Place and Church Hill Cottage. The county's most admired garden is undoubtedly Sissinghurst Castle.

Belmont

Garden of 18th-century origin with kitchen garden restored by Arabella Lennox-Boyd. English Heritage grade II. Map reference ❶

Belmont Park, Throwley, Faversham ME13 0HH, Kent; tel: 01795 890202. < www.belmont-house.org >
Opening times: *Apr–Sep Sat–Thur 2–5pm. House open Sat, Sun & BH Mons. Parties/coaches accepted.*
Admission prices: *adults £5.25, children £2.50, over-60s £4.75.*
Facilities: *parking, disabled access, shop, plants for sale, refreshments. Picnics permitted. Guide dogs only.*

A mixture of formal and informal, herbaceous and woodland, fruit and vegetable, there is something for everyone at Belmont. To the east and south of the house large formal lawns (including croquet lawns) are dotted with fine specimen trees, including a 100-year-old tulip tree and a Cedar of Lebanon. There is a woodland area and pinetum, plus a shell grotto and a small walled garden bordering the courtyard. The latter has extensive long borders, magnificent wisteria and a large rose border. The new kitchen garden was designed by Arabella Lennox-Boyd.

History: The gardens have been evolving since they were laid out in the 1790s.

Local pubs: The Albion Tavern, Faversham; George Pub, Newnham.

Chartwell

Winston Churchill's family home. English Heritage Grade II*. Map reference ❷

Westerham TN16 1PS, Kent, tel: 01732 866368; fax: 01732 868 193. < www.nationaltrust.org.uk >

PRECEDING PAGES: Bateman's, Sussex.

OPPOSITE: the borders at Great Dixter, East Sussex.

ABOVE: detail at Chartwell.

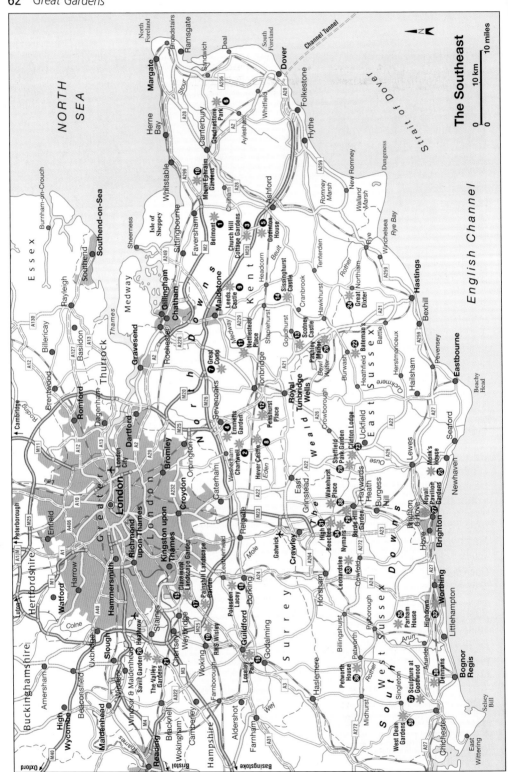

The Southeast

NORTH SEA

English Channel

Strait of Dover

North Foreland
South Foreland
Broadstairs
Ramsgate
Margate
Sandwich
Deal
Dover
Channel Tunnel
Herne Bay
Whitstable
Isle of Sheppey
Sheerness
Whitfield
Folkestone
Hythe
Canterbury
Goodnestone Park ❻
Faversham
Sittingbourne
Mount Ephraim Gardens ❿
Ashford
New Romney
Dungeness
Romney Marsh
Walland Marsh
Maidstone
Belmont ❶
Church Hill Cottage Gardens ❸
Godinton House ❺
Headcorn
Gillingham
Chatham
Rochester
Gravesend
Leeds Castle ❾
Nettlestead Place ⓫
Sissinghurst Castle ⓮
Tenterden
Rye
Winchelsea
Rye Bay
Hastings
Bexhill
Cranbrook
Hawkhurst
Great Dixter ㉑
Great Comp ❼
Scotney Castle ⓭
Pashley Manor ㉓
Batemans ㉒
Heathfield
Herstmonceux
Pevensey
Eastbourne
Beachy Head
Romford
Dagenham
Dartford
Bromley
Orpington
Sevenoaks
Chartwell ❹
Emmetts Garden ❹
Hever Castle ❷
Westerham
Penshurst Place ⓬
Royal Tunbridge Wells
Crowborough
Uckfield
Clinton Lodge ㉘
Monk's House ㉖
Lewes
Seaford
Newhaven
London
London City
Croydon
Caterham
Reigate
Redhill
East Grinstead
Sheffield Park Garden ㉙
Wakehurst Place ㉚
Haywards Heath
Burgess Hill
Royal Pavilion Gardens ㉗
Brighton & Hove
Gatwick
Crawley
High Beeches ㉜
Borde Hill Garden ㉛
Nymans ㉝
Leonardslee ㉞
Cowfold
Worthing
Littlehampton
Bognor Regis
Selsey Bill
East Wittering
Chichester
Arundel
West Dean Gardens ㊴
Sculpture at Goodwood ㊱
Singleton
Midhurst
Petworth House ㊳
Parham House ㊵
Highdown ㊲
Denmans ㊶
Pulborough
Billingshurst
Horsham
Haslemere
Farnham
Aldershot
Camberley
Woking
RHS Wisley ⓳
Guildford
Loseley Park ㉒
Godalming
Leatherhead
Dorking
Polesden Lacey ⓲
Claremont Landscape Garden ⓯
Painshill Landscape Garden ⓰
Weybridge
Chertsey
Savill Garden ⓴
The Valley Gardens
Windsor & Maidenhead
Slough
Maidenhead
High Wycombe
Beaconsfield
Amersham
Watford
Harrow
Hammersmith
Richmond upon Thames
Kingston upon Thames
Staines
Reading
Wokingham
Bracknell
Basingstoke

Essex
Kent
East Sussex
West Sussex
Surrey
Hampshire
Hertfordshire
Buckinghamshire
North Downs
The Weald
South Downs

0   10 km
0   10 miles

Opening times: last week in Mar–Oct Wed–Sat (plus Tues & Aug BH) 11am–5pm (last admission 4.15pm). National Garden Scheme days. House open. Parties/coaches may view by appointment (tel: 01732 868381).
Admission prices: house & garden: adults £6.50, children £3.25, family £16.25; garden & Churchill's studio: adults £3.25, children £1.60.
Facilities: parking, disabled access, shop, plants for sale, refreshments. No picnics. Dogs allowed on leads.

Commanding unrivalled views over the Weald of Kent, Chartwell contains lakes, a water garden, golden orfe pools and a rose garden. Among the highlights is the Golden Rose Walk given to Sir Winston and Lady Churchill by their children on their golden wedding anniversary. Best viewed from the terrace above, it features 32 varieties of yellow and golden roses. Nearby is a Wendy house built for their daughter Mary Soames. Visitors can see evidence of Sir Winston's own handiwork in the brick walls he erected in the 1920s and '30s.

History: The planting and overall design were largely the responsibility of Lady Churchill, assisted by Victor Vincent, her head gardener from the end of World War II until 1979. After Churchill's death in 1965, the property was administered by the National Trust, which employed Lanning Roper to re-design parts of the garden in co-operation with Mary Soames.

Local pubs: Harrow Inn, Igtham Common; George & Dragon, Igtham.

Church Hill Cottage Gardens

Informal cottage gardens with many unusual plants. Map reference ❸

Charing Heath, Ashford TN27 0BU, Kent; tel: 01233 712522; fax: 01233 712522.

Opening times: last week Mar–Sep Tues–Sun 10am–5pm. National Garden Scheme days. Parties/coaches accepted. House closed.
Admission prices: adults £2, children free.
Facilities: parking, disabled access, shop, plants for sale, refreshments. Picnics permitted. Dogs allowed on leads.

A quiet and peaceful 1½-acre (0.6-hectare) garden surrounding a 16th-century cottage, Church Hill is arranged as a series of interconnecting areas linked by winding paths. Many unusual plants, mainly perennials planted alongside the paths, and clever use of colour, give a very natural feel to the garden. The garden has particularly fine collections of dianthus, ferns, hostas and violas.

Accommodation: Ringlestone Inn, Harrietsham (tel: 01622 859900; ££); Eastwell Manor, Boughton Lees (tel: 01233 213000; ££££).
Local pubs: Red Lion, Charing Heath; Dering Arms, Pluckley.

ABOVE: down the garden path at Church Hill Cottage.

spring flowers, both in the garden and in the surrounding woodland, which in autumn is spectacular. The garden is also attractive for its outstanding views over the Weald of Kent.

History: Emmett's design was influenced by William Robinson, an advisor to Frederick Lubbock, the owner of the house from 1890 to 1926. It was given to the National Trust in 1964 by Charles Boise, an American geologist who oversaw a programme of plantings intended to ensure botanical continuity.

Local pubs: Harrow Inn, Igtham Common; George & Dragon, Igtham.

Godinton House

Jacobean mansion with a garden designed in the 1920s by Sir Reginald Blomfield. English Heritage Grade I. Map reference ❺

The Godinton House Preservation Trust, Godinton Lane, Ashford TN23 3BP, Kent; tel: 01233 620773, fax: 01233 647351.
< www.godinton-house-gardens.co.uk >
***Opening times:** year-round: house & gardens Fri, Sat & Sun 2–5.30pm (last tour 4.30pm); gardens: Thur–Sun 2–5.30pm. National Garden Scheme days. Parties of 12 or more must view by appointment.*
***Admission prices:** house & gardens: £6, gardens: £3; children free.*

Emmetts Garden

Hilltop garden with views over the Weald of Kent. English Heritage Grade II. National Trust. Map reference ❹

Ide Hill, Sevenoaks TN14 6AY, Kent; tel: 01732-750490.
***Opening times:** last week in Mar–Jun Wed–Sun 11am–5pm; Jul–Oct Wed, Sat, Sun & BH Mon 11am–5pm. National Garden Scheme day. Parties/coaches accepted. House closed.*
***Facilities:** parking, disabled access, plants for sale, refreshments. Picnics permitted. Dogs allowed on leads.*

ABOVE: Emmetts House and Garden.

RIGHT: graceful Godinton.

Acharming and informal garden laid out in the 19th century, Emmetts contains exotic and unusual plants and shrubs from many parts of the world. It also has the highest treetop in Kent. There are glorious displays of flowering shrubs and

Facilities: parking, limited disabled access, plants for sale, refreshments (teas). Picnics permitted. No disabled access. No dogs.

Map: page 62

The great boundary hedge of Godinton House is one of the largest in the country. Behind the long yew hedge, shaped to mirror the gables on the house, is the formal garden featuring lawns, topiary, pond, terraces and the Pan Garden. In spring, other notable features include daffodils, a large tulip tree and cherry trees. Numerous varieties of clematis grow up the walls and fruit trees. The delphinium borders were planted by the Delphinium Society.

History: This glorious Jacobean mansion was reworked in the 1920s by the architect and garden designer Sir Reginald Blomfield, who also created the Italian garden with statuary, loggia and summerhouse. Restoration is ongoing.

*Accommodation: The Lime Tree, Lenham (tel: 01622 859509; £–££), Dering Arms, Pluckley (tel: 01233 840371; ££). **Local pub:** Bell Inn, Smarden.*

Goodnestone Park

An 8th-century estate which has associations with Jane Austen. English Heritage Grade II*. Map reference ➏

Goodnestone, Canterbury CT3 1PL, Kent; tel: 01304 840107.
< www.kenttourism.co.uk/goodnestone >
Opening times: third week Mar–third week Oct Mon, Wed–Fri 11am–5pm, Sun noon–6pm. National Garden Scheme Days, including in Feb to see snowdrops. May book to see house.
Admission prices: adults £3.30, children 50p, over-60s £2.80, family (2 adults and 2 children) £5.60, season £14.50.
Facilities: parking, disabled access, plants for sale, refreshments. Picnics permitted. No dogs.

Covering about 14 acres (6 hectares), the gardens surround a fine Palladian mansion. The formal area around the house has fine specimen trees and a parterre planted for the millennium. This leads through a small arboretum to the woodland area, with a 1920s rockery and pond, rhododendrons, magnolias, camellias, cornus and a large collection of hellebores.

The lovely Walled Garden, with some parts of the wall dating from the 17th century, was redesigned over the past 30 years. It is filled with clematis, old red roses and many herbaceous plants.

History: Goodnestone House was built in 1700 by Brook Bridges and enlarged by his great-grandson, whose daughter married Jane Austen's brother, prompting many references to Goodnestone in the author's letters. The garden nearest the house dates from the 16th century, with 17th-century additions and 18th-century parkland. The woodland was laid out in the 1920s.

*Accommodation: Magnolia House, Canterbury (tel: 01227 765121; ££); Hotel Continental (tel: 01227 280280; ££–£££). **Local pub:** Griffins Head, Chillenden.*

ABOVE: an abundance of peonies in the Walled Garden at Goodnestone Park.

Great Comp

Plantsman's garden and 17th-century manor house. Map reference ❼

RIGHT: *Platt, Borough Green, Sevenoaks TN15* topiary at *8QS, Kent; tel: 01732 886154.* Hever Castle. *< www.greatcomp.co.uk >*
Opening times: Apr–Oct 11am–6pm.
BELOW: *National Garden Scheme days.*
Great Comp *Parties/coaches accepted. House closed.* has a vast *Admission prices: adults £4, children* collection of *£1, season £12, over-60s season £8.* plants from *Facilities: parking, disabled access,* all over the *shop, plants for sale, refreshments.* world. *Picnics permitted. Guide dogs only.*

Hever Castle

Award-winning gardens surrounding a romantic castle that was the childhood home of Anne Boleyn. English Heritage Grade I. Map reference ❽

Hever, Edenbridge TN8 7NG, Kent; tel: 01732 865224.
< www.hevercastle.co.uk >
Opening times: Mar–Nov daily; gardens: 11am–6pm (castle from noon), last admission 5pm. No parties/coaches.
Admission prices: gardens & castle: adults £8.40, children £4.60 (under-5s free), over-60s £7.10, family (2 adults and 2 children) £21.40; gardens: adults £6.70, children £4.40, over-60s £5.70, family £17.30.
Facilities: parking, disabled access, shop, plants for sale, refreshments. Picnics permitted. Dogs allowed on leads.

Developed over more than 40 years by the present owners Roderick and Joy Cameron, Great Comp provides interest throughout the year with its vast and varied plant collection from all over the world. Grass paths meander some 7 acres (3 hectares), culminating in the Italian Garden. Several ruins, devised by the owners, are used to great effect. Among the many plants, the large collection of salvias is of particular note, as are the 70 magnolias in 30 varieties. There is also a nursery selling many unusual plants.

Local pub: Harrow Inn, Igtham.

Hever Castle dates from the 13th century, but the gardens were laid out in Edwardian times at the behest of the American William Waldorf Astor. The large number of different areas and features offer colour and life all year round, from snowdrops and winter crocus in March to dahlia borders and spectacular foliage in autumn. It has good formal gardens, including the majestic Italian Garden, which has an outstanding collection of Roman statuary assembled by Astor during his time as the American ambassador to Italy. Among the garden's other outstanding features are the yew maze, the splashing water maze and a 35-acre (14-hectare) lake. Notable topiary near the castle and in the Chess Garden, and a large rose garden complete the picture.

History: The gardens were laid out between 1904 and 1908 by Joseph Cheal & Son. They have been evolving ever since and are still maturing.

Accommodation: Merzie Meadows, Tonbridge (tel: 01622 820500; £). **Local pubs:** *Henry VIII Inn, Hever; Castle Inn, Chiddingstone.*

Leeds Castle

Historic castle with extensive grounds. English Heritage Grade II*. Map reference ❾

Maidstone ME17 1PL Kent; tel: 01622 765400, fax: 01622 735616. < www.leeds-castle.co.uk >
National collection: Monarda.
Opening times: Mar–Oct 10am–5pm, Nov–Feb 10am–3pm. Parties/coaches accepted.
Admission prices: Mar–Oct adults £11, children £7.50, concessions £9.50; Nov–Feb adults £9.50, children £6, concessions £8; special rates for groups of 15 +).
Facilities: parking, disabled access, shop, plants for sale, refreshments. Picnics permitted. Dogs allowed on leads.

Leeds Castle is a major tourist attraction and popular all year round. Though the castle itself tends to be the main attraction, the gardens and grounds are well worth exploring. They begin (from the car park) with the Wood Garden beside the River Len, which is filled with daffodils and anemones in spring and then flowering summer shrubs such as rhododendrons and azaleas.

Map: page 62

There are several garden areas. The Culpeper Garden, containing the National Collection of monarda (bergamot) was created by the painter and garden designer Russell Page (1906–85). It features traditional neat box hedges surrounding colourful perennials and roses, pinks, lupins and poppies. The Mediterranean-style "Lady Baillie Garden" includes terraces planted with palms, olives, pomegranate, mimosa, vines, hedychium and echiums, all more usually found in warmer climates.

There are 13 greenhouses, containing a renowned collection of pelargonium, fuchsia and fan-trained, hand-pollinated peaches and nectarines. In the 1730s Lord Fairfax sent ginseng and wild olives from Virginia to be grown in the castle's hothouses. There is also an important vineyard producing more than 8,000 bottles of wine a year.

History: The park was established in the

LEFT:
Leeds Castle nestling in deepest Kent.

Middle Ages, when Leeds Castle was an important royal residence. There is documented evidence of a vineyard at the castle in a Register of Royal Expenses dated 1291–93 for Edward I and Queen Eleanor of Castile. Russell Page was responsible for many of the features evident in today's grounds, including the lake and the duckery, as well as the Culpeper Garden.

Local pub: Ringlestone Inn, Harrietsham (tel: 01622 859900; ££–£££).

Mount Ephraim Gardens

Mixed garden with many features including topiary and water garden. Map reference ⑩

Hernhill, Faversham ME13 9TX, Kent; tel: 01227 751496.
< www.mountephraimgardens.co.uk >
Opening times: May–Sep Mon, Wed, Thur, Sat & Sun 1–6pm, BH weekends 11am–6pm. National Garden Scheme days. Parties/coaches accepted. House open for groups by appointment.
Admission prices: adults £3, children £1, groups £2.50 pp, season £8.
Facilities: parking, disabled access, shop, plants for sale, refreshments. Picnics permitted. Dogs allowed on leads.

BELOW: Mount Ephraim.

Mount Ephraim's 9 acres (3.6 hectares) of gardens are set in the heart of an 800-acre (325-hectare) fruit farm. Remarkable for their variety, they are set against a backdrop of trees of outstanding shapes and contrasts, and include a topiary and water garden. Magnificent views extend over the Swale and Thames, and rose terraces enclosed by yew hedges slope down to a lake with a woodland area behind. Planting throughout is intensive, giving colour and interest throughout the year. The Japanese Rock Garden, ornamented with stone huterns and based on a series of pools, follows a gently winding route.

History: Mount Ephraim has belonged to the Dawes family for 300 years. The existing house was built in 1876 by Sir Edwyn Sandys Dawes, a wealthy and successful ship owner, on the site of his family home.

Accommodation: The Garden Hotel, Boughton (tel: 01227 751411; £–££). The White Horse, Boughton (tel: 01227 751343; ££). Local pubs: Three Horseshoes and Red Lion, Hernhill; Dove, Dargate; Shipwrights Arms, Oare.

Nettlestead Place

Plantsman's garden surrounding 13th-century manor house. Map reference ⑪

Nettlestead, Maidstone ME18 5HA, Kent; tel: 01622 812205.
Opening times: National Garden Scheme days in June, Jul & Sep. Parties/coaches accepted. House closed.
Admission prices: adults £3, children free.
Facilities: parking, disabled access, refreshments. Picnics permitted. No dogs.

Nettlestead Place, a medieval manor house that was recorded in the Domesday Book, is set in 7 acres (3 hectares) of grounds. An early 14th-century gatehouse leads through an avenue of Irish yews to the courtyard. Kentish ragstone walls, yew, thuja, beech, and box hedges surround the various garden rooms.

Across the main drive is the Walnut Tree Lawn, which is named after the very old

walnut tree. Other trees include tulip trees, various varieties of camellia and cryptomeria. From here a path to the Rose Garden leads through a small shady garden, with abundant plantings of dwarf narcissi and daffodils, hosta, shade-loving geranium and ferns.

On the east side of the house an 80-yd/metre-long terraced gravel garden is planted with rock plants and dwarf bulbs. A daffodil meadow separates the area from a series of small canals leading to the Glen Garden, a valley area with a natural stream planted with primula, meconopsis, ferns, hosta, shade geraniums and dwarf pines.

Local pub: Hop Pole Inn, Maidstone.

Penshurst Place

Elizabethan garden. English Heritage Grade I. Map reference ⑫

The Lord De L'Isle, Penshurst, Tonbridge TN11 8DG, Kent; tel: 01892 870307. < www.penshurstplace.com >
Opening times: *Apr–Oct 10.30am–6pm. House open noon–5.30pm (until 4pm Sat). Parties/coaches accepted.*
Admission prices: *house & garden: adults £6.50, children £4.50, family £18; garden: adults £5, children £4, over-60s £4.50, family £15, season £30.*
Facilities: *parking, disabled access, shop, plants for sale, refreshments. Picnics permitted. No dogs.*

Among the oldest gardens in private ownership, the gardens of Penshurst Place remain much as they were in Elizabethan times. The 11-acre (4.5-hectare) formal walled gardens offer a variety in form, foliage and bloom throughout the year, passing from bulbs in spring, through summer roses and exuberant herbaceous borders, to mellow orchard fruits and a blaze of colour in autumn. Winter starkness reveals the garden's shape and structure.

History: There has been a garden at Penshurst since the 14th century (earliest records show 1346), but the present gardens were laid out by Sir Henry Sidney in the 16th century. Central to his original design was the acclaimed Italian Garden, a project that involved shifting thousands of tons of earth and building an ingenious system of walls and terraces.

Later, in the 19th century, the second Lord De L'Isle and Robert Dudley set about restoring the formality of the garden, dividing the garden and orchards into a series of small self-contained garden rooms, separated by yew hedges. The process has been continued in modern times by some of the leading garden designers, including Lanning Roper and John Codrington.

Accommodation: Hotel Du Vin, Royal Tunbridge Wells (tel: 01892 526455; ££–£££); Danehurst House, Royal Tunbridge Wells (tel: 01892 527739; £–££). Local pub: Leicester Arms, Penshurst.

Map: page 62

Above: the gardens and manor at Nettlestead Place.

Below: the Elizabethan garden at Penshurst Place.

Scotney Castle

**Moated castle with romantic gardens
and woodland. English Heritage
Grade I. National Trust. Map
reference ⑬**

*Lamberhurst, Tunbridge Wells TN3 8JN,
Kent; tel: 01892 891081, fax: 01892
890110. < www.nationaltrust.org.uk >*
Opening times: *garden: last week
Mar–Oct Wed–Sun (and BH Mons)
11am–6pm. National Garden Scheme
days. Castle: May–mid Sep. Estate open
all year. Coaches/parties accepted.*
Admission prices: *adults £4.40, children
£2.20, family £11.*
Facilities: *parking, disabled access, shop.
Picnics permitted. Guide dogs only.*

Deep in the hills around Lamberhurst,
the ruins of Scotney Castle create a
picturesque focus for its gardens.
Good views from the bastion lead across the
Quarry Garden to the valley and woodlands
beyond. Ghent azaleas and rhododendrons
provide spectacular colour in May and June,
while the great trees, including liquidambar
and tulip trees, and many flowering shrubs

ABOVE:
picturesque
Scotney
Castle.

take on rich colours in autumn, as do the
woodlands of the surrounding 700-acre
(280-hectare) estate. Near the lake there is a
reclining figure in bronze by Henry Moore.

History: Edward Hussey, with advice
from William Sawrey Gilpin, created the
garden in the picturesque style of the mid-
19th century. The castle, really a fortified
manor house with 16th- and 17th-century
additions, was considered uninhabitable and
was selectively demolished to leave romantic walls and towers. In the mid-20th
century additional planting was initiated by
Christopher Hussey.

*Accommodation: Hotel Du Vin, Tunbridge Wells
(tel: 01892 526455; ££–£££); Danehurst House,
Tunbridge Wells (tel: 01892 527739; £–££).*
Local pub: Green Cross Inn, Goudhurst.

Sissinghurst Castle

**Famous garden created by Vita
Sackville-West and her husband
Harold Nicolson. English Heritage
Grade I. Map reference ⑭**

*Sissinghurst, Cranbrook TN17 2AB, Kent;
tel: 01580 710 700, Infoline: 01580 710*

701, fax: 01580 710 702.
< *www.nationaltrust.org.uk* >
Opening times: *last week Mar–Oct Mon, Tues, Fri 11am–6.30pm, Sat–Sun & BH 10am–6.30pm (last admission 5.30pm or 30 mins before dusk). Parties/coaches accepted. House open (library and writing room only).*
Admission prices: *adults £6.50, children £3, over-60s £6.50, family (two adults and three children) £16.*
Facilities: *parking, disabled access, shop, plants for sale, refreshments. Picnics permitted. Dogs allowed on leads in estate.*

Sissinghurst Castle Garden, created by the English aristocrats Vita Sackville-West and Harold Nicolson in the 1930s, is set around the remains of an Elizabethan manor house in unspoilt Wealden countryside. The garden, described by Harold Nicolson as "a succession of privacies" successfully combines contrasting elements in the couple's characters. Nicolson, a classicist, liked formality and clean lines, while Vita, a romantic, favoured profusion and surprise. She wrote, on first seeing the castle, "I fell in love; love at first sight. I saw what could be made of it. It was Sleeping Beauty's Castle, but a castle running away into sordidness and squalor, and a garden crying out for rescue." It is the combination of these two apparent opposite

characters that has made the garden a major influence on modern garden design.

Map: page 62

The garden can best be described as a sequence of 10 separate gardens linked by vistas. These include the White Garden, Rose Garden, Lime Walk, Cottage Garden, Tower Lawn and Yew Walk, Herb Garden, the Moat Walk and the Nuttery and the Orchard. Sissinghurst is of international importance and repute due to its historic interest, horticultural significance and superb collection of plants.

History: The 16th-century manor house was built by Sir John Baker on the site of a medieval manor house. The tower, in which Vita later wrote, dates from 1573 and was built for a visit by Elizabeth I. During the Seven Years' War (1756–63) the property served as a prison for captured French soldiers and became known as Sissinghurst Castle; from 1794 it served as a work farm for the poor. Sackville-West and Nicolson bought Sissinghurst in 1930 and immediately set about renovating the ruined manor, dismantling the lean-to additions, and planning their garden. At the base of the tower a tablet simply says "To Vita Sackville-West, who made this garden."

Accommodation: *Sissinghurst Castle Farm (tel: 01580 712885; £–££); Cloth Hall Oast, Cranbrook (tel: 01580 527739; ££).* ***Local pubs:*** *The Bull, Sissinghurst; Three Chimneys, Biddenden; Langley Oast, Langley.*

LEFT: the Tower Lawn. Sissinghurst castle.

SURREY

Like Kent, Surrey is richly endowed with gardens. In addition to significant landscape gardens, such as Claremont and Painshill, it has two of the finest woodland gardens, Savill and Valley, both in Windsor Great Park. Perhaps its greatest horticultural asset is RHS Wisley, a vast demonstration garden run by the Royal Horticultural Society.

Claremont Landscape Garden

Historic landscape garden. English Heritage Grade I. National Trust. Map reference ⓯

Portsmouth Road, Esher KT10 9JG, Surrey; tel: 01372-467806.
< www.nationaltrust.org.uk >
Opening times: *Apr–Oct Mon–Fri 10am–6pm, weekends & BH Mons 10am–7pm (late-night opening on selected dates in May and June); Nov–Mar 10am–5pm or sunset if earlier. National Garden Scheme days. Belvedere Tower open first weekend in the month Apr–Oct. Parties/coaches must view by appointment (no coaches Sun or BHs). House closed.*
Admission prices: *adults £3.80, family £9.50, groups of 15 min £3.20 pp.*
Facilities: *parking, disabled access,*

Above: the grass amphitheatre at Claremont.

shop, plants for sale, refreshments. Picnics permitted. Dogs allowed on leads Nov–Mar only.

C laremont was once described as "the noblest of any [landscape] in Europe". It has numerous grand features. From the belvedere, built by John Vanbrugh in 1715, views extend over the bastions to a bowling green and the Lime Avenue. Another superb vantage point is the immense grass amphitheatre offering views of the lake and woods. The grotto of sandstone and chalk next to the lake was probably built by Joseph and Josiah Lane, designers of the grotto at Painswick *(see page 130)*.

History: Almost all the great landscape designers have worked on Claremont. It was first laid out by Lord Clare in 1715 around a castellated palace designed by Vanbrugh. Charles Bridgeman, the leading landscape gardener at the time, who had co-operated with Vanbrugh on Stowe, built the grass amphitheatre in about 1726. William Kent remodelled the landscape in front of the amphitheatre in the early 1730s in the fashionable natural form. Lord Clive (Clive of India) bought the estate in 1768 and replaced Vanbrugh's palace with a neo-classical house designed by Capability Brown, who made the landscape less formal and disguised the amphitheatre by covering it in trees and shrubs. The estate was bought in 1816 by the royal family to provide a home for Princess Charlotte, the only daughter of the Prince Regent, and remained a royal property until 1922. The National Trust purchased it in 1975.

Accommodation: Hilton National Hotel, Cobham (tel: 01932 864471; ££–£££) . Local pub: King William IV, Mickleham (south of Leatherhead).

Map: page 62

Loseley Park

Elizabethan house with a large walled garden based upon a Gertrude Jekyll design. Map reference ⓰

Guildford GU3 1HS, Surrey; tel: 01483 304440, fax: 01483 302036. < www.loseley-park.com >
Opening times: *garden: early May–Sep Wed–Sun (plus summer BHs) 11am–5pm. National Garden Scheme days. House: early Jun–late Aug Wed–Sun. Parties/coaches (min 10) may also view by appointment.*
Admission prices: *house & garden: adults £6, children £3, over-60s £5. Garden: adults £3, children £1.50, over-60s £2.50, season garden ticket (ticket holder plus one guest) £15.*
Facilities: *parking, disabled access, shop, plants for sale, refreshments. Picnics permitted. Guide dogs only.*

L oseley Park comprises five gardens, each with its own theme and character, including the award-winning Rose Garden containing over 1,000 rose bushes, the bold and fiery Fruit and Flavour Garden and the peaceful Fountain Garden filled with plants of a cream, white and silver theme. There is also a Vine Walk, a vegetable and flower garden and a delightful Moat Walk. There is plenty of interest and colour throughout the season, though June is a particularly good month to visit on account of the roses.

History: The current garden, based on a Gertrude Jekyll design, was designed by Serena Smith. The original 2½-acre (1-hectare) walled garden was laid out formally in the 1500s and partly redesigned by Gertrude Jekyll at the turn of the 20th century. Sadly, by the end of the World War II the garden had become overgrown and neglected. Since then it has progressed through the years as an organic market garden. In 1991, the present owners set about restoring the walled garden to its 16th-century glory.

Accommodation: *The Angel Posting House, Guildford (tel: 01483 564555; £££).* **Local pub:** *Red Lion Inn, Shamley Green.*

Painshill Landscape Garden

One of Europe's finest 18th-century landscape gardens. English Heritage Grade I. Map reference ⓱

Portsmouth Road, Cobham KT11 1JE, Surrey; tel: 01932 864674, information: 01932 868 001; < www.painshill.co.uk >.
Opening times: *Apr–Oct Tues–Sun and BH 10.30am–6pm; Nov–Mar Tues–Thur, weekends & BHs 11am–4pm (or dusk if earlier). Parties/coaches accepted. House closed.*
Admission prices: *adults £4.50, children (5–16) £2, over-60s £4, individual season £20, family season £40.*
Facilities: *parking, disabled access, shop, refreshments. Picnics permitted. No dogs.*

Aʙᴏᴠᴇ: the Moat Walk at Loseley Park.

Bᴇʟᴏᴡ: landscape as theatre at Painshill.

Covering over 160 acres (65 hectares), Painshill has been described as "landscape theatre", in which the spectator moves from scene to scene. Staged around a huge serpentine lake, it offers new interest at every turn – a Gothic temple provides the garden's focal point, a Chinese bridge leads to a grotto, and a ruined abbey, a Turkish tent, a Gothic tower and a waterwheel provide further surprises. The great Cedar of Lebanon is reputedly the largest in Europe.

As well as the buildings, hills and towering cedars, Painshill has authentic 18th-century plantings and a working vineyard.

History: The garden was created by Charles Hamilton, plantsman, painter and designer, between 1738 and 1773. He transformed barren heathland into ornamental pleasure grounds and parkland of dramatic beauty and contrasting scenery, dominated by a 14-acre (5.6-hecatre) serpentine lake fed from the river by an immense waterwheel.

*Accommodation: Hilton National Hotel, Cobham (tel: 01932 864471; ££–£££). **Local pub:** King William IV, Mickleham.*

Polesden Lacey

Regency-cum-Edwardian house with fine gardens and walks. National Trust. Map reference ⓲

Great Bookham, Dorking RH5 6BD, Surrey; tel: 01372 452048, information: 01372 458203, fax: 01372 452023. < www.nationaltrust.org.uk >

BELOW: the pergolas are a feature at Polesden Lacey.

Opening times: garden and walk: daily 11am–6pm; house: last week Mar–Oct Wed–Sun 11am–5pm. Coaches/parties accepted.
Admission prices: walks and garden: adults £4, children £2, family £10; house and garden £7; children £3.50, family £17.50
Facilities: parking, disabled access, shop, plants for sale, refreshments. Picnics permitted. Dogs allowed on leads on walk only.

This is a 30-acre (12-hectare) garden with lawns, borders and a walled rose garden with over-arching pergolas. It offers lovely walks through the estate, with stunning views of the North Downs.

History: The dramatist Richard Sheridan owned Polesden Lacey in the early 19th century and extended its finest feature, the Long Walk. The speculative builder Thomas Cubitt (1788–1855) built the house in the Greek classical style for Joseph Bonsor, a wealthy stationer and bookseller, who also planted 20,000 trees. The garden was remodelled in 1906 by Mrs Greville, a well-known Edwardian hostess, and in 1923 King George VI and Queen Elizabeth (the Queen Mother) spent part of their honeymoon here. Polesden Lacey was given to the National Trust in 1944.

*Accommodation: Hilton National Hotel, Cobham (tel: 01932 864471; ££–£££). **Local pub:** Red Lion Inn, Shamley Green.*

RHS Wisley

Sumptuous garden and educative horticultural centre. English Heritage Grade II*. Map reference ⓳

Woking GU23 6QB, Surrey; tel: 01483 224234. < www.rhs.org.uk >
National Collection: crocus, colchicum, daboecia, epimedium, erica, daphne, galanthus, hosta and pulmonaria.
Opening times: all year Mon–Sat

10am–4.30pm or sunset (6pm during British Summer Time), Sun 9am–4.30pm or sunset (6pm during British Summer Time). House closed. Parties/coaches accepted but no viewing by appointment.
Admission prices: *adults £6, children (6–16) £2, under-6s free, groups (min 10) adults £5 pp, children £1.60 pp. RHS members (plus one guest) free. Companion to disabled free.*
Facilities: *parking, disabled access, shop, plants for sale, refreshments. Picnics permitted. No dogs.*

With its romantic half-timbered Tudor-style buildings and a canal designed by Sir Geoffrey Jellicoe, Wisley is a particularly beautiful garden. The soil is mainly acid sand which is poor in nutrients and fast draining, but there is a wide range of very different garden areas. There is a rock garden, formal and walled gardens by Lanning Roper, herbaceous borders, a rose garden, summer garden, winter garden and woodland garden, a fruit field, glasshouses and an arboretum, as well as alpine gardens, vegetable gardens and a new country garden designed by Penelope Hobhouse.

Any gardening speciality can be met at Wisley (one area even specialises in model gardens). Its purpose is to "use and occupy the Estate for the purpose of an Experimental Garden and the Encouragement and Improvement of Scientific and Practical Horticulture in all its Branches". Visitors will find trial areas of collections of cultivars, and there are laboratories for research into pests, diseases and general garden problems.

History: In 1878 George Ferguson Wilson, a businessman, scientist, inventor and keen gardener, bought the site and established the Oakwood Experimental Garden with the idea of growing difficult plants successfully. Soon the garden was renowned for its lilies, gentians, Japanese irises, primulas and waterplants. Despite changes since then, it is still true to his original concept.

In 1903, the eminent botanist Sir Thomas Hanbury, who created the famous La Mortola garden in Italy, bought the estate and presented it in trust to the RHS.

Map: page 62

ABOVE LEFT: RHS Wisley in autumn.

Accommodation: *Hilton National Hotel, Cobham (tel: 01932 864471; ££–£££).* **Local pub:** *King William IV, Mickleham.*

Below: the Savill Garden in spring.

Savill Garden (Windsor Great Park)

Woodland garden within Windsor Great Park. English Heritage Grade I. Map reference ⑳

Englefield Green SL4 2HT, Surrey (access via Wick Lane); tel: 01753 847518, fax: 01753 847536.
< www.savillgarden.co.uk >.
National Collection: *Ilex, Magnolia,*

Mahonia, Pernettya, Pieris, Rhododendron, ferns and dwarf conifers.
Opening times: *all year daily 10am–6pm (4.30pm Nov–Feb), closed Christmas Day and Boxing Day. Parties/coaches should preferably view by appointment. House closed.*
Admission prices: *adults £6, children (6–16) £2 (under 6 free), over-60s £4.50. Groups of 10 + : adults £5 pp, children £1.60 pp.*
Facilities: *parking, disabled access, shop, plants for sale, refreshments. Picnics permitted. Guide dogs only.*

A 35-acre (14-hecatre) woodland garden, Savill was created in 1932 by Sir Eric Savill from an undeveloped area of Windsor Great Park. It offers year-round interest – spectacular spring displays, a formal rose garden and herbaceous border in summer, fiery autumn colours and misty vistas in winter. A temperate house – "a piece of woodland under glass" – shelters frost-tender plants in winter. The new Golden Jubilee Garden has soft summer planting, hard landscaping and a water sculpture.

BELOW: the Valley Gardens (Windsor Great Park).

History: In 1932 Sir Eric Savill began developing the garden from a boggy area of the Great Park, encouraged by King George VI and Queen Elizabeth, the Queen Mother.

Accommodation: The Castle Hotel, Windsor (tel: 0870 4008300; £££). **Local pub:** *The Two Brewers, Windsor.*

The Valley Gardens (Windsor Great Park)

Outstanding woodland garden. Map reference ㉑

Englefield Green TW20 0VU, Surrey; tel: 01753 847518, fax: 01753 847536. < www.crownestate.co.uk/estates/ windsor/valley.html >
National Collection: *dwarf and slow growing conifers.*
Opening times: *year-round 8am–7pm or dusk if earlier. Parties/Coaches accepted (£50 to lead coach to Valley Garden from Savill Garden, by arrangement). House closed.*
Admission prices: *car park £4 (£5.50 Apr–May).*
Facilities: *parking, disabled access. No picnics. Dogs allowed on leads.*

The Valley Gardens, covering some 220 acres (90 hectares) on the north side of Virginia Water Lake, contain an unrivalled collection of rhododendrons, azaleas, camellias and magnolias. Fifty acres (8 hectares) are devoted to the largest planting of rhododendron species in the world. Several acres of daffodils and a 10-acre (4-hectare) heather garden provide interest in winter and early spring. In July and August many hundreds of hydrangeas provide a spectacular display. In autumn, Japanese maples, red oaks, cherries, tupelos and sweet gums provide superb colour.

Accommodation: The Castle Hotel, Windsor (tel: 0870 4008300; £££). **Local pub:** *The Two Brewers, Windsor.*

EAST SUSSEX

East Sussex has several exceptional gardens attached to interesting houses. Among these are Bateman's, Rudyard Kipling's former home; Great Dixter, the 15th-century home of the renowned plantsman and gardening writer Christopher Lloyd; and Monk's House, the cottage of Virginia and Leonard Woolf. Another highlight is 18th-century Sheffield Park, created by CapabilityBrown.

Map: page 62

Bateman's

Rudyard Kipling's house and garden. English Heritage Grade II. Map reference ㉒

National Trust, Burwash, Etchingham TN19 7DS, East Sussex; tel: 01435 882302, fax: 01435 882811.
Opening times: *Apr–Oct Sat–Wed 11am–5pm. House & mill (which grinds flour most Sats from 2pm) 11am–5pm. Parties/coaches accepted. National Garden Scheme days.*
Admission prices: *adults £5.20; children £2.60, family £13, pre-booked parties of 15+ £4.40 pp (excluding Sun and BHs) for house, mill and garden.*
Facilities: *parking, disabled access, shop, plants for sale, refreshments. Picnics permitted. Dogs allowed on lead.*

ateman's, a charming 17th-century house and garden that belonged to Rudyard Kipling, attracts a ready stream of visitors curious to know more of the writer's domestic circumstances. The scene is set for visitors as they pass the herb border, which is laden with spicy scents, to reach the "pear alley" where several varieties of pear share the supports with clematis, complemented by colourful underplanting. A pair of wrought-iron gates lead to a superb Chinese Snakebark maple and herbaceous borders planted with hardy plants, such as *Crocosmia citronella* and *Morina longifolia*.

South of the house broad lawns with fine trees and a pleached lime avenue are laid out with other features. Kipling's Rose Garden contains a sundial with the inscription "It is later than you think."

History: The house, dating from 1634, was bought by Kipling in 1902. It was his home until his death in 1936 and many of his best-known works were written here; the mill that features in *Puck of Pook's Hill* and *Rewards and Fairies* is reached through the Wild Garden. Kipling had the lily pond dug out to make a swimming pool for his children; in the visitors' book several guests have the initials "FIP" after their name, recording that they had "Fallen in Pond".

ABOVE: Bateman's, the former home of Rudyard Kipling.

Accommodation: Stone House, Rushlake Green, Heathfield (tel: 01435 830553; ££–££££).
Local pubs: Bull, Three Legged Cross, near Ticehurst; Star Inn, Old Heathfield (east of Heathfield)

Clinton Lodge

Modern but formal garden surrounding Carolean and Georgian house. Map reference ㉓

Fletching, Uckfield TN22 3ST, East Sussex; tel: 01825 722952.
Opening times: *National Garden Scheme days and by appointment for private groups. House closed.*
Admission prices: *NGS days: adults £3.50, children £2; groups by appointment: £5 pp (minimum £100 per group).*
Facilities: *parking, limited disabled access, refreshments. No picnics. No dogs.*

RIGHT: Great Dixter is one of the most exciting gardens of the modern age.

BELOW: focal point at Clinton Lodge.

Designed over the past 30 years by the current owners, Clinton Lodge is a 6-acre (2.4-hectare) formal and romantic garden surrounding a Carolean and Georgian house, overlooking parkland. Highlights include old roses, double herbaceous borders, yew hedges, pleached lime walks, a copy of a 17th-century herb garden, medieval-style potager, canal garden, vine and rose allée, and a wild flower garden.

Accommodation: *Ashdown Park Hotel & Country Club, Forest Row (tel: 01342 824988; £££–££££).* ***Local pub:*** *The Griffin Inn, Fletching.*

Great Dixter

Historic 15th-century house and garden belonging to the plantsman Christopher Lloyd. English Heritage Grade 1. Map reference ㉔

Dixter Road, Northiam, Rye TN31 6PH, East Sussex; tel: 01797 252878, fax: 01797-252879.
< www.greatdixter.co.uk >
Opening times: *Mar–Oct Tues–Sun 2–5pm. Parties/coaches accepted. House open.*
Admission prices: *adults £4.50, children £1, season ticket £13.50.*
Facilities: *parking, disabled access, shop, plants for sale, refreshments. Picnics permitted. Dogs allowed on leads.*

Great Dixter is the family home of the well-known plantsman and gardening writer Christopher Lloyd, who has devoted his lifetime to creating one of the most exciting gardens of the modern age. There is a wide variety of interest from yew topiary, carpets of meadow flowers, a colourful tapestry of mixed borders (including the famous Long Border), natural ponds, a formal pool and the exuberant Exotic Garden. Christopher Lloyd and head gardener Fergus Garrett are ceaselessly experimenting. The sunken garden, almost

hidden by barns and oasts, was designed by Lloyd's father, Nathaniel.

History: Built in the middle of the 15th century and then restored and enlarged by Sir Edwin Lutyens from 1910, Great Dixter is both a historic house and a family home. Nathaniel Lloyd commissioned Sir Edwin to clear the 15th-century house of the later alterations, revealing the medieval splendour of the Great Hall, the largest surviving timber-framed hall in Britain.

Accommodation: Little Orchard House, Rye (tel: 01797 223 831; ££); Jeake's House, Rye (tel: 01797 222828; ££); Mermaid Inn, Rye (tel: 01797 223065; £££). Local pub: The White Hart, Neverden.

Monk's House

The country home of Leonard and Virginia Woolf. National Trust. Map reference ㉕

Rodmell, Lewes, BN7 3HF, East Sussex; tel: 01892 890651, fax: 01892 890110.
Opening times: *Apr–Oct Wed & Sat 2–5pm. Parties/coaches may view by appointment Thur 2–5pm. House closed.*
Admission prices: *adults £2.60, children*

£1.30, season £6.50.
No facilities.

A small, white, weather-boarded cottage, Monk's House was the country home of Leonard and Virgina Woolf from 1919 until Leonard's death in 1969. The rooms reflect the literary circle in which they moved. The garden has four sections – a formal walled area, an orchard underplanted with bulbs, an open lawn and a kitchen garden. "Our orchard is the very place to sit and talk for hours in," Virginia wrote in her diary. A typical Sussex flint church lies at the bottom of the garden.

Accommodation: Shelleys, Lewes (01273 472361; £££); Nightingales, Lewes (tel: 01273 475673; £).
Local pub: Juggs, Kingston, near Lewes.

Pashley Manor

Tudor manor surrounded by classic English garden. Map reference ㉖

Ticehurst TN5 7HE, East Sussex; tel: 01580 200888.
< www.pashleymanorgardens.com >
Opening times: *mid-Apr–Sep Tues, Wed,*

Map:
page 62

LEFT: cottage garden profusion at Monk's House.

Thur, Sat and BH 11am–5pm.
Parties/coaches accepted. House closed.
Admission prices: adults £6, children £5
(under-6s free), over-60s £5, season £18,
senior season £15.
Facilities: parking, disabled access, shop,
plants for sale, refreshments. No picnics.
No dogs.

Pashley Manor, an 8-acre (3.25-hectare) garden, offers a sumptuous blend of romantic landscaping, imaginative planting and fine old trees, fountains, springs and large ponds. It is a quintessentially English garden, with exceptional views of the surrounding fields. Many eras of English history are reflected here, typifying the tradition of the English country house and its garden. The tulips and roses are wonderful in May and June.

History: The house dates from 1550, with a Georgian addition. The present owners enlisted the landscape architect Anthony du Gard Pasley to help restore the gardens.

ABOVE: the gardens at the Royal Pavilion in Brighton are typical of the Regency period.

Accommodation: Stone House, Rushlake Green, Heathfield (tel: 01435 830553; ££–££££); Hotel du Vin, Tunbridge Wells (tel: 01892 526455; £–££).
Local pubs: The Bull, Three Legged Cross, near Ticehurst; Green Cross Inn, Goudhurst.

Royal Pavilion Gardens

A Regency garden restored according to John Nash's original plan. Map reference **㉗**

Brighton BN1 1EE, East Sussex; tel:
01273 290900, fax: 01273 292871.
< www.royalpavilion.org.uk >
Opening times: grounds: year-round daily. Royal Pavilion: Apr–Sep 9.30am–5.45pm, Oct–Mar 10am–5.15pm, closed Christmas Day and Boxing Day. Parties/coaches accepted.
Admission prices: grounds free; pavilion: adults £5.35, children £3.30, over-60s £3.85, family £14.
Facilities: disabled access, shop, plants for sale, refreshments. Picnics permitted. Dogs allowed on leads.

The Royal Pavilion gardens are laid out according to John Nash's plan of the early 1820s, with flowering shrubberies typical of the Regency Period. The irregular-shaped beds are in a more natural style, comprising a mixture of trees, shrubs, herbaceous plants and bulbs.

History: A great change in landscape gardening took place in the 1730s. The previously fashionable formality of French gardens was replaced with a more natural style, with groupings of trees, shrubs and herbaceous plants. The pavilion's plantings in irregular beds along winding paths allow the visitor a succession of interesting views.

Accommodation: Paskins Town House (tel: 01273 601203; ££); Trouville Hotel, New Steine (tel: 01273 697384; ££).

Sheffield Park Garden

Grand landscaped garden incorporating four linked lakes. English Heritage Grade I. National Trust. Map reference ㉘

*Sheffield Park TN22 3QX, East Sussex, tel: 01825790231, fax: 01825 791264'.
< www.nationaltrust.org.uk >*
Opening times: *Jan–Feb weekends 10.30am–4pm, Mar–Oct Tues–Sun and BH 10.30am–6pm, Nov–Dec Tues–Sun 10.30am–4pm. Parties/coaches accepted. National Garden Scheme days. House closed.*
National Collection: *Ghent azaleas.*
Admission prices: *adults £4.80, children (5–16) £2.30, family £12.*

Facilities: *parking, disabled access (self-operated wheelchairs available), shop, plants for sale, refreshments. Picnics permitted. Dogs allowed on leads.*

**Map:
page 62**

A magnificent landscaped garden covering 120 acres (48 hectares), Sheffield Park centres upon four lakes linked by cascades and waterfalls that reflect the exquisite planting of trees and shrubs. There are dramatic shows of daffodils and bluebells in spring and the rhododendrons, azaleas and Stream Garden are spectacular in early summer. Autumn brings stunning colours from the many rare trees and shrubs, making it one of the finest gardens in Britain for autumn visits.

History: The garden was laid out in the 18th century by Capability Brown, with the aim of enhancing the grandeur of the house, which had been remodelled by James Wyatt. It was further developed in the early years of the 20th century by Arthur G. Soames at the behest of the third Earl of Sheffield. Soames introduced exotic trees and shrubs and extended the water features.

Accommodation: Ashdown Park Hotel & Country Club, Forest Row (tel: 01342 824988; £££–££££), Accommodation/pub: The Griffin Inn, Fletching (tel: 01825 722890; ££).

BELOW:
Sheffield
Park is one
of Britain's
greatest
landscape
gardens.

WEST SUSSEX

Characterised by the rolling South Downs falling away to the coast, West Sussex offers a fine setting for several first-class gardens, in particular Parham and Petworth, as well as the superb woodland gardens of Nymans and Leonardslee. Other highlights are Wakehurst Place, the site of the world's largest seed bank, and West Dean, with its fabulous pergola designed by Harold Peto.

Borde Hill Garden

Romantic garden with exotic plantings and many features.
Map reference ㉙

Balcombe Road, Haywards Heath RH16 1XP, West Sussex; tel: 01444 450326; fax: 01444 440427. < www.bordehill.co.uk >
Opening times: *daily 10am–6pm. National Garden Scheme days. House open on selected dates.*

Admission prices: *adults £5.50, children £3, over-60s £5, season £35.*
Facilities: *fishing on lake, adventure playground. No parking, disabled access, refreshments, picnics or dogs.*

ABOVE: a quiet corner at Borde Hill.

Set in 200 acres (80 hectares) of spectacular Sussex parkland in West Sussex, Borde Hill was created in the 1890s by Colonel Stephenson Clarke, with new planting by garden designer Robin Williams. Botanical interest and garden design play equally important roles. A series of intimate garden rooms offer a rich variety of seasonal colour, with trees and shrubs from as far afield as China, Asia, Tasmania and the Andes. Garden highlights include the Mediterranean and Italian gardens, the Azalea Ring, the Round and Long dells, and the Garden of Allah featuring rhododendrons and a wildlife pond. There are also award-winning Victorian greenhouses.

Accommodation*: Ockendon Manor, Cuckfield (tel: 01444 416111; £££).* **Local pubs:** *The Fountain, Handcross; the Red Lion, Handcross; Black Horse, Nuthurst.*

Denmans

Imaginative modern garden offering year-round interest. Map reference ㉚

Fontwell, Arundel, BN18 0SU, West Sussex; tel: 01243 542808, fax: 01243 544064. < www.denmans-garden.co.uk >
Opening times: *Mar–Oct daily 9am–5pm. Parties/coaches may view by appointment. Collection of rare breeds of poultry and waterfowl can be viewed by prior arrangement.*
Admission prices: *adults £2.95, children (4–16 years) £1.75, over-60s £2.65, prebooked groups of 15 or more £2.50 pp.*
Facilities: *garden tours.*
No parking, disabled access, refreshments, picnics or dogs.

Comprising nearly 4 acres (1.5 hectares), Denmans is a modern garden nestling in former farmland in the West Sussex countryside. Predominantly the work of the landscape designer John Brookes, it combines native species with many frost-tender plants. Some of the latter are housed within the Dutch light greenhouse. Other features include the Walled

Map: page 62

Garden, the dry stream bed, and the South Garden in which Brookes has experimented with texture. Year-round interest is provided by aquilegia in late spring; campanulas and ceratostigma in summer; and hellebores with *Iris foetidissima* in winter. A clock house, conservatory and locally produced statuary provide further interest.

Accommodation: Bonham's Country House, Arundel (tel: 01243 551301; £–££); Chichester Lodge, Oakwood, Chichester (01243 786560; £–££). Local pubs: Gribble Inn, Oving; George & Dragon, Burpham; The Fox Goes Free, Charlton.

High Beeches

Woodland and water garden. English Heritage Grade II. Map reference ㉛

Handcross, Near Haywards Heath RH17 6HQ, West Sussex; tel: 01444 400589, fax: 01444 401543.
< www.highbeeches.com >
National Collection: *Stewartias.*
Opening times: *Apr–Jun and Sep–Oct Thur–Tues 1–5pm; Jul–Aug Mon, Tues, Thurs, Fri and Sun 1–5pm). National Garden Scheme days. Parties/coaches accepted. House closed.*
Admission prices: *adults £5.50; children*

free; season £30 for two for 12 months.
Facilities: *parking, lavatories, plants for sale, refreshments. Picnics permitted. No disabled access. No dogs.*

High Beeches comprises about 25 acres (10 hectares) of woodland with rhododendrons, magnolias, camellias and bluebells in spring and good autumn colour. The water gardens, which extend through a wooded valley, include many ponds and streams, creating attractive

Above: an experiment in texture at Denmans.

Left: autumn foliage at High Beeches.

vistas at every turn. There is a large variety of naturalised wild plants including orchids, gentians and primulas.

History: Designed in 1906 by Colonel G.H. Loder, High Beeches is now a charitable trust, managed by Edward and Anne Boscawen, well-known horticulturalists and botanical travellers who have introduced many rare exotics.

Accommodation: Gravetye Manor, East Grinstead (tel: 01342 810567; ££); South Lodge, Lower Beeding (tel: 01403 891711; £££). Local pubs: The Fountain, Handcross; the Red Lion, Handcross.

Highdown

Garden specialising in chalk-loving plants. English Heritage Grade II*. Map reference ㉜

Littlehampton Road, Goring-by-Sea BN12 6PE, West Sussex; tel: 01903 239999/501054.
Opening times: *Apr–Sep daily 10am–6pm, Oct–Nov & Feb–Mar Mon–Fri 10am–4.30pm, Dec–Jan Mon–Fri 10am–4pm. Parties/coaches may also view by appointment. House closed.*
Admission prices: *free.*
Facilities: *refreshments nearby. No parking. No disabled access. No dogs.*

Highdown was created in a disused chalk pit by the banker Sir Frederick Stern and Lady Stern in the first half of the 20th century. The gardens, said to have begun as an experiment to discover which plants would thrive best on chalk soil, are the result of 50 years of dedicated work. Lilacs and junipers were among the first shrubs to be planted. The variety of species is a testament to the botanic innovation of the Sterns. They include species brought back from China and the Himalayan region.

In spring, the hellebore bank boasts a profusion of colour, as does the Middle Garden, planted with daffodils, crocus, snowdrops

and anemones. In summer, the highlights are peonies (May) and the rose garden and herb garden. Autumn colour is provided by the Himalayan birch bark cherry trees and paper bark maples. The Cave Pond, created on the site of a pigsty, and the Bamboo Pond provide year-round interest.

Accommodation: Kenmore Guest House, Rustington (tel: 01903 784634; £). Local pubs: Star Inn, Steyning, George & Dragon, Burpham.

Leonardslee

A grand woodland garden set around seven lakes. English Heritage Grade I. Map reference ㉝

Lower Beeding, Horsham RH13 6PP, West Sussex; tel: 01403 891212, fax: 01403 891305. < www.leonardslee.com >
Opening times: *Apr–Oct daily 9.30am–6pm. Parties/coaches (20+ adults) may view by appointment. House closed.*
Admission prices: *Apr & Jun–Oct £6, May Mon–Fri £7, May Sat, Sun & BHs £8, children £4.*
Facilities: *parking, shop, plants for sale, refreshments. Picnics permitted. No disabled access. No dogs.*

This romantic 240-acre (98-hectare) valley with walks around seven lakes has been described as the most beautiful garden in Europe during May, when the vast

RIGHT: chalk-loving plants thrive at Highdown.

collection of rhododendrons, some nearly 200 years old, and azaleas make a spectacular show, full of fragrance. The Pulhamite rock garden is planted with Japanese azaleas of every hue. Other attractions include a bonsai collection, and wallabies and deer that roam through the park.

History: The backbone of the garden was created in the first years of the 19th century, but the four generations of the Loder family who have lived at Leonardslee since 1889 have continued the design and expansion of the valley plantings.

Accommodation: Ockendon Manor, Cuckfield (tel: 01444 416111; £££). **Local pubs:** *The Fountain, Handcross; Black Horse, Nuthurst.*

Nymans

Year-round grand garden and landscaped woodland. English Heritage Grade II*. National Trust. Map reference ❸④

Handcross, Haywards Heath RH17 6EB, West Sussex; tel: 01444 400321/405250, fax: 01444 405253.
Opening times: Apr–Oct Wed–Sun 11am–6pm; Nov–Feb weekends 11am–4pm. Parties/coaches accepted.
Admission prices: adults summer £6, winter £3; children summer £5, winter £1.50.
Facilities: parking, disabled access, shop, plants for sale, refreshments, picnics permitted. Guide dogs only.

Nymans is very much a family garden with extensive views across the South Downs and wild meadows contrasting with intimate courtyards.

The main views from the garden radiate from the pinetum and towering Lime Avenue and extend to the 600-acre (240-hectare) estate of Nymans Woods. A sheltered garden walk is provided by the elegant Laurel Walk leading past the entrance to the original house, now standing as a romantic ruin after a devastating fire in 1947.

The rose and heather gardens and pergola are all striking features. The jostling colours and fragrance of the borders take the garden through the spring and summer, while the range of coloured foliage offers new interest in autumn.

Part of the old house that was saved after the 1947 fire is open to the public.

History: The framework for the garden was set out by Ludwig Messel in 1890 when the first house was constructed. It was developed by Leonard and Maud Messel, who introduced rare magnolias and exotic plants until the garden passed to the National Trust in 1953. Incredibly, there have been only three head gardeners at Nymans since 1890.

Accommodation: Ockendon Manor, Cuckfield (tel: 01444 416111; £££). **Local pubs:** *The Fountain, Handcross; the Red Lion, Handcross; Black Horse, Nuthurst; White Harte, Cuckfield.*

Map: **page 62**

LEFT: the lush gardens of Leonardslee.

BELOW: Nymans, a grand garden with many intimate corners.

Parham House

Victorian-cum-20th-century garden
with superb borders. English
Heritage Grade I. Map reference ㉟

Pulborough RH20 4HS, West Sussex;
tel: 01903-742021, fax: 01903 746557.
< www.parhaminsussex.co.uk >
Opening times: *Easter–Sep Wed, Thur,*
Sun & BH Mon, plus Tues & Fri in Aug
noon–6pm, last entry 5pm. National
Garden Scheme days. Parties/coaches
accepted. House opens at 2pm. Also look
out for the autumn flower show in early
September and garden study mornings.
Admission prices: *adults £4, children 50p.*
No facilities.

Parham House lies on a plain below the
South Downs, with magnificent views
all around. From the Lion Gate the
entrance borders are planted with osmanthus and hydrangeas and other shrubs chosen for their foliage. The long vista ends
with the classical summer house.

The orchard, which was replanted in
1992, is flanked by blue borders which lead
on to white borders and a charming Wendy
house, built into the garden wall for the

Above: spring
borders at
Parham
House.

daughters of the house in the 1920s. On the
other side of the wall is the three-arched-
summerhouse with a white marble statue.
Further on are the pleasure grounds, pond
and maze.

Within the walled garden are the gold
borders and "hot" border, the herb garden
and the Clematis Walk leading on to a large
vegetable garden.

History: The land, which originally
belonged to the Monastery of Westminster,
was acquired by the Palmer family following the Dissolution of the Monasteries in the
16th century. Since then only three families
have lived at Parham. The park is regarded
as one of England's finest surviving
medieval deer parks.

The pleasure grounds and pond were
designed in about 1863, while the garden
buildings and paths were built in the 1920s.
More recently, the garden designer Peter
Coats laid out the entrance borders and blue
and gold borders. The design of the maze,
created in 1991, is based on the intricate
16th-century embroidery on the Great Bed
in the Great Chamber in the house.

Accommodation: Moorings, Worthing (tel: 01903
*208882; £). **Local pubs:** Star Inn, Steyning, George*
and Dragon, Burpham.

Petworth House

Landscaped woodland garden. English Heritage Grade I. National Trust. Map reference ㉟

Petworth GU280AE, West Sussex; tel: 01798 342207, fax: 01798 342963. < www.nationaltrust.org.uk >
Opening times: weekends in early March and Apr–Oct Sat–Wed 11am–6pm. Parties/coaches accepted. Viewing by appointment. House open last week Mar–end Oct (closed Thursday and Friday).
Admission prices: adults £1.50, children free.
Facilities: parking, limited disabled access (wheelchairs available to rent), shop (no plants), refreshments. Picnics permitted. No dogs.

Incorporating styles from the 16th, 18th and 20th centuries, Petworth is a woodland garden coverings 40 acres (16 hectares). Paths meander among woodland, transformed by daffodils, bluebells and blossom in spring; wild flower meadows team with anemones, fritillaries and orchids.

History: The garden was created in 1585 by the ninth Earl of Northumberland (the "Wizard Earl"), who planted the Birchen Walks. Between 1688 and 1693 George London worked on the design, which was further adapted by Capability Brown from 1751. Brown added the temple and rotunda.

Accommodation: Horse Guards Inn, Tillington (tel: 01798 342332; ££). *Local pubs:* Stonemasons Arms, Petworth; Halfway Bridge Inn, Halfway Bridge; Black Horse, Byworth.

Sculpture at Goodwood

Woodland setting for modern British sculpture. Map reference ㊲

Goodwood Chichester PO18 0PQ, West Sussex; tel: 01243 538449, fax: 01243 581853. < www.sculpture.org.uk >
Opening times: end Mar/beginning Apr–Oct Thur–Sat 10.30am–4.30pm. Parties/coaches accepted. Viewing by appointment. House closed.
Admission prices: adults £10, children (6–16) £6, over-60s £6.
Facilities: parking, disabled acccess, shop. No refreshments. No picnics or dogs.

Covering some 20 acres (8 hectares) and enclosed on two sides by an historic, listed fruit wall, this garden provides a superb setting for a changing collection of modern British sculpture. The landscaped woodland in which the sculpture is displayed lies on the edge of the South Downs overlooking Chichester.

The garden's designer, Victor Shawley-Lawrence has devised an on-going plan of woodland renewal with native species of broad-leaf trees adding to the diversity of stock and providing deep background colours that change with the seasons.

The best times to visit Sculpture at Goodwood are spring for the bluebells and autumn for the colours.

Accommodation: Chichester Lodge, Oakwood, Chichester (tel: 01243 786560; ££); Marriott Goodwood Park Hotel (tel: 01243 775537; £££); Forge Hotel, Chilgrove, Chichester (tel:0800 0854030; £££). Local pubs: Anglesey Arms, Halnaker; Hurdlemakers, East Dean; The Fox Goes Free, Charlton.

Map: page 62

LEFT: relic of a bygone age of gardening.

Wakehurst Place Garden & Millennium Seed Bank

The world's largest seed bank.
English Heritage Grade II. National
Trust. Map reference ㊳

*Ardingly, Haywards Heath, West Sussex;
tel: 01444 894066. < www.kew.org >*
National Collection: *Betulas,
Hypericums, Nothofagus, Skimmas.*
Opening times: *all year except Christmas
Day and New Year's Day; Nov–Jan
10am–4pm, Feb 10am–5pm, Mar & Oct
10am–6pm, Apr–Sep 10am–7pm.
Parties/coaches accepted. House open.
Guided walks available 11.30am and
2.30pm Sat, Sun & BH Mon. National
Garden Scheme days.*
Admission prices: *adult £6.50, children
under 12 free, over-60s and students
£4.50.*
Facilities: *parking, disabled access, shop,
plants for sale, refreshments. Picnics
permitted. No dogs.*

W akehurst Place was established by
Edward Culpeper (a distant rela-
tive of the herbalist Nicholas
Culpeper) in the 16th century.

The gardens are arranged geographically:
for example, species that grow at over 9,000
ft (3,000 metres) in the Himalayas are gathered in one glade. Starting from the house,
visitors pass from the formal gardens and a
small lake to the water gardens, planted with

BELOW:
Wakehurst
Place in early
summer.

Wakehurst's Millennium Seed Bank, started in
1997, holds the largest and most diverse collection
of wild species in the world, including 90 percent of
UK flora. With the emphasis on the drylands, its
aim is to collect and conserve 10 percent of the
world's flora, some 24,000 species, by 2010, as
well as the remaining part of the UK seed-bearing
flora. The international seed collecting will be done
through international collaboration.

The species targeted include species at risk in
the wild, and species of most use to human beings.
By storing at least 10 percent of the world's flora
under optimal conditions, the Millennium Seed
Bank and its partner banks will act as a substantial
genetic asset.

irises and many other plants, and then into
the woodland areas. The latter are spectacular in late spring when the vast banks of
rhododendrons and azaleas are in bloom.

Further on, the nature reserve can only be
visited by special permit, but casual visitors
can skirt this and see the swamp, reed beds
and willows, the habitat of kingfishers.
Returning up the western valley past
Westwood Lake with its acers and liquid-
amber, the route passes groves of Douglas Fir
and Wellingtonias and some remarkable
exposed tree roots anchored to rocks.

History: Culpeper rebuilt the house on an
old site in 1590. In 1694 the estate was purchased from the last surviving member of the
Culpeper family by Dennis Lydell, a friend
of Samuel Pepys. Over the next 175 years the
house had various owners and tenants, and
many changes were made to its architecture.

In 1903, Gerald Loder bought Wakehurst
Place and began introducing many trees and
shrubs. Sir Henry Price, the owner from
1938, developed the gardens further. On his
death in 1963, the estate was bequeathed to
the National Trust who leased it to the Royal
Botanic Gardens Kew, in 1965.

*Accommodation: Ockendon Manor, Cuckfield
(tel: 01444 416111; £££).* **Local pubs:** *White Harte,
Cuckfield; The Fountain, Handcross; Black Horse,
Nuthurst.*

West Dean Gardens

Grand garden designed by Harold Peto. English Heritage Grade II. Map reference ❸❾

West Dean, Chichester PO18 0QZ, West Sussex, tel: 01243 818210/811301.
< www.westdean.org.uk >
Opening times: *Mar–Oct daily Mar, Apr & Oct 11am–5pm; May–Sep 10.30am–5pm. Parties/coaches accepted. National Garden Scheme days.*
Admission Prices: *adults £5, children £2, over-60s £4.50, family £12, season £16.50.*
Facilities: *parking, limited disabled access, shop, plants for sale, refreshments, picnics permitted. Dogs allowed on leads.*

Set in the rolling South Downs, West Dean is a 35-acre (14-hectare) garden on a grand scale which has been considerably restored in recent years. Its sweeping lawns punctuated by long-established trees help balance the scale of the plantings and relate the gardens to the landscape. The 300-ft (100-metre) pergola, designed by Harold Peto, running east–west across the north lawn and covered in roses, clematis and honeysuckle, is the most spectacular feature of the formal gardens. At its eastern end, the sunken garden with spring and summer bedding has replaced a late Victorian rose parterre.

In the spring garden a complete redevelopment of the area is underway to reinstate lost features such as the laburnum tunnel. The rustic summerhouse in the western end of the garden has been restored, using moss walls and a thatched roof, and extensive work has taken place on Regency stone and flintwork around the watercourses.

History: Dating from 1622, West Dean's rare trees were mentioned by the prolific gardening writer John Claudius Loudon in 1836. In 1891 the property was purchased by William James, who, in 1910, commissioned Harold Peto to design the magnificent pergola.

Accommodation: *Chichester Lodge, Oakwood, Chichester (tel: 01243 786560; ££); Forge Hotel, Chilgrove, Chichester (tel:01243 535333; ££).*
Local inns: *The Fox Goes Free, Charlton; the White Horse, Chilgrove.*

Above: West Dean Gardens.

Map: page 62

Dorset,
Hampshire
& Wiltshire

*Large areas of this region
have fast-draining chalky soil,
ideal for alkaline-loving plants
and best suited to spring and
early summer visiting before
conditions become too dry.
However, sandy spots near the
coast and elsewhere sometimes
allow ericaceous plants
to flourish*

DORSET

In spite of the prevailing chalk soil, Dorset has a wide range of gardens. On the coast at Weymouth is Abbotsbury, a subtropical paradise hosting rare and exotic plants from all over the world, while inland, near the border with Hampshire, is Cranborne Manor, established in the 17th century with plants supplied by the early plant collector John Tradescant. Another highlight is Sticky Wicket, an organically managed wildlife garden.

Abbotsbury Subtropical Gardens

Wooded valley and walled garden walks. Famous for its camellia grove and magnolias. English Heritage Grade I. Map reference ❶

Abbotsbury, Weymouth DT3 4LA, Dorset; tel: 01305 871387.
< www.abbotsbury-tourism.co.uk >
National Collection: *Hebes.*
Opening times: *Mar–Oct 10am–6pm (last admission 5pm), Nov–Feb 10am–4pm (last admission 3pm). Parties/coaches accepted. House closed.*
Admission prices: *adults £5.80, children £3.50, over-60s £5.50.*
Facilities: *parking, disabled access, shop, plants for sale, refreshments. Picnics permitted. Dogs allowed on leads.*

A mixture of formal and informal, Abbotsbury has attractive walled garden walks and spectacular woodland valley views. It is world famous for its camellia groves and magnolias and noted for its rhododendron and hydrangea collections. In summer it is awash with subtropical colour.

History: Abbotsbury was established in 1765 by the first Countess of Ilchester as a kitchen garden for her nearby castle. Developed since then into a magnificent 20-acre (8-hectare) garden, it is filled with rare and exotic plants from all over the world. Many of these were new introductions to the UK, discovered by plant-hunting descendants of the countess.

Accommodation: Manor Hotel, West Bexington (tel: 01308 897616; £££). Local pubs: Elm Tree, Langton Herring.

PRECEDING PAGES: Longstock Water Gardens, Hampshire.

OPPOSITE: first signs of spring at Forde Abbey, Dorset.

ABOVE: Abbotsbury Subtropical Gardens.

Athelhampton, Dorchester DT2 7LG, Dorset; tel: 01305 848363, fax: 01305 848135. < www.athelhampton.co.uk >
Opening times: *Mar–Oct Sun–Fri 10.30am–5pm; Nov–Feb Sun only 11am–dusk; Easter & August BH Sat only 11am–4.30pm. Parties/coaches accepted. Viewing by appointment. House closed.*
Admission prices: *adults £5.75, children free, over-60s £5.50.*
Facilities: *parking, disabled access. shop, plants for sale, refreshments. Picnics permitted. Dogs allowed on leads.*

ABOVE: topiary yew pyramids in the walled garden at Athelhampton.

Athelhampton House Gardens

A great architectural garden with topiary pyramids. English Heritage Grade I. Map reference ❷

This fine 15th-century manor house is surrounded by one of England's great architectural gardens. The garden is full of vistas, and gains much from the fountains and the River Piddle flowing through its lower end.

The walled garden includes the topiary yew pyramids, over a century old and stand-

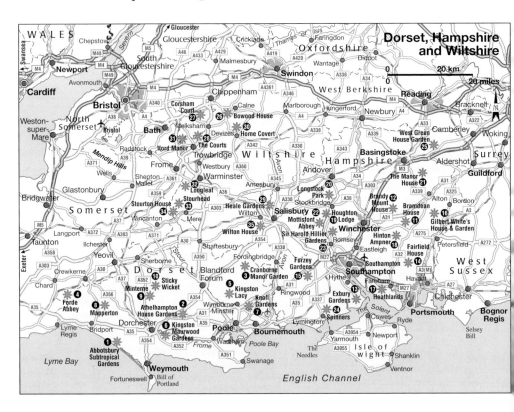

ing more than 30 ft (10 metres) high; and collections of tulips, magnolias, roses, clematis and lilies in season.

In the Octagonal Garden, pleached limes form a canopy around an octagonal pool. Another feature, the 15th-century dovecote, which in the past housed up to 1,200 birds for the manor's table, is surrounded by climbing roses.

History: Sir William Martyn, a prosperous merchant who became Lord Mayor of London, built Athelhampton in the 1480s after receiving a licence from Henry VII to enclose 160 acres (65 hectares) of deer park. The property was divided in 1595, after the last male Martyn heir died and passed through the hands of several owners. Alfred Cart de Lafontaine began restoration of the house and the design of the formal gardens in 1891, and Francis Inigo Thomas designed the four Ham-stone courts in Elizabethan style shortly afterwards.

The design of the Octagonal Garden, in 1971, was by Sir Robert Cooke (it was also used for the design of New Palace Yard at Westminster). Cooke introduced many of the superb specimen trees and plants.

*Accommodation: Casterbridge Hotel, Dorchester (tel: 01305 264043; ££). **Local pub:** Hambro Arms, Milton Abbas.*

Cranborne Manor Garden

Map: page 94

Historic garden established in the 17th century with plants supplied by John Tradescant. English Heritage Grade II*. Map reference ❸

Cranborne, Wimborne Minster BH21 5PP, Dorset; tel: 01725 517248, fax: 01725 517862. < www.cranborne.co.uk >
Opening times: *Mar–Sep Wed only 9am–5pm. National Garden Scheme days. Parties/coaches accepted. Viewing by appointment. House closed.*
Admission prices: *adults £3.50, children 50p, over-60s £3.*
Facilities: *parking, limited disabled access, plants for sale. No dogs.*

The gardens of Cranborne Manor have a long history. The clipped yew hedges, the walled garden with its espaliered fruit trees, the herb garden and wild gardens all originated in the 17th century. Spring is a particularly good time to visit, for the displays of spring bulbs and blossom in the crab apple orchard in the wild garden. The White Garden is at its best in June and July. Later in the season the herbaceous borders are a riot of colour.

LEFT:
Jacobean influences in Cranborne Manor Gardens.

History: Much of the garden, with lawns, roses and cut yews, was laid out by Mounten Jennings, with John Tradescant, gardener to King James I and Robert Cecil, supplying many of the original plants. The manor has been almost continually occupied since the early 17th century. Parts of the house, including the main walls and turret stairs, date from the Middle Ages.

*Accommodation: Alderholt Mill, Fordingbridge (tel: 01425 653130; £). **Local pubs:** Fleur de Lys, Cranborne; Rose and Thistle, Rockbourne.*

Forde Abbey

A riverside garden with superb water features and bog garden. English Heritage Grade II*. Map reference ❹

BELOW: the canal at Forde Abbey.

Chard TA20 4LU, Dorset; tel: 01460 221290, fax: 01460 220296.
< www.fordeabbey.co.uk >
***Opening times:** all year daily 10am–4.30pm (last admission). Parties/coaches accepted. House also open Apr–Oct Tues–Fri and Sun 1–4.30pm and BHs.*
***Admission prices:** house & gardens: adults £7, over-60s £6.50; gardens: adults £5.25, over-60s £4.75; season £14, children under 15 free.*
***Facilities:** parking, disabled access, shop, plants for sale in nursery, including rare specimens, refreshments. Picnics permitted. Dogs allowed on leads.*

Forde Abbey has a splendid 30-acre (12-hectare) garden surrounding the part-Jacobean-Gothic house. It is bordered on one side by the River Axe, which forms the county boundary between Somerset and Dorset. Its water features are fed by a spring and include the Great Pond, a series of smaller pools, cascades and a canal near the house. These, together with the herbaceous borders and yew trees and mature trees on sloping lawns, create a tranquil and pleasing environment. The owners have developed a bog garden with spectacular irises, primulas and hostas which can easily be inspected from the gravel paths and decking running through it.

Other features include the Beech House, a folly constructed entirely of living saplings, and the walled garden, in use since the monks were here, which has a wide variety of fruits, vegetables and cutting flowers. The arboretum has been extended since World War II and features magnificent specimens.

History: Forde was originally a Cistercian abbey, founded over 800 years ago; it has been in private hands since 1650. The rock garden was planted by alpine specialist, Jack Drake.

*Accommodation: Bellplot House Hotel, Chard (tel: 01460 626000; £–££). **Local pub:** Cotley Inn, Wambrook.*

Kingston Lacy

Formal bedding, extensive woodland and avenues of mature trees. English Heritage Grade II. National Trust. Map reference **5**

Wimborne Minster BH21 4EA, Dorset; tel: 01202 883402, fax: 01202 882402.
< www.nationaltrust.org.uk >
National Collection: *Anemone Nemorosa and Convallaria.*
Opening times: *late Mar–Oct daily 11am–6pm. National Garden Scheme day. No parties/coaches. Viewing by appointment. House open Wed–Sun.*
Admission prices: *adults £6.50, children £3, family £17.*
Facilities: *parking, disabled access, shop, plants for sale, refreshments. Picnics permitted. Dogs allowed on leads in the park only.*

The grounds at Kingston Lacy comprises 32 acres (13 hectares) of garden and woodland, with rose beds and extensive lawns totalling approximately 6 acres (2.4 hectares). It includes a parterre with formal bedding scheme, Victorian fernery and a sunken garden. Beyond the formal areas are a nursery wood and a series of walks leading to the Lime Avenue, planted in the 17th century, Laurel Walk and Cedar Avenue.

History: The garden was designed by Sir Roger Pratt in 1663 and during the 18th century it was landscaped in traditional style. The parterre was laid out in 1899. Many of the trees in the avenues were planted to commemorate the visits of illustrious guests.

Accommodation: Ashton Lodge, Wimborne Minster (tel: 01202 883423; £). **Local pub:** *Langton Arms, Tarrant Monkton.*

Kingston Maurward Gardens

Parkland and formal gardens surrounding Palladian-style house. Map reference **6**

Dorchester DT2 8PY, Dorset, tel: 01305 215003, fax: 01305 215001.
< www.kmc.ac.uk >
National Collection: *Penstemons and Salvias.*
Opening times: *Jan–mid-December daily. Parties/coaches accepted. House closed.*
Admission prices: *adults £4, children £2.50, family day ticket £12.50, family season ticket £36.*
Facilities: *parking, disabled access, refreshments, plants for sale, animal park and children's play area. Picnics permitted. No dogs.*

The parkland and pleasure gardens were originally laid out in the "Jardin Anglais" style popularised by Capability Brown. Simplicity was their hallmark, and they consisted of rolling turf, carefully placed groups of trees, a lake and a lakeside temple. These and the lovely formal gardens

ABOVE: view of Kingston Maurward.

have been carefully restored with the help of photographs taken in the 1930s, but new features have also been introduced.

The gardens now consist of a matrix of small gardens each with its own theme, tree trails, lakeside walks and a walled garden. New plantings and features are added annually.

The Animal Park is home to an interesting collection of animals, some of which can be hand-fed. There is a large picnic and play area.

History: The house was built in 1720 for George Pitt in the classic Palladian style that characterised the period. The 35-acre (14-hectare) formal gardens were created between 1915 and 1922 within the framework of the existing parkland setting.

Local pub: Wiseman, West Stafford.

Knoll Gardens and Nursery

A 4-acre (1.6-hectare) garden with modern plantings and mature trees. Map reference ❼

Hampreston, Wimborne Minster BH21 7ND, Dorset; tel: 01202 873931, fax: 01202 870842. < www.knollgardens.co.uk >
National Collections: *Deciduous Ceanothus and Phygelius.*
Opening times: *all year except Christmas week daily 10am–5pm (or dusk if earlier). Parties/coaches accepted. House closed.*
Admission prices: *adults £3.50, children £2, over-60s £3.*
Facilities: *parking, disabled access, shop, plants for sale, refreshments. Picnics permitted. Dogs allowed on leads.*

John May, who founded this 4-acre (1.6 hectare) garden, was particularly interested in plant breeding and raised many of the hybrid phygelius (Cape fuchsia) which he named Phygelius African Queen. From

within the framework of mature trees and shrubs there is a wealth of colour and form throughout the season, but above all this is a summer garden with fantastic foliage. It has some of the hottest colours around and the gravel garden is full of sun-loving, drought-tolerant plants. The water garden has several waterfalls and the Dragon Garden has a central pool with large koi carp.

History: The garden was planted in the 1970s on a carrot field and semi-wooded, overgrown area of scrub. The collection of plants increased rapidly and the garden became known as Wimborne Botanic Garden. In 1988 it was acquired by Mr and Mrs Kevin Martin, who were responsible for the water and formal gardens, and in 1994 by Neil Lucas and John and Janet Flude, who have introduced many unusual plants to form their own collection.

Accommodation: Ashton Lodge, Wimborne Minster (tel: 01202 883423; £). Local pub: Langton Arms, Tarrant Monkton.

Mapperton

Terraced valley gardens and an arboretum. English Heritage Grade II*. Map reference ❽

Beaminster DT8 3NR, Dorset; tel: 01308 862645, fax: 01308 863348. < www.mapperton.com >
Opening times: *Mar–Oct daily 2–6pm.*

Parties/coaches accepted. House open. Jun–mid-Jul Mon–Fri and spring & summer BHs.
Admission prices: *garden: adults £3.50, children under-18 £1.50; house: £3.50, children under 18 £1.50.*
Facilities: *parking, shop, plants for sale, refreshments. Picnics permitted. Disabled access to lavatories and part access to garden. No dogs.*

The terraced valley gardens of Mapperton surround a honey-coloured Jacobean manor house, stable blocks, a dovecote and a church. A walled croquet lawn on the upper levels drops down to the orangery and Italianate formal garden, with fountains, topiary, grottoes, ponds and borders. Below, there is a 17th-century summerhouse with fish ponds and topiary and access to the lower garden where there is an arboretum of mature specimen shrubs, rare trees and a spring garden. Further interest is provided by magnificent walks and views, good colour in the autumn and bulbs in the spring.

History: "There can hardly be a more enchanting manorial group" was Pevsner's opinion of Mapperton in his guide to Dorset published in the 1950s. It has been owned by the Earls of Sandwich for centuries. The gardens were laid out in the 1920s.

Accommodation: The Bridge House Hotel, Beaminster (tel: 01308 862200; ££); Watermeadow House, Hooke, Beaminster (tel: 01308 862619; £).
Local pubs: Pickwicks Inn, Beaminster; Cotley Inn, Wambrook.

Minterne

A woodland garden with a splendid Himalayan collection. English Heritage Grade II. Map reference ❾

Minterne Magna, Dorchester DT 7AU, Dorset; tel: 01300 341370.
Opening times: *Mar–early Nov daily 10am–7pm. Parties/coaches accepted. Viewing by appointment. House closed.*
Admission prices: *adults £3, accompanied children free.*
Facilities: *lavatories only. No disabled access. Dogs allowed on leads*

Although the hills are chalk, the garden at Minterne is situated on a mound of green sand, which runs for a mile down the centre of the valley. This, with the humus and dappled shade provided by the large beech trees, is the perfect setting for the rhododendrons and magnolias gathered from expeditions to the Himalayas by Ernest Henry Wilson, George Forrest and Kingdon Ward. The beech trees tower over small lakes, streams and cascades, which in summer are enhanced by primulas, astilbes and water-lilies. March sees the magnolias and early rhododendrons, April and May,

LEFT: the orangery at Mapperton.

Map: page 94

Japanese cherries and a profusion of rhododendrons and azaleas, together with *Pieris forestii* with its brilliant red shoots. In late May and June many fine specimens of *Davidia involucrata* – the pocket handkerchief tree – are a particular feature.

History: Minterne has been the home of the Churchill and Digby families for nearly 350 years. In 1768 Admiral Robert Digby, a younger son of the seventh Baron Digby of Sherborne Castle, bought Minterne from the executors of General Charles Digby. In his diary that year Robert wrote: "Visited my new estate, valley very bare, trees not thriving, house ill contrived and ill situated." He immediately set about improving it with an eye to Capability Brown's work at Sherborne Castle.

Accommodation: The King's Arms, Dorchester (tel: 01305 265353; £–££). Local pubs: Brace of Pheasants, Plush; The New Inn, Cerne Abbas; Red Lion, Cerne Abbas.

BELOW:
Minterne has
a superb
collection of
Himalayan
plants.

Sticky Wicket

A modern, organic, wildlife garden and meadowland. Map reference ❿

Buckland Newton, Dorchester DT2 7BY, Dorset; tel/fax: 01300 345476.
Opening times: *Jun–Sep Thur only 10.30am–8pm. National Garden Scheme days. Parties/coaches accepted. Viewing by appointment. House closed.*
Admission prices: *adults £3, children £1.50.*
Facilities: *parking, disabled access, shop, plants for sale, refreshments. Picnics permitted. Dogs allowed on leads.*

Blending unobtrusively into the heart of Dorset's fertile Blackmore Vale, Sticky Wicket is both a haven for wildlife and an artist's paradise. There are several different garden areas, each with a particular colour theme and focus of seasonal and wildlife interest. A small pond and bog bring a wealth of creatures to the Spring Garden.

The herb-rich Nectar Garden provides food for bees and butterflies and the soft kaleidoscope of colours are designed to peak from mid- to late summer. Grasses and autumn fruits and berries are features of the informal White Garden. The two wildflower meadows are seen to their best advantage in

Map:
page 94

aesthetic values as the owners strive to achieve a sense of beauty, harmony, peace and inspiration. There are boards to guide visitors as they explore the various aspects of the wildlife initiatives. Advice on gardening in tune with nature is also provided.

History: The 2½-acre (1-hectare) garden has been created over the past 15 years or so. In a garden context, wetland, woodland, hedgerow and grassland habitats have been created, where once neglected pasture surrounded the house and offered little diversity for wildlife. All the garden features have been fashioned out of recycled materials.

June. A glimpse into the flamboyant, vegetable garden demonstrates the essence of companion planting.

Although primarily an organically managed wildlife garden, high priority is set on

Accommodation: The Old Vicarage Hotel, Milborne Port, Sherborne (01963 251117; ££). Local pubs: Gaggle of Geese (300 yds/metres away); Brace of Pheasants, Plush; The New Inn, Cerne Abbas.

HAMPSHIRE

Among the county's highlights are Longstock, one of the loveliest water gardens in Europe, Mottisfont Abbey, famous for its large collection of old-fashioned, scented roses, and the Sir Harold Hillier Gardens and Arboretum, containing 11 national collections. Among the county's historic gardens is the Manor House, the most complete restoration of a Gertrude Jekyll garden.

Bramdean House

A sloping site on chalk soil, with mirror-image herbaceous borders and a working kitchen garden. English Heritage Grade II.
Map reference ⓫

Bramdean, Alresford SO24 0JU, Hants; tel: 01962 771214, fax: 01962 771095.
Opening times: specific Sundays throughout the summer 2–5pm; call the above number for exact dates. National Garden Scheme days. Parties/coaches accepted. Viewing by appointment. House closed.
Admission prices: adults £4, children free; NGS days £3.
Facilities: parking, refreshments, plants for sale on NGS days. No picnics. No disabled access. No dogs.

The mellow brick, 18th-century Bramdean House is well protected from the main road by a huge undulating yew and box hedge. The 5½-acre (2.2-hectare) garden on chalk slopes away from the house and is divided into three parts. The first contains the famous mirror-image herbaceous borders. Surrounding beds have a large array of common and

ABOVE: Chatelaine lupins at Sticky Wicket.

BELOW: sumptuous borders at Bramdean House.

RIGHT: **Brandy Mount.** unusual plants, shrubs, bulbs and small trees. Fine wrought-iron gates lead through into the walled working kitchen garden, cultivated entirely by hand, containing fruit and vegetables, old-fashioned sweet peas, perpetual carnations, a peony walk and a trial area for plants. Ornamental flower beds alongside a central path lead through a second wrought-iron gate into the orchard area featuring fruit trees underplanted with massed daffodils and a wild flower area. The orchard is closed off by an apple house and belfry. To the east are interesting shrubs and trees and castellations of yew. There are carpets of aconites, snowdrops, crocuses and other bulbs in the spring.

History: The owner's parents purchased the house and the garden in 1944. The garden, which has very alkaline (PH8) soil has evolved through time. It has featured in numerous gardening books and articles.

Accommodation: Hotel du Vin, Winchester (tel: 01962 841414; £££); Royal Hotel, Winchester (tel: 01962 840840; £); Wessex Hotel, Winchester (tel: 01962 841503; £££). Local pubs: Fox Inn, Bramdean; Globe on the Lake, Alresford; The Milburys, Beauworth.

Brandy Mount House

A lovely spring garden, well known for its snowdrops and daphnes. Also has an Alpine House. Map reference ⑫

Alresford SO24 9EG, Hants; tel: 01962 732189. < brandymount.co.uk >
National Collections: *Galanthus (snowdrops); daphnes.*
Opening times: *selected dates in Feb 11am–4pm and in Mar & May 2–5pm, including National Garden Scheme days. Parties/coaches accepted. Viewing by appointment in snowdrop season. House closed.*
Admission prices: *adults £2, children free.*
Facilities: *no parking (park in station car park five minutes away). No lavatories. No refreshments except teas in March and May. No picnics. No disabled access. No dogs.*

Brandy Mount House comprises about 1¼ acres (0.5 hectares) of informal gardens in a secluded location close to New Alresford High Street. The garden is at its best in spring (the chalky soil tends to be too dry in summer), as it has a wide range of bulbs, snowdrops, dwarf narcissi and anemones. Daphnes and alpines are found in terraced beds around the house and there is an alpine house with a collection of European primulas, narcissi and saxifragus. There is also a small potager with vegetables and flowers.

History: The garden at Brandy Mount was first enclosed from pasture in about 1940 when the surrounding trees, many of them apple, were planted to keep the garden cool and secluded. The present owners, who moved here about 20 years ago, have steadily improved the layout of the garden and built up the collection of daphnes and snowdrops.

Accommodation: Flower Pots Inn, Cheriton (tel: 01962 771318; £–££). Local pubs: Globe on the Lake, Alresford; Tichborne Arms, Tichborne.

Exbury Gardens

A woodland garden with flowering shrubs and exotic trees. English Heritage Grade II*. Map reference ⓭

Exbury, Southampton SO45 1AZ, Hants; tel: 023 8089 1203 or 023 8089 9422, fax: 023 8089 9940.
< www.exbury.co.uk >
***Opening times:** Mar–Oct daily 10am–5.30pm (or dusk if earlier). Parties/coaches accepted. House closed.*
***Admission prices:** Mar–mid-Jun adults £5.50, children aged 10–15 £3.50, over-60s £5; mid-Jun–Oct adults £3.50, children £2.50, over-60s £3.*

***Facilities:** parking, shop, plants for sale, refreshments, buggy tours, steam railway. Picnics permitted. Disabled access and free wheelchair loan. Dogs allowed on leads.*

Exbury is a spectacular 200-acre (81-hectare) woodland garden on the east bank of the Beaulieu River, world famous for the Rothschild collection of rhododendrons, azaleas, camellias and magnolias in spring. There is a daffodil meadow, rock garden, rose garden, ponds, cascades and exotic trees. There is a new, summer flowering Summer Lane Garden and a coal-fired steam train that takes visitors on a 1¼-mile (2-km) journey over a bridge, through a tunnel, across a pond, along the top of the rock garden and across a viaduct.

History: The gardens were created by Lionel de Rothschild (1882–1942), who bought the estate in 1919, and described himself as "a banker by hobby, a gardener by profession." His son and grandsons have continued his work.

***Accommodation:** The Montagu Arms, Beaulieu (tel: 01590 612324; £££); Master Builders' Hotel, Bucklers Hard, Beaulieu (tel: 01590 616253; ££).*
***Local pubs:** Fleur de Lys, Alley; Pilgrim Inn, Marchwood.*

Fairfield House

A splendid, private rose garden with a good display of spring bulbs. Map reference ⓮

East Street, Hambledon, Portsmouth PO7 4RY, Hants; tel: 023 9263 2431.
***Opening times:** National Garden Scheme days only 2–6pm; call above number for dates. Parties/coaches accepted. Viewing by appointment. House closed.*
***Admission prices:** adults £2.50, children free.*
***Facilities:** parking, shop, plants for sale,*

Map: page 94

L EFT: flowering shrubs at Exbury Gardens.

B ELOW: blossom time at Fairfield House.

refreshments, teas by arrangement. Picnics permitted. Disabled access. Dogs allowed on leads.

This 5-acre (2.2-hectare) informal garden lies on chalk. Designed by Lanning Roper and Peter and Edward Waket, it has extensive walls, mature trees and a large variety of shrub and climbing roses, both old-fashioned and new. There is an excellent display of bulbs in the spring as well as numerous interesting perennials.

Accommodation: Five Bells, Buriton (tel: 01730 263584; £–££). Local pubs: Bat and Ball pub, Hambledon; Five Bells, Buriton.

Furzey Gardens

An informal garden with flowering shrubs and trees of botanical interest. Map reference 15

BELOW: Furzey Gardens lie in the heart of the New Forest.

Minstead, Lyndhurst SO43 7GL, Hants; tel: 02380 812464, fax: 02380 812297. Opening times: all year daily except Christmas and Boxing day 10am–5pm (till dusk in winter). Parties/coaches accepted. House closed.

Admission prices: adults £3.50, children £1.50, over-60s £2.80, family £9. Facilities: parking, disabled access. shop, plants for sale from adjacent nursery shop, refreshments. Picnics permitted. Guide dogs only.

Set in the New Forest, Furzey is a delightful informal garden with extensive collections of azaleas and rhododendrons. There is a sensory garden, a lake, a heather garden and a host of summer and winter flowering shrubs and trees of botanical interest at all seasons. Children are kept entertained by the log play cabins.

History: There is a kitchen and original fireback and bread oven in the restored Forest Cottage which dates back to 1560. The garden was designed by Hugh Dalrymple and established in 1922.

Accommodation: Bartley Lodge, Bartley (tel: 02380 814194; £–££). Local pubs: Trusty Servant, Minstead; White Hart, Cadnam.

Gilbert White's House and Garden

Historic naturalists' garden dating from the 18th century and recently restored. Map reference 16

The Wakes, Selborne, Alton GU34 3JH, Hants; tel: 01420 511275, fax: 01420 511040. Opening times: all year except 25–31 Dec daily 11am–5pm. Parties/coaches accepted. House open Apr–Dec. Admission prices: adults £4.50, children £1, over-60s £4. Facilities: parking, disabled access, shop, plants for sale, refreshments. There is also an "unusual plant" fair on Gilbert White Day, 21 July. The attached Oates Museum commemorates Captain Lawrence Oates who journeyed to the Antarctic with Captain Scott. No picnics. No dogs.

guished naturalist and the author of *The Natural History of Selborne* (1788), which he wrote in this house.

Map: page 94

Accommodation: Hotel du Vin, Winchester; tel: 01962 841414; £££); Wykeham Arms, Winchester (tel: 01962 853834; ££). *Local pubs:* Trooper Inn, Froxfield Green; White Horse Inn, Priors Dean; Hawkley Inn, Hawkley.

Heathlands

An intimate plantsman's garden with mature trees and tender plants. Map reference ⑰

This garden was well documented by its creator, the Reverend Gilbert White (1720–93). A programme to restore it to its 18th-century form is nearly complete. The features White described and the plants of his time are displayed in "Six Quarters", a naturalists' garden and a vegetable garden. There is a quincunx, comprising a layout of five cypress trees on a mound, replicating the one originally devised by White. A revolving "wine pipe" overlooks the miniature landscape garden and magnificent beech-clad hangar. There is a good selection of plants for sale.

History: Gilbert White was a distin-

47 Locks Road, Locks Heath, Southampton SO31 6NS, Hants; tel: 01489 573598, fax: 01489 557884. **National Collection:** *Japanese anemones.* **Opening times:** *selected Sundays, including National Garden Scheme days 2–5.30pm; call above number for specific dates. No parties/coaches. Viewing by appointment. House closed.* **Admission prices:** *adults £2, children free.* **Facilities:** *parking on road, plants for sale, refreshments. Disabled access but only partial facilities. Picnics permitted. Dogs allowed on leads.*

ABOVE LEFT: Gilbert White's House and Garden.

LEFT: Heathlands.

Heathlands garden covers an area of just over 1 acre (0.2 hectares) and is surrounded by mature trees. It is divided into several parts, each with its own character. It is a plantsman's garden but plants take second place to good design. Two miles (3.5 km) from the Solent, the relatively mild climate encourages the cultivation of some less hardy plants. It is a green garden with many evergreens but there are always seasonal flowers, including daffodils, azaleas, paulownias and Japanese anemones.

History: The garden has been developed by its owner and designer, Dr John Burwell, since 1967. Widening of the road in 1972 led to the making of the Long Walk and the line of paulownias, now 40 ft (13 metres) high. Over the years there has been a great deal of development around Heathlands, and it is now a quiet oasis in a busy area.

Accommodation: Solent Hotel, Whiteley, Fareham (tel: 01489 880000; £££–££££). Local pub: The Jolly Farmer, Fleet End Road.

Hinton Ampner

A beautifully designed mid-20th-century garden based upon a Victorian design. English Heritage Grade II. National Trust. Map reference ⓲

Hinton Ampner, Bramdean, Alresford SO24 0LA, Hants; tel: 01962 771305, fax: 01962 793101.
< www.nationaltrust.org.uk >
Opening times: Apr–Sep Sat–Wed 11am–5pm. National Garden Scheme days. Parties/coaches accepted. House also open Tues & Wed pm and Aug weekends.
Admission prices: house and garden: adults £5.50, children £2.75; garden only: adults £4.50, children £2.25.

Facilities: parking, disabled access, plants for sale on occasions, refreshments. No picnics. No dogs.

Created by Ralph Dutton, the eighth and last Lord Sherborne who inherited the estate in 1935, this is one of the great gardens of the 20th century. It is a masterpiece of design based upon the bones of a Victorian garden, in which a formal layout is united with varied and informal planting in pastel shades. Topiary is a notable feature.

Hinton Ampner is also a garden of year-round interest with many scented plants and magnificent vistas over the park and surrounding countryside. The garden forms the link between the woodland and parkland planting.

History: Ralph Dutton began creating the garden in 1930. The house, which he remodelled into a small neo-Georgian manor house, was begun in 1936. It contains his fine collection of English furniture and Italian paintings. Dutton once said of his garden, "I have learned during the past years what above all I want from a garden: this is tranquillity."

Accommodation: Hotel du Vin, Winchester (tel: 01962 841414; £££); Royal Hotel, Winchester (tel: 01962 840840; £); Wessex Hotel, Winchester (tel: 01962 841503; £££). Local pubs: Hinton Arms, Hinton Ampner; The Fox, Bramdean; Globe on the Lake, Alresford.

Houghton Lodge Garden and Hydroponicum

A leading hydroponic centre, also featuring topiary, herbaceous borders and woodland. English Heritage Grade II*. Map reference ⑲

Martin Busk, Houghton, Stockbridge SO20 6LQ, Hants; tel: 01264 810912, fax: 01264 810177.
< www.houghtonlodge.co.uk >
Opening times: *Mar–Sep Mon–Fri 10am–5pm, Sat–Sun and BHs 10am–5pm. Parties/coaches accepted. House closed.*
Admission prices: *adults £5, groups of 25 + £4.50 pp.*
Facilities: *parking, disabled access, shop, plants for sale, refreshments. Picnics permitted. Dogs allowed on leads.*

Houghton Lodge Garden is set in an idyllic spot on a hillside above the River Test with extensive views of the river. It has a restored walled kitchen garden, a topiary peacock garden, a topiary dragon which puffs as you pass, splendid herbaceous borders, woodland and river walks, a hydroponic greenhouse, and an orchid house.

Hydroponics, in which Houghton Lodge specialises, is a form of gardening in which plants are grown without the use of soil. Instead, they are successfully grown in a nutrient-enriched perlite and vermiculite base. Biological, rather than chemical control is used in the hydroponicum, in the form of beneficial bugs.

Houghton also offers demonstrations of how amateur gardeners may employ hydroponics in their own garden or greenhouse in a practical way, to grow flowers, herbs, salad, vegetables, exotic plants, shrubs and even trees.

History: Houghton Lodge is an 18th-century, listed Gothic "cottage orné" set above the River Test. The original concept of cottage ornés was to provide a natural type of dwelling in sympathy with the more natural style of landscape garden fashionable in that period, avoiding the draughty and uncomfortable grandeur of the country house of the time. Typically they featured conservatories, French windows and verandahs to soften the border between house and garden.

Accommodation: Old Three Cups Hotel, Stockbridge (tel: 01264 810527; £–££); Grosvenor Hotel (tel: 01264 810606; ££).
Local pubs: Peat Spade, Longstock; John of Gaunt, Horsebridge.

Map: page 94

BELOW: Houghton Lodge, a Gothic "cottage orné".

Longstock Park Water Gardens

A delightful water garden fed by the River Test, an arboretum and the National Collection of *Clematis viticella* and buddleia.
Map reference ㉑

Longstock, Stockbridge SO20 6EH, Hants; tel: 01264 810894.
< www.longstockpark.co.uk >
National Collections: *Buddleia and Clematis viticella.*
Opening times: *1st & 3rd Sun of month Apr–Sep 2–5pm. National Garden Scheme days. Parties/coaches accepted. Viewing by appointment. House closed to visitors.*
Admission prices: *adults £3, children 50p.*
Facilities: *parking, disabled access, shop, plants for sale, refreshments. No picnics. Guide dogs only.*

ABOVE: Longstock, one of the loveliest water gardens in Britain.

These exquisite 7-acre (2.8-hectare) water gardens are fed by the River Test, which flows nearby. The winding paths and little bridges taking visitors from island to island reveal collections of water irises, lilies, astilbes, primulas and many other water-loving plants. The walled garden features herbaceous borders, a rose pergola and a collection of clematis viticella. There is also a 6-acre (2.4-hectare) arboretum. On request, the National Collection of buddleias may be visited.

History: The main lake came into being by accident. In 1870, Alfred and Arthur East, the owners of Longstock House, dredged gravel from the banks of the River Test in order to build a private road to the property, creating the lake in the process. When the Easts sold the Longstock estate in 1914, Reginald Beddington, the son of the new owner, decided to make an aesthetic feature of the water. In the 1920s, it was channelled into a central canal flanked by two small lakes and the margins were planted with perennial beds. The water garden you see today was created after John Spedan Lewis acquired the estate in 1946. With the help of botanist Terry Jones, Spedan Lewis began an ambitious redevelopment. He trebled the garden's size, adding a wealth of detail to the main lake. The water-logged soil meant all the work had to be done by hand, and it was 10 years before the project was completed.

Accommodation: Old Three Cups Hotel, Stockbridge (tel: 01264 810527; £–££).
Local pubs: Peat Spade, Longstock; Mayfly, Testcombe; White Hare, Stockbridge.

The Manor House

The most complete restoration of a Gertrude Jekyll garden, with many old roses. Map reference ㉒

Upton Grey, Basingstoke RG25 2RD, Hants; tel: 01256 861035, fax: 01256 861035.

Opening times: May–Jul, Mon–Fri (closed bank holidays) 9am–4.30pm. Parties/coaches accepted. Viewing by Appointment. House closed.
Admission prices: *£4.*
Facilities: *parking, limited disabled access, shop, refreshments available if requested in advance. No picnics. No dogs. Personal tours by the owner for groups by appointment.*

Set in just under 5 acres (2 hectares) on chalk, the Manor House includes a formal garden with typical Jekyll herbaceous borders, planted in drifts of colours running from cool to hot, a geometric Rose Lawn, and tennis and bowling lawns. Planted drystone walls are surrounded by yew hedging. There is also Gertrude Jekyll's only restored wild garden, a pond and a small planting of walnut trees.

The rambling and species roses, some of which were formerly extinct in this country, are a delight and make June one of the best time to visit. Grass steps and winding grass paths, a nuttery, an orchard and a kitchen garden all add to the many delights.

History: The garden was designed by Gertrude Jekyll in 1908, and the house is the work of Ernest Newton, a founder member of the Art Workers' Guild. Charles Home, the owner, founder and some-time editor of *The Studio*, the most important Arts & Crafts magazine, took over the property in 1893 and it remained in his hands until the 1920s. The garden has been painstakingly restored by the current owner, Mrs Ros Wallinger. Gertrude Jekyll's plans are on display, along with photographs of the restoration.

Accommodation: The Hatchings, Cliddesden, Basingstoke (tel: 01256 465279; £–££).
Local pubs: Hoddington Arms, Upton Grey; The Sun, Bentworth; Chequers Inn, Well.

Mottisfont Abbey

Extensive gardens partly designed by Geoffrey Jellicoe. English Heritage Grade II. National Trust. Map reference ㉒

Map: page 94

Mottisfont, Romsey SO51 0LP, Hants; tel: 01794 340757, fax: 01794 341492.
National Collection: *old-fashioned roses.*
Opening times: *late Mar–early Nov Sat–Wed (and Good Fri) 11am–6pm (or dusk if earlier); July also Thur 11am–6pm. Rose garden is open until 8.30pm (last admission 7.30pm) for 10-day period in mid-June. No parties/coaches. House closed.*
Admission prices: *adults £6, children £3, season £15.*
Facilities: *parking, disabled access, shop, plants for sale, refreshments. Picnics permitted. No dogs.*

Set on the west bank of the River Test, Mottisfont Abbey is surrounded by sweeping lawns with ancient trees and walled gardens. The extensive gardens were remodelled gradually during the 20th century. Norah Lindsay designed a parterre, Geoffrey Jellicoe redesigned the north front with an avenue of limes and an octagon of

BELOW: still waters at Mottisfont Abbey.

yews, and the rose garden, situated in the old walled kitchen garden, was designed in 1972 by Graham Stuart Thomas after the National Trust had taken over the property. The garden now contains the National Collection of old-fashioned roses, with over 300 varieties. A particular feature of the grounds are the old trees; one, the great plane, is thought to be the largest of its kind in the country. The rose garden is superb in the evenings during mid-summer.

History: Originally a 12th-century Augustinian foundation, the abbey, which has a drawing room decorated by Rex Whistler, was adapted many times before coming into the care of the National Trust.

Accommodation: Old Three Cups Hotel, Stockbridge (tel: 01264 810527; £–££).
Local pub: Star Inn, East Tytherley.

Sir Harold Hillier Gardens & Arboretum

Extensive arboretum which includes numerous National Collections. Map reference ㉓

Jermyns Lane, Ampfield, Romsey SO51 0QA, Hants, tel: 01794 368787; fax: 01794 368027.

BELOW: winter weather in Sir Harold Hillier Gardens & Arboretum.

< www.hillier.hants.gov.uk >
Opening times: *all year daily except Christmas and Boxing day 10.30am–6pm (or dusk if earlier). Parties/coaches accepted. House closed.*
National Collections: *11 national plant collections: Quercus (oaks), Ligustrum (privet), Cornus (dogwoods), Photinia, Lithocarpus, Pinus (pines), Cotoneaster, Hamamelis (witch hazels), Carpinus (hornbeam), Corylus (hazels), Hillier plants.*
Admission prices: *adults £5, children free, over-60s £4.50.*
Facilities: *parking, disabled access, shop, plants for sale, refreshments. Picnics permitted. Dogs allowed on leads.*

Promoted as "gardens for all seasons", the collection provides a stunning range of colour and interest throughout the year and features 11 national plant collections, the Gurkha Memorial Garden and the largest winter garden in Europe, with over 650 different types of plants. The collection of more than 40,000 plants from temperate regions around the world grow in a mixture of formal and informal landscapes set in 180 acres (73 hectares) of Hampshire countryside.

The gardens run a progressive education policy for a wide range of user groups from primary schoolchildren to horticultural experts.

History: The garden was established in 1953 by the distinguished plantsman Sir Harold Hillier. Sir Harold was born into horticulture and from an early age spent his childhood building an encyclopedic knowledge of the plant world. In 1952, he purchased Jermyn's House, an 18th-century manor house surrounded by 40 acres (16 hectares) of fertile land, in which he created a personal "stamp collection" of rare plants from all over the world. Over the next 30 years he introduced a range of new and rare species from as far afield as Japan, Korea, Mexico and South Africa. Keen to ensure that his collection was not

Map:
page 94

lost, he formed a charitable trust and, in 1977, presented the gardens to Hampshire County Council.

Accommodation: Old Three Cups Hotel, Stockbridge (tel: 01264 810527; £–££); Hotel du Vin, Winchester (tel: 01962 841414; £££). *Local Pub:* Star Inn, East Tytherley.

Spinners

A small but splendid plantsman's garden. Map reference ㉔

School Lane, Boldre, Lymington SO41 5QE, Hants; tel: 01590-673347.
National Collection: Trilliums.
Opening times: mid-Apr–mid-Sep Tues–Sat 10am–5pm; nursery and part of garden open during winter (free). Parties/coaches accepted. House closed.
Admission prices: £2 (children under 6 free).
Facilities: parking, plants for sale. events for RHS. Picnics permitted. No refreshments. No disabled access. No dogs.

This woodland garden features rare shrubs, trees and woodland plants. Rhododendrons and azaleas are the mainstay at the top of the garden, where the soil is very poor. Lower down, rodgersias and hostas thrive and in the wetter areas, ferns, primulas and irises. In front of the house, the scene changes. On the drier, sunny slopes, cranesbills (geraniums) provide foreground planting to rare shrubs, such as the purple judas tree and the silvery *Leptospermum grandifolium.*

A large collection of lacecaps and hydrangeas are at their best later in the season, followed by the Japanese maples, giving a final burst of colour.

History: This garden was designed and made entirely by Mr and Mrs P.G.G. Chappell, the owners, between 1961 and 1981, at a total cost, including plants, of around £1 per week. The nursery has a wide variety of rare plants for sale.

Accommodation: Passford House, Passford, Lymington (tel: 01590 682398; ££–£££). Local pubs: The Red Lion, Boldre, Lymington; Fleur de Lys, Pilley; East End Arms, East End.

ABOVE:
Spinners is
a true
plantsman's
garden.

West Green House Garden

A water garden with follies, a parterre and a "green theatre". National Trust. Map reference ㉕

West Green, Hartley Wintney, Hook RG27 8JB, Hants; tel: 01252 844611, fax: 01252 844611. < www.nationaltrust.org.uk >
Opening times: *late Apr–Aug Wed–Sun 11am–4.30pm (last entry); Sep weekends 11am–4.30pm. National Garden Scheme days. Parties/coaches accepted. Viewing by appointment for National Trust groups. House closed.*
Admission prices: *adults £5; children £2.50; over-60s £3. Free entry for NT members on Wed, or for pre-booked NT groups.*
Facilities: *parking, shop, plants for sale, refreshments. No disabled access. No - picnics. No dogs.*

Abbot. Eighteenth-century in origin, they are surrounded by a neoclassical park studded with follies, monuments and birdcages. The newly restored lake gives a perfect backdrop to a spectacular garden creation. A grand water garden, parterres and the "green theatre" all add to its beauty.

The unique colour combinations of the formal gardens are complemented by the decorative potagers and ornamental fruit cages, making an exciting architectural statement within the original walls. Among the other features are a collection of 10,000 liliums and an "Alice in Wonderland" garden. West Green hosts horticultural events, as well as several cultural events each year.

History: West Green is a 1720s manor house surrounded by two gardens whose origins also lie in the 18th century. Restoration of the gardens is on-going and has been featured in magazines and on television. The property is leased, but not owned, by the National Trust.

ABOVE:
West Green House, an 18th-century manor house.

The gardens of West Green House have been painstakingly restored by the renowned garden designer Marylyn

Accommodation: The Hatchings, Cliddesden, Basingstoke (tel: 01256 465279; £–££).
***Local pub:** Chequers Inn, Well.*

WILTSHIRE

Wiltshire contains several extremely grand estates, including Stourhead, Longleat and Wilton House. It also has two properties associated with the famous Edwardian architect and landscape designer Harold Peto: Heale House and Iford Manor. The latter, his home for most of his working life, has one of the finest Italianate gardens in England.

Bowood House and Gardens

Capability Brown designed parkland and outstanding rhododenron walks. English Heritage Grade I.
Map reference ㉖

Derry Hill, Calne SN11 0LZ, Wilts;
tel: 01249 812012, fax: 01249 812757.
< www.bowood-house.co.uk >
Opening times: *Apr–Oct daily 11am–6pm; rhododendron walks, including National Garden Scheme days: late Apr–early Jun daily 11am–6pm. Parties/coaches accepted. House open.*
Admission prices: *adults £6.25; children (2–4) £3.15, (5–15) £4; over-60s £5.15; season tickets available.*
Facilities: *parking, disabled access. shop, plants for sale, refreshments, adventure playground and soft play palace for under-12s. Picnics permitted. No dogs.*

The 100-acre (40-hectare) garden and park surrounding Bowood House have an important pinetum and arboretum. These, together with the Doric temple and rhododendron walks, are the most important features. The garden is particularly beautiful in spring with massed bulbs and bluebell woods.

The garden has features designed by many of the most famous English landscape gardeners and architect/designers of the 18th and 19th centuries. For example, Capability Brown created the lake and parkland, Humphry Repton the landscape, Charles Hamilton built the famous cascade and Robert Adam the orangery and mausoleum. Lately, Mary Keen has advised on the planting of the Italianate formal gardens, using box hedging and gravel to replace grass paths.

History: Today's house is only a part of the original house, as the "big house", formerly adjoining the eastern end, was demolished in 1955. The interior also contains several rooms designed by Robert Adam, who was employed by the first Marquess of Lansdowne.

Accommodation: Lansdowne Strand, Calne (tel: 01249 812488; ££). Local pubs: The Lansdowne Arms, Derry Hill; George & Dragon, Rowde; Red Lion, Laycock.

BELOW:
Bowood
House and
Gardens.

when it was built on or near the site of an ancient manor house. In 1745 it came into the hands of the Methuen family, whose fortunes were based on the Cotswold woollen industry. The flower garden dates from the 1830s, and the fourth Lord Methuen added many more exotic shrubs in the 1950s and 1960s

Accommodation: Methuen Arms, Corsham (tel: 01249 714867; ££). ***Local pubs:*** *The Royal Oak; The Red Lion, Lacock.*

Corsham Court

18th-century landscape garden. English Heritage Grade II*. Map reference ㉗

Corsham SN13 0BZ, Wilts, tel: 01249 701610.
Opening times: *late Mar–Sep Tues–Sun 2–5.30pm; Oct–Mar weekends 2–4.30pm. National Garden Scheme days. Parties/coaches accepted. House open.*
Admission prices: *grounds: adults £2, children £1, over-60s £1.50, season £10.*
Facilities: *parking, disabled access. No refreshments. Picnics permitted. Dogs allowed on leads.*

Set in a landscape designed by Capability Brown and Humphry Repton, the gardens feature ancient trees, massive undulating yew hedges and the unique Gothic bath house with its 15th-century Bradford Porch (taken from a house in Bradford-on-Avon). A fine collection of mature magnolias lends early spring a special display, as does the extensive array of primroses, bluebells and white narcissi. The Oriental plane is said to be the largest in Europe and there are fine examples of ginkgo, black walnut and sequoia, as well as tree peonies.

History: The house dates from 1582,

ABOVE: Corsham Court.

The Courts

A garden with Mediterranean overtones and a series of hedged "rooms". English Heritage Grade II. National Trust. Map reference ㉘

Holt, Trowbridge BA14 6RR, Wilts; tel/fax: 01225 782340.
< www.nationaltrust.org.uk >
Opening times: *late Mar–mid-Oct*

Sun–Fri noon–5.30pm. National Garden Scheme days. Parties/coaches accepted. Viewing out of season by appointment with head gardener. House closed.
Admission prices: *adults £4, children £2.*
Facilities: *parking, disabled access. No lavatories, no refreshments. No picnics. No dogs.*

The garden at the Courts, with its well-defined compartments, is not dissimilar to Hidcote in Gloucestershire and is just as full of delightful surprises. Against a backdrop of some good specimen trees, the planting schemes include half-moon shaped white, pink and lilac rooms, as well as blue and yellow borders, a fuchsia border and a fernery with bamboo as background. There is a lovely walk with Mediterranean touches in the orange, scarlet, yellow and silver flowers and numerous different lavenders. In the lower garden the water-loving plants predominate beside what was once the millstream. Irises, and masses of water lilies of every colour adorn the large pool and giant gunnera feature in the former mill's dyeing pool beyond. The autumn foliage (for example, acers, viburnums and Sargent's cherry) is spectacular. Finally, in the arboretum formality disappears completely as chestnuts, limes, walnuts and beech tower over the spring daffodils and, later, the snakeshead fritillarias.

History: The early Georgian house may have been the local law courts, as the property's name suggests, although this is not certain. Sir George Hastings, the architect who laid out the garden in the early 1900s, introduced interesting statuary from Ranelagh House in Barnes. After World War I his architectural scheme was elaborated on by Lady Cecile Goff, who paved the paths and terraces with slabs from Devizes Gaol, then being demolished. Her daughter, Moyra Goff, planted the arboretum in 1952.

Accommodation: Hilbury Court House, Trowbridge (tel: 01225 752949; ££).
Local pub: Tollgate Inn, Holt.

Map: page 94

BELOW: a "hedged room" at The Courts.

Heale Gardens

Planned by Harold Peto, this garden has a profusion of climbing plants and roses. English Heritage Grade II*. Map reference ㉙

Middle Woodford, Salisbury SP4 6NT, Wilts; tel: 01722 782504.
Opening times: *all year Tues–Sun & BHs 10am–5pm. National Garden Scheme day. Parties/coaches accepted. House closed. Snowdrop Sundays in early Feb. Sunrise day: June equinox 4.30–9am.*
Admission prices: *adults £3.25, children £1.50, season £13.*
Facilities: *parking, shop, plants for sale, refreshments. Picnics permitted. Disabled access. Dogs allowed on leads.*

ABOVE: Heale Gardens are known for their climbing plants

Much of the enjoyment of visiting Heale House comes from the sense of profusion and the little pockets of surprise and interest that are discovered among the 8 acres (3.2 hectares) of flowers and shrubs that fill and over-spill the beds. In the lower part of the garden a tunnel theme is achieved by a variety of climbing plants grown up larch or ash poles and trained across the paths. *Vitis coignetiae* fight it out with wine berry, *jasminum* 'Aureum' and the rose *Felicite et Perpetue*, while on one side of the lower tunnel, *Vitis purpura* competes with that unsurpassable old rose, Easlea's Golden Rambler.

The garden also has a fish pond and boat terrace facing a little waterfall. The northeast corner of the garden, which is based on plans drawn up for the Honourable Louis Greville by Harold Peto in 1910, was planted in the style of that time with very formal herbaceous plants and a tunnel of figs.

History: The original building (now the western end of the house) was completed by Sir William Greene for his daughter and son-in-law as a wedding present in 1553. Charles II hid here for six nights while waiting for a ship to arrive at Shoreham. After a devastating fire in 1835, the Honourable Louis Greville, a great-uncle of the present owner, rebuilt all except the surviving southwest wing. In the 20th century, Lady Anne Rasch created a wonderful garden over 35 years. In recent years it has developed further, with the introduction of modern design and colour.

Accommodation: Scotland Lodge Farm, Winterbourne Stoke (tel: 01980 621199; £); Salisbury Old Mill House, South Newton (tel: 01722 742458; £). **Local pub:** *Compasses Inn, Lower Chicksgrove.*

Home Covert

A plateau of 6 acres (2.4 hectares) with water gardens. Map reference ③⓪

Roundway, Devizes SN10 2JA, Wilts; tel: 01380 723407.
Opening times: *various dates throughout spring and summer including a National Garden Scheme day. Call for specific dates. Parties/coaches accepted. Viewing by appointment. House closed.*
Admission prices: *adults £2.50, children free.*
Facilities: *parking, disabled access, shop, plants for sale and refreshments on NGS open day only. Picnics permitted. Dogs allowed on leads.*

Home Covert garden has a 6-acre (2.4-hectare) plateau, with the high Downs to the north, and, on a clear day, a distant view to the southwest of Alfred's Tower at Stourhead *(see page 120)*.

It has a very wide botanical range, especially of trees and shrubs. Herbaceous borders, a white and pastel garden, as well as an old rose garden and shrub and tree walks are prominent features. There are three water gardens, 90 ft (30 metres) below the main level, each leading into another, together with a small lake and an extensive range of wet-growing plants and primulas. There are also gunneras, rodgersias, bamboos and a number of tree species including metasequoia and a Chinese tulip tree.

In late April, 33 acres (13.3 hectares) of woodland offer bluebells, and a large number of erythroniums (dog tooth violets) around the oaks in the same season make for tranquil walks.

History: The garden was designed by the present owners, Mr and Mrs John Phillips, and constructed from ancient mixed woodland which has been the amenity woodland of the Roundway estate for over 40 years.

Accommodation: The Bear Inn, Market Place, Devizes (tel: 01380 722444; ££); The Black Swan, Devizes (tel: 01380 723259; ££). **Local pubs:** *George & Dragon, Rowde; George & Dragon, Potterne.*

Map: page 94

BELOW: Home Covert has a vast range of plants.

Iford Manor

The former home of the Edwardian architect and landscape designer Harold Peto. English Heritage Grade I. Map reference ㉛

Bradford-on-Avon BA15 2BA, Wilts; tel: 01225-863146, fax: 01225 852364. < www.ifordmanor.co.uk >
Opening times: *Apr and Oct Sun & Easter Mon 2–5pm; May–Sep Tues–Thur & Sat–Sun 2–5pm. Parties/coaches accepted. Viewing by appointment. House also open.*
Admission prices: *adults £4, over-60s, students and children over 10 £3.50, under-10s free.*
Facilities: *parking, disabled access, shop, plants for sale, refreshments. Picnics permitted. Dogs allowed on leads.*

BELOW: the Italianate Garden at Iford Manor.

The award-winning Italianate Garden of Iford Manor, famous for its tranquillity and beauty, was the home of Edwardian architect and landscape gardener, Harold Peto, from 1899 to 1933. He created the unusual and romantic garden, using his vast collection of architectural fragments on a steep-sided wooded valley set beside the River Frome. Characterised by pools and terraces, statues, sculptures, evergreen planting and magnificent rural views, the garden also has a fine cloister and casita set among many plants of botanical interest. Iford garden has been the winner of the Historic Houses Association/Christie's Garden of the Year Award.

History: The site of Iford Manor has been occupied since Roman times. The manor house is medieval in origin, but its classical facade was added in the 18th century when the hanging woodlands above the garden were planted. In 1899, Harold Ainsworth Peto discovered Iford; the individuality of the garden owes everything to his eye for combining architecture and plants.

Accommodation: Limpley Stoke Hotel, Lower Limpley Stoke, Bath (tel: 01225 723333; ££).
Local pubs: The Hop Pole, Limpley Stoke; The Inn, Freshford; Tollgate Inn, Holt.

Longleat

A splendid house surrounded by Capability Brown-landscaping, with labyrinths and a maze. English Heritage Grade I. Map reference ㉜

*Warminster BA12 7NW, Wilts; tel: 01985 844400, fax: 01985 844885.
< www.longleat.co.uk >*
Opening times: *Jan–mid-Mar weekends & school holidays 11am–3.30pm, mid-Mar–Easter daily 11am–3.30pm, Easter–Sep daily 10am–5.30pm, Sep–Dec except Christmas daily 11am–3.30pm. Parties/coaches accepted. Viewing also by appointment. House open.*
Admission prices: *grounds: adults £3, over-60s and children £2; passport tickets: adults £16, children and over-60s £11.*
Facilities: *parking, disabled access, shop, plants for sale, refreshments. Picnics permitted. Dogs allowed on leads.*

Map: page 94

Nestling alongside a lake and within rolling grounds landscaped by Capability Brown, Longleat is one of the main tourist attractions of Wiltshire. It never fails to impress. Fringed by thousands of trees, the grounds include formal gardens, a "secret garden", the Pleasure Walk, a 19th-century planting of rhododendrons and azaleas, topiary and fine examples of mazes including the Love Labyrinth, the Sun Maze and the Lunar Labyrinth. One of the most recognisable features within the park is Heaven's Gate: designed by Capability Brown, this gap in the beech trees offers magnificent views across Somerset.

History: The park underwent a major refashioning by Capability Brown under the instruction of the first Marquess during the latter half off the 18th century. This work was continued by the second Marquess who employed Humphry Repton to redesign Half Mile Lake, which had originally been constructed as a canal by the first Viscount Weymouth. Repton built the island where Longleat's Lowland Gorillas, Nico and Samba, now live.

*Accommodation: Sturfford Mead, Longleat (tel: 01373 832213; £); Land End Cottage, Corsley (tel: 01373 83239; £). **Local pub:** Cross Keys, Corsley.*

Stourhead

Outstanding English landscape garden with grottoes and classical temples. English Heritage Grade I. National Trust. Map reference ㉝

Stourton, Warminster BA12 6QD, Wilts; tel: 01747 841152, fax: 01747 842005. < www.nationaltrust.org.uk >
Opening times: *grounds: all year daily 9am–7pm (or dusk if earlier). National Garden Scheme day. Parties/coaches accepted. House: Apr–Oct Fri–Tues 11am–5pm.*
Admission prices: *house & garden: adults £8.90, children £4.30, family £21.20, groups of 15+ £8.50 pp; garden or house: adults £5.10, children £2.90, family £12.70, groups of 15+ £4.60 pp.*
Facilities: *parking, shop, plants for sale, refreshments. Picnics permitted. Disabled access. Dogs allowed on leads.*

This splendid garden is an outstanding example of the English landscape style. A satisfying arrangement of formal gardens, dells, knolls, lake and parkland enfold temples to Flora and Apollo, picturesque bridges, a cascade, a Gothic cottage, a grotto and the parish church,

ABOVE: going round in circles at Longleat.

creating a delightful theatre for the drama of the changing seasons. King Alfred's Tower, a red-brick folly built in 1722 by Henry Flitcroft, is almost 165 ft (50 metres) high and offers views over the estate. Much of the 2,650 acres (1,072 hectares) of the wider estate is managed for nature conservation. There are two interesting Iron Age hill-forts, Whitesheet Hill and Park Hill Camp.

History: The gardens of Stourhead were designed by Henry Hoare II and laid out between 1741 and 1780. Horace Walpole thought the gardens "one of the most picturesque scenes in the world." The house, begun in 1721 by Colen Campbell, contains furniture by the younger Chippendale and fine paintings.

Accommodation: The Barn, Longbridge Deverill (tel: 01985 841138; £). **Local pubs:** *Horse & Groom, East Woodlands; Spread Eagle Inn, Stourton.*

Stourton House Flower Garden

A plantsman's garden with numerous kinds of hydrangeas and herbaceous borders. Map reference **34**

Stourton House, Stourton, Warmister BA12 6QF, Wilts; tel: 01747 840417. *Opening times: Apr–Nov Wed, Thur and Sun; other days by appointment 11am–6pm; Dec–Mar Mon–Fri for dried flowers and plants. National Garden Scheme days. Parties/coaches accepted. Viewing by appointment. House closed.* **Admission prices:** *adults £3, children 50p.* **Facilities:** *parking, disabled access, shop, plants for sale, refreshments. No picnics. No dogs.*

Stourton is a 4½-acre (1.8-hectare) plantsman's garden where grass paths lead through daffodils, camellias, scented azaleas and magnolias. There are majestically hedged borders, under kiwi-laden trees, down delphinium- and rose-covered walks and by pitcher plant lily ponds that host dragonflies, butterflies and birds. A ferny secret garden and woodland area with camellias and blue hydrangeas complete the picture.

History: The garden was developed by Anthony and Elizabeth Bullivant during the latter half of the 20th century. When they bought the property, the derelict garden had little to offer except some fine trees, rhododendrons and blue hydrangeas. When a huge beech tree blew down in the 1960s, the root hole was lined with 30 tons of clay to form a pond and part of the paddock was cultivated, thus beginning the transformation of the garden.

ABOVE: the classical landscape of Stourhead.

Accommodation: Old Ship, Mere (tel: 01747 860258); The Talbot, Mere (tel: 01747 860427; £).
Local pubs: Spread Eagle, Stourton; Horse & Groom, East Woodlands.

Wilton House

A mixture of parkland and small formal gardens with many special features and a fine collection of old-fashioned roses. English Heritage Grade I. Map reference ㉟

Wilton, Salisbury SP2 0BJ, Wilts;
tel: 01722 746720.
< www.wiltonhouse.com >
Opening times: mid-Apr–Oct daily 10.30am–5.30pm (last admission 4.30pm). Parties/coaches accepted. Viewing by appointment for groups. House open.
Admission prices: adults £4, children aged 2–5 £1, 5–15 £3, season from £24.
Facilities: parking, disabled access, shop, plants for sale, refreshments. Picnics permitted. No dogs.

The grounds of Wilton House are a mixture of small, formal gardens and open parkland with an interesting collection of trees. The North Forecourt Gardens, planted in 1971, comprise a rectangle of pleached limes outlining a parterre of clipped box and surrounding a central fountain.

A walk along the bank of the River Nadder from the Palladian Bridge leads past the Victorian Boathouse, Egyptian Column and loggia and then continues around the Woodland Walk before returning via the Water Garden, a series of linking ponds with aquatic and marginal plantings and Oriental-style bridges.

The tour finishes in the English Rose Garden with its fine collection of old fashioned species.

Map: page 94

Entry to the house is required to see the Inner Courtyard, which was transformed in 1995 from a plain gravel area by the creation of a new formal garden, only visible from inside the house. New features include the Laburnum Arch and the Millennium Water Feature, the latter designed by sculptor William Pye. The Inner Courtyard also contains an interesting knot garden.

History: In the 17th century, the fourth Earl of Pembroke commissioned Isaac De Caus to create a formal garden similar in layout to the Venetian gardens of the period. Various changes were introduced in the 18th century to reflect the fashions of the times, and in the 1820s Countess Worenzov (the second wife of the 11th Earl) set out a flower garden, designed by Sir Richard Westmacott, in the Italianate style. Many of the early features were removed or simplified due to the high cost of labour and the effects of two world wars. The present Earl, a keen gardener, has created several new gardens.

Accommodation: Pembroke Arms, Wilton (tel: 01722 743328; ££). Local pub: Haunch of Venison, Salisbury.

BELOW: the Water Garden at Wilton.

Gloucestershire & Oxfordshire

This area is associated with the influential Cotswold school of gardening which was allied to the Arts & Crafts movement. Among its leading lights were Charles Wade (Snowshill Manor) and Lawrence Johnston (Hidcote Manor), who favoured small-scale "garden rooms"

GLOUCESTERSHIRE

Gloucestershire has an unusually large number of very individual gardens. It has superb Arts and Crafts-style gardens, including Rodmarton Manor, Snowshill Manor and Hidcote, the Indian-inspired Sezincote, and the rococo-style garden at Painswick. Another highlight is Barnsley House, Rosemary Vercy's famous garden, which also sprang from the Arts & Crafts tradition. The county also has two notable arboretums, Batsford and Westonbirt.

Barnsley House

An intimate garden that has had a great influence on gardening styles since the 1950s. Map reference ❶

Barnsley, Cirencester GL7 5EE, Glos; tel: 01285 740421; fax: 01285 740142.
Opening times: *selected days in May, Jun, Aug & Sep 11am–5pm. In future will also be open as grounds of hotel and restaurant. National Garden Scheme days.*
Admission prices: *£5.*
Facilities: *parking, disabled access, shop, plants for sale, refreshments. Picnics permitted. Dogs allowed on leads.*

This is an important garden, the future of which, after the death of its creator Rosemary Verey in 2001, was uncertain. However, in late 2002 it was revealed that the property was to be turned into a hotel

and that the garden would be maintained.

The 4-acre (1.6-hectare) garden blends various styles in an artful and pleasing combination with subtle and beautiful colour and texture coordination. The kitchen garden has numerous small beds and features fruit trees trained against the Cotswold stone walls and box hedges edging the paths. The famous Laburnum Walk, with wisteria and purple alliums, is at its best in late May and early June.

History: The house dates from 1697 and the garden is enclosed on three sides by a stone wall dating from 1770. The garden was created by Rosemary Verey after she and her architect husband, David, inherited it from his father in 1951. It featured in many of her television gardening programmes.

Accommodation: The Village Pub, Barnsley (tel: 01285 740421; £–££); Rectory Farmhouse, Stow-on-the-Wold (tel: 01451 832351; £).

PRECEDING PAGES: Batsford Arboretum.

OPPOSITE: the Laburnum Walk at Barnsley House.

ABOVE: a scarecrow at Barnsley.

Batsford Arboretum

A peaceful and intimate place with many Oriental touches. English Heritage Grade I. Map reference ❷

Batsford Park, Moreton-in-Marsh GL56 9QB, Glos; tel: 01386 701441; fax: 01386 701827.
< www.batsford-arboretum.co.uk >
Opening times: *Feb–mid-Nov daily 10am–5pm, mid-Nov–Jan Sat–Sun 10am–4pm, plus Boxing Day 10am–3pm. National Garden Scheme day. Parties/coaches accepted. Viewing by appointment. House closed.*
Admission prices: *adults £4, children £1, over-60s £3.*
Facilities: *parking, disabled access, shop, plants for sale, refreshments. Picnics permitted. Dogs allowed on leads. Garden centre, falconry centre.*

Batsford holds a rare and beautiful collection of trees, shrubs and wild flowers, located in 55 acres (22 hectares) of spectacular Cotswold countryside. Visitors can wander along paths that meander beside streams among magnolias, candelabra primulas, and Japanese cherries. In autumn, the trees explode into reds, deep purples, yellows and golds against the evergreen foliage. There is a Japanese Rest House with views across the Evencode Valley, a bronze Buddha and a waterfall.

History: In 1897 Algernon Bertram Freeman Mitford rebuilt Batsford House and planted trees in a style that he had admired when travelling as British envoy in Japan and China, thereby establishing the Oriental style that was continued during the 20th century. In 1916 Lord Dulverton developed the arboretum with further extensive plantings. The Batsford Foundation was established in 1984 as a charitable trust.

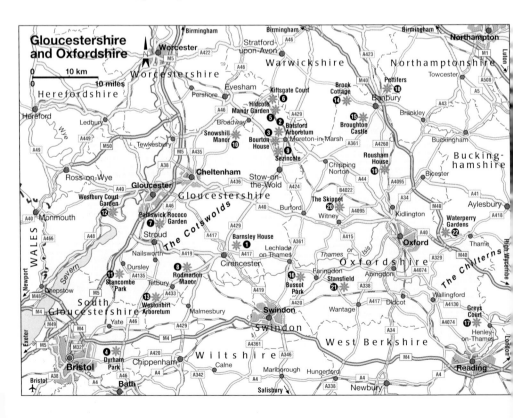

Map: page 126

Accommodation: Rectory Farmhouse, Stow-on-the-Wold (tel: 01451 832351; £); The Old Bakery, Blockley (tel: 01386 700408; £££).
Local pubs: Fox and Hounds, Great Wolford.

Bourton House

A plantsman's paradise, with tropical borders and topiary. English Heritage Grade II. Map reference ❸

Bourton-on-the-Hill, Moreton-in-Marsh GL56 9AE, Glos; tel: 01386 700754.
< www.bourtonhouse.com >
Opening times: late May–Oct Wed–Fri 10am–5pm & BH Mons. National Garden Scheme days. Parties/coaches accepted, minimum of 20 people. Viewing by appointment. House closed.
Admission prices: adults £4.50, children free.
Facilities: parking, limited disabled access, shop, plants for sale, refreshments. Picnics permitted. No dogs.

Bourton is an intensively planted 3-acre (1.2-hectare) garden surrounding an early 18th-century manor house. A number of garden rooms feature an abun-

dance of unusual plants in exciting colour, shape and textural combinations. Tender plants are used in the borders and the planted containers, which range from lead water butts to giant terracotta vases. There is some good topiary, mainly of *Buxus sempervirens*.

History: This is a modern garden, first laid out in the 1960s but largely created over the past two decades by the present owners.

Accommodation: Rectory Farmhouse, Stow-on-the-Wold (tel: 01451 832351; £); The Old Bakery, Blockley (tel: 01386 700408; £££); The Village Pub, Barnsley (tel: 01285 740421; £–££).
Local pub: Fox and Hounds, Great Wolford.

ABOVE: Batsford Arboretum in autumn.

LEFT: vibrant borders at Bourton House.

Dyrham Park

Specimen trees and a well-stocked orangery, set in an ancient deer park. English Heritage Grade II*. National Trust. Map reference ❹

Chippenham SN14 8ER; Glos; tel: 0117 9372501. < www.nationaltrust.org.uk >
Opening times: garden: late Mar–Oct Fri–Tues 11am–5.30pm (or dusk if earlier); park: all year daily (except Christmas Day) 11am–5.30pm (or dusk if earlier); house: as garden, but noon–5.30pm. National Garden Scheme days. Parties/coaches accepted.
Admission prices: house, garden & park: adults £7.90, children £3.90, family £19.50; garden & park: adults £3, children £1.50, family £7.
Facilities: parking, disabled access, shop, plants for sale, refreshments. Picnics permitted. Dogs allowed on leads.

BELOW: the statue of Neptune at Dyrham Park.

Dyrham Park occupies a remarkable setting and is notable for parkland and superb trees. It possesses one of the earliest architectural greenhouses, the orangery, where citrus fruits as well as plumbago, passion flowers, oleander and jasmine, are still grown. However, the trees are the real glory; many of them were comparatively early imports from America. Tulip trees and holm oaks, black walnut, red oak, catalphas and *Pinus strobus* all flourish here.

History: The estate was an ancient deer park and the name derives from the Saxon "deor hamm" (deer enclosure). It was acquired by William Blathwayt, William III's Secretary of War and Secretary of State, at the end of the 17th century. He demolished the Tudor manor house and built the present structure. The garden originally had a 224-step cascade, dropping down from the statue of Neptune (still in place) to the front of the house; and there was a formal garden in the Dutch style, with parterres, terraces, fountains and avenues. However the cost of upkeep was too high and in time it was all removed.

Accommodation/pub: White Hart, Ford, west of Chippenham (tel: 01249 782213; ££).

Hidcote Manor Garden

Numerous rare and interesting plants and an architectural structure. English Heritage Grade I. National Trust. Map reference ❺

Hidcote Bartrim, Chipping Campden GL55 6LR, Glos; tel: 01386 438333; fax: 01386 438817.
< www.nationaltrust.org.uk >
Opening times: Apr–Oct Tues, Wed & weekends 10.30am–5.30pm (till 4pm in Oct; last admission an hour before closing). National Garden Scheme day. Parties/coaches accepted. Viewing also by written appointment. House closed.
Admission prices: adults £5.90, children £2.90, family £14.50.
Facilities: parking, shop, plants for sale, refreshments. Picnics permitted. Disabled access. Dogs allowed on leads. Possible crowding on Sunday and bank holidays.

T he great innovation, so well executed at Hidcote, is to bring the experience of the traditional English country house garden into an area of about 10 acres (4 hectares). Lawrence Johnston achieved this by creating a series of "rooms", providing surprises at every turn. There is so much to see in the numerous compartments, with a great range of rare and interesting plants. This influential garden has been widely copied, and is, at its core, a plantsman's garden, echoing Vita Sackville-West's depiction of Johnston as a botanist and plant hunter.

History: The garden was started by Lawrence Johnston who arrived here with his mother in 1907 and developed it from exposed farmland, gradually enclosing the surrounding pastures as he progressed. Johnston took part in two major plant-hunting expeditions – with George Forrest to China and with Cherry Ingram to South Africa. In planting the garden he was assisted by his friend Norah Lindsay and had intended to leave Hidcote to her when he moved to the South of France, where he created another garden near Menton. Sadly, Norah Lindsay died in 1945, and Hidcote was acquired by the National Trust three years later. The Trust has striven to retain the spirit and content of the original garden.

Accommodation: Holly House, Chipping Campden (tel: 01386 593213; £). **Local pubs:** *Howard Arms, Ilmington; Fleece Inn, Bretforton.*

Kiftsgate Court

Famous for its roses and for its use of colour. English Heritage Grade II*. Map reference ❻

Map: page 126

Chipping Campden GL55 6LW, Glos; tel/fax: 01386 438777.
< www.kiftsgate.co.uk >
Opening times: *Apr–May & Aug–Sep Wed–Thur, Sun & BH Mons 2–6pm; Jun–Jul Wed–Thur & weekends noon–6pm. Parties/coaches by appointment. House closed.*
Admission prices: *adults £4.30, children £1.*
Facilities: *parking, plants for sale, refreshments. Picnics permitted. Dogs allowed on leads on the lawn only. No disabled access.*

K iftsgate is famous, above all, for its roses, especially *Rosa filipes*, known as the Kiftsgate rose, which grows in profusion in the rose border and is covered in a mass of white flowers in mid-July. The whole border is a delight, with old-fashioned varieties interspersed with deutzias for early colour. The yellow border is also splendid, with royal blue delphiniums making a striking contrast among yellow and orange blooms. Highlights in April

ABOVE LEFT: detail at Hidcote Manor.

BELOW: admiring the borders at Kiftsgate Court.

and early May are the bluebell wood that runs beside the drive and the *Magnolia denudata* that blooms in the forecourt. The latest addition to Kiftsgate is the water garden, a minimalist, architectural affair in shades of black, green and white.

History: Kiftsgate Court dates from the late 1880s, when it was built by Sydney Graves Hamilton, who owned nearby Mickleton Manor. The garden is the work of three generations of the Muir family: Heather Muir, who began it in the 1920s, her daughter Diana Binny who took over in 1950, and Anne Chambers and her husband, who still live here. Heather was helped by her friend Lawrence Johnston, who created the garden at Hidcote.

Accommodation: Three Ways House, Mickleton, Chipping Campden (tel: 01386 438429; ££–£££); Eight Bells, Chipping Campden (tel 01386 840371; ££). Local pubs: Volunteer, Chipping Campden.

Painswick Rococo Garden

A rococo-style garden with a stunning display of snowdrops. English Heritage Grade: II*. Map reference ❼

Painswick, GL6 6TH Glos; tel: 01452 813204; fax: 01452 814888. < www.rococogarden.co.uk >

Opening times: early Jan–Oct daily 11am–5pm. Parties/coaches accepted. House closed.
Admission prices: adults £3.60, children £1.80, over-60s £3.30, season £9.50.
Facilities: parking, limited disabled access, shop, plants for sale, refreshments. Picnics permitted. Dogs allowed on leads.

Set in a hidden valley in the Cotswolds, Painswick dates from the brief rococo period in the 18th century, known for its flamboyancy and frivolity. The garden incorporates formal vistas and informal walks; rococo architectural features have been newly restored.

Painswick is best known for its naturalised display of snowdrops and the recently planted maze. Woods of beech and other fine trees shelter wild flowers.

History: The garden was laid out by Benjamin Hyett in the 1740s and the original layout was captured by local artist Thomas Rubins in 1748. There has been a great deal of excellent restoration in recent years, by the Painswick Rococo Garden Trust, and much of this is still in progress.

Accommodation: Painswick Hotel, Painswick (tel: 01452 812160; £££–££££); Cardynham House, Painswick (tel: 01452 814006; ££–£££). Local pubs: Falcon Inn, Painswick; Royal Oak, Painswick; Seven Tuns, Chedworth; Bathurst Arms, North Cerney.

BELOW: 18th-century flamboyance at Painswick Rococo Garden.

Rodmarton Manor

A splendid example of an Arts & Crafts Movement garden. English Heritage Grade II*. Map reference ❽

Rodmarton, Cirencester GL7 6PF, Glos; tel: 01285 841253; fax: 01285 841298.
Opening times: *early May–Aug Wed, Sat & BHs 2–5pm, plus Mon 11am–5pm Jun–Jul. National Garden Scheme day. Parties/coaches of 20+ people accepted. Viewing also by appointment. House also open for guided tours (groups 20+), or by prior appointment.*
Admission prices: *house & garden: adults £6, children £3, garden: adults £3, accompanied children under 14 free. Minimum group charge £120; parties of 30+ may be divided; guided tours of garden £30 per group.*
Facilities: *disabled access, refreshments by arrangement when booking for parties of 20+. No parking, no picnics, no dogs.*

The garden at Rodmarton Manor is one of the best surviving examples of an Arts & Crafts Movement garden. It was designed as a series of outdoor rooms, each with its own character, and walled with hedges of holly, box, beech and yew. The original garden consisted of borders, lawns, topiary, two kitchen gardens and three tennis courts, as well as older trees that were already on the site.

The most recent plantings consist principally of lime, hornbeam, birch, Portuguese laurel and Irish yew. In addition, there are some fine old-fashioned roses and a wild garden.

History: At a time when mass factory and machine production had already become the norm, Rodmarton Manor was one of the last country houses to be built in the traditional style with local craftsmen using local stone and timber. Ernest Barnsley and the Cotswold group of craftsmen, who commenced building and furnishing the house for Claud and

Margaret Biddulph in 1909, were responsible for the revival of many traditional crafts which were in danger of dying out.

The garden was also designed by Barnsley and the work was directed by Margaret Biddulph and her head gardener, William Scrubery.

Map: page 126

Accommodation: *Calcot Manor, Tetbury (tel: 01666 890391; £££); Gumstool Inn, Tetbury (tel: 01666 502469; £–££); Egypt Mill, Nailsworth (tel: 01453 833449; £–££).* ***Local pub:*** *Wild Duck Inn, Ewen.*

Sezincote

Indian-style garden with water-loving plants and fine trees. English Heritage Grade I. Map reference ❾

Moreton-in-Marsh GL56 9AW, Glos (postal enquiries only).
Opening times: *Jan–Nov Thur–Fri & BH Mons 2–6pm (or dusk if earlier). Parties/coaches accepted. House also open May–Sep (no children in house).*
Admission prices: *adults £3.50, children £1, over-60s £5.50.*
Facilities: *parking, Picnics permitted. No disabled access. Guide dogs only.*

Flamboyant Sezincote house was the inspiration, in the early 1800s, for the Brighton Pavilion. A stream emerges

Above: Rodmarton Manor epitomises the ideals of the Arts & Crafts movement.

from below a temple to Surya and descends via a series of pools and fountains to a lake. The cruciform Moghul-style garden perfectly complements the Indian facade of the house. Although it looks older, it was designed relatively recently, in 1965.

The borders are planted with massed rodgersias, hostas, campanula and other water-loving plants, surrounded by unusually large trees, including cedars, copper beeches and limes. The autumn colours are wonderful. There is a curved orangery, which protects tender climbing plants, an Indian Snake Bridge and Brahmin bulls.

Sezincote also has the tallest maidenhair tree, *Ginkgo biloba* (85 ft/26 metres) in the British Isles.

History: It is thought that the surrounding parkland was designed by Humphry Repton at the beginning of the 19th century. It was restored in the 1950s by Lady Kleinwort and Graham Stuart Thomas, who later laid out the Indian Garden to the south of the house.

Accommodation: The Manor Hotel, Moreton-in-Marsh (tel: 01608 650501; £££–££££); Rectory Farmhouse, Stow-on-the-Wold (tel: 01451 832351; £); The Old Bakery, Blockley (tel: 01386 700408; £££). Local pubs: Coach and Horses, Moreton-in-Marsh; Fox and Hounds, Great Wolford.

Above: Brahmin bull at Sezincote.

Snowshill Manor

Arts & Crafts-style house and garden. National Trust. Map reference ❿

Broadway WR12 7JU, Glos; tel: 01386 852410; fax: 01386 852410.
< www.nationaltrust.org.uk >
***Opening times:** Apr–Sep Wed–Sun & BH Mons, plus Mon Jul–Aug 11am–5.30pm. House also open noon–5pm. National Garden Scheme days. Parties/coaches accepted by written appointment only.*
***Admission prices:** house & garden: adults £6.40, children £3.20, family £16; garden: adults £3.60, children £1.80.*
***Facilities:** parking, disabled access (motorised buggy available), shop, plants for sale, refreshments. Picnics permitted. Dogs allowed on leads.*

Snowshill is an extraordinary house and garden, expressing the philosophy of Charles Wade and the Arts & Crafts Movement even down to the exact shade of dark blue favoured for the garden furniture, to blend and contrast with the greens of the garden and mellow tones of the Cotswold stone. The garden is laid out as a series of "outdoor rooms", intended by Wade to be an extension of the house, and contains a variety of architectural objects. In the wider scene, the garden fits well into the Cotswold landscape, views of which cleverly counterbalance the enclosed effect of the garden.

History: Charles Wade, architect, artist and woodworker, bought Snowshill Manor in 1919 as a base to demonstrate his passion for the Arts & Crafts philosophy. He commissioned M.H. Baillie-Scott to create the garden rooms in the Hidcote style *(see page 128)*. Following its acquisition of the property, the National Trust has maintained both house and garden in the original style of Wade.

Accommodation: Churchill Arms, Paxford (tel: 01386 594000; ££). Local pubs: Crown and Trumpet, Broadway; Baker's Arms, Broad Campden.

Stancombe Park

A mixture of 19th-century mock-Gothic and modern design, lying at the head of a valley. English Heritage Grade I. Map reference ⓫

Stancombe, Dursley GL11 6AU, Glos; tel: 01453 542815.
Opening times: by appointment.
Parties/coaches accepted. House closed.
Admission prices: adults £3, children £1.
Facilities: parking, refreshments.
Picnics permitted. No disabled access.
No dogs.

Situated midway between Dursley and Wotton-under-Edge, Stancombe Park lies at the head of a valley below Stinchcombe Hill, a well-known South Gloucestershire landmark. The park comes right up to the house, and is separated from the upper garden by a sweeping drive.

The garden is clearly divided into two areas; the upper one, nearest to the house, was created out of existing parkland and showcases rose beds and well-designed mixed borders as well as a row of sweet chestnuts. The second one, the historic Gothic Folly Garden is reached by a romantic path, dropping down into the valley past ferns, grottos and two ponds to the main lake at the bottom. The path links a series of extraordinary follies.

History: The house was originally a late 18th-century structure, but a fire in the latter part of the 19th century necessitated much rebuilding, which has resulted in the two different architectural styles. Much of the excellent planting in the upper garden is modern, the work of Nadia Jennet and Lanning Roper.

Accommodation: The Swan Hotel, Wotton-under-Edge (tel: 01453 521454; ££–£££).
Local pubs: The Black Horse Inn, North Nibley; Ram Inn, South Woodchester.

LEFT: Snowshill Manor fits perfectly into the Cotswold scene.

BELOW: Stancombe Park.

Westbury Court Garden

A remarkable Dutch garden, growing only plants that were cultivated before the start of the 18th century. English Heritage Grade II*. National Trust. Map reference ⑫

Westbury-on-Severn, GL14 1PD Glos; tel: 01452 760461.
< *www.nationaltrust.org.uk* >
Opening times: *Mar–Jun & Sep–Oct Wed–Sun & BH Mon 10am–5pm; Jul–Aug daily. National Garden Scheme day. Parties/coaches accepted. Viewing by appointment Nov–Feb. House open.*
Admission prices: *adults £3, children £1.50.*
Facilities: *parking, shop, plants for sale, refreshments. Picnics permitted. Disabled access. Dogs allowed on leads.*

ABOVE: the Dutch-style garden at Westbury Court.

Remarkable restoration work conducted by the National Trust has recreated the original 17th-century Dutch Water Garden at Westbury Court, the only one to survive the era of naturalistic landscaping by the likes of Repton and Capability Brown. Although the exotic varieties of tulips from the age of "tulipomania" are long gone, Westbury is planted exclusively with species of plants available before 1700. The box parterre with conical and ball-shaped topiary contained within yew hedges provides a formal surround to the Tall Pavilion.

Many old varieties of apple and plum trees are espaliered here, along with peach , apricot and cherry trees. There is a small walled garden with a collection of 17th-century perennials. Two magnificent trees, a tulip tree and a holm oak, dominate the formal garden, the oak being one of the largest and oldest in the country.

History: The garden at Westbury Court was laid out between 1696 and 1715 by Maynard Colchester, and possibly influenced by his Dutch neighbour, Catherine Boevey of Flaxley Abbey. The T-shaped canal was the first feature he created, in 1696. The garden came to the National Trust in 1967 in a very sorry state and became its first garden restoration project, the work starting in 1971.

Accommodation: The Speech House, Coleford (tel: 0870 8304455; ££). **Local pubs:** *Red Hart Inn, Blaisdon; Red Hart Inn, Awre.*

Westonbirt Arboretum

The national arboretum. Map reference ⓭

Westonbirt, Tetbury GL8 8QS, Glos; tel: 01666 880220; fax: 01666 880559.
National Collection: *Japanese Acers, Salix (willow).*
Opening times: *year-round daily 10am–8pm, or dusk if earlier. Parties (min 12) may also view by appointment.*
Admission prices: *Apr–Nov adults £7.50, children £1, over-60s £6.50; Jan–Mar adults £5, children £1, over-60s £4. December free.*
Facilities: *parking, disabled access, refreshments, shop. Picnics permitted. Dogs allowed in some areas.*

Westonbirt contains around 18,000 numbered specimens from all over the world, covering 600 acres (240 hectares) of Cotswold countryside. Visitors can wander where they please along 17 miles (27 km) of signposted trails or simply sit and admire some of the tallest, oldest and indeed rarest trees in Britain.

Westonbirt is famous for its autumn colour, but April is good for seeing the acer glades, as is May for rhododendrons, azaleas, camellias, magnolias and bluebells.

History: Westonbirt was started in 1829 by Robert Holford. It expanded under other members of the family for 130 years before passing to the government in 1956.

Accommodation/pub: Gumstool Inn, Tetbury (tel: 01666 502469; £–££).

Map: page 126

OXFORDSHIRE

In addition to two major gardens – Rousham House, the most complete remaining work of the great 18th-century landscape designer William Kent, and Buscot Park, a water garden by Harold Peto – Oxfordshire has some outstanding modern plantsman's gardens. These include Brook Cottage, Pettifers, Stansfield and The Skippet, the latter hosting a large collection of alpines.

Brook Cottage

A delightful modern garden with colour-coordinated borders, a water garden, many varieties of clematis and roses, and a gravel garden. Map reference ⓮

Well Lane, Alkerton, Banbury OX15 6NL, Oxon; tel: 01295 670303/670590; fax: 01295 760362.
Opening times: *Easter Mon–Oct Mon–Fri 9am–6pm. Parties/coaches accepted by appointment. Viewing by appointment evening and weekends. House closed.*
Admission prices: *adults £3, children free, over-60s £2, season £6.*
Facilities: *parking, shop, plants for sale, refreshments – groups should order when making appointment. Picnics permitted. No disabled access. Dogs allowed on leads.*

This 4-acre (1.6-hectare) garden has been created by the owner, Mrs Hodges, a plantswoman, and her late husband, an architect, on the west facing slope of a valley. Groups of now-mature trees and shrubs growing in grass, merge the garden into the surrounding countryside. A

BELOW: the Water Garden at Brook Cottage.

wide variety of plants is grown, some rarely seen, including bulbs, perennials, over 200 shrub and climbing roses, flowering and foliage shrubs and water and bog plants. There is also a gravel garden.

A number of the borders are colour-coordinated: soft shades of pink and blue in one, "hot" colours in another. The White Border is seen against the yew hedge, while the Yellow Border is backed by a hedge of copper beech. The Water Garden with primulas, iris, astilbes, day-lilies and other bog plants is at its best from early June. Over 60 varieties of clematis climb over walls and shrubs.

History: Apart from a small area above the 17th-century house, the whole garden site consisted of rough pasture when Mr and Mrs Hodges began their work in 1964.

Accommodation: Easington House Hotel, Banbury (tel: 01295 270181; ££); Whately Hall, Banbury (tel: 01295 263451; £–££). Local pubs: The Bell, Shenington.

Broughton Castle

ABOVE: Buscot Park, designed by Harold Peto.

Moated castle with fine herbaceous borders and formal walled garden. English Heritage Grade II*. Map reference ⑮

Broughton, Banbury OX15 5EB, Oxon; tel: 01295 276070.
< www.broughtoncastle.demon.co.uk >
***Opening times:** mid-May–mid-Sep Wed & Sun, plus Thur in Aug and BHs, including Easter 2–5pm. Parties/coaches may also view by appointment. House open.*
***Admission prices:** house & garden: adults £5, children £2, over-60s £4.*
***Facilities:** no facilities. No disabled access. No dogs.*

The formal garden to the south features unusual fleur-de-lys-shaped box hedges with Rose Grass, an Aachen and many other old-fashioned varieties of shrub roses in the surrounding beds. In addition there are four herbaceous borders planted with shrub roses, shrubs and a variety of perennial plants – one border has a blue and yellow theme, another pink and red.

History: The home of the same family for the past 600 years, the castle was built in 1300 and rebuilt in 1550. It has a medieval Great Hall, splendid fireplaces, panelling and plaster ceilings, a collection of Civil War arms and armour and a moat.

The formal garden to the south of the house was laid out in 1890. The designer is not known, though Gertrude Jekyll is believed to have approved of the design. The remainder of the garden was re-designed and re-planted with guidance from Lanning Roper in 1970

Accommodation: Wroxton House Hotel (tel: 01295 730777; ££). *Local pub:* Red Lion Inn, Addenbury.

Buscot Park

Harold Peto's famous water garden. English Heritage Grade II*. National Trust. Map reference ⑯

Faringdon SN7 8BU, Oxon; tel: 01367 240786; fax: 01367 241794. < www.buscot-park.com >
Opening times: Apr–Sep Wed–Fri & alternate weekends 2–6pm. Parties/coaches accepted. Viewing by appointment. House also open.
Admission prices: house & garden: adults £5, children £2.50; garden: adults £4, children £2.
Facilities: refreshments. No parking. No disabled access. No picnics. No dogs.

T he sudden, surprising view through dense woods leading down to the Great Lake, with a temple on the other side, never fails to entrance visitors. Harold Peto's Water Garden, the best-known part of Buscot Park, features steps, canals, rills, still pools, cascades and a serpentine walk that leads over a pretty bridge, while statues provide interest along the way down to the lake. In a separate area, walled gardens mainly devoted to flowers, but with fruit trees growing against the walls, are designed round a formal plan with a Judas tree tunnel. There is also a secret green and white "swinging" garden, so called because of the swing seats dotted around it. This is a large garden and one that should be enjoyed at leisure.

History: Edward Loveden Townsend, the first owner of the house, was probably responsible for the two lakes and dense belts of trees, as well as the walled kitchen gardens. Harold Peto was commissioned in 1904 by Alexander Henderson, later Lord Faringdon, to create an Italianate garden to connect the neoclassical house to the 20-acre (8-hectare) lake lying below it. The second Lord Faringdon cut more avenues in the trees in the form of a *patte d'oie*, or goose foot. Peter Coats created the Parents' Walk, a sumptuous herbaceous border, in 1986.

Accommodation: The White Horse, Woolstone, Faringdon (tel: 01367 820726; £–££); The Lamb at Buckland (tel: 01367 870484; ££). Local pubs: The Trout at Tadpole Bridge, north of Buckland.

Greys Court

An arbour of ancient wisteria and old-fashioned roses are the main features of this tranquil garden. National Trust. Map reference ⑰

Rotherfield Greys, Henley-on-Thames RG9 4PG, Oxon; tel: 01491 628529. < www.nationaltrust.org.uk > Opening times: late-Mar–Sep Tues–Sat &

Map: page 126

Below: Greys Court.

BH Mons (closed Good Friday) 2–6pm.
National Garden Scheme days.
Parties/coaches accepted by appointment.
House open.
Admission prices: *house & garden:
adults £4.80, children £2.40, family £12;
garden: adults £3.20, children £1.70,
family £8.*
Facilities: *parking, refreshments (teas).
No picnics. No disabled access. Dogs
allowed on leads in car park and estate
footpaths only.*

The 14th-century ruins of a fortified house, which still sports a Great Tower, provide a peaceful background to a tranquil garden, or rather a set of gardens, of which the main feature is a spectacular arbour of ancient wisteria. The walled gardens of Greys Court are resplendent with old-fashioned roses and beds of peonies. There is an ornamental vegetable garden where unusual varieties are grown, a Nut Avenue and a peaceful White Garden. The Archbishop's Maze and the statue of St Fiacre, the patron saint of gardeners, are other interesting touches.

History: The ancient property, which had a history of court intrigue in Jacobean times, was bought by Sir Felix and Lady Brunner in 1937 and the garden, originally designed by Humphrey Waterfield, was largely developed by them before it came into the care of the National Trust.

Accommodation: *The Knoll, Shiplake (tel: 01189 402705; ££).* **Local pubs:** *Horns, Crazies Hill; Bird in Hand, Knowl Hill; Five Horseshoes, Henley-on-Thames; Anchor, Henley-on-Thames.*

Pettifers

Although only occasionally open to the public, this modern plantsman's garden is an elegant and peaceful place. Map reference ⓲

Lower Wardington, Banbury OX17 1RU, Oxon; tel: 01295 750232.

Opening times: *one National Garden Scheme Sunday in May 1–6pm, one in Sep 2–6pm. Parties/coaches accepted occasionally by appointment. House closed.*
Admission prices: *adults £3, £4 on prearranged private group visits; children free.*
Facilities: *disabled access, plants for sale, refreshments (NGS days). No parking. No picnics. No dogs.*

Pettifers garden took some 15 years to create but continues to evolve. It is a peaceful place with extraordinary views over the surrounding landscape. Now fully mature, this is a plantsman's garden. The elegant patterns made in the paths show the care that has been put into the creation by the owners, Mr J. and the Hon Mrs Price. Features include cutting gardens, a box-hedged herb garden and a new autumn border. A plan and a plant list are supplied.

Accommodation: *Old Bonhams, Wardington (tel: 01295 758069; ££).* **Local pub:** *George and Dragon, Chacombe.*

ABOVE RIGHT: brilliant colours at Pettifers, a plantsman's garden.

Rousham House

The best surviving example of William Kent's early 18th-century landscaping. English Heritage Grade I. Map reference ⓲

Steeple Aston, Bicester OX6 3QX, Oxon; tel: 01869 347110; fax: 01869 347110. < www.rousham.org >
Opening times: *all year, daily 10am–4.30pm. Parties/coaches accepted. House also open Apr–Sep Wed, Sun, BH Mons 2–4.30pm.*
Admission prices: *adults £3; no children under 15.*
Facilities: *parking, disabled access. Picnics permitted. No dogs.*

Rousham represents the first phase of English landscape design and remains almost as it was left by its designer, William Kent (1685–1748). It is one of the few gardens of this date to have escaped alteration, with many features that delighted 18th-century visitors still *in situ*. These include ponds and cascades in Venus' Vale, the Cold Bath, the seven-arched Praeneste, Townsend's Building, the Temple of the Mill and, on the skyline, a sham ruin known as the Eyecatcher.

There is also a lovely walled garden with herbaceous borders, a small parterre, a pigeon house and espaliered apple trees.

History: Rousham House, originally built in 1635 by Sir Robert Dormer, is still in the ownership of the same family. William Kent, the principal exponent of Palladian architecture in England, added the wings and stable block and made alterations to the interior. The gardens are almost entirely his work.

Map: page 126

Accommodation: *Holt Hotel, Steeple Aston (tel: 01869 340259; £££); Falkland Arms, Great Tew (tel: 01608 683653; ££).* **Local pubs:** *Horse and Groom, Caulcott; Red Lion, Steeple Aston.*

The Skippet

A plantsman's garden with a splendid collection of alpines. Map reference ⓴

Mount Skippet, Ramsden, Chipping Norton OX73AP, Oxon; tel: 01993 868253.
Opening times: *by appointment only. Parties/coaches accepted. House closed to visitors.*
Admission prices: *£1.*
Facilities: *parking, disabled access, plants for sale. Picnics permitted. No dogs. Local garden centre.*

BELOW: border in the Walled Garden at Rousham House.

The Skippet garden surrounds a 16th-century house, owned by the Rogers family for 75 years and intensively gardened by Dr Maurice Rogers for almost half that period. It features numerous unusual plants, including some tender ones that are not normally grown outdoors, and an alpine house with a huge collection.

In addition, there is an old orchard bordering a large village pool, believed to be of Roman origin, sloping lawns and spectacular views.

Maurice Rogers is a good host, welcoming enthusiasts, novices and experienced gardeners alike. Most unusually, he even permits cuttings to be taken.

History: The Cotswold stone house was converted in the 1920s and Maurice Rogers designed the garden.

ABOVE: alpines feature at Stansfield.

Accommodation: The Royal Oak, Ramsden (tel: 01993 868213; ££); Bird in Hand, Hailey Witney (tel: 01993 868321; ££). **Local pub:** *The Plough, Finstock.*

Stansfield

A small garden with a plantsman's collection of over 2,000 varieties. Map reference ㉑

49 High Street, Stanford-in-the-Vale, Faringdon SN7 8NQ, Oxon; tel: 01367 710340.
Opening times: *Apr–Sep first Tues in month 10am–4pm, plus two National Garden Scheme days in May and June, 2–6pm. Parties/coaches accepted. Viewing by appointment. House closed.*
Admission prices: *adults £1.50, accompanied children free.*
Facilities: *parking, plants for sale, refreshments. No disabled access. No lavatories. No picnics. No dogs.*

Stansfield is an informal 1-acre (0.4-hectare) plantsman's garden on alkaline soil. Although it was started only in 1979, it now contains more than 2,000 varieties. There are numerous different interlinked areas including a very productive vegetable plot. Attractive alpines are grown in sinks or troughs. The whole garden has been rabbit proofed and is surrounded by herbaceous borders, a scree garden, an architectural border, a damp garden and shade borders which all lead to a small copse underplanted with spring bulbs, lilies and hellebores.

Accommodation: The Lamb, Buckland (tel: 01367 870484; ££); The White Horse, Woolstone, Faringdon (tel: 01367 820726; £–££). **Local pubs:** *The Trout, Tadpole Bridge, north of Buckland.*

Waterperry Gardens

Waterperry has fine herbaceous borders and a waterlily canal.
Map reference ㉒

Wheatley OX33 1JZ, Oxon; tel: 01844 339226; fax: 01844 339883.
< www.waterperrygardens.co.uk >
National Collection: *Saxifraga, Porophyllum group.*
Opening times: *all year, except a few days in mid-July, daily 9am–5pm. Parties/coaches accepted. Viewing by*

appointment. *House closed.*
Admission prices: *adults £3.50, children £2 (under-10s free), over-60s £3.*
Facilities: *parking, shop, plants for sale, refreshments. Picnics permitted. No disabled access. Dogs allowed on leads.*

This well-tended 8-acre (3.2-hectare) garden is loved by plant enthusiasts for its large, well-labelled collection. Waterperry Gardens include one of the finest herbaceous borders in the country, flowering continuously and vividly from May to October, and set against a mellow brick wall. There is a tranquil rose garden, hedged in yew, alpine gardens and island beds, originally planted by Alan Bloom. A new Waterlily Canal and a river walk, where kingfishers may sometimes be seen, complete the picture. A vast and fragrant citrus tree is to be found in the walled garden.

History: A small horticultural school was started here in the 1930s by Beatrix Hovergal and there is still an emphasis on education. Mary Spiller, who designed the gardens and has worked here for 50 years, also runs amateur gardening courses.

Accommodation: Cotswold House, Oxford (tel: 01865 310558; ££). **Local pub:** *George and Dragon, Chacombe.*

LEFT:
Waterperry
Gardens, a
harmonious
combination
of fine
planting and
mellow
stone.

The Southwest

Spring comes early here, with plants several weeks in advance of those in counties further north. Providing there is protection from coastal winds, the warm, moist climate encourages dense growth of sub-tropical and "architectural" plants such as gunnera and chusan palm

CORNWALL

Cornwall is as famous for its gardens as it is for its beaches. Trebah, Trelissick, Mount Edgcumbe, the restored Lost Gardens of Heligan, and now the Eden Project, a global garden under a series of massive futuristic-looking biomes, draw visitors from all over the world. An added attraction of Trevarno, near Helston, is the National Museum of Gardening containing Britain's most comprehensive collection of antique tools.

Antony House

Formal landscaped gardens and woodland. English Heritage Grade II. National Trust. Map reference ❶

Torpoint PL11 2QA, Cornwall; tel/fax: 01752 812364.
< www.nationaltrust.org.uk >
National collection: *Hemerocallis and Camellia Japonica.*
Opening times: *formal garden & house: late Mar–Oct Tues–Thur & BH Mons 1.30–5.30pm, Jun–Aug Sun 1.30–5.30pm (last admission 4.45pm). Woodland gardens: Mar–Oct Tues, Thur, Sat, Sun & BH Mons 11am–5.30pm. Parties/coaches accepted.*
Admission prices: *combined gardens: adults £3.90; house & formal garden: adults £4.60, children £2.20.*
Facilities: *parking, disabled access, shop, refreshments. Picnics permitted. No dogs.*

Antony House gardens comprise 28 acres (11 hectares) surrounding a fine 18th-century house. There is an attractive contrast between the formal sweeping lawns, mature trees, avenues of magnolias and high yew hedges and the romantic idyll of extensive woodlands full of wildflowers and studded with rhododendrons, Asiatic magnolias and a spectacular bank of pink, red and white camellias. Near the house are tender climbing plants, assorted peach trees and a collection of day lilies.

History: The estate has been the home of the Carew family since the 15th century and the house was built for Sir William Carew in 1724. The garden was greatly influenced by Humphry Repton, who was consulted by Reginald Pole-Carew in 1792. Generations of the family extended the garden through Victorian and Edwardian times by creating formal walks, terraces and gardens. The late Sir John Carew-Pole planted the Japanese garden and woodlands, and Mrs Carew-Pole began the enclosed knot garden in 1983.

PRECEDING PAGES: inside one of the biomes of the Eden Project, Cornwall.

LEFT: lush profusion at Trebah, Cornwall.

ABOVE: Antony House.

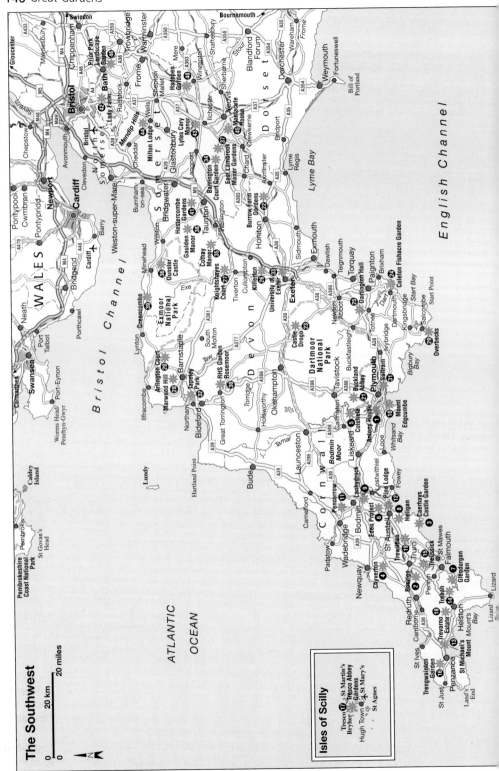

The Southwest

Map: page 146

a finished article, as the improvements have been on-going over the past 20 years.

Accommodation: Royal Hotel, Truro (tel: 01872 270345; £££); Bissick Old Mill, Ladock, Truro (tel: 01726 882557; ££). **Local pub:** *County Arms, Highertown.*

Accommodation: Tregondale Farm, Menheniot, Liskeard (tel: 01579 342407; £). **Local pub:** *Ye Olde Plough House Inn, Duloe (south of Liskeard).*

Bosvigo

Unusual herbaceous plants and a woodland garden. Map reference ❷

Bosvigo Lane, Truro TR1 3NH, Cornwall; tel: 01872 275774; fax: 01872 275774. < www.bosvigo.com >
Opening times: *Mar–Sep Thur & Fri 11am–6pm. National Garden Scheme days. Parties/coaches accepted. Viewing by appointment. House closed.*
Admission prices: *adults £3, children under 16 £1, over-60s £3.*
Facilities: *parking, refreshments, shop, small specialist nursery. Picnics permitted. Partial disabled access. Dogs allowed on leads.*

The 2 acres (0.8 hectares) of gardens feature mainly herbaceous plants in attractive colour combinations that are at their best during the summer. There are a number of hedged gardens that have their own colour themes.

The woodland garden, in contrast, planted with snowdrops, hellebores, erythroniums and wood anemones, is delightful in spring.

History: Created by the current owners Michael and Wendy Perry, this garden is a work-in-progress, rather than

Caerhays Castle Garden

Woodland garden surrounding a 19th-century castle. English Heritage Grade II*. Map reference ❸

Gorran, St Austell PL26 6LY, Cornwall; tel: 01872 501310; fax: 01872 501870. < www.caerhays.co.uk >
National Collection: Magnolias.
Opening times: *gardens: Mar–May daily 10am–5.30pm (last admission 4.30pm); house: mid-Mar–mid-May Mon–Fri 1–4pm, tours commence every 45 minutes. Also charity open days. Parties and coaches (min 15) may also view by appointment.*
Admission prices: *house & garden: adults £8, children £3.50; gardens only: adults £4.50, children £2; house only: (tours): £4.50, children under 16 £2. Charity open days: adults £2.50, children free.*
Facilities: *parking, disabled access, shop, refreshments, plants for sale. Picnics permitted. Dogs allowed on leads.*

ABOVE LEFT: Bosvigo.

BELOW: Caerhays Castle in spring.

ABOVE: Chyverton is famous for magnolias.

BELOW RIGHT: Cotehele woodland.

Extending over 100 acres (40.4 hectares), Caerhays is a superb woodland garden, the result of late 19th-century plant hunting expeditions. One find was the famous camellia Williamsii that still thrives here. Many wonderful old specimens of rhododendrons and magnolias are found in the woods. There are more than 35 record-breaking trees, including eight acer species.

History: The informal woodland garden was created by J.C Williams who sponsored various plant-hunting expeditions to China at the turn of the 19th century, and specialised in hybridising rhododendrons and camellias.

Accommodation: Nare Hotel, Carne Beach, Veryon (tel: 01872 501279; £££–££££); Wheal Lodge, Carlyon Bay (tel: 01726 815543; ££). Local pub: The Crown Inn, St Ewe.

Chyverton

Georgian landscape garden. Map reference ❹

Zelah, Truro TR4 9HD, Cornwall; tel: 01872 540324; fax: 01872 540648. Opening times: year round by appointment only. House closed. Admission prices: adults £5, children 16–18 £2 (under 16 free). Facilities: parking, disabled access, shop, refreshments, plants for sale. Picnics permitted. Dogs allowed on leads.

Chyverton is a large landscape garden of around 140 acres (57 hectares), with a lake, a bridge and statuary. A valley garden holds a magnificent collection of trees, shrubs and over 100 magnolias.

History: The house dates from the 1730s and there is a copper beech of the same date close by. The grounds were landscaped by John Thomas between 1780 and 1825 and the trees were added from 1830 to 1850. In 1924 it was bought by Trevor Holman and the present shrub garden, started in 1930, was continued after 1959 by his son, Nigel, a distinguished plantsman.

Accommodation: Carlton Hotel, Truro (tel: 01872 272450; £). Local pub: Hawkins Arms, Zelah.

Cotehele

Splendid formal garden and woodland. English Heritage Grade II. National Trust. Map reference ❺

St Dominick, Saltash PL12 6TA, Cornwall; tel: 01579 351346. < www.nationaltrust.org.uk > Opening times: all year daily 10.30am–dusk; house: open Apr–Sep Sat–Thur (and Good Fri) 11am–5pm; Oct–early Nov 11am–4.30pm. Parties/ coaches may also view by written appointment except Sun and BHs.

Map:
page 146

Admission prices: house & garden: adults £6.40, family £16; garden and mill: £3.60, family £9, parties £5.40 pp.
Facilities: parking, disabled access, shop, refreshments, plants for sale. Picnics permitted. Dogs allowed on leads on woodland walks.

Cotehele is a 14-acre (5.5 hectare) garden with a house and outbuildings at the top of a combe that drops down to the River Tamar and Cotehele Quay. The garden surrounding the house is laid out in a formal manner. The upper garden has sloping lawns, herbaceous borders, a spectacular tulip tree and tree of heaven and there is a lily pond at the centre.

There is also a dovecote and a stew pond from which a stream with pools and runnels running down to the river supports primulas, marsh marigolds and gunnera. Rhododendrons, azaleas, magnolias, camellias, enkianthus and kalmias provide a fine display during the spring.

History: Dating from medieval times, Cotehele was enlarged in the Tudor era by Sir Richard and Sir Piers Edgcumbe. Ornamental tree and shrub planting began at the head of the valley in the 1860s and screening conifers were planted when the railway viaduct was constructed in 1905.

Accommodation: Well House Hotel, Liskeard (tel: 01579 342001; ££); Tregondale Farm, Menheniot, Liskeard (tel: 01579 342407; £). *Local pub:* Ye Olde Plough House Inn, Duloe (south of Liskeard).

Eden Project

Plants from all over the world nurtured in vast glass domes.
Map reference **❻**

Bodelva, St Austell PL24 2SG, Cornwall; tel: 01726 811911; fax: 01726 811912.
< www.edenproject.com >
Opening times: all year daily except 24–25 Dec; Mar–Oct 10am–6pm (last admission 5pm); Nov–Feb 10am–4pm

(last admission 3pm). Parties/coaches accepted.
Admission prices: adults £10, children £4, over-60s £7.50, family £25.
Facilities: parking, disabled access, shop, refreshments, plants for sale. Picnics permitted. Dogs allowed on leads.

The Eden Project is a gateway to a fascinating world of plants. A dramatic global garden spreading over 37 acres (15 hectares), it nestles like a lost world in a disued china clay pit crater overlooking St Austell Bay. One of its giant conservatories simulates a majestic rainforest, full of tropical plants, while the other, the Temperate Zone, cultivates crops of the Mediterranean and the flowers of South Africa and California. Outside in the landscaped grounds, which contain a waterfall and flow-

ing river, you will find tea and lavender, sunflowers and hemp growing.

History: The spectacular Eden Project, masterminded by Tim Smit, opened in spring 2001. The aims of the project, which cost £80 million (US$126 million), include promoting an understanding of the natural world, and helping the economic regeneration of this part of Cornwall.

Accommodation: Cotswold House Hotel, Falmouth (tel: 01326 312077; £); Wheal Lodge, Carlyon Bay (tel: 01726 815543; ££); Green Lawns Hotel, Falmouth (tel: 01326 312734; ££). *Local pub:* Quayside Inn, Falmouth.

ABOVE: the Eden Project, the world's largest greenhouse.

Glendurgan Garden

Subtropical valley garden with exotic plants. English Heritage Grade II*. National Trust. Map reference ❼

Mawnan Smith, Falmouth TR11 5JZ, Cornwall; tel: 01326 250906.
< *www.nationaltrust.org.uk* >
Opening times: mid-Feb–Oct Tues–Sat (including BHs except Good Fri) 10.30am–5.30pm, last admission 4.30pm. Parties/coaches accepted. National Garden Scheme day. House closed.
Admission prices: adults £4, children £2, family £10.
Facilities: parking, disabled access, shop, refreshments, plants for sale. Picnics permitted, but garden very steep. Dogs allowed on leads.

Glendurgan, a subtropical valley garden running down to the tiny village of Durgan and its beach, was created in the 1820s. There are numerous fine trees and rare and exotic plants, with outstanding spring displays of magnolias and camellias. Late in the season a glorious display of wild flowers carpets the valley slopes. The Laurel Maze dates from 1833.

History: The garden was created in the 1820s by Alfred Fox, a Falmouth shipping agent, who introduced plants from around the world. A devout Quaker, Fox intended Glendurgan to be a "small piece of heaven on earth" and his religious beliefs are reflected in trees planted in the Holy Bank.

Accommodation: Mevdon, Falmouth (tel: 01326 25051; £–££); Burdock Vean Country House Hotel (tel: 01326 250288; £££). Local pubs: Shipwright's Arms, Helford; The Ferry Boat, Helford Passage; Red Lion, Mawnan Smith.

Heligan

Restored Victorian garden with a "Lost Valley". English Heritage Grade II. Map reference ❽

Pentewan, St Austell PL26 6EN, Cornwall; tel: 01726 845100; fax: 01726 845101. < *www.heligan.com* >
Opening times: daily except 24–25 Dec. Apr–Oct 10am–6pm (last admission 4.30pm), Nov–Mar 10am–5pm (last admission 3.30pm). Parties/coaches accepted. House closed.
Admission prices: adults £6, children £3, over-60s £5.50, family £17.
Facilities: parking, disabled access, shop, plants for sale, refreshments. Picnics permitted. Dogs allowed on leads.

Lost for over 70 years, Heligan has been described as "the garden restoration of the 20th century." Extending to over 80 acres (32 hectares) and containing a huge collection of plants from around the world, it is really a series of gardens-within-a-garden. The 35-acre (14-hectare) Northern Garden alone comprises six separate gardens, all with different themes. The Productive Gardens include acres of orchards, four walled gardens and a huge kitchen gar-

BELOW:
Glendurgan
Garden.

den now growing over 300 varieties of fruits and vegetables. Beyond this lies the 22-acre (9-hectare) Jungle garden with subtropical growth, and the 30-acre (12-hectare) Lost Valley, with lakes, pools, ancient trees and hosts of wild flowers.

History: Henry Hawkins Tremayne (1766–1829), a curate in Lostwithiel who inherited the estate, shaped the gardens. Within a short time he also inherited the Croan estate near Wadebridge and the Sydenham estates in Devon. A plan of the garden pre-1810 shows it almost as it is now. Tim Smit masterminded its restoration.

Accommodation: Nare Hotel, Carne Beach, Veryon (tel: 01872 501279; £££–££££); Wheal Lodge, Carlyon Bay (tel: 01726 815543; ££).
Local pub: The Crown Inn, St Ewe.

Lanhydrock

Formal parterres and woodland walks. English Heritage Grade II*. National Trust. Map reference ❾

Bodmin, PL30 5AD, Cornwall; tel: 01208 73320; fax: 01208 74084.
< www.nationaltrust.org.uk >
National Collection: *Crocosmias*
Opening times: *gardens: all year daily 10am–6pm (5pm from Oct–Mar); house: Apr–Oct Tues–Sun and BH Mon 11am–5.30pm, 11am–5pm in Oct. Parties/coaches accepted.*
Admission prices: *garden & grounds: adults £3.90, children £1.95; house, garden & grounds: adults £7.20, children £3.60, family £17.*
Facilities: *parking, disabled access, shop, refreshments, plants for sale. Picnics permitted. Dogs allowed on leads.*

U nusually for Cornwall, the majority of Lanhydrock gardens are laid out above the house, providing spectacular views of the rooftops from the walks through the hillside woods. Around the house are lawns with formal parterres planted with roses and bedding plants and about 30 huge topiary yews.

At the edge of the lawns there are some fine trees, among them copper beeches planted by 19th-century prime ministers, William Gladstone and Lord Roseberry, and an extraordinary field maple covered in mosses and lichens. In the Higher Garden some extremely large stands of rhododendrons and camellias provide huge splashes of colour in spring and early summer, contrasting with the magnolias, some of which form a tunnel of blossom.

History: The house dates from 1634, but was radically remodelled by George Gilbert Scott in 1857 for the first Baron Robartes. At the same time Scott laid out the garden in a formal design. This was simplified before World War II, although the parterres remain. In 1914 Lady Clifden laid out herbaceous borders surrounded by a semi-circular yew hedge. The seventh Viscount Clifden imported spectacular varieties of shrubs and trees after he inherited the property in 1930.

Accommodation: Mount Pleasant Farm House, Mount, Bodmin (tel: 01208 821342; £–££). Local pubs: Crown, Lanlivery, Royal Oak, Lostwithiel.

Map:
page 146

ABOVE LEFT: lost in the undergrowth at Heligan.

BELOW: Lanhydrock.

Mount Edgcumbe

Eighteenth-century parkland plus formal gardens. English Heritage Grade 1. Map reference ❿

Cremyll, Torpoint PL10 1HZ, Cornwall; tel: 01752 822236.
National Collection: *Camellia.*
Opening times: *Earl's Garden: Apr–Sep Sun–Thur 11am–4.30pm; park & formal garden: year-round daily 8am–dusk. House open same hours as Earl's Garden.*
Admission prices: *Earl's Garden and house: adults £4.50, children £2.25, family £10, season £7.50; park and formal gardens: free.*
Facilities: *parking, disabled access, shop, refreshments, plants for sale. Picnics permitted. Dogs allowed on leads.*

Situated on a promontory on the mouth of the Tamar river, Mount Edgcumbe overlooks the Plymouth Sound. The estate of 800 acres (320 hectares) includes 8 acres (3 hectares) of themed formal gardens (an Italian garden, an American garden, a New Zealand garden and a French garden) enclosed by high hedges to protect them from sea winds, and the 2-acre (0.8-hectare) "Earl's garden", created in the 18th century with fine herbaceous borders and a 400-year-old lime tree. Other highlights include an orangery and fern dell.

The park includes follies, temples and other focal points. Two signposted walks around the estate take in superb sea views. The woodland contains specimen trees.

History: Mount Edgcumbe was built by Sir Richard Edgcumbe of Cotehele *(see page 148)* in his deer park in the mid-16th century. The formal gardens were developed in the 18th century.

Accommodation: Well House Hotel, Liskeard (tel: 01579 342001; ££); Tregondale Farm, Menheniot, Liskeard (tel: 01579 342407; £). Local pub: Ye Olde Plough House Inn, Duloe (south of Liskeard).

Pencarrow

Rare collections of conifers, cedars and rhododendrons. English Heritage Grade II*. Map reference ⓫

Washaway, Bodmin PL30 3AG, Cornwall; tel: 01208 841369; fax: 01208 841 722.
< www.pencarrow.co.uk >

RIGHT:
Pencarrow, a
Palladian
mansion
surrounded
by fine trees.

**Map:
page 146**

Opening times: garden: Mar–Oct daily 9.30am until dusk; house: Mar–Oct Sun–Thur 11am–4pm (last tour). National Garden Scheme day. Parties/ coaches accepted.
Admission prices: garden: adults £3, children free; over-60s £3; house and garden: adults £6, children £3.
Facilities: parking, disabled access, shop, refreshments, plants for sale. Picnics permitted. Children's play area. Dogs allowed on leads.

Pencarrow has 50 acres (20 hectares) of gardens, which are justly famous for their conifers, numbering over 160 species, and the extraordinary collection of more than 570 species and hybrids of rhododendron. There are also over 60 different camellias. Many of the specimens are too tender to grow anywhere in Britain except the West Country. Two fine specimens of Chilean podocarps, one extremely rare, are to be found near the lake and the rare *Taxodium distichum* nutans, the pond cyprus, and the largest Deodar cedar in the country, stand in the Italian Gardens and East Lawn respectively.

History: The impressive Palladian mansion dates from 1760, but the gardens were designed and laid out by the radical statesman, Sir William Molesworth, from 1831, during intervals in his parliamentary sessions, until his early death in 1855. He created the Italian Garden, the rockery, the lake and the Carriage Drive and began the collection of conifers, claiming at his death that he had planted a specimen of all but 10 of those that could survive in the British Isles.

Charles Austin, a guest, named the *Araucaria araucana*, by saying "That would puzzle a monkey". Molesworth's family and descendants have continued the planting and extended the collection.

Accommodation: Mount Pleasant Farm House, Mount Pleasant, Bodmin (tel: 01208 821342; £–££). Local pubs: St Mabyn Inn, St Mabyn; Sladesbridge Country Inn; Earl of St Vincent, Egloshayle.

Pine Lodge and Nursery

Rare shrubs, a pinetum and a Japanese garden. Map reference ⑫

Cuddra, Holmbush, St Austell PL25 3RQ, Cornwall; tel: 01726 73500; fax: 01726-73500. <www.pine-lodge.co.uk>
National Collection: *Grevilleas from Australia.*
Opening times: *Apr–Oct daily 10am–6pm (last admission 5pm). Parties/coaches accepted. House closed.*
Admission prices: *£4.50, children £2.*

Facilities: parking (including coach parking), disabled access, shop, refreshments, plants for sale. Picnics permitted. Dogs allowed on leads.

ABOVE:
Pine Lodge
and Nursery.

In the woodlands and parkland of Pine Lodge and Nursery several noteworthy trees survive from the 19th century. The garden now covers 30 acres (12 hectares), with woodlands providing cover for early snowdrops, drifts of bluebells, aconites and anemones. Alpine plants include the lovely celmisias from New Zealand and miniature iris and cyclamen from Crete. Herbaceous borders show blue meconopsis and other varieties in red, white and yellow. Other herbaceous plants include the rare *Myosotidium hortensia* with blue flowers.

Shrubberies feature sycopsis, daphnes, telopea, cestrum and myoporum as well as rhododendrons, camellias, magnolias, pieris and azaleas. Water features include a wildlife pond and a larger lake added in 1994. There is also a pinetum with over 80 different conifers.

History: The garden was begun in the 1950s but the site is associated with the tin and copper mines of the mid-19th century.

Accommodation: Carlyon Bay Hotel (tel: 01726 812304; £££–££££). Local pubs: Rashleigh, Polkerris; The Crown Inn, St Ewe.

St Michael's Mount

Subtropical Mediterranean plants on castle slopes. National Trust.
Map reference ⑬

Marazion, Penzance, TR17 0EF, Cornwall; tel: 01736 710507; fax: 01736 711544. < www.nationaltrust.org.uk >
Opening times: *castle & gardens: late Apr–Oct Mon–Fri 10.30am–5.30pm (last admission 4.45pm), Jun–Sep most weekends for charity (NT members asked to pay admission), Nov–Mar tel: 01736 710507 for opening arrangements. National Garden Scheme days. Parties/ coaches accepted. Castle also open.*
Admission prices: *Apr–May gardens:*

ABOVE:
St Michael's
Mount,
a subtropical
island.

adults £2.50; castle & gardens: adults £4.50; family £13.
Facilities: *parking (in Marazion), disabled access, shop, refreshments, plants for sale. Picnics permitted. Dogs allowed on leads. Access by foot at low tide or by ferry at high tide in summer.*

The counterpart of the more famous and larger Mont St Michel in Brittany, St Michael's Mount more than holds its own in the gardening sphere, with a subtropical Mediterranean garden protected from the wind by pines, holm oaks and shrubberies of salt-tolerant plants, such as escallonia, hebe, tamarisk, fuchsia and sea buckthorn on the steep ascent to the castle. Near the summit, favoured by the sun, good drainage and lack of frost, are agapanthus, aloes and kniphofias sheltering among granite boulders, together with many other exotic plants including aeoniums, pelargoniums, callistemons, yuccas, phormiums and others usually only found in greenhouses.

History: St Michael's Mount was home of the St Aubyn family and at one time a priory and fortress. The walled garden was designed by two young female members of the family in the 18th century.

Accommodation: Queen's Hotel, Penzance (tel: 01736 362371; ££); Ennys, St Hilary, nr Penzance (tel: 01736 740262; ££).

Trebah

Ravine garden with exotic water plants, ferns and palms. English Heritage Grade II. Map reference ⑭

Mawnan Smith, Falmouth TR11 5JZ, Cornwall; tel: 01326 250448; fax: 01326 250781. < www.trebah-garden.co.uk >
Opening times: *all year daily 10.30am–5pm (last admission). Parties/coaches accepted. House closed.*
Admission prices: *adults £5, children £3, over-60s £4.50.*
Facilities: *parking, disabled access, shop, refreshments, plants for sale. Picnics permitted. Dogs allowed on leads.*

Trebah is a beautiful, 26-acre (10-hectare) Cornish ravine garden, the result of 160 years of inspired and dedicated creation. A wooded ravine descends 200 ft (61 metres) down to a secluded beach on the River Helford. A stream cascades over falls and meanders through ponds of giant koi carp and exotic water plants before winding through 2 acres (0.8 hectares) of blue and white hydrangeas to the beach. Subtropical ferns and palms mingle with trees and shrubs in ever-changing colours and scents beneath a canopy of century-old rhododendrons and magnolias.

History: Trebah was first planted in the 1840s by Charles Fox, a Quaker landowner and inspired gardener. Rare and exotic trees and plants were imported from all over the world and Fox ensured that every last sapling was placed for maximum effect. Subsequent owners continued Fox's work until World War II, when the house was sold, the estate split up, and the garden lay neglected until 1980, when Trebah was bought by the Hibbert family, who began a restoration programme. Trebah opened to the public in 1987 and three years later the family donated the house and the gardens to the Trebah Garden Trust.

Accommodation: Cotswold House Hotel, Falmouth (tel: 01326 312077; £); Dolvean House Hotel, Falmouth (tel: 01326 313658; ££).
Local pub: Shipwrights Arms, Helford.

Trelissick

Spring garden with plantsman's collection. English Heritage Grade II. National Trust. Map reference ⑮

Feock, Truro TR3 6QL, Cornwall; tel: 01872 862090; fax: 01872 865808. < www.nationaltrust.org.uk >
Opening times: *mid-Feb–early Nov daily 10.30am–5.30pm (last admission 5pm). National Garden Scheme day. Parties/coaches may also view by appointment. House closed.*
Admission prices: *adults £4.60, children £2.30, family £11.50.*
Facilities: *parking, shop, refreshments, plants for sale. Picnics permitted.*

LEFT: the ravine garden of Trebah.

ABOVE: misty morning at Trelissick.

Disabled access. Dogs allowed on leads.

The Trelissick estate, beautifully positioned at the head of the Fal estuary, commands panoramic views and has extensive park and woodland walks beside the river. At its heart is the tranquil garden, set on many levels and containing a superb collection of tender and exotic plants that bring colour throughout the year. The display of spring blossom is particularly delightful.

History: The current garden was laid out in the 1920s and 1930s by Mr and Mrs Ronald Copeland and given to the National Trust in 1955. It was designed by Graham Stuart-Thomas.

Accommodation: The Dolvean Hotel, Falmouth (tel: 01326 313658; ££). Local pub: Old Ale House, Quay Street, Truro.

Trengwainton Garden

This sheltered garden has an extensive collection of tender plants. English Heritage Grade II. National Trust. Map reference ⑯

Penzance TR20 8RZ, Cornwall; tel: 01765 362297; coach bookings tel: 01637 875404. < www.nationaltrust.org.uk >
Opening times: *mid-Feb–early Nov Sun–Thur (and Good Friday) 10.30am–5.30pm, Feb, Mar and Oct till 5pm (last admission 30 minutes before closing). National Garden Scheme days. Parties/coaches may also view by appointment. House closed.*
Admission prices: *adults £3.90, children £2, family £9, pre-arranged groups of 15 + £3.20 pp.*
Facilities: *parking, shop, refreshments, plants for sale. Picnics permitted. Disabled access. Dogs allowed on leads.*

Enjoying the mildest climate in Britain, Trengwainton has a magnificent collection of exotic plants and shrubs giving it the feel of a subtropical garden. Ferns, palms, rhododendrons, camellias, magnolias and azaleas grow in a profusion of greenery and colours with many rare and tender plants collected from Tasmania, Australia, China, Chile, New Zealand and California to surprise and delight both the expert plantsman and ordinary gardener.

History: Sir Rose Price, a Jamaican sugar planter, laid out the garden in the early 19th century. In about 1820 he built the series of small walled compartments near the entrance lodge to grow vegetables in raised brick beds, angled towards the winter sun. The Bolitho family bought the property in 1867. The exotic transfers to the garden began when Lt Col Edward Bolitho inherited the garden in 1925. As one of the sponsors of Frank Kingdon-Ward's expeditions to Assam and Burma in 1927–8, he acquired many choice specimens, some of which flowered here for the first time in the British Isles.

Accommodation: Mount Prospect Hotel, Penzance (tel: 01736 363117; ££); Ennys, St Hilary, nr Penzance (tel: 01736 740262; ££).

Tresco Abbey Gardens (Isles of Scilly)

**Outstanding collection of southern hemisphere plants on Tresco, one of the Scilly Islands, 28 miles (45 km) southwest of Land's End.
Map reference** ⓱

*Tresco, Isles of Scilly TR24 OQQ;
tel: 01720 424105; fax: 01720 422868.*
Opening times: *daily 10am–4pm.*
Admission prices: *adults £8.50, children under 15 free.*
Facilities: *disabled access, shop, plants for sale, refreshments. Picnics permitted. Dogs allowed on leads.*

Built on a series of terraces, this famous garden, favoured by a temperate climate, is home to over 20,000 exotic plants from over 80 countries, including South Africa, Australia and New Zealand. Even at the winter equinox, more than 300 plants will be in flower, so it could be said that Tresco is Kew without the protective glass – a horticultural world tour enclosed in 17 acres (7 hectares).

History: The garden was created by Augustus Smith, Lord Proprietor of the Isles of Scilly, between 1834 and 1872. It occupies the site of a 10th-century abbey on the southern tip of Tresco. The plant collections have been added to by successive generations of the Dorrien-Smith family.

Map: page 146

Accommodation/pub: Island Hotel, Tresco (tel: 01720 422883: ££–£££); New Inn, Tresco (tel: 01720 422844; ££)

Trevarno Estate and National Museum of Gardening

Victorian and Georgian gardens with a pinetum. Map reference ⓲

Trevarno Manor, Helston TR13 0RU, Cornwall; tel: 01326 574274; fax: 01326 574282.
Opening times: *daily 10.30am– 5pm. Parties/coaches accepted. House closed.*
Admission prices: *adults £4.75, children £1.75, over-60s £4.20, season £15.*
Facilities: *parking, disabled access, shop, refreshments, plants for sale. Picnics permitted. Dogs allowed on leads.*

Below: Trevarno's lake with boathouse.

The Trevarno estate combines beautiful Victorian and Georgian gardens with the splendid Fountain Garden Conservatory, an unusual range of crafts and the National Museum of Gardening. The tranquil gardens and grounds feature a cascade, lake, grotto and pinetum. Visitors can see the progress of major restoration projects and visit craft areas, including the handmade soap workshop. The site also contains Britain's most comprehensive collection of antique tools.

History: The history of Trevarno gardens dates back to 1246 when Randolphus de Trevarno first gave the estate his name. It has been privately owned since then by a succession of noble families. The present development began in 1997.

Accommodation: Alverton Manor Hotel, Truro (tel: 01872 276633; ££–£££); Colvennor Farmhouse, Helston (tel: 01326 241208; £). Local pubs: Blue Anchor, Helston; The Hazlephron Inn, Gunwalloe.

Trewithen

Woodland garden with rare trees and shrubs. English Heritage Grade: II*. Map reference ⓵

Grampound Road, Truro TR2 4DD, Cornwall; tel: 01726 883647/01726 882 764; fax: 01276 882301;
< www.trewithengardens.co.uk >
Opening times: *Mar–Sep Mon–Sat, Apr–May daily 10am–4.30pm. No parties or coaches. Viewing also by appointment. House open to public Apr–Jul Mon & Tues 2–4pm.*
Admission prices: *adults £4.25, children free, over-60s £4, groups of 20+ £4 pp.*
Facilities: *parking, disabled access, shop, refreshments, plants for sale. Picnics permitted. Dogs allowed on leads.*

The magazine *Country Life* has described Trewithen as "One of the outstanding West Country houses of the 18th century". Its fine Georgian elevations, which took 40 years to complete, perfectly complement one of the most beautiful woodland gardens in the British Isles. The Great Glade which spreads out in front of the house contains magnolias, camellias, including the original Donation (all examples of which, world-wide, stem from this plant) and rhododendrons.

There are also many rare trees and shrubs which can't be found elsewhere in the British Isles, some of which were introduced by the famous plant hunters E.H. Wilson and George Forrest.

History: Philip Hawkins purchased Trewithen in 1715 and was succeeded in 1738 by his cousin, Thomas, who planted many of the fine trees. However, there were no great developments until George Horace Johnstone (1882–1960) took the property in hand, with the spectacular results seen today. The compulsory felling of some 300 beeches to provide trench props during World War I was used by Johnstone as an opportunity to create his masterpiece, the Great Glade.

Accommodation: Alverton Manor Hotel, Truro (tel: 01872 276633; ££–£££); The Nare Hotel, Carne Beach, Veryon (tel: 01872 501279; £££–££££); Carlyon Bay Hotel, St Austell (tel: 01726 8122304; £££–££££). Local pubs: Crown, St Ewe; The Dolphin, Grampound; The Wheel Inn, Tresillion; Hawking Arms, Probus.

DEVON

Map: page 146

Rich soil and a mild climate make Devon one of the most fertile counties in Britain. Its best gardens tend to surround large country houses and manor houses rather than belong to vast estates, though the county does include 18th-century Killerton estate and Castle Drogo, the last castle to be built in Britain. Among its outstanding gardens are Knightshayes Court, Marwood Hill and RHS Rosemoor.

Arlington Court

Informal grounds surrounding a Georgian house, with a Victorian garden. English Heritage Grade II. National Trust. Map reference ⑳

Arlington, Barnstaple EX31 4LP, Devon; tel: 01271 850296.
< *www.nationaltrust.org.uk* >
Opening times: *garden: late Mar–early Nov Wed–Mon 10.30am–5.30pm (last admission 4.30pm); house & carriage collection: 11am–5.30pm; Nov–late Mar grounds open during daylight hours. National Garden Scheme days. Parties/coaches accepted.*
Admission prices: *house, carriage collection & garden: adults £5.80, children £2.90, family £14.50; garden: adults £3.80, children £1.90.*
Facilities: *parking, disabled access, shop, refreshments, plants for sale. No picnics. Dogs allowed on leads.*

T he grounds at Arlington Court are largely informal, with large clumps of rhododendrons, hydrangeas, specimen trees and drifts of wildflowers in spring. The exception is the Victorian garden, which extends across three levels of grass with a conservatory as its centrepiece. The latter is planted with plumbago, lilies, *Daphne odora*, *Solanum jasminoides*, *Cestrum newellii*, plus a collection of liriope, tender fuchsia and *Jasminum polyanthum,* which fills the air with its heady scent when in flower. The herbaceous borders beside the conservatory are full of colour in the summer while the high wall behind hides a partially restored kitchen garden. Circular flower beds have been cut into one of the terraces to recreate basket beds filled with bedding plants, and enclosed by ironwork frames through which cobaea grow. The looped pattern is echoed by the arches of honeysuckle that flank a goldfish pond and fountain on the middle terrace of the garden.

To the south of the Victorian garden are spectacular clumps of red, pink and white rhododendrons, ferns, pampas grass and gunnera.

History: The house is Georgian and is surrounded by what was originally conceived by Rosalie Chichester as a wildlife sanctuary, with a lakeside nature reserve at its heart. The Victorian flower garden was laid out in 1865.

Accommodation:Highcliffe House, Lynton (tel: 0159 752235; £–££). **Local pub:** *Ring O'Bells, Prixford, Barnstaple.*

BELOW: the Victorian conservatory at Arlington Court.

Buckland Abbey

Herb garden and new Elizabethan garden. National Trust. Map reference ㉑

Yelverton PL20 6EY, Devon; tel: 01822 853607, < www.nationaltrust.org.uk >
Opening times: *mid-Apr–early Nov Fri–Wed 10.30am–5.30pm, Nov–23rd Dec and late Feb–mid-Apr weekends 2–5pm (last admission 45 minutes before closing). Parties/coaches accepted. House also open.*
Admission prices: *abbey & grounds: adults £5, children £2, family £12.50.*
Facilities: *parking, disabled access (but the garden is steep), shop, refreshments. Picnics allowed. No dogs.*

The garden at Buckland Abbey is a tranquil spot and it is not hard to imagine that Cistercian monks once walked here, but it is largely a 20th-century creation. The irregular shaped beds, edged with dwarf box, contain 54 different culinary and medicinal herbs, and are redolent with the hum of bees and the scents of plants in high summer. A more recent planting is the thyme garden, tucked around the corner. The planting around the abbey's lawns is an informal mix of eucryphia, camellia, azalea, rhododendron and acer with some more unusual plants. To the north of the abbey, the destruction of the ancient yew walk by gales and root disease has given the National Trust the opportunity to create the new Elizabethan garden, which includes a circular pool, granite steps and topiary bushes, box-edged beds containing examples of plants that would have been grown in Tudor times, a grassy meadow and an orchard planted with old fruit varieties.

History: The Great Barn dates from the 13th century and Sir Francis Drake bought the abbey in 1580, after the dissolution of the monasteries. Vita Sackville-West, during a visit in 1953, suggested creating a herb garden beyond the barn.

Accommodation: Harrabeer Country House Hotel, Yelverton (tel: 01822 853302; £). Local pub: Peter Tavy Inn, off A386, north of Tavistock.

BELOW: Buckland Abbey.

Burrow Farm Gardens

Woodland garden, terrace garden and pergola walk. Map reference ㉒

Dalwood, Axminster EX13 7ET, Devon; tel: 01404 831285; fax: 01404 831445. < www.burrowfarmgardens.co.uk >
Opening times: *Apr–Sep daily 10am–7pm. Parties/coaches accepted. House closed.*
Admission prices: *adults £3.50, children 50p, season £9.*
Facilities: *parking, disabled access, shop, refreshments, plants for sale. Picnics permitted. Dogs allowed on leads.*

The beautifully landscaped 7-acre (2.8-hectare) Burrow Farm Gardens have wonderful views and numerous interesting features, including a woodland

Map: page 146

garden that has been created in a former Roman clay pit with ponds and a host of moisture-loving plants such as candelabra primulas, and wild flowers.

Old roses and herbaceous plants feature in the Pergola Walk. The terrace garden specialises in later summer flowering perennials. New for the millennium was the Rill Garden with traditional stone summer house and water features combined with unusual plants. The stunning colour combinations are a plantsman's delight.

History: The present owner, Mary Benger, has planted and sculpted the garden over the course of 35 years.

Accommodation: Home Farm Hotel, Wilmington, near Honiton (tel: 01404 831278; ££). **Local pub:** *Tuckers Arms, Dalwood, near Axminster.*

Opening times: garden: all year daily 10.30am–dusk; castle: late Mar–early Nov Wed–Mon 11am–5.30pm; guided tours: late Jul–end Aug Fri 11am, 1pm and 3pm. Parties/coaches accepted.

Admission prices: *castle & gardens: adults £5.90, children £2.90; gardens: adults £3, children £1.50.*

Facilities: *parking, disabled access, shop, refreshments, plants for sale. Picnics permitted. Dogs allowed on leads but only in car park and on the estate walks.*

Castle Drogo

Edwardian castle and formal gardens with sunken rose garden. English Heritage Grade II*. National Trust. Map reference ㉓

Drewsteignton EX6 6PB, Devon; tel: 01647 433306; fax: 01647 433186. < www.nationaltrust.org.uk >

ABOVE: Burrow Farm Gardens.

LEFT: Castle Drogo.

Castle Drogo is sited on a rocky outcrop with fine views of Dartmoor. The 20th-century formal garden – the highest garden owned by the National Trust – lies to the north-east of the castle and is linked to it by yew hedges. The centrepiece is the sunken rose garden, where hybrid teas and floribundas flourish. On either side are stunning herbaceous borders, at their best in late June and July, with yew arbours roofed with Persian Ironwood *(Parrotia persica pendula)* at each end.

Steps lead to a formal herb garden, from where the path passes between shrub borders to a vast circular croquet lawn. Closer to the castle is the rhododendron garden, which gives spring interest from a variety of specimens as well as cherries and magnolias.

History: The castle, a Norman fantasy, was designed by Edwin Lutyens for Julius Drewe. However, although Lutyens' influence can be seen in features such as the yew hedges and serpentine paths, the garden is likely to have been planned by George Dillistone, a designer from Kent.

Accommodation: Blackaller Hotel, Moretonhampsted (tel: 01647 440322; ££); Oxenham Arms, South Zeal, Okehampton (tel: 01837 840244; £). Local pub: Drewe Arms, Drewsteignton.

Coleton Fishacre Garden

A humid valley garden with tender and exotic species. English Heritage Grade II. National Trust. Map reference ㉔

Brownstone Road, Kingswear, Dartmouth TQ6 0EQ, Devon; tel: 01803 752466; fax: 01803 753 017.
< www.nationaltrust.org.uk >
Opening times: *garden: Mar Sat–Sun 11am–5pm, Apr–Oct Wed–Sun & BHs 10.30am–5.30pm; house: Apr–Oct Wed–Sun 11am–4.30pm. National Garden Scheme days. Parties/coaches accepted.*
Admission prices: *house & garden: adults £5, children £2.50, family £12.50; garden: adults £3.90, children £1.90.*
Facilities: *parking, disabled access, shop, refreshments, plants for sale. Picnics permitted. Dogs allowed on leads only on surrounding NT land.*

The garden lies in a stream-fed valley above the South Devon coast. The mild climate, shelter belts and high humidity make the garden suitable for a wide range of plants, including some which can only survive in conservatories elsewhere in Britain. In spring and early summer, wild flowers abound amid colourful displays of rhododendrons, camellias and azaleas planted among a collection of tender and exotic plants.

The formal terraces and Rill Garden provide summer-long interest from half-hardy perennials and unusual climbers, including the coral plant *(Berberidopsis corallina)* and the Chilean Mitre Flower *(Mitraria coccinea)*. Paths wind through clumps of bamboo, groves of mimosa, magnolias and other shrubs down to a small sea cove.

Anyone who loves plants is likely to be entranced by this garden.

History: Rupert and Lady Dorothy D'Oyly Carte commissioned Oswald Milne, a pupil of Lutyens, to design the house and gardens after they purchased the estate in 1924. The D'Oyly Cartes chose the site after seeing it from the sea while sailing between Brixham and Dartmouth. Enthusiastic gardeners, they experimented with trees and shrubs from around the world, a tradition that the National Trust continues.

Accommodation: Broome Court, Dartmouth (tel: 01803 834275; £). **Local pub:** *Green Dragon, Stoke Fleming.*

Facilities: parking, disabled access, shop, refreshments, plants for sale. Picnics are permitted. Dogs allowed on leads. Conference centre facilities.

Map: page 146

The gardens at Dartington Hall are steeped in history. The tournament ground or Tiltyard, reputed to be medieval in origin, stands as a sunken lawn and was much restored during the second quarter of the 20th century.

The southwest side of the Tiltyard is flanked by a series of grassy banks, each with a flat terrace stepping up to a row of ancient chestnut trees where a reclining

Dartington Hall

Terraced grounds with ancient trees and modern sculpture. English Heritage Grade II*. Map reference ㉕

Totnes TQ9 6EL, Devon; tel/fax: 01803 862367; < www.dartington.u-net.com >. **Opening times:** *all year dawn to dusk. Parties/coaches accepted. House open when not in use.* **Admission prices:** *£2 donation per person requested.*

figure by Henry Moore spends her days. A lawn, three more terraces, and a row of 12 Irish yew trees, known as the Twelve Apostles, separate this area from the 14th-century hall.

Still evolving, this modern garden set within an ancient landscape is known for quiet walks, great vistas, spring flowers and summer meadows. The Japanese garden provides somewhere quiet for visitors to sit and contemplate.

History: John Holand, a half-brother of King Richard II, created a manor house on

ABOVE LEFT: colour-coordinated borders at Dartington Hall.

the hillside overlooking the River Dart in the 1390s. Thereafter the property shuffled between the Crown and a number of owners until 1559 when it was bought by Sir Arthur Champernowne, Vice-Admiral of the West under Elizabeth I, who was a man of energy and ambition. Champernowne's successors lived at Dartington Hall for over 300 years. On buying the estate in 1925, Leonard and Dorothy Elmhurst set about creating the garden. Avray Tipping acted as garden advisor from 1925 to 1930, a time when the hall itself was restored from a ruin.

Until the outbreak of World War II, Beatrice Farrand, a noted American garden designer, acted as consultant. She was responsible for the courtyard, which is the only example of her work outside the USA. After the war, Percy Cane was made an advisor and went on to develop the outer reaches of the garden.

*Accommodation: Durant Arms, Totnes (tel: 01803 732240; £–££); The Old Forge, Totnes (tel: 01803 862174; £–££). **Local pubs:** The Cott Inn, Dartington; Tally Ho!, Littlehempston.*

BELOW: Killerton's magnificent borders.

Killerton

An all-year garden with a plants-man's collection. English Heritage Grade II*. National Trust. Map reference 26

Broadclyst, Exeter EX5 3LE, Devon; tel: 01392 881345; fax: 01392 883112. < www.nationaltrust.org.uk >
Opening times: park & garden: daily 10.30am–dusk; house: Apr–Nov Wed–Mon 11am–5pm, daily in Aug. National Garden Scheme days. Parties/coaches may also view by appointment (introductory talks by arrangement).
Admission prices: house & garden: adults £5.50, children £2.70, booked parties £4.60 pp; garden and park only: adults £3.90, children £2.
Facilities: parking, disabled access (buggies available), shop, plants for sale, refreshments. Picnics permitted. Dogs allowed on leads in parkland.

Killerton is a beautiful hillside garden for all seasons. In early spring, the grass slopes are carpeted with spring bulbs and wild flowers, while magnolia, crimson and pink rhododendrons and sweetly scented azaleas flower above. The herbaceous and tender borders are at their best in summer and in autumn the specimen trees flame into colour.

There are rare trees and shrubs from around the world, many of them the first of their kind to be planted in the UK. Other special features include the rustic-style summerhouse known as the Bear's Hut (which once housed a Canadian black bear), a rock garden and an ice house, used in Victorian times for storing ice cut from ponds on the estate.

The surrounding parkland of over 6,100 acres (2,500 hectares) has signposted walks.

History: Sir Thomas Dyke Acland started ed the collection of trees at Killerton when he planned a landscape park to surround the

National Garden Scheme days. Parties/coaches accepted. **Admission prices:** *house & garden: adults £5.70, children £2.80, family £14.20; garden only: £4.10, children £2.* **Facilities:** *parking, disabled access, shop, plants for sale, refreshments. Picnics permitted. Dogs allowed on leads.*

Knightshayes' garden (50 acres/20 hectares) has been described as embodying "all that is best in modern gardening," and includes formal gardens, summer flowering borders, drifts of spring bulbs, topiary, a pool garden and a "garden in the wood". Near the house are the formal areas: terraces, a paved garden, topiary cut in the yew hedge, and the delightful pool garden *(see picture on page 2)*, with its round, lily-covered pond overlooked by a Victorian sculpture of a bather and a weeping silver pear tree.

The most admired planting is the "garden in the wood", where camellias and azaleas are underplanted with geraniums, hellebores, trilliums and pulmonaria. Glades display tree magnolia and rhododendron and an arboretum of ornamental trees such as clethra, aralia and acer. The walled kitchen garden (near the stables) was laid out in 1879. It supplied the house with fruit and vegetables until the 1960s, when it became uneconomical. It is currently being restored as an exemplar of modern organic gardening practice and will supply Knightshayes' restaurant.

History: The garden was originally designed by the celebrated landscaper Edward Kemp in the 1870s. It owes much to Sir John and Lady Heathcoat-Amory, who gave Knightshayes to the National Trust in 1972. The house was designed by William Burges and built between 1869 and 1874.

Accommodation: Lower Collipriest Farm, Tiverton (tel: 01884 252321; £–££).

house, built in the 1770s. His gardener and land steward, John Veitch, developed into an exceptional landscaper. The Veitch family, who started a nursery at nearby Budlake, were among the first to send plant hunters to gather new species from the wild and, in fact the association between the Aclands and Veitches, whereby new plants were continually added to the collection at Killerton, was maintained until 1939. A giant sequoia from the west coast of America was grown from seed sent back by Veitch's collector William Lobb in the 1850s.

Accommodation: Weir Mill Farm, Willand, Cullompton (tel: 01884 820803). Local pubs: Five Bells, Clyst Hydon; Jack in the Green, Rockbeare.

Knightshayes Court

A woodland garden, with formal areas, lily ponds, topiary and terraces. English Heritage Grade II*. National Trust. Map reference ㉗

Bolham, Tiverton EX16 7RQ, Devon; tel: 01884 254665 (Property Manager), 01884 253264.
< www.nationaltrust.org.uk >
Opening times: *garden: last weekend in Feb and first three weekends in Mar, late Mar–early Nov daily 11am–5pm; house: late Mar–Sep Sat–Thur (and Good Fri) 11am–5.30pm, Oct daily 11am–4pm.*

Above: *Hesperis matronalis* and Rosa 'Bourbon Queen' at Knightshayes Court.

Marwood Hill

A fine plantsman's collection with an unusual bog garden, good winter interest and superb climbers.
Map reference ㉘

Marwood, Barnstaple EX31 4EB, Devon; tel: 01271 342528.
National Collection: *Astilbe, Clematis, Iris ensata, Tulbaghia.*
Opening times: *daily except Christmas Day dawn–dusk. Parties/coaches accepted. House closed.*
Admission prices: *adults £3, children free.*
Facilities: *parking, disabled access. shop, plants for sale, refreshments. Picnics permitted. Dogs allowed on leads.*

ABOVE: waterside planting at Marwood Hill.

The 20-acre (8-hectare) garden at Marwood Hill has three lakes and a stream with waterside planting. It has a huge variety of plants and contains several National Collections.

Great care has been taken to create a garden of real year-round interest, with striking colours and textures. The season begins with snowdrops in February followed by naturalised daffodils and bluebells. Magnolias bloom in March and April, along with a collection of camellias grown both outside and in a greenhouse. Chery trees are in flower by Easter, followed by candelabra primulas, astilbes and irises in the bog garden, along with other herbaceous plants.

Climbers are also a strong feature at Marwood, with a magnificent wisteria pergola, a collection of clematis and plenty of old-fashioned roses. In addition there is a rockery and alpine scree. There is also plenty of good autumn colour.

History: The garden was started and designed by its present owner, Dr J.A Smart, in 1950 and has evolved from its initial state as rough pastureland to the present, but still changing, flower garden. A small stream running through a field was dammed in 1968 to form two lakes. The original 8-acre (3.2-hectare) garden was increased to its present size by the purchase of an adjoining field in 1980.

Accommodation: Highcliffe House, Lynton (tel: 01598 752235; £–££). Local pub: Ring O'Bells, Prixford, near Barnstaple.

Overbecks Museum and Gardens

Subtropical and tender plants in a series of enclosures surrounding the home of the scientist Otto Overbeck. National Trust. Map reference ㉙

Sharpitor, Salcombe TQ8 8LW, Devon; tel: 01548 842893.
< www.nationaltrust.org.uk >
***Opening times:** gardens: all year daily; museum: late Mar–end Jul & Sep Fri–Sun 11am–5.30pm, Aug daily 11am–5.30pm, Oct Sun–Thur 11am–5pm. National Garden Scheme days. Parties accepted, but roads leading to Overbecks are too narrow for coaches. House open.*
***Admission prices:** museum & garden: adults £4.20, children £2.10, family £10.50; garden: adults £3, children £1.50.*
***Facilities:** parking, disabled access, shop, plants for sale, refreshments. Picnics permitted. Dogs allowed on leads only on coastal walks from car park.*

Spectacularly situated beside Salcombe Estuary, Overbecks enjoys a mild micro-climate providing ideal growing conditions for many tender plants. The series of enclosures and terraces was laid out at the beginning of the 20th century and subsequently planted with sub-tropical plants from around the world, including palms, cypresses, and olive trees. An exotic note is struck right at the entrance by an avenue of Chusan palms *(Trachycarpus fortunei)*, which are also planted throughout the garden.

The borders near the house contain South African plants, including crinum, agapanthus and *Echium pininana*, with its 5-metre (16-ft) tall lavender-blue flower spikes. The formal area of the garden is presided over by a bronze statue surrounded by four herbaceous borders. Another small garden looks down on a parterre of dwarf box and coloured gravel, where orange and lemon trees in pots are placed in the summer and banana trees *(Musa basjoo)* grow throughout the year.

Many tender plants add to the exotic feel, although native wildflowers are plentiful; in spring, bluebells, primroses, anemones and daffodils grow on the rough grass banks. The most spectacular sight is the late-winter flowering of the deep pink blossoms of the 100-year-old *Magnolia campbelli*.

The house has been turned into a museum devoted to the scientist Otto Overbeck who lived here between 1928 and 1937, and the ship-building history of the area. Its eclectic collection includes birds' eggs, fossils, butterflies and insects, shipwrights' tools and inventions of Overbeck.

History: In the early 1900s Edric Hopkins designed the basic layout of walls that divide the site into small enclosures. Mr and Mrs George Medlicott Vereker extended the planting after purchasing the property in 1913 and Otto Overbeck developed and expanded it from 1928 onwards, boasting, in a letter to a friend in 1933, "I grow bananas, oranges and pomegranates in the open garden and have 3,000 palm trees planted in my woods and garden."

Accommodation: Grafton Towers, Salcombe (tel: 01548 842882; ££); Buckland-Tout-Saints, Kingsbridge (tel: 01548 853055; £££).
Local pub: The Sloop Inn, Bantham; Crabshell, Kingsbridge.

Map: page 146

LEFT:
a corner of Overbecks.

Right: a rhubarb forcer at work.

RHS Garden Rosemoor

A vast collection of plants and styles in established and newly planted gardens, which include a gorge and lake. Run by the Royal Horticultural Society. Map reference ㉚

Great Torrington, EX38 8PH, Devon; tel: 01805 624067. < www.rhs.org.uk >
National Collection: *Cornus and Ilex*
Opening times: *all year daily except Christmas, Apr–Sep 10am–6pm, Oct–Mar 10am–5pm. Parties/coaches accepted. House closed.*
Admission prices: *adults £5, children £1, parties of 10 or more adults £4 pp; RHS members free.*
Facilities: *parking, disabled access, shop, plants for sale, refreshments. Picnics permitted. No dogs.*

Few other gardens balance to such effect the old and new or demonstrate such a wide range of interest throughout the year as RHS Garden Rosemoor. Created over just a few years, it is connected to the mature planting of designer Lady Anne Berry's garden by a winding rock gorge, planted with a variety of ferns and bamboos. The stream running from the gorge and the bog garden leads to an enchanting lake.

The original garden at Rosemoor, tucked into the northeast corner of the estate, is very much a plantsman's garden, created by Lady Anne over a period of some 30 years. Dominated by the surrounding woodlands, it contains a number of areas where choice subjects take full advantage of the warmth and shelter offered by the southwesterly aspect and high ground to the north. The new areas, with a great diversity of styles and something of interest for gardeners throughout the year, complement and contrast with the original.

The new garden area is still in the early stages of development. So far the emphasis has been upon relatively intensive and highly ornamental gardens, with roses, shrubs, perennials and bulbs, stream and bog plants and produce of all kinds. In years to come, visitors will find a garden of natural woodland hinterland surrounding more open arboretum, parkland and woodland garden areas, themselves enclosing the formal garden, Anne's Garden, the Stream Garden and lake and the fruit and vegetable garden.

History: Originally the property of Lorde Rolle, a local land and mill owner, the house, dating from the 1780s, was bought by Lady Anne Berry's father in 1923 as a family fishing lodge to be used only from March to May. Following the death of her father in 1931, Lady Anne moved to Rosemoor and with the help of her mother began landscaping the grounds.

However, it was not until 1959 that she met Collingwood "Cherry" Ingram, who opened her eyes to the possibilities of plant collecting and starting a garden of her own. Lady Anne subsequently travelled widely in South America, Papua New Guinea, New Zealand, the United States and Japan to build up the collection of 4,000 plants in her garden, which she generously presented to the RHS in 1988.

The bequest comprised 8 acres (3.2 hectares) around the house and a further 32 acres (13 hectares) of pastureland. The architects for the RHS are Elizabeth Banks Associates.

Accommodation: Halmpstone Manor. Bishop's Tawton, nr Barnstaple (tel: 01271 830321; ££); The Pines, Eastleigh (tel: 01271 860561; ££). Local pub: The Union Inn, Dolton.

Saltram

An 18th- and 19th-century landscape garden noted for its fine specimen trees and shrubs. English Heritage Grade II*. National Trust. Map reference ③

Plympton PL7 1UH, Devon; tel: 01752 333500; fax: 01752 336474, < www.nationaltrust.org.uk >
Opening times: *garden: Apr–Oct Sat–Thur (and Good Fri) noon–4.30pm, Nov–Mar Sat–Thur 11.30am–3.30pm; art gallery: same hours as garden, summer only; house: Apr–Sep Sat–Thur (and Good Fri noon–4.30pm; Oct 11.30am–3.30pm. National Garden Scheme days. Parties/coaches accepted.*
Admission prices: *house, gallery & garden: adults £6.30, children £3.30, family £15; garden: adults £3.50, children £1.50.*
Facilities: *parking, disabled access, shop, plants for sale, refreshments. Picnics permitted. Dogs on leads allowed in park.*

The original 18th-century landscape of Saltram garden has been overlaid with later influences of shrub borders and fine specimen trees planted in spacious lawns. Paths lead along parallel lines, each revealing a special plant or glimpse of building along its route. The Lime Avenue, which dates from the late 19th century, is underplanted with bulbs and wildflowers.

Half-hardy shrubs such as Hoheria Glory of Amlwch, *Acca sellowiana* (pineapple guava), loquat and the cinnamon suede trunked myrtle grow among the glades. The orangery is home to potted citrus trees during the winter months which are moved out to the orange grove in May. The Mediterranean flavour here is enhanced with chusan palm, yucca and Italian cypress.

History: Saltram was built for John and Lady Catherine Parker in the 1740s. Its panoramic views originally encompassed the estuary, the citadel, tiers of hills and the woods of Mount Edgcumbe but have been ruined by housing and bypass developments. The diarist Fanny Burney, who visited Saltram in 1789 as part of the entourage of George III, has a vantage point, Fanny's Bower, named after her.

Accommodation: Elfordleigh Hotel, Colebrook, Plymouth (tel: 01752 336428; ££). Local pub: China House, Plymouth.

LEFT: mature planting at RHS Garden Rosemoor.

Tapeley Park

Italian terraces and walled kitchen garden. English Heritage Grade II*. Map reference ㉜

Instow, EX39 4NT, Devon; tel: 01271 342558. < www.tapeley-park.uk-homepage.com > . *Opening times:* mid-Mar–Oct Sun–Fri

ABOVE: facade and gardens, Tapeley Park. *10am–6pm. Parties/coaches accepted. House open to pre-booked parties only. Admission prices: adults £4, children £2.50, over-60s £3.50. Facilities: parking, limited disabled access, shop, plants for sale, refreshments. No picnics. Dogs allowed on leads.*

There are five distinct areas in this 45-acre (18-hectare) garden. It is best known for the formal Italian terraces renovated by Mary Keen and Carl Klein in the mid-1990s; the sheltered south-facing site means rare and tender plants can be grown. The walled kitchen garden, which is worked traditionally, is full of fruit and vegetables. In contrast, there is a new vibrant permaculture garden demonstrating the benefits of companion planting to reduce pests and diseases.

Next to the permaculture area is the wild garden with a children's play area, plus a field of Highland cattle. Rare breed Berkshire pigs, peacocks and birds of prey can be found dotted around. The lake at the bottom of a ravine through the woods and surrounded by massive *Thuja plicata* trees is for many the most magical area. The newest addition is a granite labyrinth with views over the estuary.

History: Lady Rosa Christie, the present owner's great-grandmother, called in Sir John Belcher to design the garden at the end of the 19th century. The three Italian terraces were dug out at that time and the greenhouse that ran the length of the kitchen garden was erected. The lake – which had a natural clay bottom – had been dug out prior to this and surrounded with the massive Thuja Plicata trees from Canada.

Accommodation: Commodore Hotel, Instow (tel: 01271 860347; ££); Hoops Inn, Horns' Cross, Clovelly (tel: 01237 451222; ££). Local pub: Hoops Inn, Horns' Cross.

University of Exeter

A botanical landscape with terraces, a pinetum, rock garden, glasshouses, lakes and ponds. Map reference ㉝

Streatham Farm, Prince of Wales Road, Exeter EX4 4PX, Devon; tel: 01392 263059; fax: 01392 264547. < www.ex.ac.uk/univ/tours.htm > *National Collection: Azaras. Opening times: all year daily. Parties/coaches accepted. House closed. Admission prices: free. Facilities: parking, disabled access, shop, plants for sale, refreshments. Picnics permitted. Dogs allowed on leads.*

Comprising around 300 acres (120 hectares), the central estate is situated on hills to the northwest of Exeter. There are three streams flowing down valleys, which have been dammed to create a

series of ponds. The campus is planted with a wide range of trees, shrubs and herbaceous plants. It includes a series of lakes, some wingnut trees dating from 1860 and palm trees from 10 years earlier. The azaras, evergreens with scented yellow flowers from Chile, form the National Collection.

The garden includes four parallel ranges of glasshouses containing succulents, ferns, mosses and plants from tropical zones and temperate zones. Among the frost-tender plants is the Exeter hybrid acacia, which was raised by John Veitch, who created the garden.

Map: page 146

History: The original 15-acre (6-hectare) Victorian garden was designed by Veitch during the 1860s for an East India Company nabob. The lion's share of the estate has been designed since the 1920s by various architects to a brief provided by the university.

Accommodation: Great Western Hotel, Exeter (tel: 01392 274039; £); Royal Clarence, Exeter (tel: 01392 319955; £££). Local pub: The Ship Inn.

ABOVE LEFT: the grounds of the University of Exeter are among the finest university grounds in the country.

BELOW: the working kitchen garden at Barrington Court.

SOMERSET

Like Devon, Somerset has the advantages of rich soil and a clement climate. In particular it has good 20th-century gardens, including highly scented and colourful cottage gardens such as East Lambrook Manor, created by Margery Fish, and gardens by Sir Edwin Lutyens and Gertrude Jekyll, such as Barrington Court (Jekyll) and the Edwardian gardens at Hestercombe (Lutyens and Jekyll).

Barrington Court Garden

A Jekyll-influenced garden, with a working kitchen garden. English Heritage Grade II*. National Trust. Map reference ㉞

Barrington, Ilminster, TA19 0NQ, Somerset; tel: 01460 241938.
< www.nationaltrust.org.uk >
Opening times: *Mar & Oct Thur–Sun 11am–4.30pm, Apr–Jun Sat–Thur 11am–5.30pm, Jul & Aug daily 11am–5.30pm. National Garden Scheme days in Apr, May, Jun & Sep. Parties/coaches accepted. House also open except Fri.*
Admission prices: *adults £5.20, children £2.50, family £12.*
Facilities: *parking, disabled access, shop, refreshments, plants for sale. Picnics permitted. No dogs.*

Barrington Court is an enchanting formal garden influenced by Gertrude Jekyll and laid out in a series of walled rooms, including the White Garden, the rose

and iris garden and the lily garden. The working kitchen garden has espaliered apple, pear and plum trees trained along stone walls.

History: The moated manor house was built in the 16th century and restored in the 1920s by the Lyle family, who commissioned Gertrude Jekyll to design the garden.

Accommodation: *The Shubbery, Ilminster (tel: 01460 52108; ££).* ***Local pubs:*** *The Royal Oak, Barrington; The Royal Oak of Stratton.*

Cothay Manor

A plantsman's garden, with an impressive yew walk. English Heritage Grade II*. Map reference ㉟

Greenham, Wellington TA21 0JR, Somerset; tel: 01823 672283; fax: 01823 672345.
Opening times: *May–Sep Wed, Thur, Sun, BHs 2–6pm. National Garden Scheme day. Parties/coaches: groups of 20+ by appointment only. House open.*
Admission prices: *gardens: adults £3.50; house: adults £4.50; children under 12 free.*
Facilities: *parking, disabled access, shop, refreshments, plants for sale. Picnics permitted. Dogs allowed on leads.*

BELOW: the cottage garden at Cothay Manor.

This is a plantsman's paradise of 12 acres (4.8 hectares) set around what is said to be the most perfect example of a small medieval manor. Many garden rooms lead off from the 200-yd/metre yew walk. In addition there is a bog garden with azaleas and drifts of primuli, fine trees, a cottage garden, courtyards, and a river walk.

History: The gardens were laid out in the 1920s by Colonel Reginald Cooper, friend of Harold Nicolson (of Sissinghurst, see page 70), Lawrence Johnston (Hidcote, see page 128) and Sir Edwin Lutyens. This band of gardeners liked to exchange ideas: Harold Nicolson's diaries record how "Reggie came to stay and advised me on the length of the bowling green."

In 1993 the present owners, Alastair and Mary-Anne Robb, gutted the gardens but retained their original structure. The yew hedges were restored and the garden rooms redesigned. New gardens have been created, including a bog garden in the oxbow lake, formed when Reggie Cooper moved the River Tone to save his favourite pine trees from erosion. An arboretum has been planted, a small lake dug, a mound created and a wild flower meadow sown.

Accommodation: *Rumwell Manor Hotel, Rumwell, Taunton (tel: 01823 461902; ££–£££).* ***Local pub:*** *The Globe, Appley.*

Dunster Castle

Subtropical plants and a woodland garden. English Heritage Grade I. National Trust. Map reference ㊱

Dunster, Minehead TA24 6SL, Somerset; tel: 01643 821314; fax: 01643 823000.
National Collection: *Arbutus.*
Opening times: *end Mar–third week in Oct 10am–5pm, end Oct–Mar 11am–4pm. National Garden Scheme day. Parties/coaches accepted by appointment, Mar–Nov. House open.*
Admission prices: *adults £3.50, children £1.50; family £8.*

Accommodation: Luttrell Arms, Dunster (tel: 01643 821555; ££); Yarn Market Hotel, Dunster (tel: 01643 821425; ££). *Local pubs:* The Stag's Head, Dunster; Forester's Arms, Dunster.

Map: page 146

Facilities: parking, disabled access, shop, refreshments, plants for sale. Picnics permitted. Dogs allowed on leads.

The 17 acres (7 hectares) of Dunster Castle gardens are testament to the planting of generations of the Luttrell family. The Keep Garden is oval in shape with borders of cistus, hebes, day lilies and sedums. The South Terrace is home to Dunster's most famous resident, a century-old lemon tree. The terrace's south-eastern aspect and the shelter afforded it by the house creates a micro-climate. A line of towering *Trachycarpus fortunei* border the South Terrace path. Along Mill Walk can be seen blue hydrangeas, a small collection of foxglove trees, towering wellingtonia, as well as Japanese cedar and metasequoia.

History: The castle and grounds were owned by the Luttrell family for generations. The Keep Garden was a bowling green from 1870–1900.

East Lambrook Manor Gardens

Outstanding example of a cottage garden. English Heritage Grade I. Map reference ㊲

South Petherton TA13 5HH, Somerset; tel: 01460 240328; fax: 01460 242344. < www.eastlambrook.com >
National Collection: hardy geraniums.
Opening times: Feb–Oct daily 10am–5pm. National Garden Scheme days. Parties/coaches accepted. House closed.
Admission prices: adults £3.95, children £1, over-60s £3.50.
Facilities: parking, limited disabled access, shop, refreshments, plants for sale. Picnics permitted. Dogs allowed on leads. RHS courses.

The Margery Fish garden at East Lambrook Manor is a magnet for garden lovers from all over the world, particularly for the crooked stone paths

ABOVE LEFT: Dunster Castle has many magnificent trees.

LEFT: East Lambrook Manor's grounds, designed by the well-known gardening writer Margery Fish.

through the cottage-style design with a profusion of colour and scent. The garden is overflowing with plants, many of which were saved from extinction.

History: This was Margery Fish's first major project as a novice gardener. From the publication of her first book in 1956, until her death 13 years later, she wrote in a practical way of her successes and failures, communicating her deep understanding of plants. She was one of the most admired gardeners and garden writers of her day and since her death, her reputation as one of Britain's leading and most innovative gardeners has increased steadily.

The gardens she created here have become known as the premier example of English cottage gardening.

Accommodation: The Walnut Tree Hotel, North Petherton, Bridgwater (tel: 01278 662255; ££). Local pubs: Royal Oak, Over Stratton; King's Arms, Montacute.

Gaulden Manor

A modern garden with roses and herbs. Map reference ❸

Tolland, Lydeard St Lawrence, Taunton, TA4 3PN, Somerset; tel/fax: 01984 667213; fax: 01984 667213.
Opening times: Jun–Aug, Sun, Thur and BHs 2–5pm. National Garden Scheme days. Viewing by appointment. No parties/coaches. House also open for groups of 15 + by appointment.
Admission prices: adults £3.50, children £1.
Facilities: parking, shop, plants for sale. No refreshments. Picnics not permitted. No dogs except guide dogs.

These 2 acres (0.8 hectares) of well-designed modern gardens include roses, herbs, scented flowers and numerous butterflies that are attracted to them. There is also a pretty "secret garden" beyond Moulks fishpond and island, where gunneras and ferns flourish.

Accommodation: Northam Mill, Stogumber (tel: 01984 656916; £). Local pubs: Fitzhead Inn, Fitzhead; Blue Ball Inn, Triscombe.

Greencombe

Woodland and an organic plantsman's garden. Map reference ❸

Porlock TA24 8NU, Somerset; tel: 01643 862363.
National Collection: Erythronium, Gaultheria, Polystichum and Vaccinium.
Opening times: Apr–Jul Sat–Wed 2–6pm. Parties/coaches accepted. Viewing by appointment. House closed.
Admission prices: adults £4, children 50p.
Facilities: parking, disabled access, shop, plants for sale, refreshments. No picnics. No dogs.

Essentially Greencombe consists of a magnificent woodland with trees 90 ft (27 metres) high, making it seem like a great cathedral housing azaleas, rhododendrons and camellias. Erythronium, trillium and myriads of ferns grow on moss-covered slopes. There are glimpses of the sea to the north and of ancient forest to the south. In the Middle Ages this was part of one of the only two deer parks on Exmoor and the ditch and wall, built to keep the deer in, are still here.

Map: page 146

The garden is brilliant in spring; rich with roses, clematis and lilies in summer; and has splendid autumn colour.

History: This is a post-war garden that celebrated its 50-year anniversary in 1996. It was designed by Horace Stroud.

Accommodation: Andrews on the Weir, Porlock (tel: 01643 863300; ££); The Crown Hotel, Exford (tel: 01643 831554; ££–£££).

Hadspen Garden and Nursery

A modern, colour-themed garden with many unusual plantings. Map reference �40

Castle Cary BA7 7NG, Somerset; tel/fax: 01749 813707; Fax: 01749 813707. < www.hadspengarden.co.uk >
Opening times: *Mar–Sep Thur–Sun and BHs. National Garden Scheme day. Parties/coaches accepted. House closed.*
Admission prices: *adults £3, children 50p, season £25.*
Facilities: *parking, disabled access, shop, plants for sale, refreshments. Picnics permitted. Dogs allowed on leads.*

Hadspen specialises in contemporary colour-themed rose, shrub and herbaceous borders within the framework of a Victorian walled garden, surrounded by mature woodland. Nori and Sandra Pope, the present owners, have redesigned Penelope Hobhouse's original garden to great effect. There are some rare plants in the grounds and some on sale.

Accommodation: The George Hotel, Castle Cary (tel: 01963 350761; ££). **Local pubs:** *Stag Inn, Yarlington; Montague Inn, Shepton Montague.*

Hestercombe Gardens

Landscaped garden with design and plantings by Lutyens and Gertrude Jekyll. English Heritage Grade II*. Map reference �41

Cheddon Fitzpaine, Taunton TA2 8LG, Somerset; tel: 01823 413923; fax: 01823 413747; < www.hestercombegardens.com >
Opening times: *all year 10am–6pm (last admission 5pm). National Garden Scheme days in March and June. Parties/coaches (minimum of 20) accepted. House closed.*
Admission prices: *adults £5, children £1.20, over-60s £4.70, groups £4.70 pp.*
Facilities: *parking, disabled access, shop, plants for sale, refreshments. Picnics permitted. Dogs allowed on leads.*

At Hestercombe you can lose yourself in 40 acres (16 hectares) of walks, streams and temples. The formal terraces, woodlands, lakes and cascades offer fabulous views.

Hestercombe is a rare combination of three period gardens. The Georgian landscape garden was created in the 1750s by Coplestone Warre Bampfylde, and later complemented by a Victorian terrace and shrubbery. The Edwardian gardens were designed by Sir Edwin Lutyens and Gertrude Jekyll. All were once abandoned but are now being restored.

LEFT: *allée* at Hadspen.

ABOVE: Hestercombe Gardens, designed by Lutyens and Jekyll.

BELOW RIGHT: the spring-fed stream at Lady Farm.

History: Hestercombe was first mentioned in an Anglo-Saxon charter of 854, and from 1391 until 1872 was continuously owned by the Warres family. In 1731 John Bampfylde, MP for Exeter, who had married Sir Francis' daughter Margaret in 1718, commissioned plans for a garden from a Mr Brown of London. Coplestone Warre Bampfylde designed and laid out the landscape garden we know today after inheriting the estate from his father in 1750. In the 20th century Lutyens and Jekyll laid out the Edwardian gardens.

Accommodation: Bashford's Farmhouse, West Bagborough (tel: 01823 432015; £); Saltmoor House, Burrowbridge (tel: 01823 698092; ££–£££). Local pubs: Rose & Crown, Woodhill, Stoke St Gregory; Rose & Crown, East Lyng; Fitzhead Inn, Fitzhead.

Lady Farm

Modern garden with a spring-fed watercourse and cottage garden. Map reference ❷

Chelwood, Bristol BS39 4NN, Somerset; tel: 01761 490770; fax: 01761 490877.
Opening times: *Jul–Sep Sun 2–6pm. National Garden Scheme days. Parties/coaches of 10 or*
more on other days by appointment. House closed.
Admission prices: *adults £4, children under 14 free.*
Facilities: *parking, disabled access, shop, plants for sale, refreshments. Picnics permitted. Dogs allowed on leads.*

Lady Farm garden, begun in the early 1990s, has been highly acclaimed by critics. It encompasses 8 acres (3.2 hectares) in all, its key feature being a spring-fed watercourse which flows into two lakes with adjacent rock features. There is a new formal cottage garden with colour-themed perennials, and spectacular rambling roses line a hosta and allium walk.

History: The removal of 3 acres (1.2 hectares) of farm buildings in 1990–91 necessitated some serious landscaping. The chance discovery of the source of the spring water led to the formation of the lakes and water features. Anthony Archer-Wills created the rock features and cave and Mary Payne was inspirational in the grasses and prairie plantings.

Accommodation: Chelwood House Hotel, Chelwood (tel: 01761 490730; ££). Local pub: Carpenter's Arms, Stanton Wick.

Lytes Cary Manor

Colourful borders and an ornamental orchard. English Heritage Grade II. National Trust. Map reference **43**

Map: page 146

Charlton Mackrell, Somerton TA11 7HU, Somerset; tel: 01458 223297 and 01458 224471. < www.nationaltrust.org.uk >
Opening times: *garden: mid-Apr–Oct Mon, Wed, Fri & Sun 11am–5pm, or dusk if earlier; house: daily except Wed & Thur 1–5pm (BHs 11am–5pm; timed tickets). Parties/small coaches (max. 7.5m, 30 people) may also view by appointment.*
Admission prices: *adults £4.60, children £2.*
Facilities: *parking, disabled access. No picnics. Dogs allowed on leads only in car park and on river walk.*

The garden at Lytes Cary Manor, with its multitude of shades of green and low yew hedges sets off the golden colours of the house and walls in the flat Somerset farmland. The main beds display a colour sequence with berberis, achillea, aster, purple sage and many floribunda roses, leading into the White Garden with iceberg roses and philadelphus.

Sweeping lawns, more yew hedges, clumps of pink and white rugosa roses and an ornamental orchard with crab apple trees, medlars, quinces and walnuts, underplanted with daffodils and wildflowers – spectacular in spring – complete the picture. Enclosures with a hornbeam tunnel, a tranquil pool, and a lawn with a stone seat make this a lovely place for quiet contemplation.

History: Lytes Cary was the home of the Lyte family from 1286 until the late 18th century. One of the family, Henry Lyte, translated Dodoen's text on herbs, *The Cruedboek*, from Flemish in 1569. A copy of this is on display in the Great Hall. Sir Walter Jenner acquired the property in 1907 and set about restoring the house and transforming the garden. He planned a series of enclosures with simple but effective themes which Christopher Hussey called "a necklace of garden rooms strung on green corridors". The National Trust used his design after inheriting the property in 1963 and began replanting the main beds in a scheme reminiscent of Gertrude Jekyll's designs.

*Accommodation: Somerton Court Country House, Somerton (tel: 01458 274694; £–££). **Local pub:** Kingsdon Inn, Kingsdon.*

Milton Lodge

Terraced garden with fine trees and shrubs. English Heritage Grade II. Map reference 44

Wells, BA5 3AQ, Somerset; tel: 01749 672168.
Opening times: *Easter–end Oct Tues, Wed, Sun & BHs 2–5pm. Parties/coaches may view only by appointment. House closed.*
Admission prices: *adults £2.50, children under 14 free.*

Above: Lytes Cary Manor.

Facilities: parking, shop, plants for sale, refreshments. Picnics permitted. Disabled access. Dogs allowed on leads.

The entrance from the drive of Milton Lodge leads past a huge cedar, planted soon after the central part of the house was built at the end of the 18th century. Below the terrace, a variety of trees are underplanted with naturalised bulbs and wild flowers which provide a colourful display from March to May. Among the trees and shrubs are Malus (golden hornet), Sorbus (Chinese-lace) and *Diospyros lotus* (date plum). At the end of the house, the stone path merges into a grass walk along the uppermost of the four terraces.

History: The garden was conceived in about 1900 by Mr Charles Tudway, the present owner's grandfather. Over a period of about 10 years and with the assistance of a garden design firm, Tudway transformed the sloping ground to the west of the house into the existing series of architectural terraces, specifically to capitalise on the glorious views of Wells Cathedral.

Accommodation: Tynings House, Wells (tel: 01749 675368; £); Riverside Grange, Wells (tel: 01749 890761; £). Local pub: Bull Terrier, Croscombe.

Montacute House

Formal garden with colourful planting. English Heritage Grade I. National Trust. Map reference ⑤

Montacute TA15 6XP, Somerset; tel/fax: 01935 823289.
< www.nationaltrust.org.uk >
***Opening times:** Apr–Oct Wed–Mon 11am–6pm. No parties/coaches. Viewing by appointment. House also open 11am–5pm.*
***Admission prices:** house & garden: adults £6.50, children £3; garden: adults £3.50, children £1.50.*
***Facilities:** parking, disabled access, shop, plants for sale, refreshments, tours. Picnics permitted. Dogs allowed on leads. Large park with dog walk.*

This formal, Elizabethan garden of terraces and yew topiary has been constructed and enhanced over some 400 years. It is the garden's architecture – two pavilions and a garden house – that gives the property its visual impact, and the planting is designed to enhance this idea. It is not a flamboyant garden, though there is plenty of interest.

History: Various gardeners have tended this garden over the years, but the main influence was Pridheum, an 18th-century designer who is not widely known but was highly

BELOW: mellow scene at Milton Lodge.

Map:
page 146

thought of in his day. The house was once the home of Lord Curzon and Elinor Glyn.

Accommodation: King's Arms, Montacute (tel: 01935 822513; £–££). Local pub: Pelipe Arms, Montacute.

Prior Park Landscape Garden

Eighteenth-century landscape garden with links to Alexander Pope. English Heritage Grade: I. National Trust. Map reference ⑯

*Ralph Allen Drive, Bath, BA2 5AH, Somerset; tel/fax: 01225 833422.
< www.nationaltrust.org.uk >
Opening times: Easter–Nov daily 11am–5.30pm (or dusk if earlier), Dec–Jan Fri–Sun 11am–dusk. Feb–Easter daily 11am–5.30pm (or dusk if earlier). Parties/coaches may also view by appointment. House also open (not NT). Admission prices: adults £4, children £2, over-60s £2, £1 discount off all prices with a valid public transport ticket.*

Facilities: disabled access, shop, plants for sale, refreshments. Picnics permitted. Dogs allowed on leads. No car parking on site except for disabled visitors. Buses from Bath every 20 minutes.

This intimate 18th-century landscape garden is set in a sweeping valley with views of the city of Bath. The many interesting features include an extraordinary Palladian bridge and three lakes. The tranquil, tree-lined walk around the garden is 1 mile (2 km) long, with steep gradients. The wilderness area, which was suggested by the poet Alexander Pope, is being restored.

History: The house was built for Ralph Allen, a local entrepreneur, to a design by John Wood in 1735. Capability Brown was among those who provided designs for the garden, which was developed over about 30 years. The Palladian bridge dates from 1755.

Accommodation: Menzies Waterside, Widcome (tel: 01225 338855; ££££); The Ayrlington, Bath (tel: 01225 425495; ££). Local pubs: Hope & Anchor Inn, Midford; The Horseshoe, Combe Down.

ABOVE: Elizabethan Montacute House

East Anglia

The flat counties of East Anglia have a mixture of soil types, including sand and clay loam. Exposure to east coast winds is a factor for some gardens, but tender plants flourish in sheltered spots and the climate is sufficiently benign to support an award-winning vineyard

Map:
page 184

Edinburgh

Dublin

London

CAMBRIDGESHIRE

In the University Botanic Garden, Cambridge has one of the most comprehensive collections of plants in the country – 8,000 species and six national collections. The county also has a number of well-maintained historic gardens and, in complete contrast, the intensively planted 20th-century Crossing House Garden, bursting with colour and ideas, and right beside the main railway line.

Abbots Ripton Hall

Fine old trees, old-fashioned roses and architectural features in an historic setting. Map reference ❶

Abbots Ripton, Huntingdon PE28 2PQ, Cambs; tel: 01487 773555; fax: 01487 773545.
Opening times: *selected Sundays in spring and summer 2–5pm. Parties/coaches accepted. Viewing by appointment for parties of 12 or more. House closed.*
Admission price: *£8.*
Facilities: *parking, disabled access, plants for sale, refreshments. No picnics. No dogs.*

The gardens of Abbots Ripton Hall contain many fine old trees, including elms (injected annually against Dutch elm disease) and some rare ones, such as the lovely *Acer cappadocicum* and the *Fraxinus*

angustifolia 'Raywood', the leaves of which turn deep purple in autumn. Spectacular roses include Rosa Shailer's White Moss, first recorded in 1788 and replanted in 1940 in the herbaceous border by the mother of Lord de Ramsey, the present owner.

History: Abbots Ripton estate totals some 5,700 acres (2,280 hectares). When Lord de Ramsey's father took up residence in 1937, the fine old trees provided the ideal framework for building up the gardens to the 8 acres (3.2 hectares) seen today. In the 1950s, Humphrey Waterfield designed the Rose Circle and Grey Border and added rare trees to the arboretum. Other plantings were undertaken by Lanning Roper and Jim Russell. Peter Foster, surveyor to Westminster Abbey, designed the architectural features including the Gothic trellis and the Constable Pavilion.

Accommodation: Old Bridge Hotel, Huntingdon (tel: 01480 424300; £££). **Local pub:** *Elephant and Castle, Abbots Ripton.*

PRECEDING PAGES: Bradenham Hall.

OPPOSITE: a tranquil corner of the garden at Helmingham Hall.

ABOVE: Abbots Ripton Hall in winter.

Anglesey Abbey

A 19th-century garden with sweeping lawns, herbaceous borders and very strong colour. English Heritage Grade II*. National Trust. Map reference ❷

Lode, Cambridge CB5 9EJ, Cambs; tel: 01223 811200.
< www.nationaltrust.org.uk/angleseyabbey >
Opening times: *Apr–Jun & Sep–Oct Wed–Sun 10.30am–5.30pm (closed Good Fri); Jul–Aug daily 10.30am–5.30pm, Thur till 8pm; Nov–Mar Wed–Sun 10.30am–4.30pm (or dusk if earlier); house also open Apr–Nov Wed–Sun (and BHs) 1–5pm. National Garden Scheme days. Parties/coaches accepted except Sun and BHs. Viewing by appointment.*
Admission prices: *house, garden and*

mill: adults £6.40, family discounts; groups £5.25 pp; garden & mill: £4; groups £3.35 pp (£3.25 in winter).
Facilities: *parking, disabled access, shop, plants for sale, refreshments. Picnics permitted. Dogs allowed on leads in car park and on public footpaths.*

Anglesey Abbey has one of the most remarkable gardens in England. Laid out almost in its entirety in the 19th century, it encompasses almost 100 acres (40.4 hectares), including some 30 acres (12 hectares) of mown lawn. The clever and subtle garden design of avenues and walks is not centred on the house, but rather is laid out in an intricate design that presents unexpected vistas and shows off the statuary collected by the first Lord Fairhaven.

The collection of bulbs and border plants matches the extravagance of the overall

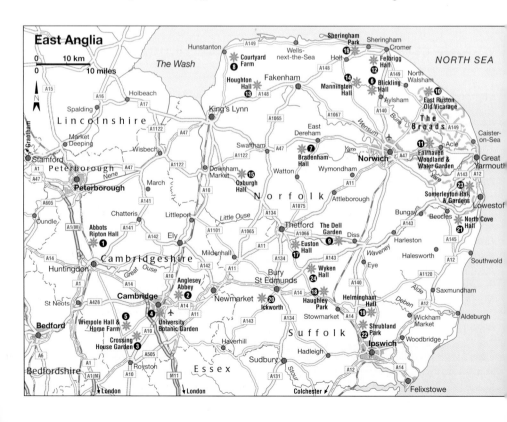

design and the herbaceous borders, with their patches of delphiniums, are splendid in high summer. The Rose Garden was a favourite of Lord Fairhaven and features many modern roses, but it is rivalled by the Hyacinth Garden and the Dahlia Garden. These areas of bright colour contrast with the deep greens of yew, box and ivy and the swathes of grass and trees. But this is not just a summer garden, as there are snow-drops in January and February and marvel-lous colours in autumn.

History: The abbey was formerly an Augustinian priory and the garden was orig-inally laid out in the 1860s by the Rev. John Hailstone, with some fine trees, including cedars and weeping lime. Huttleston Broughton, the first Lord Fairhaven, pur-chased the property in 1926 and greatly expanded the garden, taking in nearby meadows.

Much of the statuary dates from the 18th century, but some is much older, including a Roman urn of Egyptian porphyry. Lord Fairhaven also planted thousands of bulbs and plants, often in a mass of one species set in a particular enclosure. Sadly, Dutch elm disease killed some 4,000 of the mature trees; the National Trust has replanted much of the garden as a result.

Accommodation: University Arms Hotel, Cambridge (tel: 01223 351241; ££–£££). Local pub: White Pheasant, Fordham.

Crossing House Garden

This is a plantsman's garden, compact, intensively planted, full of surprises and many rare plants. Map reference ❸

78 Meldreth Road, Shepreth, Royston SG8 6PS, Cambs; tel: 01763 261071.
Opening times: all year, daily dawn–dusk. No coaches. Small parties travelling by car are welcome. House closed.
Admission prices: free.
Facilities: parking on grass verge, disabled access to most paths. Picnics permitted. Dogs allowed on leads.

Above: weathered statuary is a feature of the garden at Anglesey Abbey.

Map: page 184

ABOVE: Crossing House Garden next to the King's Cross to Cambridge railway line.

University Botanic Garden

A beautifully maintained botanic garden with important horticultural collections. Map reference ❹

Cory Lodge, Bateman Street, Cambridge CB2 1JF, Cambs; tel: 01223 336265; fax: 01223 336278.
< www.botanic.cam.ac.uk >
National Collections: *hardy geranium, Tulipa, Aalchemilla, Saxifraga, Fritillaria and shrubby Lonicera.*
Opening times: *2 Jan–24 Dec daily; garden: Feb & Oct 10am–5pm, Mar–Sep 10am–6pm, Nov–Jan 10am–4pm; glasshouses: Feb–Oct 10am–4.30pm, Nov–Jan 10am–3.45pm. National Garden Scheme days. Parties/coaches strictly by appointment. House closed.*
Admission prices: *free Mon–Fri; weekends & BH Mons: adults £2.50, children £2, over-60s £2; Friends of Cambridge University Botanic Garden with valid card (single £20; family £35) and Cambridge University students with valid university card: free at all times.*
Facilities: *disabled access, shop, refreshments. Picnics permitted. No parking. Guide dogs only.*

Crossing House Garden covers just over ¼ acre (0.1 hectare) lying beside the King's Cross to Cambridge railway line. It features an extensive range of plants, both rare specimens and old favourites, crammed into box-edged beds. There are a number of ponds stocked with water plants and wildlife.

In the alpine house the auriculas and lewisias are at their best in April (there are six raised beds full of alpines as well). Two heated greenhouses feature mainly orchids and tender bulbs. The garden soil is alkaline but there is a large acid bed, housing winter-flowering *Camellia sasanqua* as well as rhododendrons. Seats are scattered round the garden, making it suitable for people who are not able to walk far. A cider mill in front of the garden is filled with water in summer and pots of plants in winter.

History: This is a level-crossing house, built around 1850 as a bungalow, with the upper storey added about 50 years later. The present owners have lived here since 1959 and have been working on the garden for more than 30 years.

Accommodation: Riverside Guest House, Melbourn, Royston (tel: 01763 226062; ££); Sheen Mill Hotel, Melbourn (tel: 01763 261393; £££). Local pubs: The Plough, Shepreth; The Chequers, Fowlmere.

The garden was opened in its present location in 1846 and now holds approximately 8,000 plant species. It includes a rock garden, displaying alpine plants from every continent; winter and autumn gardens, tropical rainforest; seasonal displays in the glasshouses; historic systemic beds displaying hardy representatives of more than 80 families of flowering plants; and the finest collection of trees in the east of England.

It has been designed so that some parts of it look or smell wonderful at any time of the year. After discovering the remarkable use of berry, bark and foliage in the winter garden, visitors can warm up in the glasshouses and travel from the tropics to the desert in search of cacti, carnivorous plants, orchards and the extraordinary jade vine (in flower from February to March). The herbaceous borders, scented gardens and Dry Garden are a colourful summer highlight, while spring brings a carpet of bulbs and early alpines in the woodland and rock gardens.

History: Founded in 1762 on a 5-acre (2-hectare) site in the centre of the city, the garden was a typical Renaissance physic garden modelled on London's Chelsea Physic Garden and grew mainly herbaceous plants. It was enlarged by John Stevens Henslow, Professor of Botany from 1825–60 (perhaps best remembered as the teacher and mentor of Charles Darwin), and again in the 1950s when the eastern part was added. Thematic rather than species-centred, the latter has a very different feel from the western Victorian garden.

Accommodation: Cambridge Garden House (tel: 01223 259988; £££); University Arms Hotel, Cambridge (tel: 01223 351241; ££–£££); Arundel Hotel (tel: 01223 367701; ££–£££). **Local pubs:** *The Anchor; Cambridge Blue; The Eagle.*

Wimpole Hall & Home Farm

Map:
page 184

Informal pleasure grounds with rare trees and working kitchen garden. English Heritage Grade I. National Trust. Map reference ❺

Arrington, Royston SG8 0BW, Cambs; tel: 01223 207257; fax: 01223 207838. < www.nationaltrust.org.uk >
National Collection: *Juglans (walnut trees).*
Opening times: *garden: late Mar–Oct Tues–Thur (plus weekends and Fri in Aug) 10.30am–5pm; park: all year dawn–dusk; hall: same dates as garden 1–5pm (4pm in winter). National Garden Scheme day. Parties/coaches accepted. Tours available by appointment.*
Admission prices: *hall & garden: adults £6.20, children £2.80; hall, garden & farm: adults £9, children £4.50, family £22.*

BELOW: University Botanic Garden is a delight at all seasons of the year.

Facilities: *parking, disabled access, shop, plants for sale, refreshments. Picnics permitted. Dogs allowed on leads in park.*

Visitors to Wimpole Hall usually begin in the West Garden, with its fine specimen trees, and the Dutch Garden, where anemones and fuchsias bloom in season, before reaching the Victorian parterre, laid out in the pattern of a Union Jack. This is ringed by topiary yews, stone vases and lead urns. To the northeast of the house, enclosed by a ha-ha, lie the 19th-century pleasure grounds, with good specimen trees, including redwoods, holm oaks and a Cornelian cherry. Around the edge of the walled garden stands the National Collection of walnut trees and there is a beautiful display of daffodils and wild flowers in spring.

The walled garden is gradually being restored and its layout will shortly have box hedging enclosing the fruit trees and vegetable beds. The glasshouses have recently been completed as a replica of Sir John Soane's original design, found in the Soane Museum in London.

History: Wimpole provides a case-book history of English gardening from 1690 to 1830. There were five main periods of activity. From 1693 to about 1700, the second Earl of Radnor created an elaborate formal garden to the north of Sir Thomas Chichley's 17th-century house. This was greatly extended to the south by Charles Bridgeman, working for Lord Harley in the 1720s, with a system of great axial avenues and a series of canalised ponds. The naturalisation of the landscape was begun by the first Earl of Hardwicke who, between 1749 and 1754, employed Robert Greening to grass over the old parterre beds on the north side of the house.

In 1767 Capability Brown was employed by the second Earl of Hardwicke to further naturalise the landscape with belts of trees, turning the fishpond into serpentine lakes and building the Gothic tower on Johnson's Hill, which was designed years earlier by Sanderson Miller. The last important changes were made by Humphry Repton for the third Earl of Hardwicke between 1801 and 1809.

Accommodation/pub: The Old Bull Inn, Royston (tel: 01763 242003; ££).

Map:
page 184

NORFOLK

Norfolk has a huge variety of garden styles, from the rolling parkland and topiary of Blickling Hall to the exotic and innovative planting at East Ruston; from the wild flowers at organic Courtyard Farm and the water gardens at Fairhaven, to the stunning 19th-century parterre at Oxburgh Hall and the thousands of old-fashioned classic roses at Mannington Hall.

Blickling Hall

Rolling parkland, impressive topiary and a well-planted 19th-century parterre surrounding a Jacobean mansion. English Heritage Grade II*. National Trust. Map reference ❻

Aylsham, Norwich NR11 6NF, Norfolk; tel: 01263 738030; fax: 01263 731660. < www.nationaltrust.org >
Opening times: Apr–Oct Wed–Sun and BH Mons 10.15am–5.30pm, plus Tues in Aug; Nov–Christmas and early Jan–late Mar Sat–Sun 11am–4pm; park & woods: daily dawn–dusk; house: Mar–Sep Wed–Sun and BH Mons plus Tues in Aug 1–5pm; Oct–Nov 1–4pm. National Garden Scheme days. Parties/coaches accepted by appointment by sending s.a.e. to the Property Office. Taster tours of house at noon on most house open days (check on day for availability).
Admission prices: *house & garden: adults £6.90, children £3.45; garden: £3.90, children £1.95; family and group discounts available; car parking charge.*
Facilities: *parking, disabled access, shop, plants for sale, refreshments. Picnics permitted. Dogs allowed on leads in park only. Coarse fishing in lake; permits from warden, tel: 01263 734181.*

Incorporating elements created by leading garden designers over the past three centuries, the grounds include a large and well-planted parterre. It is complemented by some fantastic topiary, including the famous grand pianos. The dry moat contains plants seldom found in this part of the world, including buddleia, auriculata, ceanothus and camellias.

The rolling parkland, with fine stands of oak, beech and chestnut, is reached after leaving the parterre. Its main feature is the lake with huge Oriental plane trees and the venerable turkey oak nearby, their feet covered in spring by bulbs and wild flowers.

History: The house was built by Sir Henry Hobart, but little remains of his early 17th-century garden. His great grandson, the first Earl of Buckinghamshire, redesigned the garden in the early 18th century and the central axis and grand vista, looking up to the Doric Temple, is still there.

His son, the second Earl, living at the height of the Landscape Movement, concentrated on creating a park with rolling pasture, the great lake and the orangery, probably built by Sir Matthew Digby Wyatt and built in 1782. It is known that Humphry Repton suggested some of these improvements and his son, John, was employed after 1823, working on garden furniture and

BELOW: manicured lawns and fine stands of trees at Blickling Hall.

other features. In the 1860s the eighth Marquess of Lothian created the present grid pattern for the formal areas of the garden. He employed Markham Nesfield, the son of William Andrews Nesfield who did a great deal of work at Kew, to excavate the 2-acre (0.8-hectare) parterre, although Lady Lothian dictated the interior planting.

The present-day planting there was carried out by Norah Lindsay between the two world wars and has been continued by the National Trust.

Accommodation: Shrublands Farm, Northrepps, south of Cromer (tel: 01263 579297; £). **Local** *pubs: Buckinghamshire Arms, Blickling; Walpole Arms, Itteringham.*

Bradenham Hall

An extensive arboretum, a walled kitchen garden and an old-fashioned rose garden, plus views over Norfolk. Map reference ❼

West Bradenham, Thetford, IP25 7QP, Norfolk; tel: 01362 687243/687279; fax: 01362 687669. < *www.bradenhamhall.co.uk* >

BELOW: climbers cover the south-facing walls of Bradenham Hall.

Opening times: Apr–Sep, 2nd and 4th Sun 2–5.30pm. National Garden Scheme days. Parties/coaches accepted. Viewing by appointment. House closed. *Admission prices: adults £3, children free.* *Facilities: parking, plants for sale, refreshments. Picnics permitted. Disabled access. No dogs.*

The 27-acre (11-hectare) gardens of Bradenham Hall are situated on one of Norfolk's few high points and although the position affords a lovely view to the south over surrounding farmland, the site is consequently very windy. The owners have protected the long herbaceous borders, the shrubs and the Philosophers' Walk with stout yew hedges, which also shelter the Paved Garden, and borders containing a plantsman's collection.

On the walls of the house and garden a wide range of shrubs, climbers and fruit are grown. There is also a walled kitchen garden, an attractive old barn and an aviary. The arboretum, which was only begun in 1955, has some 800 different trees, including numerous rare and interesting specimens, underplanted with naturalised daffodils. Each tree is labelled.

History: Bradenham Hall is an early Georgian house, facing almost due south. Built in about 1740, it was owned chiefly by the Smyth, Haggard and Penrose families until 1951, when the Allhusens bought it, together with 1,500 acres (600 hectares) of surrounding land. At this time there was virtually no garden, other than the disused and weed-ridden walled garden and courtyard. The house was dilapidated and its occupation by army units during World War II had left a legacy of thousands of broken medicine bottles and the foundations of several dozen concrete Nissen huts. Other items to be removed included over 200 wasps' nests.

Accommodation: Darby's, Swanton Morley, near Dereham (tel: 01362 637647: £). *Local pubs: Ostrich Inn, Castle Acre; George and Dragon, Newton; Dolphin, Thetford.*

> Map:
> page 184

Courtyard Farm

An organic farm and garden with an expanse of wild flowers, accessible via two circular walks.
Map reference ❽

Ringstead PE36 5LQ, Norfolk; tel: 01485 525369.
Opening times: *all year, daily. House closed.*
Admission prices: *free.*
Facilities: *parking, disabled access, shop, plants for sale, refreshments. Picnics permitted. Dogs allowed on leads.*

This fully organic farm is famous for its wild flowers and abundant wildlife. The 150 acres (60 hectares) of wild flowers, mainly perennials, include about 10 different grasses and 40 wild flower species, including cowslips, harebells, dropwort, tufted vetch, clustered bell flower, scabius knapweeds and grass vetchling. In smaller areas there are annual wild flowers such as cornflowers, corn marigold, corn chamomile, poppies, corncockle, prickly poppy, Venus' looking glass and night flowering catchfly. The wild flowers are best between May and October.

The wild flower areas are crossed by two circular walks, one of 2 miles (3.2 km) and one of 6½ miles (10 km) on public footpaths. Farm leaflets with maps are available at three designated parking areas.

History: The farm and garden belong to Lord Melchett, a former Greenpeace chairman and an advocate of organic methods.

Accommodation: Le Strange Arms, Old Hunstanton (tel: 08701 253535; ££). **Local pub:** *Gintrap Pub, Ringstead.*

The Dell Garden, Bressingham

A superb collection of hardy perennials. Map reference ❾

Bressingham, Diss IP22 2AB, Norfolk; tel: 01379 687386/687382; fax: 01379 688085. < www.bressingham.co.uk >
Opening times: *late Mar–Oct daily 10.30am–5.30pm(4.30pm in Oct). National Garden Scheme days. Parties/coaches accepted. Viewing by appointment. House closed.*
Admission prices: *adults £7, children (3–16) £5, under-3s free, over-60s £6; adult season £20, family £21.*

ABOVE: the free-form herbaceous beds at The Dell Garden, Bressingham

Facilities: *parking, disabled access, shop, plants for sale, refreshments. Picnics permitted. Dogs allowed on leads. There is also a Railway Locomotive Museum including 5 miles (8 km) of narrow-gauge track.*

Strictly speaking, The Dell is a name that applies to only part of Bressingham Garden. Long ago this was where clay was dug for brick-making; now it makes for grassy slopes with mature trees as an added attraction. The whole area lies between the hall and the A1066. It is laid out with grass paths and free-form herbaceous "island" beds containing about 5,000 species, including alpines and hardy perennials.

History: The hall was built in 1760. The garden's owner and designer, Alan Bloom, is renowned for growing herbaceous and alpine plants. Just a few hundred yards from the Dell is another garden, Foggy Bottom (also open to the public), created over the past 30 years by Alan's son, Adrian. He specialises in trees, shrubs, perennials and ornamental grasses.

*Accommodation: The Park Hotel, Diss (tel: 01379 642244; ££); Bressingham Hall, on-site B&B (tel: 01379 687243; ££). **Local pubs:** The Chequers, Bressingham; Old Ram Coaching Inn, Tivetshall St Mary.*

East Ruston Old Vicarage

An exciting, still evolving, modern garden with exotic and tender plants. Map reference ⑩

East Ruston, Norwich, NR12 9HN, Norfolk; tel: 01692 650432; fax: 01692 651246. < www.e-ruston-oldvicaragegar dens.co.uk >
Opening times: *Apr–Oct Wed, Fri–Sun 2–5.30pm. National Garden Scheme days. Parties/coaches accepted. Viewing by appointment. House closed.*
Admission prices: *adults £3.80, children £1, season £12.*
Facilities: *parking, disabled access, plants for sale, refreshments. Picnics permitted. No dogs.*

This remarkable 18-acre (7.2-hectare) exotic garden is a feast of formal design, decorative exuberance and brilliant planting. It was only begun in 1988 and has been continually enhanced with new projects. Although it is quite close to the sea it is well protected from the full blast of the wind by demi-windbreaks, making it possible to grow remarkably tender plants. Clustering about the East Ruston Old Vicarage, walled and hedged compartments

BELOW: formal design and geometric topiary at East Ruston Old Vicarage.

vary strongly in mood, from cool formality to explosions of colour and form. Much of this is inward-looking, but occasionally there are exhilarating vistas of distant church towers or the Happisburgh lighthouse. Sculptures, lavishly planted pots and finely detailed walls and gates also play a decorative part. The "desert wash" (created in 2000) supports drought-tolerant plants, including palms.

History: This garden was designed by its owners Alan Gray and Graham Robeson in the grounds of a 1913 Arts & Crafts house, on a site that originally comprised tall, tussocky grass. The shelter belts, established in 1989, are an important and fundamental feature, allowing this exotic style of gardening to function.

Accommodation: Wayford Bridge Hotel, Wayford Bridge, near Stalham (tel: 01692 582414; ££); Beechwood Hotel, North Walsham (tel: 01692 403231; ££–£££). Local pubs: Fur and Feather Inn, Woodbastwick; Nelson's Head, Horsey; Fisherman's Return, Winterton-on-Sea.

Fairhaven Woodland and Water Garden

A natural woodland and water garden with wild flowers and water birds, as well as azaleas and rhododendrons. Map reference ⓫

School Road, South Walsham, Norwich NR13 6DZ, Norfolk; tel/fax: 01603 27044. < www.norfolkbroads.com/fairhaven >
Opening times: all year, daily (except Christmas Day) 10am–5pm; May–Aug Wed–Thur 10am–9pm. National Garden Scheme days. Parties/coaches accepted. House closed.
Admission prices: adults £3.50, children £1.25, over-60s £3; annual family membership £30, single £12.50.
Facilities: parking, disabled access, shop, plants for sale, refreshments. Picnics permitted. Dogs allowed on leads. Guided tours for groups. Boat trips on private Broad, May–August.

Map: page 184

This is a delightful natural woodland and water garden of over 180 acres (73 hectares) with its own private inner Broad (shallow lake).

There is plenty to see at Fairhaven at all times of the year: snowdrops and camellias in January and February, daffodils and narcissi in March, carpets of primroses and *Lysichitum Americanum* (skunk cabbage) in April, followed by bluebells, azaleas and rhododendrons in May and June, and a collection of naturalised candelabra primulas throughout May. Wild flowers and flowering shrubs appear in summer, attracting a host of butterflies and dragonflies.

In addition, 95 species of woodland and water birds are here all year round, including the three native species of woodpecker, creepers, herons, ducks, coots and kingfishers. In autumn the colours are wonderful, and winter walks offer attractive views of the Broads, which tend to be obscured by vegetation during summer. The garden is organically managed.

History: Fairhaven was designed by the second Lord Fairhaven, Henry Broughton, during the 1960s. It is based on the Savill garden at Windsor *(see page 75)*, which was designed by Fairhaven's great friend, Sir Eric Savill.

Accommodation: Fisherman's Return, Winterton-on-Sea (tel: 01493 393305; ££); South Walsham Hall, South Walsham (tel: 01603 270378; ££). Local pubs: Kings Arms and The Ship, South Walsham.

ABOVE: candelabra primulas at Fairhaven Garden.

Felbrigg Hall

A walled garden with espaliered fruit trees is the focus of this fine estate. English Heritage Grade II*. National Trust. Map reference ⑫

Felbrigg, Norwich NR11 8PR, Norfolk; tel: 01263 837444; fax: 01263 837032. < www.nationaltrust.org.uk >

Above: the mellow walled garden at Felbrigg Hall.

Opening times: garden: Apr–Oct Sat–Wed 11am–5.30pm. National Garden Scheme days. Parties/coaches accepted by appointment. Guided garden tours available for pre-booked groups. House open 1–5pm.
Admission prices: adults £2.50, children £1.
Facilities: parking, disabled access, shop, plants for sale, refreshments. Picnics permitted. Dogs allowed on leads only in park and woods.

The garden at Felbrigg Hall comprises two distinct halves. The West Garden, which creates a formal link between the hall and the greater landscape in which it is set, is typical of the 18th-century Landscape Movement. Given a Victorian overlay, focusing on the play between light and shade, it features a ha-ha and orangery, a shrubbery and many trees of transatlantic origin. The Walled Garden has borders of herbs, mixed shrubs, roses and herbaceous plants.

The kitchen garden is a mix of flowers, fruit and vegetables, with a dovecote and pond. The walls are clothed with espaliered pears, peaches, apples, apricots and cherries, and there is a new orchard planted with varieties of fruit known to have been grown here during the 19th century.

History: The Jacobean Hall was built by Thomas Windham and it is likely that it was his great-great grandson, William Windham III, patron of the young Humphry Repton from the mid-1770s, who gave the famous garden designer his first opportunity. During World War I, many of the fine trees sheltering the garden from the fierce east winds from the North Sea were felled for timber but they were largely replaced by Robert Wyndham Ketton-Cremer, who also added the "Victory V" rides in the Coronation group of beeches to commemorate VE-Day. He later bequeathed the estate to the National Trust.

Accommodation: White Horse Hotel, Blakeney (tel: 01263 740574; ££); Shrublands Farm, Northrepps. Cromer (tel: 01263 579297; £); Blakeney Hotel, Blakeney (tel: 01263 740797; ££–£££). Local pubs: George and Dragon Hotel, Cley-next-the-Sea; White Horse Hotel, Blakeney.

Houghton Hall

Lengthy herbaceous borders and a splendid kitchen garden in the grounds of an 18th-century hall. Map reference ⑬

King's Lynn PE316UE, Norfolk; tel: 01485 528569. < www.houghtonlhall.co.uk >
Opening times: garden Apr–Sep Thur, Sun and BH Mons, Jun–Sep also Wed 2–5.30pm. National Garden Scheme day. Parties/coaches accepted. Viewing by

Norfolk **195**

appointment. *House open as garden, but 2–5.30pm.*
Admission prices: house & garden: £6; garden: £3.50.
Facilities: parking, disabled access, shop, plants for sale, refreshments. Picnics permitted. Dogs allowed on leads.

Houghton Hall, one of the gems of English country houses, was built between 1721 and 1735. Its grounds contain a splendid 5-acre (2-hectare) walled garden which has been substantially renovated over the past decade. The garden is divided by yew hedges into a number of garden rooms. Herbaceous borders run the length of the garden from the glasshouse on the south-facing wall to a rustic temple on the north-facing wall. The rose parterre with a sunken pool is modelled on the ceiling design in the White Drawing Room of the hall.

The kitchen garden consists of areas of vegetables and soft fruits divided by trained fruit trees. Almost 100 varieties of apples are grown here. A north-facing border containing numerous ferns, hostas and grasses, together with an east-facing aster border, provide interest throughout the season, though June and July are the best months for seeing the roses.

History: The original layout was by Mrs Pamela Lane-Smith; the herbaceous borders and Rose Garden by Paul Underwood, the previous head gardener; the kitchen garden was designed by the present head gardener, Simon Martin; the aster border, the peony border and several garden features were the work of Julian and Isabel Bannerman; and the Laburnum Garden and Memorial Garden were designed by the present owner, the Marquess of Cholmondeley.

Accommodation: Congham Hall, King's Lynn (tel: 01485 600250; ££–£££).
Local pub: Freebridge Farm, West Lynn.

Mannington Hall

An outstanding collection of roses and extensive areas of parkland. English Heritage Grade II.
Map reference **⑭**

Saxthorpe, Norwich NR11 7BB, Norfolk; tel: 01263 584175.
< www.manningtongardens.co.uk >
Opening times: May & Sep Sun noon–5pm; Jun–Aug Wed–Fri 11am–5pm. National Garden Scheme days. Parties/coaches accepted. Viewing by appointment. House closed.
Admission prices: adults £3, children free, over-60s £2.50, family £12.
Facilities: parking, disabled access, shop, plants for sale, refreshments. Picnics permitted. No dogs.

The gardens around this moated manor house feature a wide variety of plants, trees and shrubs in a variety of settings. There are thousands of roses, especially classic varieties. In the Heritage Rose Garden and the Twentieth-Century Rose Garden roses are planted in designs that reflect their date of origin from the 15th century to the present day.

Below: water lilies bloom in the garden at Mannington Hall.

RIGHT: the scrolled design in the parterre at Oxburgh Hall.

The wider park covers about 20 acres (8 hectares). The depressions in the ground, two near the chapel and one to the right of the main drive, are unusual. A contemporary description of 1717 says "to the astonishment of those that were present, first single oak with roots and ground about was seen to subside and sink into the earth" and continues by saying that another two trees then disappeared, leaving large pits. This alarming event probably occurred because of changes in the course of the underground springs which still feed the lakes and moat.

History: Mentioned as a substantial property in the Domesday Book, much of the present hall was built in the 15th century and a map of 1565 shows it as a self-sufficient manorial community. After it was purchased by the first Lord Walpole in the mid-18th century, the fourth Earl of Orford established the gardens with battlemented walls and yew hedges, as well as planting the now massive cedar trees. Substantial tree planting has taken place in the past 30 years.

Accommodation: Shrublands Farm, Northrepps, south of Cromer (tel: 01263 579297; £). **Local pubs:** *Buckinghamshire Arms, Blickling; Walpole Arms, Itteringham,*

Oxburgh Hall

The garden features a lime avenue, mature trees, and a stunning 19th-century parterre. English Heritage Grade II. National Trust.
Map reference ⓯

Oxborough, King's Lynn PE33 9PS, Norfolk; tel: 01366 328258; fax: 01366 328066. < www.nationaltrust.org.uk >.
Opening times: gardem: early–mid-Mar & weekends 11am–4pm, late Mar–Oct Sat–Wed, and daily in Aug 11am–5.30pm; house: late Mar–Oct Sat–Wed 1–5pm, BH Mons 11am–5pm. National Garden Scheme days. Parties/coaches accepted. Viewing by appointment.

Admission prices: house & garden: adults £5.50, children £2.80, family £14.50, pre-booked parties £4.50 pp (except BHs); garden only: £2.80.
Facilities: parking, disabled access, shop, plants for sale, refreshments. Picnics permitted. No dogs.

The pride of Oxburgh Hall garden is the extraordinary parterre which has a scrolled design and uses large quantities of bedding plants each year. In such a flat landscape this sets off the hall and moat to advantage and combines effectively with oaks, beeches, cedars and Wellingtonias planted near the house. Other notable features include a lime avenue and a recently restored Victorian wilderness. On the other side of the parterre, beyond the yew hedges, is a herbaceous border and beyond that the walled kitchen garden planted with plums, gages, medlars, pears and quinces.

Further on, a wooden drawbridge leads into My Lady's Wood, where a thatched summerhouse sits among the oaks, beeches and sycamore. This area is partiuclarly pretty in spring when it is covered with snowdrops, violets and wildflowers.

History: The hall was originally built as a fortified house for Sir Edmund Bedingfield in about 1482. The sixth baronet, Sir Henry Paston Bedingfield, and his wife, Margaret, imported a design for a parterre from Paris in 1845 and, remarkably, it survives almost intact to this day, although flowers have replaced the original gravel and crushed stone, such as chalk and black stone, providing the necessary colour.

The large Victorian walled garden has been replaced by an orchard for practical reasons.

*Accommodation: Stuart House Hotel, King's Lynn (tel: 01553 772169; ££). **Local pub:** Spread Eagle, Barton Brendish.*

Sheringham Park

A stunning collection of rhododendrons in a Humphry Repton landscape. English Heritage Grade II*. National Trust. Map reference ⓰

Upper Sheringham NR26 8TB, Norfolk; tel/fax: 01263 823778. < www.nationaltrust.org.uk >
Opening times: *all year, daily dawn–dusk. National Garden Scheme days. Parties/coaches by appointment. House open only by appointment.*
Admission prices: *per vehicle £2.70, season £15; coaches £8.10.*

Facilities: parking, disabled access, shop, plants for sale, refreshments. Picnics permitted. Dogs allowed on leads.

Map:
page 184

Set in Sheringham Park's 1,000-acre (405-hectare) estate are 50 acres (20 hectares) of cultivated land preserved as a wild garden. There is a collection of broad-leaved conifers, but the pride of the gardens is the extensive collection of rhododendrons, azaleas, magnolias and camellias. There are stunning views of the countryside and the coast (just 1½ miles/2 km away) from the viewing towers and a number of delightful way-marked walks, including a route to the North Norfolk Railway Station (a private full-gauge steam railway).

History: The planting at Sheringham began in the 1700s and continued throughout subsequent centuries. The garden is considered to be one of Humphry Repton's greatest achievements. E.H. Wilson added a collection of plants from China in the early 20th century.

*Accommodation: White Horse Hotel, Blakeney (tel: 01263 740574; ££). **Local pubs:** Red Lion, Upper Sheringham; George and Dragon Hotel, Cley-next-the-Sea.*

BELOW:
view from
the temple at
Sheringham
Park.

Map: page 184

SUFFOLK

Suffolk is proud of the number of English Heritage Grade I gardens within its borders, including Haughley Park, with its bluebell walks, and Helmingham Hall, where there is a collection of rambling roses. Ungraded, but delightful, are the traditional gardens surrounding Elizabethan Wyken Hall and the natural lily pond at North Cove Hall.

Euston Hall

Formal rose gardens set within an 18th-century landscape. English Heritage Grade II*. Map reference ⑰

Thetford P24 2QP, Suffolk (Norfolk border); tel: 01842 766366; fax: 01842 766764.
< www.eustonhall.co.uk >
Opening times: *mid-Jun–late Sep Thur 2.30–5pm; also selected Sundays. Parties/coaches accepted. Viewing by appointment. House open.*
Admission prices: *house & garden: adults £4, children £2, over-60s £3; garden: adults £2, children £1.*
Facilities: *parking, shop, refreshments. No picnics. No disabled access. No dogs.*

The garden comprises 10 acres (4 hectares) of classical pleasure grounds with formal rose gardens and herbaceous borders, close to Euston Hall. William Kent (1685–1748) designed the domed temple positioned on a mound and the garden house in the formal garden. The original layout is discernible in the Great Avenue and in the rides through the yew trees in the pleasure grounds that have grown up since it was first designed.

History: The pleasure grounds were laid out by the diarist John Evelyn (1620–1706), who was also a noted landscape gardener and an expert on trees. His designs for Euston included the walk through the pleasure grounds that can still be enjoyed today. The landscaped park and the river layout were designed by William Kent and are considered one of his greatest works. The project was modified and completed by Capability Brown.

Accommodation: Broom Hall Country Hotel, Thetford (tel: 01953 882125; ££). **Local pubs:** *Grafton Arms Pub, Barnham, near Thetford; Six Bells Pub, Bardwell, near Bury St Edmunds.*

Haughley Park

Bluebell walks, ancient trees and the largest *Magnolia grandiflora* in England. English Heritage Grade I. Map reference ⑱

Stowmarket P14 3JY, Suffolk; tel: 01359 240701.
Opening times: *garden:May–Sep Tues 2–5.30pm plus Bluebell Sundays until last Sun in April or first Sun in May. Parties/coaches accepted. Viewing by appointment. House open by appointment only.*

RIGHT: the bluebell walk in the woodland at Haughley Park.

Admission prices: adults £3, children free.
Facilities: parking, plants for sale, refreshments. Picnics permitted. Disabled access. Dogs allowed.

Haughley Park is an imposing red-brick Jacobean manor house, set in gardens, park and woodland. It has an unaltered three-storey east front with five gables topped with crow-steps and finials. There are three woodland walks through old broad-leaf and pine woodland with bluebells, lily-of-the-valley and camellias (in May) and rhododendrons and azaleas (in June). A walled garden features a rose arbor as well as vegetables and fruit trees. An interesting experiment has been carried out in the West Woods following the devastation of the great storm of 1987. Some areas were undamaged and have been left; one damaged area has been left to recover naturally; another has had its stumps left in place to shoot as coppice timber; and several areas were cleared and replanted between 1992 and 1996.

History: Some of the grounds retain the historic layout, but they were partly re-designed in the 1960s by Fred Barcock, a well-known local horticulturalist. The house dates from 1620 but the north end was rebuilt in Georgian style in 1820.

Accommodation: Ravenwood Hall Hotel, Rougham (tel: 01359 270345; ££–£££).
Local pubs: Brewers Arms, Rattlesden; Sorrel Horse, Barham.

Helmingham Hall

Moated manor house with extensive deer park, rambling roses and herbaceous borders. English Heritage Grade I. Map reference ⑨

Helmingham, Stowmarket IP14 6EF, Suffolk; tel: 01473 890363.

< *www.helmingham.com* >
Opening times: garden: May–mid-Sep Sun 2–6pm, Wed 2–5pm for individuals and parties by appointment. National Garden Scheme day. Parties/coaches accepted. House closed.
Admission prices: adults £4, children £2, parties of 30+ £3.75 pp.
Facilities: disabled access, refreshments. No parking. Picnics permitted. Dogs allowed on leads. Occasional safari rides to see red deer, cattle and Soay sheep.

It would be hard to exaggerate the impact of Helmingham Hall's beautiful 400-acre (162-hectare) park. A moated house in mellow red brick and a marvellous walled garden combine to give an impression of a place unchanged for generations. Two rose gardens, a parterre and a knot garden are situated on one side of the house. On the other lies a stunning walled garden with beds of vegetables fronted by a trellis of sweet peas, rambling roses and herbaceous borders on either side of the central path. The colour combinations are both subtle and beautiful.

Produce from the walled garden is sold to visitors on Sundays.

History: The Tollemache family, who

ABOVE: runner beans, grown for ornament as well as the table at Helmingham Hall.

migrated from France at the time of the Norman Conquest, have lived at Helmingham since 1487 and rebuilt the hall in 1510. The main walled garden predates the house and is probably of Saxon origin.

The parterre was redesigned in 1978 and the Rose Garden beyond it, in 1965. The second rose garden to the east of the house was designed in 1982, as was the knot garden. The influence of garden designer, Lady Xa Tollemache, wife of the present owner, is apparent. The house's two drawbridges are raised every evening.

Accommodation: Bridge Guest House, Ipswich (tel: 01473 601760; £); Claydon Country House Hotel, Ipswich (tel: 01473 830382; ££).
Local pubs: Moon and Mushroom Inn, Swilland; Sorrel Horse, Barham.

Ickworth

Wooded parkland plus Italian-style house and gardens, an ornamental canal and a vineyard. English Heritage Grade II*. National Trust. Map reference ⑳

Horringer, Bury St Edmunds IP29 5QE, Suffolk; tel: 01284 735270.
< www.nationaltrust.org.uk >.
Opening times: Apr–Oct Mon, Tues, Fri, weekends & BH Mons; garden: 10am–5pm; park: dawn–dusk; house: 1–5pm. National Garden Scheme day. Parties/coaches accepted. Viewing by appointment.
Admission prices: house, park & gardens: adults £6.10, children £2.75, under-5s free; gardens: adults £2.80, children 80p, discounts for families and pre-booked groups of 12 + .
Facilities: parking, disabled access, shop, plants for sale, refreshments. Picnics permitted. Dogs allowed on leads.

The gardens surrounding Ickworth House were created in the first half of the 19th century by the first Marquess of Bristol. The formal, Italian-style section to the south of the house features the Gold and Silver gardens, a Victorian stumpery and the Temple Rose Garden. A raised terrace walk separates the south garden from the park. Beyond the church are the remnants of an 18th-century garden created by the first Earl. His summerhouse (*circa* 1703) and ornamental canal still survive.

The kitchen garden, protected by high brick walls, is now a vineyard producing Ickworth wines (available in the National Trust shop at Ickworth).

The 1,800 acres (730 hectares) of wooded parkland, created in part by Capability Brown, is a living landscape rich in plant, animal and bird life. Some parts are cultivated and grazed, but there is much that can be explored and enjoyed.

History: The present house at Ickworth was begun in 1795, the creation of a famously eccentric Hervey, Frederick the fourth Earl of Bristol and Bishop of Derry. Inspired by Italian architecture, Ickworth's extraordinary central rotunda and curving wings were intended to house treasures the Earl Bishop collected from all over Europe. Today, the magnificent state rooms display Old Masters, including works by Titian, Velázquez and Gainsborough. Ickworth is also noted for its Georgian silver and Regency furniture.

Accommodation: Six Bells Country Inn, Bardwell, Bury St Edmunds (tel: 01359 250820; ££).
Local pub: The Pykkerell, Ickworth.

North Cove Hall

**A natural water lily pond plus a walled garden and woodland walks.
Map reference ㉑**

*North Cove, Beccles, NR34 7PH Suffolk;
tel: 01502 476631.*
Opening times: *National Garden Scheme days. Also viewing by appointment for individuals and parties/coaches. House open.*
Admission prices: *adults £2.50, children under 17 free.*
Facilities: *parking, disabled access, plants for sale. Picnics permitted. Dogs allowed on leads. No refreshments.*

The 5-acre (2-hectare) garden surrounding the red-brick Georgian house is noted for its large natural pond covered with water lilies and a small stream with waterfalls, surrounded by trees and shrubs. Vegetables and fruit grow in a walled garden and there are some good herbaceous borders and woodland walks.

History: The Everitt family, who played an important part in modernising the harbour facilities at Lowestoft in the mid-19th century, used to own North Cove Hall. The present owners, the Blower family, have lived here since the 1940s.

Accommodation: *Abbe House Hotel, Lowestoft (tel: 01502 581083; £); The Albany Hotel, Lowestoft (tel: 01502 574394; £–££).*
Local pubs: *Reedham Ferry Inn, Reedham.*

Shrubland Park

**A Victorian garden, with Italianate terraces. English Heritage Grade I.
Map reference ㉒**

*Coddenham, Ipswich IP69QQ, Suffolk;
tel: 01473 830221; fax: 01473 832202.
< www.shrublandpark.co.uk >*
Opening times: *early Apr–mid-Sep Sun and BH Mons 2–5pm. Parties/coaches accepted. Viewing by appointment. House closed.*
Admission prices: *adults £3, children £2, over-60s £2.*
Facilities: *parking, disabled access but only limited facilities. Picnics permitted in the park. No refreshments. No dogs.*

The extraordinary Grand Descent, an Italianate parade of steps leading down from the house through several

BELOW: the view down the Grand Descent at Shrubland Park.

ABOVE: the sweeping lawns of Somerleyton Hall.

terraces to the gardens below, dominates the scene at Shrubland Park. Off the first terrace are the fine, 18th-century French blue gates and at the foot is the main fountain and formal beds, with a loggia beyond. An authentic Swiss chalet, with an alpine rockery, is found near the Witches' Circle, a set of stone basins and a raised flower bed. On the other side of the grand descent is a terrace lined with magnificent old chestnuts, some reputed to be 800 years old. An unusual "hot wall", intended to accelerate the growing of fruits, has been restored.

History: The hall was designed by James Paine in the 1770s. Gandy Deering designed extensive alterations in the 1840s, while Donald Beaton helped with the garden design. Sir Charles Barry completed the additions to the hall and assisted with the redesign of the gardens, particularly the Grand Descent. William Robinson was consulted by Lord de Saumarez in the 1880s and assisted with the planting.

Accommodation: Mockbeggars Hall, Claydon, Ipswich (tel: 01473 830239; £). Local pubs: Sorrel Horse, Claydon; Moon and Mushroom Inn, Swilland.

Somerleyton Hall and Gardens

One of the finest yew mazes in Britain, walled and sunken gardens, and magnificent specimen trees. English Heritage Grade II*. Map reference ㉓

Somerleyton, Lowestoft Suffolk, NR32 5QQ, Suffolk; tel. 01502 730224; fax: 01502 732143.
< www.somerleyton.co.uk >.

Opening times: *Apr–Jun and Sep Thur, Sun & BH Mons; Jul–Aug Tues–Thur & Sun; Oct Sun; gardens: 12.30–5.30pm; hall: 1–5pm. National Garden Scheme days. Parties/coaches accepted. Private tours by prior arrangement. Also viewing by appointment.*

Admission prices: *adults £5.80, children £2.90, over-60s £5.50, family £16.40; season £18, parties of 20+ £5.30 pp.*

Facilities: *parking, shop, plants for sale, refreshments. Picnics permitted. Disabled access. Guide dogs only. Miniature railway.*

Sweeping lawns and formal gardens combine well with majestic statuary and ornamentation, while a sense of depth is given by elegant yew hedges, topiary and numerous mature trees from around the world, including a giant redwood *(Sequoia giganteum)*. The present sunken garden was once the site of a grand, glass-domed winter garden. The walled garden, now planted with a variety of fruit trees and two huge herbaceous borders, dominates the gardens' northern end.

One of the most popular features is the yew maze; designed by William Nesfield and planted in 1846, it is still one of the finest in Britain. It covers approximately 1 acre (0.4 hectares) of the gardens, and an enchanting small pagoda, perched on a grassy mound, stands at the centre. In spring the ground is covered with a multitude of flowering bulbs, while summer brings a wonderful show of colour in the herbaceous borders and rose beds.

History: Somerleyton Hall is the family home of Lord and Lady Somerleyton and has been in their family since 1863 when Lord Somerleyton's great-grandfather, carpet manufacturer Sir Francis Crossley, purchased the hall from Sir Morton Peto. The gardens were laid out at the same time as the hall was rebuilt (1844–51) by Sir Morton Peto and retain much of their original Victorian appearance.

Accommodation: Abbe House Hotel, Lowestoft (tel: 01502 581083; £); The Albany Hotel, Lowestoft (tel: 01502 574394; £–££).
Local pubs: The Dukes Head, Somerleyton; Village Maid, Lound.

Wyken Hall

A series of well-maintained, traditional gardens complement an Elizabethan house. Map reference ㉔

Stanton, Bury St Edmunds IP31 2DW, Suffolk; tel: 01359 250287/40; fax: 01359 252256.
Opening times: *Apr–Sep Mon–Fri & Sun*

2–6pm. National Garden Scheme day. Parties/coaches accepted. Viewing by appointment. House closed.
Admission prices: *adults £2.50, children free, over-60s £2.*
Facilities: *parking, disabled access, shop, plants for sale, refreshments. No dogs. Vineyard and woodland walk.*

The grounds at Wyken Hall are cleverly designed as a set of traditional gardens organised as rooms to complement the Elizabethan house. They include a knot garden and a herb garden designed by Arabella Lennox-Boyd. There is an English kitchen garden as well as wildflower meadows, a nuttery with a gazebo and a copper beech maze.

Beautifully maintained, this is one of the finest private gardens to be developed in recent years in Britain. Its features include the woodland garden, roses both new and old-fashioned, a plantsman's collection of perennials, herbs, fruit and shrubs, and good herbaceous borders. There is an award-winning 7-acre (2.8-hectare) vineyard, and a new pond has recently been created.

History: This garden was designed by the owners, Sir Kenneth and Lady Carlisle and by Arabella Lennox-Boyd. The improvements to the garden began in 1979 and are still continuing.

Accommodation: The Angel, Bury St Edmunds (tel: 01284 714000; ££); Six Bells Country Inn, Bardwell, Bury St Edmunds (tel: 01359 250820; ££). Local pub: The Pykkerell, Ixworth.

BELOW:
Wyken Hall's traditional but modern gardens.

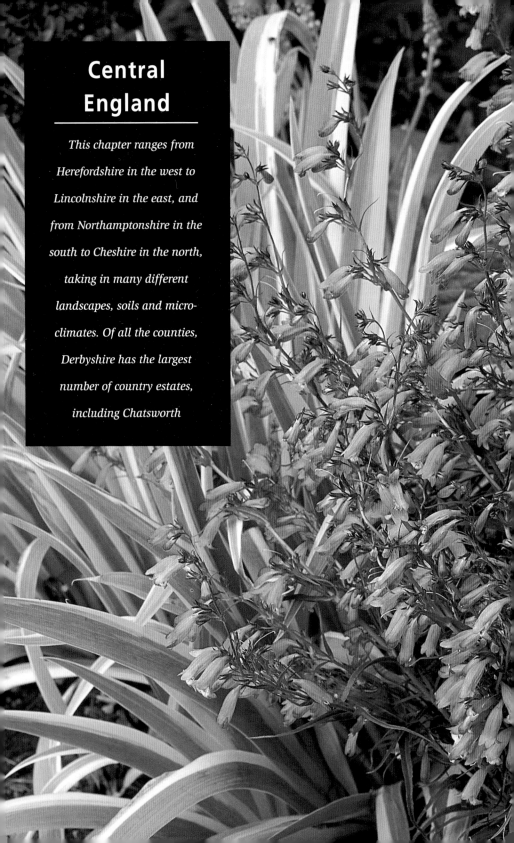

Central England

This chapter ranges from Herefordshire in the west to Lincolnshire in the east, and from Northamptonshire in the south to Cheshire in the north, taking in many different landscapes, soils and micro-climates. Of all the counties, Derbyshire has the largest number of country estates, including Chatsworth

Map:
pages
208-9

BIRMINGHAM AREA

With two major botanical gardens and the meticulously restored 18th-century gardens at Castle Bromwich Hall, the Birmingham area has far more to offer the garden lover than one might expect to find in a city. The Birmingham Botanical Gardens contain the National Collection of bonsai, while the University Botanic Garden has a collection on the history of the rose as well as an Arts & Crafts garden.

Birmingham Botanical Gardens & Glasshouses

A Victorian creation with historic gardens, tropical plants in Victorian glasshouses, and the National Collection of bonsai. English Heritage Grade II*. Map reference ❶

Westbourne Road, Edgbaston B15 3TR, Birmingham; tel: 0121 454 1860. < www. birminghambotanicalgardens.org.uk >
National Collection: *Bonsai.*
Opening times: *all year daily (except Christmas Day) Mon–Sat 9am–7pm (or dusk if earlier), Sun 10am–7pm (or dusk if earlier). Parties/coaches accepted. House closed.*
Admission prices: *adults £5.50, children & over-60s £3, season £50.*
Facilities: *parking, disabled access, shop,*

plants for sale, refreshments. Picnics permitted. Guide dogs only. Band performances on summer Sundays and BHs.

A tranquil oasis, designed by J.C. Loudon and opened in 1832, the Birmingham Botanical Gardens and Glasshouses are easily reached by road from the motorway networks and by rail from Birmingham city centre.

The general layout is still much the same as the original design, with a formal terrace, a sweeping main lawn with a Victorian bandstand, and 15 acres (6 hectares) of magnificent ornamental gardens. These include separate rhododendron, herb, rock, alpine, rose and formal Japanese gardens, plus three historic gardens from different eras.

There are four glasshouses providing plenty of year-round interest. An organic garden and a children's discovery garden

PRECEDING PAGES: Chatsworth, one of England's great country estates.

OPPOSITE: *Penstemon* 'Evelyn' makes a fine show.

ABOVE: the Subtropical House at the Birmingham Botanical Garden, a quiet oasis in a busy city.

are the most recent additions to the complex.

History: The gardens were laid out by John Claudius Loudon, a leading garden planner, horticultural journalist and publisher in the first half of the 19th century. It is owned by the Birmingham Botanical and Horticultural Society.

Accommodation: Hyatt Regency Hotel (tel: 0121 6431234: ££££); Jonathans, Oldbury, Birmingham (tel: 0121 4293757; £££); New Hall Thistle Hotel, Sutton Coldfield (tel: 0121 3782442; £££).

Castle Bromwich Hall Gardens

A restored 18th-century formal garden featuring a sizeable collection of rare plants and a holly maze. English Heritage Grade II*. Map reference ❷

Chester Road, Castle Bromwich B36 9BT, Birmingham; tel/fax: 0121 7494100.
< www.cbhgt.swinternet.co.uk >
Opening times: *Apr–Oct Tues–Thur 1.30–4.30pm, Sat–Sun and BH Mons 2–6pm. National Garden Scheme day. Parties/coaches accepted and may also view by appointment. House closed.*
Admission prices: *adults £3.50, children £1.50, over-60s £2.50.*
Facilities: *parking, disabled access, shop, plants for sale, refreshments. No picnics. Dogs allowed on leads. Special events throughout the season.*

Set within 10 acres (4.5 hectares), the formal gardens of Castle Bromwich Hall have been restored to their former, early 18th-century glory, offering an oasis of tranquillity within their walls. They

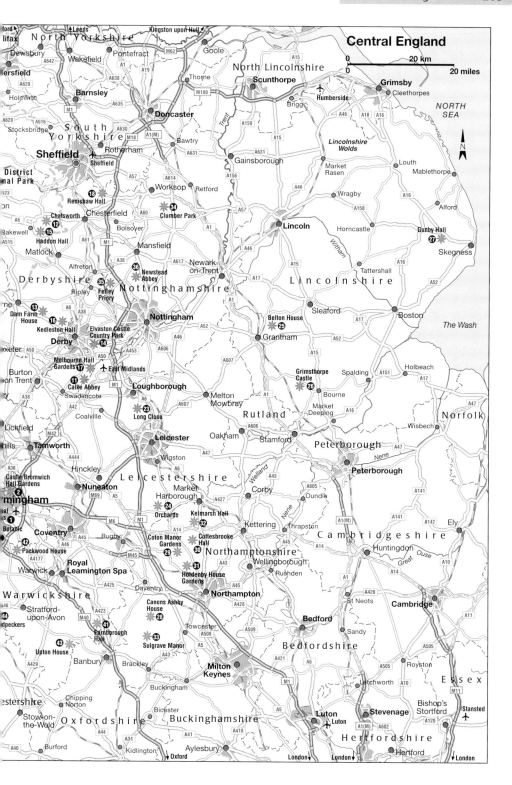

Central England

0   20 km
0   20 miles

NORTH SEA

N

ford
lifax
Halifax
North Yorkshire   ▲Leeds   Kingston upon Hull
Dewsbury   A642   Wakefield   Pontefract   M62   Goole
ersfield   A19   A638
A629   Holmfirth
Barnsley   Thorne   **North Lincolnshire**   A15
A628   A616   M1   A635   **Scunthorpe**   **Grimsby**
Stocksbridge   **South**   A630   **Doncaster**   M180   Brigg   **Humberside**   Cleethorpes
Yorkshire   M18   A1(M)   Bawtry   **Humberside**
Sheffield   Rotherham   A631   A46   A18   A16
Sheffield   A57   Gainsborough   **Lincolnshire Wolds**   Louth   Mablethorpe
District   A614   Worksop   Retford   Market Rasen
nal Park   **18**   Renishaw Hall   A156   A46   Wragby   A16   Alford
on   **Chatsworth** Chesterfield   A60   **34** Clumber Park   A57   A158
A6   **12**   Bolsover   A1   **Lincoln**   Horncastle   **Gunby Hall** **27**
Bakewell   **15**   Haddon Hall   A61   M1   Mansfield   Skegness
A515   **Haddon Hall**   A38   Newark-   A15   Tattershall   A16
Matlock   Alfreton   **36** Newstead Abbey   on-Trent   A617   A17   A52
ne   **13**   **Derbyshire**   Ripley   **35** Felley Priory   **Nottinghamshire**   A1   Sleaford   **Boston**
Dam Farm House   A6   A38   Belton House   A17   **The Wash**
Kedleston Hall   Elvaston Castle   **Nottingham**   A52   **25**   A52
16   Country Park   A46   Grantham   A15
xeter   A50   **Derby**   A453   A606   A607   Grimsthorpe Castle   Spalding   A151   Holbeach
Burton   A50   Melbourne Hall Gardens   **17**   ✈ East Midlands   **28**   Bourne   A17
on Trent   **11**   M1   **Loughborough**   A1   Market Deeping   A47
ey   A38   Calke Abbey   Swadlincote   A6   Melton Mowbray   A16   Wisbech   **Norfolk**
A42   Coalville   **23** Long Close   A607   **Rutland**
Lichfield   M42   Oakham   A606   Stamford   **Peterborough**   A47
nills   **Tamworth**   **Leicester**   A47   **Peterborough**
A38   A444   Wigston   Nene   A141
Castle Bromwich Hall Gardens   Hinckley   **Leicestershire**   A6   A43   Corby   A605   Oundle
2   **Nuneaton**   Market   **24**   A427   A1(M)   A141   A142   Ely
mingham   M69   A5   Harborough   Orchards   Kelmarsh Hall   Kettering   Thrapston   **Cambridgeshire**
ial   **1**   M6   M1   A14   **32**   A45   Huntingdon   A10
Botanic   **42** **Coventry**   A45   Rugby   Coton Manor   Cottesbrooke Hall   A14   Ouse   A14
Packwood House   A46   Gardens   **30**   **Northamptonshire**   Wellingborough   A1
A4177   M45   **29**   **31**   A43   Rushden   A14
Warwick   **Royal**   Holdenby House Gardens   A45   A428   St Neots   **Cambridge**
Leamington Spa   A425   Daventry   **Northampton**   A428   A11
Warwickshire   Canons Ashby House   A428   **Bedford**   St Neots
46   Stratford-   A423   **41**   Towcester   A509   Sandy   A505   Royston
dpeckers   upon-Avon   M40   **28**   A508   A421   A6   A505   **Essex**
44   Farnborough Hall   **33** Sulgrave Manor   A5   **Bedfordshire**   M11
43 Upton House   A43   Banbury   Brackley   A421   A6   Letchworth   A10   Bishop's   Stansted
A429   Chipping   Buckingham   **Milton Keynes**   M1   A505   Stortford
estershire   Norton   Bicester   A5   **Luton** ✈ **Stevenage**   A120
Stow-on-the-Wold   **Oxfordshire**   **Buckinghamshire**   Luton   A1(M)   A602
A40   Burford   A44   A34   A41   A418   **Hertfordshire**
A40   Kidlington ▼Oxford   Aylesbury   London▼   London▼   Hertford   London▼

University Botanic Garden

An Edwardian Arts & Crafts garden and a national rose collection close to Birmingham University campus. Map reference ❸

Winterbourne, 58 Edgbaston Park Road, B15 2TT, Birmingham; tel: 0121 4144944. < www.botanic.bham.ac.uk >
National Collection: *History of the Rose.*
Opening times: *all year (except BHs, Easter and Christmas) Mon–Fri 11am–4pm. National Garden Scheme days every Thur. Parties/coaches accepted. House closed.*

contain a large collection of unusual plants – species that would have been available in the mid-1700s – and a 19th-century holly maze, the mirror image of the maze at Hampton Court. There is an elegant summerhouse and greenhouse standing at each end of the broad Holly Walk.

In the formal vegetable garden, numerous historic varieties of vegetables and herbs are grown, including unusual ones like the Black "Congo" potato and the white carrot. There are many trained fruit trees, too, including apple, pear, apricot, fig and cherry.

History: The hall was built in 1599 by Sir Edward Devereaux and extended by Sir John Bridgeman about a century later. The baroque gardens were designed by Captain William Winde (died 1772) and George London and Henry Wise (designers of the Hampton Court maze), while the architect and garden designer Batty Langley (1696–1751), author of *New Principles of Gardening* (1728), was responsible for the vegetable garden. The gardens, which were developed over the years by successive generations of the Bridgeman family, were restored by the Castle Bromwich Hall Garden Trust in 1985.

Accommodation: Hyatt Regency Hotel (tel: 0121 6431234: ££££); Jonathans, Oldbury, Birmingham (tel: 0121 4293757; £££); New Hall Thistle Hotel, Sutton Coldfield (tel: 0121 3782442; £££).
Local pubs: Bradford Arms, Chester Road, Castle Bromwich.

ABOVE: exuberant natural planting, Castle Bromwich Hall.

RIGHT: the University Botanical Garden.

Admission prices: *adults £2, children free.*
Facilities: *parking, disabled access, plants for sale on selected days, refreshments. No picnics. No dogs.*

The Botanic Garden at Winterbourne occupies an attractive, gently sloping site quite close to the centre of Birmingham University campus. Beyond it lie the woodlands and lake of Edgbaston Park, an area of natural beauty, part of which is a nature reserve supervised by the Birmingham Natural History Society.

The Edwardian Arts & Crafts-style garden covers 6 acres (1.9 hectares) and com-

Map: pages 208–9

bines themed gardens and plant collections ranging from scree gardens to herbaceous borders, a perennial meadow, a bog garden, a nut walk and an arboretum. The rose plantings in the Walled Garden, which document the history of the rose from remote times to the present day, have now been registered with the NCCPG as a national rose collection.

History: Winterbourne House, also in the Arts & Crafts style, was built in 1903 by J.S. Nettlefold (of the Birmingham metal merchants Guest, Keen and Nettlefold). The gardens were designed by his wife, Margaret (née Chamberlain). The property was bequeathed to the university in 1943.

The Botanic Garden was later built up as a focus for the horticultural teaching courses provided by the university's School of Education.

Accommodation: Hyatt Regency Hotel (tel: 0121 6431234; ££££); Jonathans, Oldbury, Birmingham (tel: 0121 4293757; £££); New Hall Thistle Hotel, Sutton Coldfield (tel: 0121 378 2442; £££).

CHESHIRE

A famous Japanese garden at Tatton Park, a splendid orangery at Lyme Park, the National Collection of willows at Ness Botanic Garden, a Humphry Repton landscape at Rode Hall and the award-winning gardens of Arley Hall are among the horticultural highlights of Cheshire.

Arley Hall & Gardens

Award-winning gardens, created by generations of the same family. Famous for its herbaceous borders. English Heritage Grade II*. Map reference ❹

Great Budworth, Northwich CW9 6NA, Cheshire; tel: 01565 777353.
Opening times: garden: Apr–Sep Tues–Sun and BH Mons 11am–5pm, Oct weekends 11am–5pm. National Garden Scheme days. Parties/coaches accepted by appointment (min. 15 people). House: Tues & Sun noon–4.30pm.
Admission prices: adults £4.50, children, £2.25, over-60s £3.90, family £11.25, season £19.
Facilities: parking, disabled access, shop, plants for sale, refreshments. Picnics permitted. Dogs allowed on leads. Specialist tours, garden courses, garden lectures.

O verlooking a beautiful park, the award-winning gardens of Arley Hall have been created by successive generations of the same family. Features include the double herbaceous borders, first laid out in 1846, the pleached Lime Avenue, the avenue of *Quercus ilex*, fine yew hedges and topiary. There is also a good collection of shrub roses, rhododendrons and azaleas, as well as walled gardens and a herb garden.

Lastly, the Grove is a more informal area, with spring bulbs, a large collection of rhododendrons and azaleas and other flowering shrubs and trees.

History: The earliest records of Arley gardens appear on a map of 1744. When Sir Peter and Lady Elizabeth Warburton lived here (from 1743) they built the first walled gardens and laid out a large pleasure ground of shrubberies and walks on the east side of the house. In 1846 Rowland and Mary Egerton-Warburton created the garden that

BELOW: the double herbaceous borders at the award-winning Arley Hall Gardens.

we see today. The double herbaceous border was laid out in that year, long before William Robinson made such borders popular. The Rootree was also created at this time, an area of stumps and rocks popular in the Victorian period; as were the Furlong Walk and Tea Cottage garden (so named for the tea parties held here). It was Rowland's love of trees that led him to create the pleached lime avenue and other avenues on the estate.

In 1900 Antoinette Egerton-Warburton, Rowland's daughter-in-law, created the Flag Garden as an enclosed sanctum featuring roses, lavender and other fragrant plants. In 1930 the Fish Garden, with a small central pond, was created, taking the place of a former bowling green.

*Accommodation: Hanover International, Stretton (tel: 01925 730706; £££); Cottons, Knutsford (tel: 01565 650333: £££). **Local pubs:** The Thorn, Appleton; George and Dragon, Great Budworth.*

BELOW: rhododendrons and azaleas flourish at Hare Hill Gardens.

Hare Hill Gardens

A woodland garden with splendid rhododendrons and a large collection of unusual hollies. National Trust. Map reference ❺

Over Alderley, Macclesfield SK10 4QB, Cheshire; tel: 01625 828981.
< www.nationaltrust.org.uk >
Opening times: Apr–Oct Wed–Thur, weekends plus BH Mons 10am–5.30pm; mid–late May daily (for rhododendrons and azaleas). Parties/coaches accepted by written appointment or by telephoning Gardener-in-Charge (tel: 01625 828981). House closed.
Admission prices: adults £2.75, children £1.50 (car-park charge of £1.50 is refundable on entry to garden).
Facilities: parking. No refreshments. No picnics. No dogs.

Hare Hill estate consists principally of rolling parkland. The gardens were created in the 1820s but their present form is due chiefly to a 20th-century owner, Colonel Charles Brocklehurst, who was a great rhododendron enthusiast. He steadily introduced them into the gardens from 1960 onwards and the climate and soil have allowed them to flourish here. The National Trust has replaced many of the common purple variety with more colourful and exotic varieties and has extended the season for visiting the garden by planting roses, lacecaps, eucryphia and hydrangeas, and early interest is sustained by snowdrops, daffodils, a huge *Clematis montana*, skunk cabbage and magnolia.

The main feature of the garden, however, is the collection of more than 50 hollies, including silver- and golden-leaved and yellow- and orange-berried varieties, plus the rare Highclere holly.

History: Hare Hill was owned by Colonel Charles Brocklehurst, who was advised in horticultural matters by the plantsman James Russell. The colonel presented the estate to the National Trust in 1978, three years before his death.

*Accommodation: Dog Inn, Over Peover (tel: 01625 861421; ££). **Local pubs:** Sutton Hall, Sutton Lane Ends, 2 miles (3 km) south of Macclesfield; Bells of Peover, Lower Peover.*

Map:
pages
208–9

Lyme Park

A sunken Dutch Garden, a splendid orangery and a collection of Vicary Gibbs plants. English Heritage Grade II*. National Trust. Map reference ❻

Disley, Stockport SK12 2NX, Cheshire; tel: 01663 762023/766492; fax: 01663 765035. < www.nationaltrust.org.uk >
Opening times: *garden: Apr–Oct Fri–Tues 11am–5pm, Wed–Thur 1–5pm, Nov–mid-Dec weekends noon–3pm. Parties/coaches accepted. View by appointment. House: Apr–Oct Fri–Tues 1–5pm plus BH Mons 11am–5pm.*
Admission prices: *house & garden: adults £5.50, children £2.25; house: adults £4, children £2; garden: £2.50, children £1.20.*
Facilities: *parking, disabled access, shop, plants for sale, refreshments. Picnics permitted. Dogs allowed on leads.*

Some 15 acres (6 hectares) of garden and parkland surround Lyme Park, one of England's best-preserved Palladian houses. Of particular note, to the west of the

house, is the vast sunken Dutch Garden, which, although destroyed in a flood in 1973, has been restored to the original design, with a central fountain and intricate seasonal plantings edged in ivy.

The orangery, designed by Lewis Wyatt in 1815 and remade by Alfred Derbyshire in 1865, contains a fig tree and two spectacular camellias. It is fronted by terrace beds displaying *Penstemon rubicundus*, first raised at Lyme in 1906. There is a smaller Sunken Garden to the north commemorating the renowned gardener Vicary Gibbs.

The garden features a large lake designed to reflect the view of the house and numerous fine trees lead the eye to the Lanthorn Tower folly. Rhododendrons, azaleas and ferns abound in the area known as Killtime. A deer park of almost 1,400 acres (565 hectares) surrounds the property.

History: Owned for almost 600 years by the Legh family, the original house was Tudor but was rebuilt to an Italianate design by Giacomo Leoni in the early 18th century.

Accommodation: Waltzing Weasel, Birch Vale, near Hayfield (tel: 01663 743402; ££).
Local pub: The Sportsman, Hayfield.

ABOVE: the sunken Dutch Garden at Lyme Park.

Ness Botanic Gardens

The botanic gardens include temperate, arid and tropical glasshouses, an orchid display and the national collection of willows. English Heritage Grade II. Map reference ❼

University of Liverpool, Neston Road, Ness CH64 4AY, Cheshire; tel: 0151 3530123; fax: 0151 3531004. < www.merseyworld.com/nessgardens >

National Collection: willows.
Opening times: daily except Christmas Day, Mar–Oct 9.30am–5pm; Nov–Feb 9.30am–4pm. Parties/coaches accepted, preferably by appointment. House closed.
Admission prices: adults £4.70 (winter rate £3.70), accompanied children under 18 free, over-60s £4.30; 10 percent discount for parties of 20 + . Friends annual membership: single adult £20, double £35 (concessions: single £17, double £30).
Facilities: parking, disabled access, shop, plants for sale, refreshments. Picnics permitted. No dogs allowed.

ABOVE: Ness Botanic Garden.

Entering Ness Botanic Garden, the first thing visitors encounter is the Jubilee Garden and the sorbus lawn featuring what was once one of only three *Sorbus forestii* in the country. After the conservatory, with acacias and a group of *Echium pininana*, comes the rhododendron border and the historically important specimen lawn with magnolia, sorbus and *Pieris formosa forrestii*, all from the 19th-century golden age of plant collecting.

The glasshouses are divided into temperate, arid and tropical zones and include displays of orchids. Other features include a rose garden, azalea border and herbaceous area, a heather garden, rock garden, woodland garden, water garden and arboretum. On the perimeter of the grounds is the willow collection.

History: Arthur Kilpin Bulley, a Liverpool seed merchant, set about creating the garden in 1898. He was interested in introducing new plant species from abroad and in particular believed that Himalayan and Chinese mountain plants could be established in Britain. He tested this by sponsoring numerous expeditions to the Far East and thereby launched the careers of renowned plant collectors such as George Forrest and Frank Kingdon Ward. Some of his rhododendron and camellia introductions were used for hybridisation; this, together with his propagation programme, resulted in his company, Bees Ltd, offering newly introduced species to the public from 1911.

Accommodation: Britannia Adelphi Hotel, Liverpool (tel: 0151 709 7200; ££–££££). Local pub: Fox and Hounds, Barnston.

Norton Priory Museum and Gardens

Woodland garden with a walled garden, a sculpture trail and the National Collection of tree quinces. Map reference ❽

The Norton Priory Museum Trust, Tudor Road, Manor Park, Runcorn WA7 1SX, Cheshire; tel: 01928-569895. < www.nortonpriory.org >

Rode Hall

A formal garden and a walled kitchen garden, set in a Humphry Repton landscape. English Heritage Grade II. Map reference ❾

Map: pages 208–9

Church Lane, Scholar Green, Stoke-on-Trent ST7 3QP, Cheshire; tel: 01270 882961; fax: 01270 882962.
Opening times: Apr–Sep Tues–Thur and BH Mons. National Garden Scheme days. Parties/coaches accepted. Viewing by appointment. House open Wed 2–5pm.
Admission prices: house & garden: adults £5, children & over-60s £3; garden: adults £3, children & over-60s £2; season (garden only) £15, over-60s £12.
Facilities: parking, plants for sale, refreshments (teas). No picnics. No disabled access. Dogs allowed on leads.

National Collection: Cydonia oblonga (tree quince).
Opening times: Apr–Oct Mon–Fri noon–5pm, Sat–Sun and BH Mon noon–6pm; Nov–Mar noon–4pm; walled garden: Apr–Oct daily 1.30–4.30pm (guided tours only by prior appointment). National Garden Scheme day. Parties/coaches accepted. House closed.
Admission prices: adults £3.95, children £2.75, over-60s £2.75, family £10.
Facilities: parking, disabled access, shop, plants for sale, refreshments. Picnics permitted. Dogs allowed on leads.

The gardens are set in 38 acres (15 hectares) of tranquil woodland and contain the excavated remains of the 800-year-old priory and a purpose-built museum. The St Christopher statue – one of the great treasures of medieval Europe, and over 600 years old – is displayed in a special gallery. The garden itself has a sculpture trail, attractive arbours, some made of apple trees, and an award-winning walled garden with the National Collection of tree quinces, herbs, roses, vegetables and fruit.

History: The Augustinian priory was founded in the 13th century and survived for 400 years. The property was acquired by the Brooke family in the early 17th century. They built the walled garden between 1757 and 1770 as a kitchen garden to provide fresh produce for the mansion.

Accommodation: Daresbury Park Hotel (tel: 01925 267331; £££). Local pub: Ring O' Bells, Daresbury.

Rode Hall gardens are set in a landscape designed by Humphry Repton in 1790. In February, the garden is a delight, with snowdrops, hellebores and early varieties of rhododendrons. From early April, the woodland garden, which includes a terraced rock garden and a grotto, is full of rhododendrons and azaleas, and bluebells and lily of the valley are in abundance. The old stew pond is the background to a water garden planted with hostas and primulas. The formal garden, dating from

ABOVE LEFT: on the sculpture trail at Norton Priory Gardens.

BELOW: Rode Hall's woodland garden.

the 19th century, has herbaceous borders and roses set in a garden of clipped yews and gravel paths still faithful to the original design. The large, walled kitchen garden is home to numerous varieties of prize-winning gooseberries.

History: The kitchen garden was probably built in the 1750s when the main house was completed. In 1800 John Webb was commissioned to complete the work recommended by Repton; this took about a decade and included the creation of Rode Pool and the terraced rock garden. The formal garden was designed by W. Nesfield in 1860.

*Accommodation: Manor House, Alsager (tel: 01270 884000; ££–£££). **Local pubs:** Bleeding Wolf, Scholar Green; Egerton Arms, Astbury.*

Tatton Park

One of the top Japanese gardens in Britain sits within 1,000 acres of park-land. English Heritage Grade II*. National Trust. Map reference ⑩

Knutsford WA16 6QN, Cheshire; tel: 01625 534400; fax: 01625 534400. < www.tattonpark.org.uk >
Opening times: *garden: all year except Christmas Day, Apr–Oct Tues–Sun 10.30am–6pm, Nov–Mar 11am–4pm. Parties/coaches accepted by appointment (tel: 01623 534428). House: Apr–Oct Tues–Sun.*

ABOVE: the formal terraced garden at Tatton Park.

Admission prices: *adults £3, children £2, family £8, group rates for 12 +.*
Park: £3.60 per car.
Facilities: *parking, disabled access, shop, plants for sale, refreshments. Picnics permitted. Dogs allowed on leads in park; only guide dogs in gardens.*

Tatton Park's 50 acres (20 hectares) of grounds are among the finest historic gardens in England. They are well known for their rhododendrons and azaleas and for their Japanese gardens, fully restored in 2001 to the original 1913 design. The grounds also include an Italian garden, a maze, topiary, small lakes, an Edwardian rose garden, herbaceous borders and buildings for tropical ferns and orange trees. The walled kitchen garden has been renovated.

History: The neoclassical mansion was home to the Egerton family for over 200 years. It contains masterpieces by Canaletto and Van Dyck and original furniture by Gillows of Lancaster. Lewis Wyatt built the orangery and other renowned designers, including Joseph Paxton (1801–65), best known for his work at Chatsworth, were responsible for designing the gardens and associated buildings. The property is set in 1,000 acres (400 hectares) of parkland with herds of red and fallow deer.

*Accommodation: Cottons Hotel, Knutsford (tel: 01565 650333; £££). **Local pubs:** The Thorn, Appleton; George and Dragon, Great Budworth.*

DERBYSHIRE

Derbyshire is rich in historic gardens, from the rolling acres of Chatsworth, to the Le Nôtre influences at Melbourne Hall, and Robert Adam touches at Kedleston Hall. But the new garden at Dam Farm should not be overlooked, nor should the wonderful roses at Renishaw Hall.

Map: pages 208–9

Calke Abbey

Late 18th-century garden surrounded by woods, pastures and lakes. English Heritage Grade II*. National Trust. Map reference ⓫

Ticknall DE73 1LE, Derbyshire; tel: 01332 863822; fax: 01332 865272. < www.nationaltrust.org >
Opening times: garden & church: Apr–Oct Sat–Wed and BH Mons 11am–5.30pm; house: 1–5.30pm; park: all year daily till 9pm (or dusk if earlier). National Garden Scheme days. Parties/coaches accepted.
Admission prices: house & garden: adults £5.60, children £2.80, family £14; garden: adults £3.20, children £1.60, family £8.
Facilities: parking, disabled access, refreshments. Picnics permitted. No dogs.

I n the late 18th century the flower and kitchen gardens at Calke Abbey were moved away from the house to enable it to sit in a more natural landscape, with the result that the ancient woods, pasture and lakes provide a tranquil setting for the house. The pleasure ground has been renovated and planted with wild flowers and bulbs. Lady Crewe's Garden has been restored and the curious design of 22 small beds in the lawn planted with annuals and exotics, such as cordylines and chusan palms.

An extraordinary "Auricula Theatre" for displaying auriculas and other summer pot plants, is located in the northwest corner of the garden, giving these plants, which belong to the primula family, plenty of fresh air, while shading them from rain and noon-day sun. The physic garden, now a working kitchen garden with an assortment of

frames, hot beds and glasshouses, and the vinery, have also been restored. The gardener's bothy, with its collection of original tools and seed cabinet, is also interesting.

History: Calke Abbey was the home of the eccentric and reclusive Harpur-Crewe family from 1622. The Rev. Harpur-Crewe,

who died in 1883, was a notable gardener and plant collector and rector of Drayton Beauchamp in Buckinghamshire. A yellow wallflower named after him, Cheiranthus Harpur Crewe, is grown here.

Accommodation: Limeyard Stables, Ticknall (tel: 01332 864802; £). Local pub: John Thompson, Ingleby.

Chatsworth

Grand country estate where Joseph Paxton worked as head gardener. English Heritage Grade I. Map reference ⓬

Bakewell, Derbyshire DE45 1PP, Derby; tel: 01246 582204; fax: 01246 583536;

ABOVE: the auricula theatre at Calke Abbey.

style between 1686 and 1707. The park was landscaped by the fourth Duke, who was resident here from 1720–64, and who commissioned Capability Brown to transform the formal garden into a more natural one. In the 19th century, the sixth Duke engaged Joseph Paxton as head gardener; he was responsible for the Emperor fountain, the glasshouses and the now-demolished Great Conservatory. Both house and garden remain little changed since that time.

Accommodation: Cavendish Hotel, Baslow (tel: 01246 582311; ££££); Riber Hall, Matlock (tel: 01629 582795; ££££). *Local pubs:* Eyre Arms, Hassop; Packhorse Inn, Little Longstone; Devonshire Arms, Pilsley.

< www.chatsworth.org >
Opening times: mid-Mar–Oct, daily 11am–6pm. Parties/coaches accepted. Viewing by appointment. House open.
Admission prices: garden: adults £4.50, children £2, over-60s £3.50, season £11.
Facilities: parking, disabled access. shop, plants for sale, refreshments. Picnics permitted. Dogs allowed.

Temples, sculptures, fountains, bridges, streams, cascades and ponds abound in this 1,000-acre (400-hectare) park on the banks of the River Derwent. The gardens are set in a 100-acre (40-hectare) area mainly to the south and west of the house, with the spectacular Emperor fountain ascending to 275 ft (84 metres) as the centrepiece. The highest gravity-fed fountain in the world, it emerges in the canal which leads from the house and is the foreground to a beautiful vista of the Derbyshire hills, opened up by Capability Brown.

Other features include a mature yew maze, the cottage garden and an impressive rockery. The Old Conservatory Garden, kitchen garden and colour-matched borders will give endless pleasure, as will the arboretum, pinetum and beech hedges.

History: The first Duke of Devonshire rebuilt the 16th-century house in classsical

ABOVE:
Chatsworth
gardens,
unchanged
since the
19th century.

Dam Farm House

A relatively new garden with some bold planting, rare varieties and an arboretum. Map reference ⓭

Yeldersley Lane, Ednaston, Ashbourne DE6 3BA, Derbyshire; tel: 01335 360291.
Opening times: selected days in Apr, Jun, Aug & Sep. National Garden Scheme days. Parties/coaches accepted. Viewing also by appointment Apr–Oct. House closed.
Admission prices: adults £3, children free
Facilities: parking, plants for sale, refreshments. Picnics permitted. No disabled access. No dogs.

The garden at Dam Farm House began as a field in 1980 and has been developed over the years. It is designed as a series of rooms, each consisting of mixed borders and shrubs surrounded by beech and yew hedges, including a "tapestry" hedge. A scree garden in front of the house provides colour all year. There are a number of rare plants, and a semi-mature arboretum.

History: This is is still a young garden in which the plants and trees are gradually maturing.

Accommodation: *Callow Hall, Ashbourne (tel: 01335 343403; £££–££££); Omnia Somnia, Ashbourne (tel: 01335 300145; ££).*
Local pubs: *Red Lion, Hollington; Shoulder of Mutton, Osmaston.*

Elvaston Castle Country Park

A winter garden, based on a 19th-century design, with tender specimen trees. English Heritage Grade II*. Map reference ⓴

Borrowash Road, Elvaston DE72 3EP, Derbyshire; tel: 01332 571342; fax: 01332 758751.

Opening times: *park: all year daily 9am–dusk; Old English Garden: summer 10am–5pm, winter 10am–3.30pm. Parties/coaches accepted. House closed.*
Admission prices: *free (small charge for car park).*
Facilities: *parking, disabled access, shop, refreshments. Picnics permitted. Dogs allowed on leads.*

Based on the remains of the formal garden designed by William Barron in the 1830s for the fourth Earl of Harrington, the grounds of Elvaston Castle comprise 200 acres (81 hectares) of avenues and gardens. It has a winter theme, as Barron intended, with numerous conifers,

including yew, sequoia and fir trees. The Old English Garden is a modern walled garden with herbaceous borders, a herb garden and exotic trees. The four main avenues are lined with trees from around the world.

History: Barron came to Elvaston in 1830 and, after a programme of tree clearing, created a 16-acre (6.5-hectare) pinetum. Barron got on well with Lord Harrington, whom he described as "a nobleman, every inch of him. He never treated me like a servant, but more as a brother." Their partnership lasted until the Earl's death in 1850.

Map: pages 208–9

Accommodation: *Marriott Breadsall Priory Country Club, Morley (tel: 01332 832235; ££–£££); Midland Hotel, Derby (tel: 01332 345894; £££).* **Local pubs:** *Old Crown, Cavendish Bridge; Malt Shovel, Shardlow.*

Haddon Hall

The riverside gardens of a medieval hall. English Heritage Grade I. Map reference ⓯

Bakewell, DE45 1LA, Derbyshire; tel: 01629 812855.
< www.haddonhall.co.uk >
Opening times: *garden: Apr–Sep daily 10.30am–5pm, Oct Thur–Sun 10.30am–4.30pm. National Garden Scheme days. Parties/coaches accepted. Viewing by appointment. House open same hours as garden.*

LEFT: one of the great avenues at Elvaston Castle Country Park.

BELOW: Haddon Hall's gardens are known for their roses.

Admission prices: *adults £7.25, children (5–16) £3.75, over-60s £6.25, family £19.* **Facilities:** *parking, shop, refreshments. No picnics. No disabled access. No dogs.*

The grounds at Haddon Hall consist of a series of terraced, stone-walled gardens overlooking the River Wye. They are best known for their collection of roses, including ramblers, hybrid teas and many others, both old varieties and new. The garden also features splendid old yew trees and strongly planted borders, in which the delphiniums are outstanding.

History: Haddon Hall is a castellated Elizabethan house with thick stone walls. The neo-Tudor gardens were reconstructed, and the roses planted by the ninth Duchess of Rutland in the early 20th century.

Accommodation: *Cavendish Hotel, Baslow (tel: 01246 582311; ££££); Riber Hall, Matlock (tel: 01629 582795; ££££).* **Local pubs:** *Eyre Arms, Hassop; Packhorse Inn, Little Longstone; Devonshire Arms, Pilsley.*

Kedleston Hall

BELOW: ancient trees shade a walled corner at Kedleston Hall.

Massive rhododendrons, ancient trees and a Robert Adam orangery. English Heritage Grade I. National Trust. Map reference 🔟

Kedleston, Derby, DE22 5JH, Derby; tel: 01332 842191.

< www.nationaltrust.org.uk >
Opening times: *garden: end Mar–Oct, daily 10am–6pm. National Garden Scheme day. Parties/coaches accepted. House open Sat–Wed noon–4.30pm.* **Admission prices:** *house, park & gardens: adults £5.50, children £2.70, family £13.70; park & gardens: adults £2.50, children £1.20.* **Facilities:** *parking, disabled access,.shop, plants for sale, refreshments. Picnics permitted. Dogs allowed on leads.*

The gardens lie immediately to the south and west of Kedleston Hall and contain a mixture of expansive lawns, massive rhododendrons and ancient trees with newly created beds, all designed to complement the grandeur of the house and parkland. At the western end the Long Walk – a 3-mile (5-km) woodland and glade circuit – is currently undergoing extensive work to restore it to its semi-natural splendour. Bold plantings have been introduced to existing beds and there are new beds where evergreens predominate. The subtle mix of colours is one of the pleasures of the gardens; and the spring show of snowdrops, daffodils and bluebells, heralding the blazing colour of rhododendrons and azaleas in May and June, are stunning.

History: Kedleston Hall is a neoclassical palace designed by Robert Adam (1728–92) for the Curzon family. The gardens were landscaped at the same time and Adam designed the orangery and summerhouse.

Accommodation: *Kedleston Country House Hotel (tel: 01332 559202; ££).* **Local pubs:** *Cock Inn, Mugginton; Black Swan, Idridgehay.*

Melbourne Hall Gardens

A splendid 18th-century garden, influenced by Le Nôtre. English Heritage Grade I. Map reference 🔟

Melbourne DE73 1EN, Derby; tel: 01332 862502; fax: 01332 862263.

designer Le Nôtre, have been restored in the formal style of the time. Today, it is regarded as an exemplary 18th-century garden.

Accommodation: Park Farmhouse Hotel, Castle Donington (tel: 01332 862409; ££). **Local pubs:** *The Packhorse, Kings Newton; The Lamb, Melbourne.*

Renishaw Hall

Romantic garden famed for its roses.
English Heritage Grade II*.
Map reference ⑱

Renishaw, nr Sheffield S21 3WB, Derbyshire; tel: 01246 432310; fax: 01246 430760. < www.sitwell.co.uk >
National Collection: *yuccas.*
Opening times: *Apr–Sep Fri–Sun & BH Mons 10.30am–4.30pm. National Garden Scheme days. Parties/coaches accepted. Viewing by appointment. House open by appointment only.*
Admission prices: *adults £3.50, children free, over-60s £2.50, season £20.*
Facilities: *parking, disabled access, shop, plants for sale, refreshments. Picnics permitted. Dogs allowed on leads.*

LEFT: 18th-century statuary at Melbourne Hall Gardens.

BELOW: water lilies at romantic Renishaw.

Opening times: *gardens: Apr–Sep Wed, weekends & BH Mons 1.30–5.30pm. Parties/coaches accepted. Viewing by appointment. House open in Aug.*
Admission prices: *adults £3, children (5–15) £2, over-60s £2, family £8.*
Facilities: *shop, refreshments. No parking. No picnics. No disabled access. No dogs.*

Renishaw is an oasis of beauty and the arts in an area dominated by industry and mining. The gardens are divided into 12 by yew hedges, each garden having its own character. There are three rose gardens containing historic varieties under-

The garden retains its original style and layout, and features avenues leading to statuary, fountains, a grotto, lime palisades and a series of terraces leading down to a lake called the Great Basin. There is also, at the end of a long yew walk, a rare, wrought-iron birdcage arbour.

History: The original design of the garden dates from 1704, reflecting the enthusiasm of Thomas Coke when he inherited the property in 1696. The walks, vistas and statuary, much favoured in the early 18th century, and influenced by French

planted with clematis, peonies, lilies and geraniums, interplanted with shrubs. Lush herbaceous borders flank the middle lawn, which leads to the White Garden and the Ballroom Garden containing blue, yellow and white flowers. There is also a secret garden with a pocket handkerchief tree and an Indian bean tree. These, and the wealth of roses (over 1,000) make Renishaw a particularly romantic garden.

The south-facing Bottom Terrace in which rare and tender shrubs and flowers flourish, is in marked contrast to the Fishpond Garden, where water, yew hedges and grass have been laid out with geometric precision.

To either side of the formal gardens there are walks through a more natural landscape; one of these leads to Renishaw's three lakes.

History: The formal garden was laid out in 1895 by Sir George Sitwell (1860–1943) in the classical Italianate style. In 1909 he published *On the Making of Gardens*, attacking Augustan formalism in garden design. He was ambitious in the changes that he made. His eldest son Osbert said of him: "He abolished small hills, created lakes and particularly liked to alter the levels at which full grown trees were standing. Two old yew trees in front of the dining-room window at Renishaw were regularly heightened and lowered; a process which I believe could have been shown to chart, like a thermometer, the temperature of his mood."

Accommodation: Sitwell Arms, Renishaw (tel: 01246 435226; ££). Local pub: The Mossbrook, Eckington.

HEREFORDSHIRE & WORCESTERSHIRE

There is something for everyone here, from the stylish modern gardens at Burford House, which hold a National Collection of clematis, to the cottage garden delights at Eastgrove; a plantsman's paradise at Stone House Cottage Garden and Nursery; and some of the finest rhododendrons in the country, along with record trees, at Hergest Croft.

Burford House Gardens

BELOW: fluid design at Burford House Gardens.

A modern garden with good herbaceous borders and a National Collection of clematis. Map reference ❿

Tenbury Wells WR15 8HQ, Worcs; tel: 01584 810777; fax: 01584 810673.
National Collection: Clematis.
Opening times: all year daily 10am–5pm. Parties/coaches accepted. House closed.
Admission prices: adults £3.95, children £1, over-60s £3.50; season: single £10, family £17.50.
Facilities: parking, disabled access, shop, plants for sale, including clematis, refreshments, garden centre. Picnics permitted. Dogs allowed on leads only in car park and garden centre.

The stylish 7-acre (2.8-hectare) garden at Burford was created to complement the handsome Georgian house, and has now reached maturity. The fluid design is enhanced by interesting plants, imaginatively used and comprehensively labelled. There is a good collection of roses as well as herbaceous borders and a pleasing series of water gardens. But clematis is what Burford is best known for. Its National Collection comprises some 350 varieties, all cleverly trained and displayed among shrubs as well as in the new clematis maze near the coach house.

There are more new developments on the other side of the river, too, with bulbs and wild flower plantings.

History: The garden was originally designed by John Treasure in the 1950s. Charles Chesshire, the current designer, is renewing and reordering some of the planting, with excellent early results.

Accommodation: Court Farm, Tenbury Wells (tel: 01885 410265; £). Local pubs: Peacock Inn, Boraston; Roebuck Inn, Brimfield.

Eastgrove Cottage Garden

A delightful cottage garden, created by the owners over the past 30 years. Map reference ㉔

Sankyns Green, Shrawley, Little Witley, WR6 6LQ, Worcs; tel: 01299 896389. < www.eastgrove.co.uk > Opening times: mid-Apr–Jul Thur–Sun & BH Mons 2–5pm; Sep–mid-Oct Thur–Sat. National Garden Scheme days. Parties/coaches accepted. Viewing by appointment. House closed. Admission prices: adults £3, children free. Facilities: parking, disabled access, plants for sale, refreshments. Picnics permitted in car park only. No dogs.

This perfumed garden surrounds a 17th-century, half-timbered farmhouse. The beds and borders are bursting with old cottage-garden favourites – tumbling roses, pinks, violas, aquilegias, irises and lavender, to name but a few. Full of flowing curves, the whole is held together by a meticulously clipped *Lonicera nitida* hedge. This is the backbone of the flower garden and leads into the Secret Garden, with a carefully chosen colour theme of pink, mauve, silver and burgundy. A rose tunnel leads to the so-called Great Wall of China, a raised bed where unusual rock and alpine plants hold sway.

There are short mown paths leading into the small arboretum known as The Glade and then to the The Grove, which blends beautifully with the surrounding countryside. There is more sophisticated planting around the splendid 40-ft (13-m) long timber and brick medieval barn. Several parts of the garden are linked by brick paths, and the whole is surrounded by 5 acres (2 hectares) of unspoilt meadow and woodland.

Accommodation: Crown and Sandys Arms, Ombersley (tel: 01905 620252; ££). Local pub: Whitley Court (English Heritage).

Aʙᴏᴠᴇ: at Eastgrove wisteria forms a backdrop to the cottage-garden favourites.

Hergest Croft Gardens

One of the finest gardens in the country for rhododendrons and rare and record trees. English Heritage Grade II*. Map reference **㉑**

Kington HR5 3EG, Herefordshire; tel/fax: 01544 230160. < www.hergest.co.uk >
National Collection: *Maples, Birches and Zelkova.*

RIGHT: brick folly at Stone House Cottage.

Opening times: *Apr & Jul–Oct daily 12.30–5.30pm, May & Jun daily noon–6pm. Parties/coaches accepted. Viewing by appointment. House closed.*
Admission prices: *adults £4, children free, season £15.*

BELOW: Hergest Croft Gardens have splendid colour throughout the year.

Facilities: *parking, disabled access, shop, plants for sale, refreshments. No picnics. Dogs allowed on leads.*

From spring bulbs to autumn colour, this is a garden for all seasons. With over 60 record trees and shrubs, and numerous rare species, Hergest Croft Gardens are recognised to have one of the best collections of plants held in private ownership. The rhododendrons and azaleas are spectacular in spring, and the large kitchen garden, with the long, double herbaceous borders, rose garden and spring borders are a great attraction. In autumn, the colours are superb.

History: The garden was designed by William Hartland Banks (1867–1930) and his wife Dorothy Alford, beginning in 1896. They used no professional help but were influenced by the writings of William Robinson, especially *The English Garden.*

Accommodation: Harp Inn, Old Radnor (tel: 01544 350655; ££–£££). **Local pubs:** *Stagg Inn, Titley; Harp Inn, Old Radnor.*

Stone House Cottage Garden and Nursery

A garden for plantsmen, with unusual climbers, herbaceous plants and roses. Map reference **㉒**

Stone, Kidderminster DY10 4BG, Worcs; tel: 01562 69902; fax: 01562 69960. < www.shcn.co.uk >
Opening times: *Mar–Sep Wed–Sat 10am–5.30pm. Parties/coaches accepted. Viewing by appointment. House closed.*
Admission prices: *adults £2.50, children free.*
Facilities: *parking, disabled access, plants for sale. No refreshments. Picnics permitted. No dogs.*

Set in an old walled kitchen garden, this is a romantic place, as well as a delight for plantsmen. The area is only ¾ acre (0.3 hectares) but seems much larger. Hedges divide it into different compartments, thereby creating diverse habitats in which to grow the vast selection of rare and unusual plants for which the garden and nursery are renowned. Mellow brick walls and follies are attractive in themselves and are covered with roses and the many other climbing and hanging plants in which Stone House specialises. In the adjoining nursery you can buy plants of almost all the species found in the garden. The list of shrubs and climbers includes many that are rarely available in this country.

Map: pages 208–9

Accommodation: Stone Manor Hotel, Stone (tel: 01562 777555; £££–££££); Brockencote Hall, Chaddesley Corbett (tel: 01562 777876; £££).
Local pubs: The Dog, Harrington; Little Packhorse, Bewdley; Horse and Jockey, Far Forest.

LEICESTERSHIRE

Visitors flock to Long Close for its wonderful display of rhododendrons and azaleas, planted in the 1930s; and to the formal, modern garden at Orchards, where the emphasis is on form and texture.

Long Close

A modern garden surrounding a 17th-century house, with rhododendrons and azaleas, a snowdrop tree and a collection of penstemons. Map reference ㉓

60 Main Street, Woodhouse Eaves, Loughborough LE12 8RZ, Leics; tel: 01509 890616 (9am–5pm).
Opening times: Mar–Jul and Sep–Oct Mon–Sat 9.30am–1pm & 2–5.30pm; tickets from Pene Craft Gift shop, opposite garden. National Garden Scheme day. Parties/coaches accepted. Viewing by appointment. House closed.
Admission prices: adults £2.50, children free.
Facilities: parking, disabled access, shop, plants for sale, refreshments. Picnics permitted. Dogs allowed on leads.

The garden at Long Close lies behind the house, which is the oldest in the village, and leads via a series of three terraces down to an informal garden and meadow walk. On the top terrace, 15 varieties of rhododendron are on display and there is a fine view of the garden. Further down, in the orchard bed, a rare *Paulownia*

fargesii flowers every year alongside a rhododendron Polar Bear and a Halesia (snowdrop tree). There is also a secret garden, with numerous rare plants, hidden behind a high, protective wall, plus herbaceous borders, penstemons, a potager, lily ponds and a parterre.

History: The house dates from the 17th century or earlier but the garden was started in earnest in the 20th century by a Colonel Heygate who, in the early 1930s, purchased a whole stand of rhododendrons and azaleas when the Royal Agricultural Show came to Leicester. He used this to form the perimeter of the garden.

Accommodation: Swan in the Rushes, Loughborough (tel: 01509 217014; ££); Great Central Hotel, Loughborough (tel: 01509 263405; £). Local pub: Pear Tree, Woodhouse Eaves; Wheatsheaf, Woodhouse Eaves.

LEFT:
the top terrace at Long Close has a fine collection of rhododendrons.

Orchards

A modern garden with an emphasis on texture. Map reference ㉔

Hall Lane, Walton, Lutterworth LE17 5RP, Leics; tel: 01455 556958.
Opening times: *early Jun–late Aug Sun 2–5pm. National Garden Scheme days. Parties/coaches accepted. Viewing by appointment. House closed.*
Admission prices: *adults £2, children free.*
Facilities: *parking, plants for sale, refreshments (teas). Picnics permitted. No disabled access. No dogs.*

This is a lush, green garden, where the colour comes from carefully selected flowers rather than from foliage plants. The interesting design is modern and formal; the planting is underpinned with a basis of natural plants, and a great deal of attention is given to form and texture.

The garden is just over 1 acre (0.4 hectares) in extent and the soil is sandy loam. Lovely views over the surrounding farmland can be admired from different points in the garden.

Accommodation: Denbigh Arms, Lutterworth (tel: 01455 553537; £). Local pubs: Bell Inn, East Langton; Baker's Arms, Thorpe Langton.

LINCOLNSHIRE

The county has three notable gardens. The renovated formal gardens at Belton House and the intricate parterre, topiary and herbaceous borders at Grimsthorpe Castle make a striking contrast with the walled herb and vegetable gardens that are the pride of Gunby Hall.

Belton House

Well-renovated formal gardens and a wild flower area in a huge woodland estate. English Heritage Grade I. National Trust. Map reference ㉕

Belton, Grantham NG32 2LS, Lincs; tel: 01476 566116; fax: 01476 579071.
< www.nationaltrust.org.uk >
Opening times: *gardens: late Apr–Oct*

BELOW: the immaculately restored gardens at Belton House.

Wed–Sun 11am–5.30pm; house: 12.30–5.30pm. National Garden Scheme days. Parties/coaches accepted; group rates available for pre-booked parties.
Admission prices: *adults £5.80, children £2.90, family £14.50.*
Facilities: *parking, shop, plants for sale, refreshments. Picnics permitted in park only. Disabled access. No dogs except guide dogs. Evening guided tours by prior arrangement with the head gardener. Adventure playground.*

The formal gardens that form part of the 1,000-acre (400-hectare) Belton House estate have recently been returned to their earlier glory. The Wyatville orangery has been renovated and replanted; walls and garden features have been restored and repaired; the Statue Walk and Box Maze have been re-created and there has been extensive replanting of the shrubberies. There are also some splendid cedars and maples, and the Dutch Garden, with shades of green and golden yew, is particularly delightful.

Map: pages 208–9

History: The original 17th-century gardens, designed by George London and Henry Wise, who also designed the famous maze at Hampton Court, were devastated by flooding in the mid-18th century. In the 1850s, in the wake of Capability Brown's Landscape Movement, the highly elaborate formal gardens were removed. The only feature to survive from the original gardens, and still there today, is the small canal to the northeast of the house.

The 18th century saw the re-creation of the Wilderness Garden and planting of specimen trees. In the early 19th century the first Earl Brownlow commissioned Sir Jeffrey Wyatville to design the orangery and the sunken Italian garden. In 1880, the third Earl was responsible for the recreation of the early 17th-century garden, and the Dutch Garden was created to harmonise with the north front of the house.

The estate remained in the hands of the Brownlow family until 1984, when it was entrusted to the National Trust. It has been extensively restored in recent years.

Accommodation: De Vere Belton Woods, Hotel and Country Club, Belton (tel: 0161 8354080; £££–££££). Local pub: The Stag, Barkston.

Grimsthorpe Castle

A medieval deer park is the setting for topiary, herbaceous borders and an ornamental vegetable garden. English Heritage Grade I.
Map reference 26

Grimsthorpe, near Bourne PE10 0NB, Lincs; tel: 01778 591205; fax: 01778 591259. < www.grimsthorpe.co.uk >
Opening times: *garden: Apr–Jul and Sep Sun, Thur, and BH Mons; Aug Sun–Thur 11am–6pm. Ranger tours in a Land Rover most Sun & Thur. National Garden Scheme days. Parties/coaches accepted. Viewing by appointment. House: 1–4.30pm.*
Admission prices: *adults £3, children £2, over-60s £2.50, family £8.*
Facilities: *parking, disabled access, shop, refreshments. Picnics permitted. Dogs allowed on leads in park.*

ABOVE: the intricate parterres of Grimsthorpe Castle.

G rimsthorpe Castle is the centrepiece in a 3,000-acre (1.214-hectare) park of rolling pastures, landscaped lakes and historic woodland. The medieval deer

RIGHT: old-fashioned roses are a feature of Gunby Hall garden.

park, with herds of red, fallow and muntjac deer, and the Tudor oak park are crossed by fine avenues of trees.

The formal flower and topiary garden blends imperceptibly into the woodland garden and provides a fine setting for the ornamental vegetable garden and orchard, created in the 1960s by the Countess of Ancaster and Peter Coates. Intricate parterres marked with box hedges lie close to the castle, and a dramatic herbaceous border frames views across the lake.

History: Grimsthorpe has been the home of the De Eresby family since 1516, when it was granted by Henry VIII to the 10th Baron Willoughby de Eresby when he married Maria de Salinas, lady-in-waiting to Catherine of Aragon. The North Front is the last work of Sir John Vanbrugh. It was commissioned in 1715 by his friend, Robert Bertie, the 16th Baron Willoughby de Eresby, to celebrate his enoblement as the first Duke of Ancaster and Kesteven.

Accommodation/pub: Black Horse Inn, Grimsthorpe (tel: 01778 591247; ££). Local pub: Wishing Well, Dyke.

Gunby Hall

Walled herb and vegetable gardens are the pride of this estate. English Heritage Grade II. National Trust. Map reference ㉗

Spilsby PE23 5SS, Lincs; tel: 01909 486411. < www.gunbyhall.ic24.net >
Opening times: *garden: Apr–Sep Wed–Thur plus occasional Sun 2–6pm. National Garden Scheme day. Parties/coaches accepted. Viewing by appointment. House: Wed only.*
Admission prices: *house & garden: adults £3.80, children £1.90; garden: adults £2.70, children £1.30, family £6.70.*
Facilities: *parking, disabled access, shop, plants for sale, refreshments. Picnics permitted. Dogs allowed on leads.*

The Gunby Hall estate consists of 8 acres (3.2 hectares) of walled gardens including a working kitchen garden, a herb garden, sweeping lawns and a well stocked fish pond. There is an old orchard, many fine herbaceous borders, abundant old-fashioned roses, a wildflower walk and formal frontage. In addition, the Orchard Gallery displays contemporary paintings with floral themes.

History: The Hall was built in 1700 by Sir William Massingberd, based on the style of Sir Christopher Wren. It inspired Alfred, Lord Tennyson to write his poem *Haunt of Ancient Peace*.

Accommodation: The Shades Hotel, Spilsby (tel: 01790 752200; £). Local pub: King's Head, Gunby; Bell, Halton Holegate.

NORTHAMPTONSHIRE

Map: pages 208–9

Northamptonshire has a huge variety of gardens. Rosemary Verey re-created the Elizabethan garden at Holdenby House, Geoffrey Jellicoe influenced the design of Kelmarsh Hall gardens; Canons Ashby epitomises 18th-century elegance, while the roses, clematis and luxuriant herbaceous borders at Coton Manor have earned it an English Heritage Grade I listing.

Canons Ashby House

A lime avenue, topiared yews and a wealth of fruit bushes and shrubs in a well-restored setting. English Heritage Grade II*. National Trust. Map reference ㉘

Daventry NN11 3SD, Northants; tel: 01327 860044.
< www.nationaltrust.org.uk >
***Opening times:** Apr–Oct Sat–Wed, Nov–Dec weekends only: gardens, park and church: 11am–5.30pm (till 4.30pm in Oct, 3pm Dec); house: Apr–Sep 1–5.30pm, Oct noon–4.30pm); Parties/coaches accepted. Viewing by written appointment with property man-ager (s.a.e.).*
***Admission prices:** house, gardens, park & church: adults £5.40, children £2.70, family £13.50; garden: £1.*
***Facilities:** parking, disabled access, shop, plants for sale, refreshments. Picnics permitted. Dogs allowed on leads in home paddock only.*

This is a romantic garden set in rolling Northamptonshire countryside sur-rounding an elegant country house faced in the golden-brown stone found in the area. The terraces, now restored by the National Trust, are full of fruit bushes, vines and apple trees mingled with flowers and shrubs. Remarkably, one of the original four great cedars planted in 1781 survives, guarding the main axis leading down past lawns, roses, yews and lilacs to the Lion Gates with their fine baroque gate piers. Beyond these, an avenue of limes connects the garden to the church and passes the wild flower gardens. The West Court, containing eight topiaried yews, was once the main entrance to the house but its sweep of lawn, espaliered walls and statue of a shepherd boy demonstrate the elegance of an early 18th-century garden.

History: A Tudor house with a pele tower was refaced in 1710 by Edward Dryden, who had begun work on the garden two years earlier, using a simple but elegant design with walls to shelter the plants from winds, and terraces and avenues leading down towards the church and into the park.

***Accommodation:** The Windmill, Badby (tel: 01327 702363; ££); George and Dragon, Chacombe (tel: 01295 711500; ££). **Local pub:** Kings Arms, Farthingstone.*

BELOW: the statue of a shepherd boy at Canons Ashby House.

Coton Manor Gardens

A 20th-century garden surrounding a 17th-century manor house. English Heritage Grade I. Map reference ㉙

Guilsborough NN6 8RQ, Northants; tel: 01604 740219; fax: 01604 740838.
< www.cotonmanor.co.uk >
Opening times: Apr–Sep Tues–Sat plus Sun in Apr & May noon–5.30pm.
Parties/coaches accepted. Viewing by appointment. House closed.
Admission prices: adults £4; children £2; over-60s £3.50.
Facilities: parking, disabled access to terraces, shop, plants for sale, refreshments. Picnics permitted in car park. No dogs.

BELOW: the walls of Coton Manor support unusual climbing roses.

Coton Manor lies in peaceful Northamptonshire countryside which provides an ideal setting for the 10-acre (4-hectare) garden. This is, in fact, a conglomeration of small gardens, each providing surprises and contrasts as they gradually unfold. The walls of the 17th-century manor house support unusual climbing roses, mainly old varieties, clematis and shrubs, while the luxuriant borders, with some vivid colour plantings, will delight the plant enthusiast. Further away from the house, a newly established wild flower meadow and a 5-acre (2-hectare) bluebell wood offer pleasant walks in spring.

History: The garden was originally laid out in 1925 by the grandparents of the present owners, the Pasley-Tylers, and has been lovingly developed ever since.

Accommodation: Olde Coach House Inn, Ashby St Ledgers (tel: 01788 890349; ££). Local pub: Red Lion, East Haddon·

Cottesbrooke Hall

A Queen Anne-style house surrounded by formal and wild gardens. English Heritage Grade II. Map reference ㉚

Cottesbrooke NN6 8PF, Northants; tel: 01604 505808; fax: 01604 505619.
< www.cottesbrookehall.co.uk >
Opening times: garden: May–Sep Thur, Sun & Mon including BH Mons 2–5.30pm. National Garden Scheme days. Parties/coaches accepted. Viewing by appointment. House: Easter–Sep Tue–Wed & Fri and 1st Sun of month.
Admission prices: house & garden: adults £6, children £3; gardens: adults £4, children £2.
Facilities: parking, disabled access, plants for sale, refreshments by arrange-ment. Picnics permitted. No dogs.

Cottesbrooke Hall is a magnificent Queen Anne house reputed to be the model for Jane Austen's *Mansfield Park*, and surrounded by formal and wild gardens. Wandering in the gardens, visitors will see huge 300-year-old Cedars of

Map: pages 208–9

Lebanon, double herbaceous borders, pools and lily ponds. There is a Yew Statue Walk with pergolas, a rose garden and, on the south front, formal parterres framing the vista towards the ancient church. In spring the Wild Garden, planted along the course of a running stream with stepping stones, cascades and arched bridges, comes alive with spring bulbs; later in the season, the acers and rhododendrons with bamboos and gunneras are a delight. In mid-summer, an array of planters in the individually planted courtyard gardens come into their own.

History: A number of distinguished landscape designers have been involved in developing the gardens. They include Edward Schultz in the early 20th century, Sir Geoffrey Jellicoe between the two world wars, and Dame Sylvia Crowe after World War II. The main inspiration came from Lady Macdonald-Buchanan.

Accommodation: Broomhill Hotel, Spratton (tel: 01604 845959; ££). Local pubs: The Spencer Arms, Chapel Brampton; King's Arms, Farthingstone; Boat Inn, Stoke Bruerne; Red Lion, East Haddon.

Holdenby House Gardens

A miniature Elizabethan garden planned by the late Rosemary Verey. English Heritage Grade II*. Map reference ③

Holdenby NN6 8DJ, Northants; tel: 01604 770074; fax: 01604 770962. < www.holdenby.com >

Opening times: *Easter–Sep Sun 1–5pm plus Jul–Aug Sun–Fri 1–5pm; BHs 1–6pm. National Garden Scheme day. Parties/coaches accepted. Viewing by appointment for house tours for groups on selected days.*

Admission prices: *adults £4.50 (BHs £6), children £3.50 (BHs £4), over-60s £4 (BHs £5); prices include falconry centre.*

Facilities: *parking, disabled access, shop, plants for sale, refreshments (teas). Picnics permitted. Dogs allowed on leads. Falconry centre; 17th-century farmstead and play area.*

ABOVE: summer planting in borders and containers at Cottesbrooke Hall.

RIGHT: the garden at Holdenby House gave solace to Charles I.

Positioned high on a hill, Holdenby overlooks rural Northamptonshire. The view from the garden lawns, with their extensive yew hedging, is stunning. The miniature Elizabethan Garden was planned by gardening expert Mrs Rosemary Verey in 1980, using only plants that were available in the 1580s, when the palace was completed. The croquet lawn is sunk into the foundations of the West Wing of Sir Christopher Hatton's great palace, demolished in the 1650s. King Charles's Walk, once part of the old garden, has been incorporated into the new garden. It recalls the period of Charles I's imprisonment at Holdenby in 1647, before his execution. Tradition has it that this was his favourite part of the garden. The Tous Tous Border has survived from the Victorian period. Recently redesigned by Rupert Golby, it contains plants chosen for their scent. The silver border hosts a wide range of silver and grey foliage plants collected by the current owner, Mr James Lowther.

History: There are two gardens at Holdenby. The inner, or new garden is contained within the remains of the early palace and comprises the Victorian Garden and a 20th-century one, which includes a re-cre-

ation, in miniature, of the Elizabethan original. The second is the older or outer garden, the original Elizabethan one, the outlines of which are still visible as you walk around the grounds.

Accommodation: Broomhill Hotel, Spratton (tel: 01604 845959; ££). Local pub: Red Lion, East Haddon.

Kelmarsh Hall

A 20th-century garden whose design owes much to Nancy Lancaster and Geoffrey Jellicoe. Map reference ㉜

Kelmarsh NN6 9LU, Northants; tel: 01604 686543; fax: 01604 686485.
< www.kelmarsh.com >
Opening times: Apr–Sep Mon–Thur, Sat & BH Mons 2.30–5pm. National Garden Scheme days. Parties/coaches accepted. Viewing by appointment. House open Apr–Sep Sun & BH Mons and Thur in Aug.
Admission prices: house & garden: adults £4, children (5–16) £2, over-60s £3.50; garden only: adults £3, children under 16 free, over-60s £2.50.

Facilities: parking, disabled access, refreshments (teas) Sun and BH Mons only. No picnics. No dogs.

Kelmarsh Hall gardens are 20th century in origin and design, and they are largely attributable to Nancy Lancaster. During the 1920s and '30s, Nancy worked with Norah Lindsay laying out the flower beds in the topiary garden and the Long Border.

It was probably through Nancy that Geoffrey Jellicoe became involved here in 1936–8, when he laid out the terrace walks, pleached limes and red horse chestnuts on the west front. There are some interesting old yews, a sunken garden with white plantings and a garden devoted to old-fashioned roses.

History: Palladian Kelmarsh Hall was built between 1728 and 1732 to a design by James Gibbs for William Hanbury. The Hanburys remained here until 1865 when the house was sold to a banker from Liverpool. In 1902 Mr G.G. Lancaster bought the estate, introducing the British White cattle whose descendants graze the parkland.

Accommodation: Kettering Park Hotel (01536 416666; £££); Bull's Head, Clipston (tel: 01858 525268; £). Local pub: The George, Gt Oxendon

Sulgrave Manor

Tudor manor house and garden associated with the ancestors of George Washington. English Heritage Grade II. Map reference ㉝

Sulgrave, Banbury OX17 2SD, Northants; tel: 01295 760205; fax: 01295 768056. < www.sulgravemanor.org.uk >
Opening times: house & garden: Apr–Oct Tues, Wed, Thur, Sat, Sun and BHs 2–5.30pm. Parties/coaches accepted. Viewing by appointment essential for parties numbering 15 +. Admission prices: adults £5, children £2.50.
Facilities: parking, lavatories, shop, plants for sale, refreshments. Picnics permitted. Disabled access. Dogs allowed on leads.

A significant motive for many visitors to Sulgrave's house and garden is its connections with the family of George Washington. But its gardens, though modest, are worth visiting for their own sake. They include herbaceous borders, topiary, an Elizabethan knot garden with traditional herbs, an orchard, underplanted with thousands of daffodils, lawns and yew

LEFT:
Kelmarsh
Hall garden,
influenced by
Geoffrey
Jellicoe.

hedges. Herbs and unusual perennials are sold in the courtyard from Easter to September.

History: The garden was designed as a setting for the Tudor house, built in 1539 by Lawrence Washington on land purchased from Henry VIII. His descendants lived here for 120 years and in 1656 his great, great grandson, Colonel John Washington, left England to take up land in Virginia, where he created what later became Mount Vernon. Colonel Washington was the great grandfather of George Washington, first President of the United Sates.

In 1914 Sulgrave Manor was presented by a body of subscribers to the Peoples of Great Britain and the United States in celebration of 100 years of peace between the nations.

Accommodation: Banbury House, Banbury (tel: 01295 259361; ££); Cromwell Lodge (tel: 01295 259781; ££–£££); George and Dragon, Chacombe (tel: 01295 711500; ££).
Local pub: Star Inn, Sulgrave.

NOTTINGHAMSHIRE

Many people visit Newstead Abbey for its Byronic connections, but are captivated by its Spanish and Japanese gardens. Clumber Park is renowned for its mature limes, rhododenrons and serpentine lake, while old-fashiond roses are the highlight of Felley Priory.

ABOVE: Clumber Park.

Clumber Park

A huge wooded park with mature limes, cedars and rhododendrons. English Heritage Grade I. National Trust. Map reference **34**

ABOVE: *Worksop S80 3AZ, Notts; tel: 01909 476592; fax: 01909 500721.*
< www.nationaltrust.org.uk >

Opening times: park: daily all year; walled kitchen garden: Apr–Sep Wed–Thur 10.30am–5.30pm, weekends & BH Mons 10.30am–6pm. Parties/coaches accepted and may also view by appointment. House closed.
Admission prices: park: cars and motorbikes £3.50; minibuses and caravans £4.60; walled kitchen garden: adults £1.
Facilities: parking, disabled access, shop, plant sales, refreshments. No picnics. Dogs allowed on leads in park.

A wonderful 2-mile (3-km) avenue of mature limes leads to a large, artificial serpentine lake beside which stands a huge Gothic chapel and some pretty stable blocks. The enormous trees and rhododendrons set in the 3,800 acres (1,530 hectares) of rolling parkland around the lake are probably the best part of the garden.

There is an impressive avenue of cedars leading to a walled garden which has a good range of glasshouses and a collection of early garden implements. The Lincoln Terrace beside the lake provides an enjoyable stroll, concluding at a dock where a pleasure boat was once kept.

History: Clumber Park was one of the "Dukeries", created in the 18th and 19th centuries for a number of newly created noblemen on land annexed from Sherwood Forest. Clumber was originally laid out in 1760 with a substantial mansion, which burnt down in 1879. Rebuilding commenced immediately but only the foundation stones survive from the house that stood here until 1938, when it was demolished to save the owner from paying tax on it. The National Trust took on the estate after World War II.

Accommodation: Dukeries Park Hotel, Worksop (tel: 01909 476674; £–££).

Felley Priory

A delightful garden designed in the 1970s, with old-fashioned roses, pergolas and knot gardens.
Map reference ❸❺

Underwood NG16 5FL, Notts; tel: 01773 810230; fax: 01773 580440.
Opening times: all year Tues–Wed & Fri 9am–2.30pm; also Mar–Oct, 2nd & 4th Wed 9am–4pm and every 3rd Sun 11am–4pm. National Garden Scheme day. Parties/coaches accepted and may also view by appointment. House closed.
Admission prices: adults £2, children free.
Facilities: parking, disabled access, plants for sale, refreshments. No picnics. No dogs.

Each part of Felley Priory garden is planted differently. The south- and east-facing borders are for slightly tender plants, which thrive surprisingly well here. The pergolas are mainly covered with roses, vines, clematis and honeysuckle, and the knot gardens are full of neat architectural box. The borders are planted with a mixture of small trees and shrubs underplanted by hellebores, hostas, digitalis, meconopsis and geraniums. The rose garden is full of

old-fashioned roses, among them gallicas, bourbons, moss roses, damasks, albas and chinensis. In the borders under the old Elizabethan wall are various types of agapanthus and some tender shrubs, interplanted with the roses.

History: Felley Priory was founded in 1156 but dissolved by Henry VIII in 1536. Later that century a new house was built, and this was enlarged in 1886. The garden was designed by the present owner, the Hon. Mrs Chaworth-Musters, who started the planting in 1976.

Map: pages 208–9

Accommodation: Hole in the Wall, Underwood (01773 713936; £). **Local pub:** *Black Swan, Idridgehay.*

Newstead Abbey

Briefly the estate of Lord Byron, Newstead has sub-tropical bamboo gardens and an excellent Japanese garden. Map reference ❸❻

Newstead Abbey Park, Nottingham NG15 8GE, Notts; tel: 01623 455900; fax: 01623 455904.
< www.newsteadabbey.org.uk >
Opening times: grounds: all year, daily

ABOVE: a mass of midsummer colour at Felley Priory.

except last Fri in Nov 9am–dusk; house: Apr–Sep noon–5pm, last admission 4pm. Parties/coaches accepted.
Admission prices: *house & garden: adults £4, children £2.50, over-60s £2.50; garden: adults £2, children £1.50; over-60s £1.50, groups of 10+ £1.50 pp.*
Facilities: *parking, limited disabled access, shop, refreshments. Picnics permitted. Dogs allowed on leads.*

The north terrace walk at Newstead Abbey, 720 ft (220 metres) in length, runs parallel to a grand herbaceous border created by the Webbs, the 19th-century owners, some time before 1876. Nearer to the house the poet Lord Byron (1788–1824), who inherited and briefly owned the property, had built a monument to his favourite dog Boatswain. To the south of this is the Spanish Garden, named after the well-head at its centre which originated in Spain; the thick box hedges form a geometrical pattern for bright flower beds.

The sub-tropical or bamboo gardens, recently restored, are thought to be the work of the Webb sisters, Geraldine and Ethel, and contemporary with the rockery. The rose garden, created in 1965, contains early roses and recent cultivars. It was formerly the kitchen garden that supplied the Webb household with fruit and vegetables. Two statues representing a family of satyrs were brought here from Italy by the fifth Lord Byron ("The Wicked Lord", Byron's great-uncle) to ornament a grove of trees to the east of the pond. The grove, thereafter known as Devil's Wood, was eventually cleared and has been recently replanted.

Newstead owes much of its tranquil beauty to the River Leen. Since monastic times its waters have fed the lakes, ponds and water cascades.

History: Newstead Abbey was founded as a monastic house in the late 12th century. The estate was bought by Sir John Byron in 1540. The large formal garden to the east of the house is thought to have been created by the fourth Lord Byron, probably no later than 1720, in a style that had been fashionable a generation earlier. Newstead's most famous owner, the sixth Lord Byron, inherited the debt-ridden property, but sold it in 1818. The Spanish Garden was designed by Miss Geraldine Webb in 1896 and the Japanese Garden was laid out for Ethel Webb in 1907 by a Japanese landscape architect.

Accommodation: The Gateway, Newstead (tel: 01159 794949; ££–£££); Portland Hall Hotel, Mansfield (tel: 01623 452525; £–££).
Local pub: The Hutt, Ravenshead.

RIGHT: the Japanese Garden at Newstead Abbey.

Map: pages 208-9

SHROPSHIRE

Shropshire has few great gardens, but Hodnet Hall is one that has much to offer all year round: rhododendrons flourish in early summer and the autumn foliage and berries are colourful, while the series of ponds, fed by underground springs, are the home of interesting bog plants.

Hodnet Hall Gardens

Pools and water gardens, mature trees and a wealth of colour characterise this estate. English Heritage Grade II. Map reference ❸

Hodnet, Market Drayton TF9 3NN, Salop; tel: 01630 685202; fax: 01630 685853.
Opening times: *Apr–Sep Tues–Sun and BH Mons noon–5pm. National Garden Scheme days. Parties/coaches accepted by appointment, minimum of 25 people. House closed.*
Admission prices: *adults £3.50, children £1.50, over-60s £3, season £19.50.*
Facilities: *parking, disabled access, shop, plants for sale, refreshments. Picnics permitted. Dogs allowed on leads.*

A daisy chain of water on different levels provides the central axis of the garden at Hodnet Hall. As the soil is lime-free, there is scope for rhododrons, camellias and other ericaceous plants, which flourish in the acid soil. The 26 inches (660 mm) of rain each year and the moistness resulting from the presence of pools and streams are ideal for candelabra primulas, irises and bog plants. It is supposed that the pools, fed by numerous underground springs, moderate the temperature, as they seldom freeze over.

The favourable soil and temperate climate also allow trees such as beeches, oaks, sycamores and limes to attain great size.

Hodnet Hall is of interest as a garden that has been carefully planted to provide a show of colour throughout the seasons. Daffodils and blossom in early spring are followed by a burst of rhododendrons, Exbury azaleas, laburnums and lilacs, and then by peonies and roses, astilbes and primulas. The summer borders, the masses of hydrangeas and the late summer shrubs follow on, and in the autumn there is brilliant foliage and berries.

History: Hodnet has had a park and gar-

ABOVE: vivid kniphofia flourish in the borders at Hodnet Hall Gardens.

den for many centuries, and the design and size have been adapted to the three different sites of the houses in which the Heber-Percy family have lived.

The oldest landscape plantings of trees can still be seen surrounding the earthworks of the Norman castle near the visitors' car park. The beech avenue led down to the second house, a large 16th-century half-timbered building complete with a terraced walk and circular garden. In the 1920s

Brigadier A.G.W. Heber-Percy embarked on building a series of pools and terraces, and in so doing joined the formal gardens, enclosed in a yew hedge around the house, with those already existing around the old family house in the valley.

Accommodation: Tern Hill Hall Farmhouse, near Market Drayton (tel: 01630 638984; £); Stafford Court, Market Drayton (tel: 01630 652646; £–££). ***Local pub:*** *The Bear Hotel, Hodnet.*

STAFFORDSHIRE

Three gardens are featured from this county: the splendid Chinese Water Garden at Biddulph Grange the elegant neoclassical garden of Shugborough and the spectacular waterfall and alpine scree plants in the Dorothy Clive Garden.

Biddulph Grange Garden

BELOW: the Chinese Water Garden at Biddulph Grange.

A highly unusual estate, with a themed gardens, statuary and a rock garden, linked by subterranean paths. English Heritage Grade I. National Trust. Map reference ㊳

Grange Road, Biddulph, Stoke-on-Trent, ST8 7SD, Staffs; tel: 01782 517999; fax: 01782 510624.
< www.nationaltrust.org.co.uk >
Opening times: *gardens: Apr–Oct Wed–Fri noon–5.30pm, weekends and BH Mons 11am–5.30pm; Nov–Christmas, weekends noon–4pm (or dusk if earlier). Parties/coaches accepted. May also view by appointment. House also open.*
Admission prices: *adults £4.60, children £2.30, family £11.50, pre-booked groups of 15 + £3.90 pp; mid-Nov–Christmas free.*
Facilities: *parking, disabled access, shop, plants for sale, refreshments. Picnics permitted. Dogs allowed on leads in car park only.*

The 15-acre (6-hectare) garden at Biddulph Grange, set in a somewhat unpromising industrialised landscape, has just about everything, and in extraordinary measure. Where else would you find an Egyptian tomb, a Scottish glen, a Chinese Water Garden with a familiar willow pattern design, complete with pagoda, an imitation Great Wall, a stumpery, a half-timbered Cheshire cottage leading into a pyramid, an avenue of wellingtonias, a gilded water buffalo under a canopy and an enormous stone frog? All these elements are cleverly linked by subterranean pathways, stepping stones across water and narrow paths around rock faces, each hidden from the other so that walking round the garden brings a series of surprises. This was one of the most influential gardens of the 19th century and its originality and beauty still capture the imagination.

History: James Bateman, a keen plantsman, and his wife, Maria, moved to Biddulph Grange in 1840. The estate had been acquired by his grandfather, originally for coal mining, but they recognised the potential to create a spectacular garden. They were assisted by their friend, the marine artist, Edward Cooke, who designed many of the architectural features and rock work.

The Batemans drew heavily on the results of the early Himalayan plant-hunting expeditions by Joseph Hooker in 1849–51 and Robert Fortune's expeditions to China and Japan in the 1840s and 1850s, as well as acquiring wellingtonias from Veitch in 1853. Robert Heath bought the property from the Batemans in 1871 and continued the programme of planting.

Accommodation: The North Stafford, Stoke-on-Trent (tel: 01782 744477; ££–£££); Victoria House, Tunstall (tel: 01782 835964; £). **Local pubs:** *Black Lion, Butterton; The Ship Inn, Wincle.*

The Dorothy Clive Garden

Woodland plants and colourful summer borders are among the highlights here. Map reference ❸❾

Willoughbridge, Market Drayton TF9 4EU, Staffs; tel: 01630 647237; fax: 01630 647902.
< www.dorothyclivegarden.co.uk >

Map: pages 208–9

Opening times: Apr–Oct daily 10am–5.30pm. Parties/coaches accepted. House closed.
Admission prices: adults £3.20, children £1 (under-11s free), over-65s £2.70.
Facilities: parking, disabled access, refreshments. Picnics permitted. Dogs allowed on leads.

This south-facing hillside garden, with views over the surrounding country-side, is best known for its beautiful woodland plantings, established in a disused gravel quarry. A spectacular waterfall cascades between mature rhododendrons, azaleas and choice woodland plants. An alpine scree garden, water features and colourful summer borders are among the delights.

History: Colonel Clive and his friends, John Codrington, Kenneth Midgley, a landscape designer, and Frank Knight, the director of Wisley, set about creating this peaceful garden in 1940, in memory of Dorothy, the colonel's wife.

Accommodation: Corbet Arms, Market Drayton (tel: 01630 652037; ££); Stafford Court, Market Drayton (tel: 01630 652646; £–££). **Local pubs:** *Bhurtpore Inn, Aston; The Chetwode Arms, Pipe Gate, Shropshire; The Falcon, Woore.*

Aʙᴏᴠᴇ: the spectacular waterfall in the Dorothy Clive Garden.

Shugborough

An 18th-century landscape garden containing a host of neoclassical monuments of national importance. English Heritage Grade I. Map reference ⓵

Milford, Stafford ST17 0XB, Staffs; tel: 01889 881388; fax: 01889 881323. < www.staffordshire.gov.uk >
Opening times: *garden: Apr–Sep Tues–Sun 11am–5pm; Oct Sun only 11am–5pm, Nov–Mar pre-booked parties only Mon–Fri 10.30am–4pm and BH Mons. Parties/coaches accepted. Viewing by appointment. House open.*
Admission prices: *grounds & gardens: £2 per vehicle; house & museum: adults £6, children £4; farm: adults £4.50, children £3.*
Facilities: *parking, disabled access, shop, refreshments. Picnics permitted. Dogs allowed in park only.*

ABOVE: neoclassical elegance at Shugborough.

There are few places in Staffordshire where the seasons are more apparent than on the Shugborough estate. Whether it is the blanket of daffodils on the banks of the River Sow in spring, the gentle fragrance of lavender in the formal gardens in summer, or the riot of autumn colours on the woodland drive in October, the gardens and parkland are a timeless tribute to the neoclassical age.

The lawns on the northwest side of the house were the site of Thomas Anson's bowling green, the lawn in front of the Doric Temple was once the family tennis court. Other features include the blue bridge at the end of the Wild Garden (formerly Thomas Anson's shrubbery), a red bridge beside the Chinese House, the boy and swan fountain by the landing stage and the remains of a Gothic dovecote.

History: Eight monuments of national importance are situated in the 900 acres (360 hectares) of parkland. Built by Thomas Wright of Durham and James "Athenian" Stuart during the mid-18th century, they reflect the English landowner's fascination with classical architecture.

*Accommodation: Oak Tree Farm, Tamworth (01827 56807; £). **Local pub:** Royal Oak, Abbots Bromley; Bagot Arms, Abbots Bromley.*

WARWICKSHIRE

Map:
pages
208–9

Garden visitors are often drawn to Warwickshire chiefly to see the astonishing topiary at Packwood House, but while in the county it would be a great pity to miss the water features at Farnborough Hall, the bog garden at Upton House and the delightful colour-themed cottage garden at Woodpeckers.

Farnborough Hall

Pools, ponds and pavilions, ever-green shrubs and a long terrace walk on an old family estate. English Heritage Grade I. National Trust. Map reference **④**

Banbury OX17 1DU, Warwicks; tel: 01295 690002.
< www.nationaltrust.org.uk >
***Opening times:** house and garden: Apr–Sep Wed & Sat plus two days in early May 2–6pm; Terrace Walk: Thur–Fri 2–6pm by prior arrangement. National Garden Scheme days. Parties/coaches accepted by written appointment only.*
***Admission prices:** house, garden & Terrace Walk: adults £3.50; garden and terrace walk: £1.75; Terrace Walk only: £1.*
***Facilities:** parking. No refreshments. No picnics. No disabled access. Dogs allowed on leads.*

A highlight of Farnborough is the lovely serpentine uphill walk along a ¾-mile (1.5-km) grass terrace, terminating in a lofty obelisk. The walk, which passes an Ionic temple and an oval-shaped pavilion with a blue and white rococo interior, is flanked by trees and evergreen shrubs on one side and on the other by a laurel hedge with 33 bastions, from which the Malvern Hills and Edge Hill can be seen, as well as Holbech's river pool. Returning by the hexagonal game larder and stew ponds, visitors encounter the Sourland Pool and a cascade into the river pool, then a parterre of bush roses and an alcove seat, which makes a satisfying finish to the garden tour.

History: Farnborough Hall estate has been in the Holbech family for more than 300 years and the honey-coloured Palladian villa was built in 1745 by William Holbech, replacing the former manor house. Like many well-connected gentlemen of the time, he had undertaken the Grand Tour and immersed himself in Italian art and architecture, the influences of which can be seen here. The garden and its buildings were designed with the help of his friend, landscape gardener Sanderson Miller, and were completed in about 1751.

***Accommodation:** Easington House, Banbury (tel: 01295 270181; ££); Whately Hall, Banbury (tel: 01295 263451; £–£££).* ***Local pubs:** Castle, Edge Hill; George and Dragon, Chacombe.*

BELOW: glorious delphiniums.

Packwood House

Spectacular topiary and a beautiful sunken garden in an historic setting. English Heritage Grade I. National Trust. Map reference ❹

Lapworth, Solihull B94 6AT, Warwicks; tel: 01564 782024; fax: 01564 782706. < www.nationaltrust.org.uk >
Opening times: *gardens: Mar–Oct Wed–Sun & BH Mons 11am–4.30pm (till 5.30pm May–Sep); house: noon–4.30pm; park and woodland walks: all year, daily. National Garden Scheme day. Parties/coaches accepted by written appointment only (15+ people).*
Admission prices: *house & garden: adults £5.40, children £2.70, family £15; garden only: adults £2.70, children £1.35.*
Facilities: *parking, disabled access, shop, plants for sale, refreshments. Picnics permitted. Dogs allowed on leads.*

ABOVE: topiary, roses and herbaceous borders at Packwood House.

RIGHT: playful Pan at Upton House.

The glory of this garden is its topiary, the extraordinary standing figures traditionally held to represent the Sermon on the Mount, with the Master on the summit of the mound, the 12 Apostles and four Evangelists below, and the assembled multitude on the lawn. Some of the figures are over 50 ft (12 metres) high.

Two other major features are the lovely, mellowed brickwork of the gazebos, walkways, walls and flights of steps, and the beautifully planted sunken garden and herbaceous borders.

History: The original 16th-century house was redesigned in the late 17th century by John Fetherston and his son, who began laying out the rectangular enclosures, the raised terracing and the gazebo, which is shown in a drawing of 1756. It is believed that the topiary was begun much later, in the mid-19th century. Graham Baron Ash, whose father, an industrialist and racehorse owner, bought Packwood for him in 1905, created the South Garden and restored the gazebos.

Accommodation: Renaissance Solihull Hotel (tel: 0121 711 3000; ££–£££); Haseley House, Warwick (tel: 01926 484222; £–££). **Local pub:** *The Boot, Lapworth.*

Upton House

Terraces, herbaceous borders and a bog garden surround a 17th-century house. English Heritage Grade II*. National Trust. Map reference ❹

Banbury OX15 6HT, Oxon; tel: 01295 670266; fax: 01295 670266. < www.nationaltrust.org.uk >
National Collection: *Asters.*
Opening times: *Apr–Oct Sat–Wed 12.30–5pm; Nov–mid-Dec weekends noon–4pm. Parties/coaches by written appointment. House open late Mar–Oct.*
Admission prices: *house & garden: adults £6.40, children £3.20 family £15.50; garden: adults £3.20, children £1.60.*
Facilities: *parking, shop, plants for sale, refreshments. No picnics. Disabled access. No dogs.*

Standing near the site of the Civil War battle of Edgehill, Upton House gardens are impressive for the expanse of lawn and a series of terraces descending to a large lake. The bog garden, where numerous water-loving plants grow, and a pair of colourful herbaceous borders complement the kitchen garden alongside the terraces.

The house holds an extraordinary collection of Old Masters, including works by Stubbs, Constable, Canaletto and Breughel.

History: The garden was created at the end of the 17th century. The banker, Robert Child, owned the property during the 18th century and added a lake and temple in 1775. The second Lord Bearsted and his wife further developed it in the 1920s and 1930s with the help of architect, Percy Morley Holder. More recent design is by Kitty Lloyd-Jones.

Accommodation: Banbury House, Banbury (tel: 01295 259361; ££); Cromwell Lodge, Banbury (tel: 01295 259781; ££–£££). **Local pubs:** *The Bell, Shenington; The Plough, Bodicote.*

Woodpeckers

Colour-themed borders, a knot garden and a potager in a modern garden. Map reference ⑭

The Bank, Marlcliff, Bidford-on-Avon B50 4NT, Warwicks; tel: 01789 773416.
Opening times: all year, daily by appointment only. Parties/coaches accepted. House closed.
Admission prices: adults £3, children free.
Facilities: parking, plants for sale, refreshments. No lavatories. Picnics permitted. Disabled access; wheelchair users must be accompanied. No dogs.

Woodpeckers is a country garden of 25 acres (11 hectares) with open views over surrounding pastures. Designed to be of interest throug the year, the garden has a mixed border devoted to plants that look their best in winter and trees chosen for the colour of their bark in winter. The Meadow Garden provides interest in spring, followed by an explosion of flowers in the colour-themed borders in summer. Old roses and numerous varieties of clematis are other summer highlights. The garden is largely informal, but a knot garden and a potager with unusual vegetables and old varieties of apple fit happily into the scene.

History: The owners, Mr and Mrs A J Cox, built a house here in 1965 and have created and maintained the garden unaided. The aim was to create a garden in sympathy with the surrounding countryside.

Accommodation: Glebe Farm House, Stratford-upon-Avon (tel: 01789 842501; ££); Loxley Farm, Stratford-upon-Avon (tel: 01789 840265: £–££). **Local pubs:** *Blue Boar, Temple Grafton; Three Horseshoes, Wixford; The King Arms, Cleeve Prior.*

Above: Woodpeckers, the perfect cottage garden.

Map: pages 208–9

The North

England's northern counties
– Cumbria, Durham,
Lancashire, Merseyside,
Northumbria and Yorkshire –
have many fine gardens
belonging to historic estates.
They include Northumbria's
Alnwick Castle, whose gardens
have received one of the most
ambitious and expensive
redesigns of the modern age

CUMBRIA

The best of Cumbria's gardens are concentrated around Lake Windermere and Morecambe Bay, sharing spectacular lakeland and coastal settings. Exotic plants from all over the world thrive in the gardens of Holker Hall, Muncaster Castle and Charney Well, all of which benefit from a mild climate influenced by the Gulf Stream. Levens Hall is renowned for its topiary garden dating from the 17th century.

Charney Well

Tiered garden overlooking Morecambe Bay with a profusion of exotic plants, including a National Collection of phormiums.
Map reference ❶

Hampsfell Road, Grange-over-Sands LA11 6BE, Cumbria; tel: 01539 534526; fax: 01539 535 765.
< www.charneywell.com >
Opening times: *viewing by appointment only. Parties/coaches accepted. House closed.*
National Collection: *Phormium.*
Admission prices: *adults £2.50, children free.*
Facilities*: plants for sale, refreshments. No parking. No disabled access. No dogs.*

Designed by Christopher Holliday and developed by the owners, Charney Well is a south-facing tiered garden with thinly covered steep limestone slopes, bordered on three sides by high limestone walls. Its sheltered position and the benefits of the Gulf Stream create the perfect microclimate for the growth of exotic plants. European fan palms, acacias, callistemons and many sub-tropical plants from the southern hemisphere thrive here.

Over 200 phormiums, or New Zealand flax, form the National Collection and are the pride of the owners. Views over Morecambe Bay are magnificent.

Accommodation: Mayfields, Grange-over-Sands (tel: 01539 534730; £–££); Aynsome Manor, Cartmel (tel: 015395 36653; ££–£££).
Local pubs: Cavendish Arms, Cartmel; King's Arms, Cartmel; Wheatsheaf, Beetham.

PRECEDING PAGES: the pool at Lancashire's Gresgarth Hall.

OPPOSITE: Holker Hall in Cumbria.

ABOVE: phormiums at Charney Well.

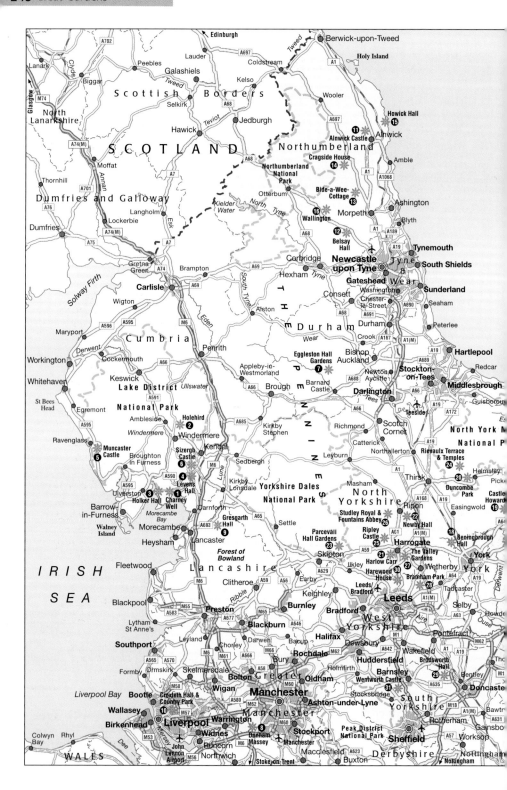

The North

0   20 km
0   20 miles

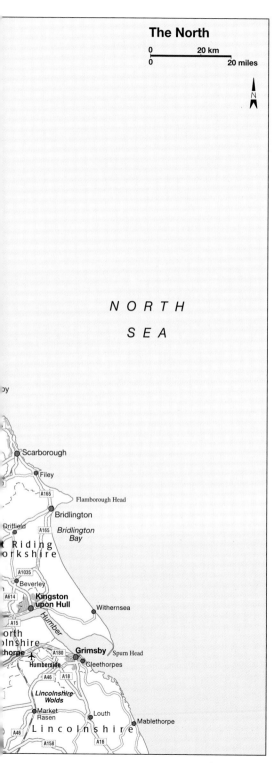

N O R T H

S E A

Scarborough

Filey

A165

Flamborough Head

Bridlington

Driffield   A165   *Bridlington Bay*

Riding
orkshire

A1035

Beverley

A614   **Kingston upon Hull**

Withernsea

A15

orth
Inshire
thorpe   A180   **Grimsby**   Spurn Head
Humberside   Cleethorpes

A46   A18

Lincolnshire Wolds

Market Rasen   Louth   Mablethorpe

A46   L i n c o l n s h i r e

A158   A15

Holehird

Formal gardens with outstanding Lakeland setting. Map reference ❷

Lakeland Horticultural Society, Patterdale Road, Windermere LA23 1NP, Cumbria; tel: 01539 446008.
< www.cragview.demon.co.uk >
Opening times: *garden: year-round dawn–dusk. National Garden Scheme day. Parties/coaches accepted. Viewing also by appointment. House open.*
National Collections: *Astilbe, Hydrangeas and Polystichum ferns.*
Admission prices: *£2 donation suggested for adults.*
Facilities: *parking, limited disabled access, shop, plants for sale. Picnics permitted. No dogs.*

These 9-acre (3½-hectare) formal gardens surround a Grade II listed building. On a hillside at the southern end of the Troutbeck Valley near Windermere village, they are enhanced by their spectacular setting and offer views across the lake to the fells beyond. The Lakeland Horticultural Society tends the formal gardens, including the Victorian walled garden. The upkeep of the gardens are undertaken entirely by the members on a voluntary basis.

History: The Lakeland Horticultural Society was founded in 1969 to "promote and develop the science, practice and art of horticulture, particularly with regard to conditions prevailing in the Lake District".

Accommodation: Holbeck Ghyll, Windermere (tel: 01539 432375; £££–££££); Newstead Guesthouse, Windermere (tel: 01539 444485; £–££).
Local pub: Hole in't Wall, Bowness-on-Windermere.

Holker Hall

Gulf Stream garden and arboretum hosting plants from all over the world. English Heritage Grade II*. Map reference ❸

Cark-in-Cartmel, Grange-over-Sands LA11 7PL, Cumbria; tel: 015395 558328. < www.holker-hall.co.uk >
Opening times: *house & garden: last week Mar–early Nov Sun–Fri 10am–6pm (last entry 4.30pm). National Garden Scheme day. Parties/coaches accepted. Viewing by appointment. Holker Garden Festival held end May/beginning June.*
National Collection: *styracaceae.*
Admission prices: *house & garden: adults £8.25, children £4.65; gardens: adults £3.95, children (ages 6–15) £2.25, family ticket £11.95. Season tickets.*
Facilities: *parking, disabled access, shop, plants for sale, refreshments. Picnics permitted. Dogs allowed on leads.*

Holker Hall includes formal and woodland areas covering 25 acres (10 hectares). The range of many rare and beautiful plants and shrubs reflect the sheer passion for plants of the owners, Lord and Lady Cavendish. The climatic benefits of the Gulf Stream ensure a fantastic micro-climate for plants from throughout the world. Specimens of particular note include the *Halesia carolina, Halesia monticola, Styrax hemsleyanum* and *Styrax obassia*. The gardens provide interest for gardeners and non-gardeners from March to October. Among the highlights are the Moghul-style cascade, the old croquet lawn planted as garden room and the spectacular arboretum with over 1,000 varieties of trees.

Accommodation: Mayfields, Grange-over-Sands (tel: 01539 534730; £–££); Aynsome Manor, Cartmel (tel: 015395 36653). **Local pub:** *Masons Arms, Cartmel.*

Levens Hall

17th-century garden famous for its topiary. English Heritage Grade I. Map reference ❹

Kendal, LA8 0PD Cumbria; tel: 01539 560321; fax: 01539 560669. < www.levenshall.co.uk >
Opening times: *mid-Apr–mid-Oct Sun–Thur, gardens 10am–5pm, house noon–5pm. National Garden Scheme days. Parties/coaches accepted. Viewing by appointment.*

RIGHT: Holker Hall, part woodland, part formal garden.

Map: pages 248–9

Admission prices: house & gardens: adults £7, children £3.50, family £20; gardens only: adults £5.50, children £2.50, family £15.
Facilities: parking, disabled access, shop, plants for sale, refreshments. Picnics permitted. Guide dogs only.

This 300-year old garden covers 10 acres (4 hectares) and includes the world-famous Topiary Garden, a magnificent beech circle, formal bedding, herbaceous borders, mixed borders, an orchard, a rose garden, a nuttery, a vegetable garden and a formal water feature.

History: The gardens were designed in 1694 by Guillaume Beaumont, a pupil of Le Nôtre who had landscaped the gardens at Versailles and Hampton Court. His patron, Col. Grahme, former Privy Purse to James II, moved to the Elizabethan mansion when the king abdicated. Beaumont's Topiary Garden has been meticulously maintained ever since.

Accommodation: Lindeth Fell, Bowness-on-Windermere (tel: 015394 43286; ££). Blue Bell, Heversham (tel: 01539 562018; ££). Local pubs: Punch Bowl Inn, Crosthwaite; Hole in't Wall, Bowness-on-Windermere.

Muncaster Castle

Woodland garden with many rare plants and trees from around the world. English Heritage Grade II*. Map reference ❺.

Ravenglass CA18 1RQ, Cumbria; tel: 01229 717614.
< www.muncastercastle.co.uk >
Opening times: gardens year-round 10.30am–6pm; castle 2nd week Mar–Oct. Parties/coaches accepted. Viewing by appointment.
Admission prices: gardens: adults £5.70, children £3.70, family £17; castle: adults £7.80, children £5, family £21.
Facilities: parking, disabled access, shop, plants for sale, refreshments. Picnics permitted. Dogs allowed on leads.

Set in the dramatic grandeur of the fells, these wild and extensive woodland gardens contain an incredible collection of rare and beautiful plants, many of which are now highly endangered in their native habitats. Thousands of specimens, particularly from China and the Far East,

ABOVE: the 300-year-old Topiary Garden at Levens Hall.

have been grown from seed collected on recent expeditions. British plants also flourish. The bluebells in the high woods should not be missed in late April and early May.

The view from the castle and terrace was described by John Ruskin, the 19th-century father of the conservation movement, as the "Gateway to Paradise". The gardens are especially colourful during May and June when the rhododendrons are in bloom.

History: In the 1780s John, Lord Muncaster, planted several thousand hardwood trees, beech, chestnut, elm and oak throughout the estate. Many of these original trees still provide the framework for the gardens and protection from the elements.

Rhododendrons were first planted around 1840. A decade later Joseph Hooker began collecting rhododendrons in Sikkim and started a passion for the plants that has lasted to this day.

Sir John Ramsden inherited Muncaster in 1917 and soon realised that the gardens provided one of the best sites in the country for growing new species. Together with Lionel de Rothschild and others he helped finance expeditions to southwest China and Tibet. George Forrest and Frank Kingdon-Ward made many separate journeys into the remote mountains and collected thousands of plants and seeds. They were followed by Ludlow and Sherriff and the American Joseph Rock.

Accommodation/pub: Bay Horse Hotel, Ulverston (tel: 01229 583972; ££££).

Sizergh Castle

Rocky garden, particularly notable for its climbers, roses, ferns and conifers. English Heritage Grade II*. National Trust. Map reference ❻

Kendal, LA8 8AE, Cumbria; tel: 01539 560070. < www.nationaltrust.org.uk >
Opening times: castle & garden: Apr–Oct 12.30–5pm, last admission 5pm. National Garden Scheme day. Parties/coaches accepted.
Admission prices: castle and garden: adults £5, children £2.50, family £12.50, parties of 15 + £4pp; garden: adults £2.50, children £1.20.
Facilities: parking, disabled access (manual and powered buggies available), shop, plants for sale, refreshments, guided walks. Picnics permitted. Guide dogs only.

Two of the chief features in this garden are the 14th-century Pele tower covered in climbers, which in autumn glows a fiery red, and the Rock Garden, set in a dell fed by streams, pools and waterfalls from the lake above and rightly regarded as one of the best in the country. When first planted, it was quite open, but encroaching conifers have made it more secluded as time has passed. These conifers, many of them dwarf varieties, are features in themselves and help make the numerous winding walks even more delightful. The original alpines have been replaced by damp-loving plants,

BELOW: autumn display at Muncaster Castle.

Map: pages 248–9

Nearer to the castle, the terraces, planted with shrubs and climbers, are glorious in autumn, while the spectacular maples and recently restored Dutch Garden full of flowering cherries make for fine spring viewing.

History: Sizergh Castle was originally built as a bastion against the Scots on one of the few passable routes for invading bands. It was the home of the Strickland family for 750 years before being acquired by the National Trust. In 1926 the firm of T. R. Hayes of Ambleside was commissioned to design and build the Rock Garden using natural local limestone materials.

especially ferns, making this one of the best collections in Britain. The Rock Garden sits well amongst the limestone outcrops, screes and cliffs that abound on the large 1,500 acre (600-hectare) estate.

Accommodation: Crosthwaite House, Crosthwaite (tel: 01539 568264; £–££). **Local pub:** *Punch Bowl Inn, Crosthwaite.*

D U R H A M

County Durham has two fine botanic gardens, one attached to the university and the other a teaching facility for Houghall College. Of the historic gardens, Eggleston Hall has the most charm.

Eggleston Hall Gardens

Rare plants and shrubs and a traditional kitchen garden.
Map reference ❼

Barnard Castle DL12 0AG, Durham; tel: 01833 650115; fax: 01833 650971.
< www.egglestonhallgardens.com >
Opening times: *year-round daily 10am–5pm. Parties/coaches accepted. Viewing by appointment. House closed.*
Admission prices: *adults £1, children free, season £5. Evening tours in summer.*
Facilities: *parking, disabled access, shop, plants for sale, refreshments. No picnics. Dogs allowed on leads.*

Eggleston's enchanting Victorian gardens are bisected by a moorland stream and planted with rare herbaceous plants and shrubs visible from the winding paths. A high wall encloses the original kitchen gardens – its fruit and vegetables are still cultivated using traditional methods.

History: There has been a house on the site for almost 400 years. Old diaries record crops of apples, pears, cherries, plums, apricots, walnuts, gooseberries, strawberries, artichokes and other vegetables.

Accommodation: Rose & Crown, Romaldkirk (tel: 01833 650213; ££–£££); George Hotel, Piercebridge (tel: 01325 374576; £££–££££).

ABOVE LEFT: red hot pokers at Sizergh Castle.

BELOW: purple-sprouting broccoli from Eggleston Hall's kitchen garden.

GREATER MANCHESTER

Apart from a handful of well-designed municipal parks, this highly industrialised part of the country has few historic gardens to speak of. Dunham Massey just south of the city is exceptional.

Dunham Massey

Plantsman's garden surrounding 18th-century house. English Heritage Grade II*. National Trust.
Map reference **❽**

Altrincham, Manchester WA14 4SJ, Greater Manchester; tel: 0161 9411025; fax: 0161 929 7508.
< www.nationaltrust.org.uk >
Opening times: *Apr–end Oct/beginning Nov daily 11am–5.30pm (4.30pm last week of season).*
National Garden Scheme day. Parties/coaches accepted. Viewing by appointment. House open.
Admission prices: *house or garden: adults £3.80, children £1.90 (under-5s*

BELOW: Dunham Massey's manicured gardens.

free); house & garden: £5.80, children £2.90, family £14.
Facilities: *parking, disabled access, shop, plants for sale, refreshments.*

Dunham Massey is a great plantsman's garden with interesting historic features such as an orangery, pump house, Victorian bark house and the remains of the Elizabethan Mount. Acid conditions and a varied site provide for a wide range of unusual shade- and moisture-loving plants including giant Chinese lilies, Himalayan blue poppies and rare late-flowering azaleas, all set amongst manicured lawns, mixed borders and cool woodland.

History: The Elizabethan Mount formed part of the garden created at the start of the 17th century. The second Earl of Warrington removed the walled enclosures and created an enormous park which included terraces, parterres, and two productive gardens. In the 18th century the fifth Earl of Stamford was responsible for the flowing lawns and more naturalistic planting seen today. He also planted purple beech, two specimens of which still survive near the orangery. His son, Lord Grey of Groby, collected trees and plants of all kinds, as did the seventh Earl, who doubled the expenditure on the gardens in the mid-19th century. Standards began to slip by the end of the century, but the ninth Earl took a keen interest in the gardens and laid out a parterre by the north front and a rose garden. After World War II the garden lost many of its features (the workforce diminished from 10 to 2) and it was not until the National Trust took it over with a generous bequest from the 10th and last Earl of Stamford in 1976 that restoration began.

Accommodation: *Quality Hotel, Altrincham (tel: 0161 928 7121; ££).* **Local pub:** *The Spread Eagle, Lymm.*

Map:
pages
248–9

LANCASHIRE

The weather in this corner of the Northwest can be harsh and great gardens are few and far between. The Lennox-Boyd estate is the pick of the bunch; the variety of plants that flourish here is remarkable.

Gresgarth Hall

A large and impressive garden designed by Arabella Lennox-Boyd. Map reference ❾

Caton LA2 9BN, Lancs; tel: 01524 770313.
< www.arabellalennoxboyd.com >
***Opening hours:** Apr–Sep: 2nd Sunday in the month 11am–5pm. Parties/coaches accepted on open days. No viewing by appointment. House closed.*
***Admission prices:** adults £3.50, children free but must be accompanied.*
***Facilities:** parking, disabled access, shop, plants for sale, refreshments. Guide dogs only.*

One of the largest gardens in the northwest, Gresgarth has been extensively relandscaped and planted by Sir Mark and Lady Lennox-Boyd over the past 20 years. Straddling the Artle Beck, a tributary of the Lune, it includes herbaceous borders, terraces, a rose collection, a water garden, the Lilac Walk, a bluebell wood, the Serpentine Walk, an orchard, a nuttery, the ornamental kitchen garden, greenhouses and a rhododendron collection. In all, there are several thousand plants and trees.

History: There has been a Pele Tower on this site for many years, possibly as early as 1330 under the Curwen family. The house has been altered several times subsequently, particularly by Thomas Edmondson in 1805–1810 when the building was enlarged and given its present landscape in the romantic style. Many of the fine trees were planted by his descendants. The Lennox-Boyds purchased it in 1978.

***Accommodation:** Posthouse Hotel, Lancaster (tel: 0870 4009047; ££–£££). **Local pubs:** Snooty Fox, Kirby Lonsdale; Pheasant Inn, Casterton.*

ABOVE: Gresgarth Hall, one of the largest gardens in the region.

MERSEYSIDE

Liverpool boasts many fine public parks. The Botanic Gardens of Calderstone Park, historic Sefton Park and Birkenhead Park across the Mersey are among the country's finest urban green spaces. Croxteth Hall has been singled out here for its exceptional Victorian walled garden.

Croxteth Hall and Country Park

Victorian walled garden within extensive city park. English Heritage Grade II. Map reference ➓

Croxteth Hall Lane, Liverpool L12 0HB, Merseyside; tel: 0151 2285311.
***Opening times:** house: Easter–Sep daily 10.30am–5pm. Parties/coaches accepted. Viewing by appointment. House open.*
***National Collection:** hardy fuchsias*
***Admission prices:** adults £4, children & over-60s £2, family £9.90. Discount for booked groups of 20 +.*
***Facilities:** parking, disabled access, shop, plants for sale, refreshments. Picnics permitted. Guide dogs only.*

The house, farm and gardens are part of an historic estate 6 miles (9.5 km) outside Liverpool city centre, comprising parkland and woodland extending to over 500 acres (80 hectares). Its centrepiece is the Victorian Walled Garden, which retains many period features, including heated flue walls, a mushroom house and elaborately trained fruit trees. The high walls provide a sheltered environment to grow vegetables, soft fruit, etc. There are also colourful borders of perennials, an organic plot and greenhouses with tropical plants and cacti.

There's a working farm on the estate with a collection of rare farm breeds, which children love to visit. A network of paths criss-crosses the woodlands, which are filled with wild flowers and grazing livestock.

History: The garden traditionally supplied produce to Croxteth Hall. The house, once part of a country estate covering hundreds of square miles, was the ancestral home of the Earls of Sefton from 1575 until the death of the last earl in 1972. Today the estate is managed by the City of Liverpool and is one of the major heritage centres of the Northwest.

Accommodation: Trials Hotel, Castle St, Liverpool (tel: 0151 2271021; £££) Local pub: Fox & Hounds, Barnston.

RIGHT:
Trained apple trees in Croxteth Hall's Victorian Garden.

NORTHUMBERLAND

Map: pages 248–9

Northumberland has two Grade I properties. Belsay's main attraction is its enchanting quarry garden, while the contemporary water garden is Alnwick's spectacular centrepiece. Other regional highlights include the vast rockery and carpet bedding at Cragside and Wallington's walled garden.

Alnwick Castle

Contemporary landscaping with spectacular water features and fine ornamental garden. English Heritage Grade I. Map reference ⓫

Denwick Lane, Alnwick NE66 1YU, Northumberland; tel: 01665 511133. < www.alnwickgarden.com >
Opening times: *garden: year-round 10am–5pm/dusk; castle: Easter–Oct. Parties/coaches accepted.*
Admission prices: *adults £4, children under 16 free, concessions £3.50, parties £3.50 pp.*
Facilities: *parking, disabled access, shop, refreshments. Picnics permitted. Dogs on leads in grounds. Guide dogs only in park.*

The garden is the inspiration of Jane, Duchess of Northumberland, whose vision is to develop it into a contemporary space that integrates water and light into a "theatre of gardens". Its dramatic main feature is the Grand Cascade, which is a magnificent tumbling mass of water ending in an eruption of fountains sending 77 gallons (350 litres) of water into the air every second. The sensational displays are synchronised by computer system in a sequence lasting 12 minutes.

Above the Cascade is the Ornamental Garden, a symmetrical, structured garden with a strong Continental influence, utilising box and yew. There are places to sit and catch the sun, with inviting doorways on to flower beds and golden amber coloured paths past lavender and fruit trees. The

ABOVE: the Grand Cascade, Alnwick Castle.

central point, surrounded by a wooden pergola, is the dark source pool with pebbled rills inviting visitors to explore.

The Rose Garden is a gentle mixture of pergola paths and grassy walkways covered in shrub and climbing roses mixed with glorious clematis and honeysuckle. Star among the roses is the Alnwick Castle Rose launched at Chelsea in 2001.

The Alnwick Garden opened to the paying public in April 2002 and was soon overwhelmed by its success. Projected to receive 300,000 visitors in its first year, it has become the second largest attraction in the Northeast (after Beamish).

History: The garden is the seventh on this site, which is set in the Capability Brown landscape of the grounds of Alnwick Castle. (Details of its antecedents are available on request). The Alnwick Garden is the first UK commission of Wirtz International NV, an internationally renowned Belgian landscape garden practice.

ABOVE: the Quarry Garden, Belsay Hall. *Accommodation:White Swan Hotel, Alnwick (tel: 01665 602109, ££); The Old Manse, Chatton (tel: 01668 215343, £); Percy Arms, Chatton (tel: 01668 215244; £).* **Local pub:** *Tankerville Arms, Eglingham.*

Belsay Hall

Picturesque-style gardens surrounding a castle and manor house. English Heritage Grade I. Map reference ⑫

Belsay, Newcastle-on-Tyne NE20 0DX; tel: 01661 881636; fax: 01661 881043.
< english-heritage.org.uk >
Opening times: *garden: Apr–Sep daily 10am–6pm, Oct 10am–5pm, Nov–Mar 10am–4pm. Parties/coaches accepted. Viewing by appointment. House open.*
Admission prices: *adults £4.50, children £2.30 (under-5s free), concessions £3.40, English Heritage members free.*
Facilities: *parking, disabled access, refreshments (summer only), plants for sale (summer only). Picnics permitted. Dogs allowed on leads in grounds.*

Belsay's garden is in the Picturesque style. It consists of formal terraces to the south of the 19th-century Greek Revival hall, with many original plantings surviving, overlooking a rhododendron garden full of colour from the end of May through June. The terraces lead on to the

Magnolia Terrace, where the restored rose border flowers well into October. Parallel to this runs another long border planted with interesting herbaceous plants. To the west is a winter garden with spring- and summer-flowering heathers, scented tree heathers and long-established Douglas firs.

The Quarry Garden was carefully planted by Sir Charles Monck, who created a series of ravines, corridors and pinnacles supporting rare and exotic plants. Species of rhododendrons flower here from November to August, climbers scramble 30 ft (10 metres) up the quarry faces, spring bulbs carpet the meadow and species lilies, the aristocrats of the garden, flower from May to September.

History: In the early 17th century a formal walled garden was created in front of the manor house and castle. This was replaced in the 18th century, when parkland was developed. Around the mid-19th century Sir Charles Monck developed the gardens in the Picturesque style. His grandson, Sir Arthur Middleton, introduced many new plants and created the Rhododendron Garden.

Local pubs: The Waggon Inn, on the A696; The Highlander Inn, A696; The Beresford Arms, Walton.

Bide-a-Wee-Cottage

Delightful small garden created out of a disused quarry. Map reference ⑬

Stanton, Netherwitton, Morpeth NE65 8PR, Northumberland; tel: 01670 772262.
Opening times: *May–Aug Wed & Sat 1.30–5pm. Parties/coaches accepted. Viewing by appointment. House closed.*
National Collection: *centaurea.*
Admission prices: *£2; free to RHS members on production of card.*
Facilities: *parking, disabled access, plants for sale, refreshments. No picnics. Guide dogs only.*

Set on an exposed hillside above the Font Valley, this 2-acre (1 hectare) garden was created out of a small disused sandstone quarry. It features large drifts of unusual perennials, grasses and ferns. Paths and steps meander through natural rock and dry stone walls. A pond and small stream form the focus of the quarry; the damp margins are planted with bog plants and primula. The cool humid atmosphere on the north bank of the quarry is perfect for cardiocrinum, the giant Himalayan lily. It has a large collection of Centaurea, all distributed within the matrix of planting. Adjacent to the garden is a wild flower meadow with beehives.

Local pub: The Beresford Arms, Whalton.

Cragside House

Formal Victorian gardens and vast rockery. English Heritage Grade II*. National Trust. Map reference ⑭

Rothbury, Morpeth NE65 7PX, Northumberland; tel: 01669 620333; fax: 01669 620066.
< www.nationaltrust.org.uk >
Opening times: *garden: last week Apr–Oct Nov Tues–Sun (plus BH Mons) 10.30am–7pm, last admission 5pm; Nov–mid-Dec Wed–Sun 11am–4pm. House: last week Apr–Sep 1–5.30pm, last admission 4.30pm; Oct 1–4.30pm, last admission 3.30pm. Parties/coaches accepted. Viewing by appointment.*

BELOW: the Cragside House rockery.

Map: pages 248–9

Admission prices: *house & gardens: adults £7.20, children £3.60, family £18, booked parties £6.10 pp; gardens: adults £4.80, family £12, booked parties £3.80 pp.*
Facilities: *parking, disabled access, shop, plants for sale, refreshments. Picnics permitted. Dogs allowed on leads.*

The focus of this garden is the vast rockery installed by Lord Armstrong in the 19th century and restored by the National Trust. Alpine and moorland plants flourish in the crevices of the giant boulders. A range of rhododendrons, azaleas, brooms, berberis, roses and rowans have been planted to add variety and colour to the Debdon Gorge scenery. In the lower reaches of the gorge an open arboretum includes specimen North American conifers which, in the favourable damp conditions, have attained enormous heights and girths.

The Trust has also restored the Orchard House with its system of rotating pots towards the light to provide balanced growth, as well as the Display House and Palm House. But the glory of the formal gardens is the Victorian carpet bedding – almost literally "carpet" in this case, as several of the beds copy the pattern of carpets in the house.

History: The great Victorian inventor Lord Armstrong built this huge house in 1864 after blasting the site out of the solid rock. He created a landscape out of the empty moorland, laying 31 miles (50 km) of roads and paths, digging out four lakes and planting 7 million trees and shrubs. He used his inventiveness and engineering skill to supply the house with electricity from his hydraulic schemes (it was the first house in the world to be electrified), as well as moving water about the gardens to produce cascades and pools and to operate machinery.

Accommodation: *Saddle Hotel, Alnmouth (tel: 01665 830476; £–££).* **Local pub:** *Cook and Barker Inn.*

Howick Hall

East-coast garden supporting many tender varieties of plants.
Map reference ⑮.

Howick, Alnwick NE66 3LB, Northumberland; tel: 01665 577285.
Opening times: *Apr–Oct daily 1–6pm. Parties/coaches accepted. Viewing by appointment. House closed.*
Admission prices: *adults £3, children free, over-60s £2.*
Facilities: *parking, limited disabled access, plants for sale, refreshments. Guide dogs only.*

The emphasis in the garden is on pleasant informality in the style of William Robinson, an Irish gardener and horticultural writer. Being only 1 mile (2 km) from the sea, the garden supports many tender plants. *Eucryphia cordifolia*, *Drimys winteri*, *Embothrium coccineum* and *Rhododendron fragrantissimum* are just some of the plants that one would not expect to see on the east coast of Northumberland.

The herbaceous borders were planted by Lady Grey in the 1920s, with the agapanthus on the second terrace being a special feature. There is a Long

BELOW:
Howick Hall.

Walk which starts at the end of the Woodland Garden and winds down to the sea.

History: Howick was the family home of the Grey family from 1319 until the death of the fifth Earl Grey in 1963. It then passed to his eldest daughter, Lady Mary Howick, and then to his grandson, the present Lord Howick of Glendale. The second Earl Grey, the prime minister responsible for passing the Great Reform Bill of 1832, was a keen gardener and planted many of the hardwoods.

*Accommodation: Dunstanburgh Castle Hotel, Embleton (tel: 01665 576111; ££). **Local pubs:** Cottage Inn, Dunstan; Burnside, Longhoughton; Saddle Hotel, Alnmouth; Jolly Fisherman, Craster.*

National Collection: Elders.
Opening times: walled garden: Apr–Sep daily 10am–7pm, Oct 10am–6pm, Nov–Mar 10am–4pm; grounds: daily in daylight; house: last week in Mar–Sep Wed–Mon 1–5.30pm. Parties/coaches accepted. Viewing by appointment.
Admission prices: walled garden & grounds only: adults £4.10, booked parties £3.60 pp; house & walled garden: adults £5.70, children £2.85, family £14.25, booked parties £5.20.
Facilities: parking, disabled access, shop, plants for sale, refreshments. Picnics permitted. Dogs allowed on leads in grounds.

Wallington

Spectacular walled garden. English Heritage Grade II*. National Trust. Map reference ⓰

*Cambo, Morpeth NE61 4AR, Northumberland; tel: 01670 774283; fax: 01670 774420.
< www.nationaltrust.org.uk >*

Wallington's rolling parkland is crossed by straight and serpentine walks leading to ponds with waterlilies and plenty of birdlife. Nearer to the house are open views across the ha-ha towards Hadrian's Wall and the Shaftoe Crags further off. Statuary and urns are placed to attract the eye, as are mixed shrubberies planted in Victorian times for colour and variety. The highlight, however, is the

ABOVE:
Wallington's
conservatory,
home of the
90-year old
fuchsia 'Rose
of Castile
Improved'.

impressive Walled Garden with its terraced borders, lead statues, nearby conservatories and original follies. Clever planting with an air of informality sets off the garden against the backdrop of parkland and woods. In the parts of the garden near the stream water irises, hostas and the National Collection of elders thrive. In the conservatory a spectacular Edwardian planting scheme survives, but the highlight is the 90-year-old fuchsia, "Rose of Castile Improved".

History: The Palladian mansion was built for Sir Walter Calverley Blackett in the mid-1730s. The garden design possibly benefited from the assistance of "Capability " Brown, whose childhood home was just a mile away. There is also a bridge by James Paine dating from 1755. Sir George Otto Trevelyan inherited the estate in 1886. Being an enthusiastic gardener, he adapted Sir Walter's design for the Walled Garden and built a large conservatory. When the National Trust took over years later it reinstated Sir George's designs.

Accommodation: Linden Hall Hotel, Longhorsley, Morpeth (tel: 01670 516611, £££–££££).

NORTH & EAST YORKSHIRE

Yorkshire is a county of grand historic estates. Castle Howard, Duncombe Park and Studley Royal are among the finest examples of 18th-century landscape gardens in the country, characterised by baroque styling and carefully planned vistas of the majestic Yorkshire countryside. Among the more recently established gardens, Harlow Carr, Newby Hall and Parcevall Hall are of great horticultural interest.

Aldby Park

Historic park and garden on the site of King Edwin's 7th-century castle. Map reference ⓱

Aldby Park, Buttercrambe, York YO41 1XU, N. Yorks; tel: 01759 371398.
Opening times: *open by appointment, 1–5pm. National Garden Scheme days. Parties/coaches accepted. House closed.*
Admission prices: *adults £3, children & over-60s £1.*
ABOVE: **Facilities:** *parking, disabled access,*
tools of the *shop, plants for sale. Picnics permitted.*
trade. *Dogs allowed on leads.*

This superb ancient site has been extensively remodelled and replanted. The terraces by the river hold primulas and ferns; the Saxon Mound features yuccas, day lilies and agapanthus; the mound north of the sarcophagus is white and yellow, contrasting well with the yew and box. *Hypericum* 'Hydcote' and corkscrew hazel add interest.

History: The garden's twin mounds and dry moat indicate the site of King Edwin's 7th-century castle. In 1557 William Darley bought the manor of Buttercrambe from the Earl of Westminister; an early estate map dated 1633 shows a Tudor house situated 25 yards/metres east of the present one. The present house was built in 1726 by John Brewster Darley, probably to his own design. His son and heir, Henry, continued to work on the house and employed Thomas Knowlton to remodel the park and garden, laying out the terraces leading down the steep bank to the Derwent, the walk along the top of the bank, and the paths winding round the Saxon Mound.

Accommodation: Burythorpe House Hotel, Burythorpe, Malton (tel: 01653 658200; ££).
Local pub: Gold Cup Inn, Low Catton.

Beningbrough Hall

A delightful and restful garden. National Trust. English Heritage Grade II. Map reference ⓲

Shipton-by-Beningbrough, York YO30 1DD, N. Yorks; tel: 01904 470666; fax: 01904 470002.
< www.nationaltrust.org.uk >
Opening times: *last week Apr–Jun & Sep–Oct Sat–Wed (but open Good Fri), July & Aug daily except Thur 11am–5.30pm (house noon–5pm). National Garden Scheme days. Parties/coaches accepted. Viewing by appointment.*
Admission prices: *house & garden: adults £5.20, children £2.70, family £13.50; garden & exhibition only: adults £4, children £2, family £10.*
Facilities: *parking, disabled access, shop, plants for sale, refreshments. Picnics permitted. No dogs.*

E arly plans of Beningbrough show it at the centre of avenues radiating out in a formal landscape design, but this was soon replaced by a more natural scheme with open parkland and clumps of trees. The Walled Garden is now less of a kitchen garden than it used to be, but it still features a range of fruit on its walls and the original pear alley at its centre. Elsewhere double borders have an Edwardian theme with cool midsummer colours of whites and blues repeating along their length. In the two small formal gardens one has cobbles and York flagstones, and the other box hedging enclosing miniature roses.

History: The estate records are lost but it is known that the very capable Thomas Foster became Head Gardener in 1827. After 1916 the Earl and Countess of Chesterfield owned the property. Being keen racehorse and stud owners, they ensured that the main feature of the garden, the long South Border, was in full bloom in late September for the St Leger meeting at Doncaster.

Local pubs: Three Hares, Bilborough; Crown, Great Ouseburn.

Castle Howard

Grand 18th-century landscape garden. English Heritage Grade I. Map reference ⓳.

York YO60 7DA, N. Yorks; tel: 01653 648444; fax: 01653 648501.
< www.castlehoward.co.uk >
Opening times: *mid-Feb–Oct daily 10am–6.30pm (house 11am– 4.30pm).*

Map: pages 248–9

BELOW: borders at Beningbrough.

RIGHT: *Coaches/parties accepted.*
temple at *Viewing by appointment.*
Duncombe **Admission prices:** *house &*
Park. *grounds: adults £8, children*
£5.50, over-60s & students
£7.25; gardens and grounds:
adults £5, children (4–16)
£3.50; season: adults £30,
children £16. Group
reductions available.
Facilities: *parking, disabled*
access, shop, plants for sale,
refreshments. Picnics
permitted. Dogs allowed on
leads in park.

A major feature of Castle Howard is its rose collection of over 2,000 varieties in the old walled garden near the house. It actually consists of three adjoining gardens: one dedicated to the memory of Lady Cecilia Howard, contains old roses, many quite rare; the other two were replanted in 1994 and 1995 and contain modern roses, including David Austin's English roses.

Ray Wood, which originally held a remarkable collection of plants and ornamental statuary, was felled in 1940 and re-planted in 1970 by George Howard to the design of James Russell. It contains one of the largest and best collections of rhododendrons – over 800 varieties – and banks of pieris, rare magnolias, hydrangeas, viburnums, maples and rowans offering colour from spring to autumn.

The park contains a collection of lead statuary of Classical Greek and Roman figures, recently restored, and many interesting stone structures, such as bridges, temples, obelisks, pyramids, mock fortifications and not least the Grand Mausoleum. In all there are 125 acres (50 hectares) of parkland set in the 10,000-acre (4,000-hectare) estate.

History: The home of the Howard family since its completion, Castle Howard was Sir John Vanbrugh's first and perhaps finest creation, with considerable assistance from Nicholas Hawksmoor. It was built in a flam-

boyant baroque style over the course of 10 years from the first drawings in 1699, but it was added to continually for almost 100 years after that, culminating in the Palladian-style west wing in 1777.

The original garden was intended purely to provide fruit and vegetables for the house but a major tree-planting programme was soon initiated, the south parterre laid out and ornamental statuary installed. By the middle of the 18th century the walled garden had been doubled in size to 11 acres (4.5 hectares). A hundred years later W.A. Nesfield redesigned the garden in a much more elaborate pattern, with the Atlas fountain at its centre. At the end of the 19th century this was simplified by Lady Rosalind to be less high-maintenance.

Accommodation: Grange Farm, Bulmer (tel: 01653 618600, £). Green Man, Malton (tel: 01653 600370, ££). Local pubs: Stone Trough, Kirkham; Gold Cup Inn, Low Catton.

Duncombe Park

One of the finest baroque landscapes in England. English Heritage Grade I. Map reference ⓴

Helmsley YO62 5EB,N. Yorks; tel: 01439 770213/01439 771115; fax: 01439 771114. < www.duncombepark.com >

Opening times: gardens & grounds: May–Oct Sun–Thur 11am–5pm; house by guided tour only 12.30–3.30pm. Parties/coaches must pre-book to visit house (11am–4pm).
Admission prices: house & garden: adults £6, children (over 10) £3, over-60s £5; garden: adults £3, children £1.50, over-60s £3; parkland: adults £2, children £1, over-60s £2; season: £20 per family, £10 per adult.
Facilities: parking, disabled access, shop, refreshments. Picnics permitted. Dogs allowed on leads in parkland only.

Vast terraces with classical temples, woodland walks, breathtaking parterres and a Secret Garden, all set within a National Nature Reserve, make Duncombe Park a particularly enjoyable garden to visit. Other features include a ha-ha and an orangery.

History: It is thought that the 35-acre (14-hectare) gardens, which pre-date the era of Capability Brown and Humphry Repton by some 60 years and comprise one of the finest baroque landscapes in England, were completed between 1713 and 1730 to the designs of either Charles Bridgeman or Stephen Switzer, or both. The green gardens were created within an ancient parkland on a virgin plateau 184 ft (56 metres) above Helmsley Castle and the Arcadian Valley of the River Rye, and were the incentive

behind the choice of site for Duncombe's Great House, which was completed by 1718. Duncombe was much praised in *English Gardens and Landscapes 1700–1750* by Christopher Hussey, "The grass terraces of Duncombe and Rievaulx are unique, and perhaps the most spectacularly beautiful among English landscape conceptions of the 18th century." It is thought that there may have been plans to link up with the later terrace created by the Duncombes above Rievaulx Abbey.

Accommodation: Black Swan, Helmsley (tel: 01439-770466 £££–££££). **Local pub:** *Feversham Arms, Helmsley.*

Map: pages 248–9

Harlow Carr

The longest streamside garden in the UK. RHS Garden. Map reference ㉑

Crag Lane, Harrogate HG3 1QB, N. Yorks; tel: 01423 565418; fax: 01423 530663. < www.rhs.org.uk >
Opening times: year-round 9.30am–6pm (or dusk, if sooner). National Garden Scheme days. Parties/coaches accepted, preferably by appointment. House closed.
National Collections: rhubarb, polypodium and Dryopteris ferns, Fuchsia Section Quelusia (provisional) and Calluna vulgaris (heather) (provisional).
Admission prices: adults £4.50, children

LEFT:
the RHS
garden of
Harlow Carr.

11–16 £1 (under-11s free), over-60s £3.50, students £2, groups of 20+ £3.50 pp.
Facilities: *parking, disabled access, shop, plants for sale, refreshments. Picnics permitted. No dogs. Extensive programme of annual events, activities, guided walks and courses.*

Harlow Carr is an inspiration for all tastes and all ages. The woodland, filled with beech and oak underplanted with rhododendrons and azaleas, and arboretum are havens for naturalists. The spectacular swathe of Harlow Carr hybrid candelabra primulas, astilbes and hostas along the cultivated streamside is one of the garden's chief highlights. Sandstone and limestone rock gardens, contemporary grass borders, scented, herb, winter and foliage gardens, flower and vegetable trials and alpine houses are just a few of the garden's other features. The Old Gatehouse is now home to a museum of gardening with over 1,000 objects from tools to seed packets.

History: The gardens were established in 1950 by Colonel Charles Grey as a showcase for northern gardeners. His aim was to provide a garden setting to assess the suitability of plants for northern climates.

Accommodation: Ashley House, Harrogate (tel: 01423 507474; ££); Kimberley Hotel, Harrogate (tel: 01423 505613, ££). Local pubs: Malt Shovel, Brearton.

Newby Hall & Gardens

Award-winning gardens with the longest double herbaceous borders in Europe. English Heritage Grade II*. Map reference ㉒

Ripon HG4 5AE, N. Yorks; tel: 01423 322583; fax: 01423 324 452. < www.newbyhall.com >
National Collection: *cornus.*
Opening times: *Apr–Sep Tues–Sun & BHs, garden 11am–5.30pm, house noon–5pm. Parties/coaches accepted. Viewing by appointment.*
Admission prices: *adults £5.70, children £4.20 (under-4s free), over-60s £4.70.*
Facilities: *parking, disabled access, shop, plants for sale, refreshments, children's adventure playground and miniature railway. Picnics permitted. Dogs allowed in special exercise area only.*

These 40-acre (16-hectare) gardens fan out from a main axis running from the south front of the house down to the River Ure. The axis consists of double herbaceous borders with double yew hedges and a broad grass walk down the centre. On either side are rooms of formal design, each filled with plants planned to be at their best at different times of the year. They include a rose garden, tropical garden, white garden, water garden, autumn garden and orchard

BELOW: the double herbaceous borders at Newby Hall.

Map: pages 248-9

Accommodation: Swinton Park, Masham (tel 01765 680900; ££££); Boars' Head, Ripley (tel: 01423 771 888; £££); Bay Tree Farm, Aldfield (tel:01765 620394; £). Local pubs: The Crown, Roecliffe; Sawley Arms, Sawley.

Parcevall Hall Gardens

Early 20th-century plantsman's garden. Map reference ㉓

Skyreholme, Skipton BD23 6DE, N. Yorks; tel: 01756 720311. < www.parcevallhallgardens.co.uk > Opening times: Apr–Oct daily 10am–6pm, last admission 5pm. National Garden Scheme day. Coaches/parties accepted. Viewing by appointment. House closed. Admission prices: adults £3, children 50p. Facilities: parking, shop, plants for sale, refreshments. Picnics permitted. No disabled access. Dogs allowed on leads.

The gardens at Parcevall Hall feature an extraordinary architectural layout as well as stunning views of the Yorkshire Dales. Sir William Milner was largely responsible for their design and planting in 1927. They benefit from a wide variety of soils, including limestone and gritstone, which allows rhododendrons (many of which originate from China) and camellias to grow alongside limestone outcrops. It is also a plantsman's garden with naturalised daffodils, including "W.F. Milner", and beside the lily pond are naturalised *Primula florindae* given by Kingdon Ward. The Woodland Walk is a delight. There are also fish ponds, a rock garden and the Stations of the Cross in the grounds.

History: The gardens were laid out between 1927 and 1930. The original part of the hall dates back to 1597 but was extended in the late 1920s by Sir William Milner. The gardens are gradually being restored.

Accommodation: Low Skibeden House, Skipton (tel: 01756 793849; £–££). Local pub: Malt Shovel, Brearton.

garden. A national collection of cornus is also here.

History: Newby Hall was built between 1685–1695. The owner, Sir Edward Blackett, employed Peter Aram as Head Gardener, who laid out the formal gardens and avenues in the style of the period. This design was superseded in 1921 by that of Major Edward Compton, who was influenced by Lawrence Johnston's Hidcote Manor. The Major died in 1977 leaving his son, Richard Compton, to renovate and replant the garden.

ABOVE LEFT: faithfully restored, Parcevall Hall Gardens.

Rievaulx Terrace and Temples

Landscaped terrace running between two temples. National Trust. Map reference ㉔

Rievaulx, Helmsley, YO62 5LJ, N. Yorks; tel: 01439-798340.
< www.nationaltrust.org.uk >
Opening times: *last week Mar–end Oct/beginning Nov daily 10.30am–6pm (5pm in Oct/Nov). Last admission one hour before closing.*
Parties/coaches accepted. Viewing by appointment. House closed.
Admission prices: *adults £3.30, children £1.50, family £8, groups £2.80 pp.*
Facilities: *parking, disabled access, shop (ice creams only). Picnics permitted. Dogs allowed on leads.*

ABOVE:
Rievaulx
Terrace.

RIGHT:
Ripley Castle
gardens.

This half-mile (1-km) serpentine walk, with Ionic and Doric temples at either end, offers stunning and unexpected views through the trees of the ruins of the 12th-century Cistercian abbey at Rievaulx below. Also revealed is the arched bridge over the River Rye, with its valley and the rolling Hambledon Hills around it. Beech and other deciduous trees line the walk and the ground is carpeted with clumps of primroses, cowslips, lilies, orchids, oxlips and clovers amongst many others.

History: In the 1750s Thomas Duncombe III decided to create a similar ride to the one his father had created at Duncombe Park *(see page 264)* some 40 years before, but using a less formal plan with a more winding path. It is thought it was his intention to link the two rides with a viaduct, but this was never built.

Accommodation: Black Swan, Helmsley (tel: 01439 770466; £££–££££). **Local pubs:** *Star Inn, Harome; Malt Shovel, Oswaldkirk.*

Ripley Castle

An 18th-century landscape garden with fine formal areas and a walled garden. English Heritage Grade II. Map reference ㉕.

Harrogate HG3 3AY, Yorks; tel: 01423 770152; fax: 01423 771745.
< www.ripleycastle.co.uk >

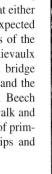

National Collection: Hyacinths.
Opening times: garden: daily 9am–5pm;
castle: Jun–Aug daily 10.30am–3pm,
Sep–May Tues, Thur, weekends
10.30am–3pm. Parties/coaches accepted.
Admission prices: castle & gardens:
adults £6, children £3.50, over-60s £5;
gardens: adults £3.50, children £2,
over-60s £3.
Facilities: parking, disabled access, shop,
plants for sale, refreshments. Picnics
permitted. Guide dogs only.

Ripley Castle's gardens are particularly impressive in spring when the hyacinths (40 varieties) are in bloom in the Walled Garden. The remainder of this area is filled with lawns, beds and borders; rare fruit trees; and vegetables, herbs and spices for the castle's table. The herbaceous borders are some of the longest in Britain.

The hot houses, renovated in 1991, contain a huge variety of cacti, ferns and tropical plants including citrus, begonias and bananas. In the centre is an orangery-cum-palm house crowned by a roof of curved glass. In the Pleasure Grounds, a walk around the lake skirts the deer park where fallow and red deer graze under oak trees.

History: The gardens were intended to supply the castle with fruit and vegetables to complement the home farm's supply of meat and dairy produce. When Sir John Ingilby's over-ambitious plans for rebuilding the castle forced him into exile in France in the 1780s, gardening remained his consolation; he even requested his agent to bring him seeds from Ripley.

His son, Sir William, embarked upon a massive scheme to improve the estate in the 1820s, with a walled garden of 4 acres (1.5 hectares) separated into formal, flower and vegetable gardens, the Pleasure Grounds of 8 acres (3 hectares) and the hot houses.

Accommodation: The Boar's Head Hotel, Ripley (tel: 01423 771888; £££); General Tarleton, Ferrensby (tel: 01423 340284; ££–£££).
Local pubs: Malt Shovel, Brearton; Sawley Arms, Sawley.

Studley Royal and Fountains Abbey

Map: pages 248–9

Grand garden in early English landscape style. English Heritage Grade I. National Trust. Map reference ㉖

Ripon HG4 3DY. N. Yorks; tel: 01765 608888. < www.nationaltrust.org.uk >
Opening times: abbey, Fountains Hall & water garden: daily (except Fri in Nov, Dec & Jan) Apr–Sep 10am–6pm, Oct–Mar 10am–4pm or dusk if earlier. Parties/coaches accepted. Viewing by appointment. House closed.

Admission prices: abbey, water garden & mill: adult £5, children £3, family £14. Booked groups of 31+ £4 pp, children £2.20 pp; groups of 31+ £3.80 pp, children £2.10 pp. Deer park: £2 car park.
Facilities: parking, disabled access, shop, plants for sale, refreshments. Picnics permitted. No dogs.

This famous garden encapsulates much of the early English Landscape style, though none of the famous gardeners of the period worked on it. Typical of the Yorkshire spirit, John Aislabie, its designer, felt he could do it without them and it is clear that he and his son William, succeeded.

ABOVE: the Temple of Piety, Fountains Abbey.

Starting at the formal Water Garden, which is the basis for John Aislabie's creation, visitors proceed past a sequence of curved and semi-circular ponds, with the beautiful Temple of Piety and a number of classical statues set in front of the wooded hillsides, and follows serpentine paths past other buildings, all with lovely views down the valley.

On one side of the valley is the Banqueting Hall, on the other the Octagon Tower, Temple of Fame and Anne Boleyn's Seat. The latter features the famous surprise view up the river to Fountains Abbey. Tiers of trees, mostly native species of oak, lime and beech, reach up either side of the valley. Further down, Aislabie accentuated the wildness of the landscape by exposing rocks and planting cleverly to reveal the contours of the land and twists of the river to produce one of the earliest examples of the Picturesque style in England. The landscaping culminates in a view of the towers of Ripon Minster framed in the gateway of the East Gate, by which visitors leave the garden.

History: John Aislabie designed the garden from 1716 after his expulsion from Parliament as Chancellor of the Exchequer during the South Sea Bubble affair, England's first great stock market crash. He continued to develop the garden until his death in 1742 and was followed by his son, William, who completed the project by acquiring Fountains Abbey itself.

Accommodation: St George's Court, Grantley, Ripon (tel: 01765 620618; ££). **Local pub:** *Sawley Arms, Sawley.*

The Valley Gardens

Outstanding public park with spa wells, pump house, sun pavilion and colonnades. English Heritage Grade II. Map reference ㉗

Valley Drive, Harrogate, N. Yorks; tel: 01423 500600; fax: 01423 556720. < www.harrogate.gov.uk > **Opening times:** *year-round until dusk.* **Admission prices:** *free* **Facilities:** *parking, disabled access, refreshments, boating pool.*

This grand 17-acre (7-hectare) public park displays alpine rarities in spring, a romantic rhododendron dell, seasonal bedding displays, good roses and a magnificent dahlia display in late summer. Part of the Valley Gardens is known as Bog's Field; it is believed that a greater number of mineral springs come to the surface here than in any other place on earth (36 of Harrogate's 88 mineral wells are found here).

History: In 1778 Bog's Field became part of Harrogate's Stray – a large piece of common land in the town centre. A path was laid down in 1847 and a pump room followed in 1858. Bog's Field was much improved in the 1920s with the addition of flower beds. After World War II a wide variety of new plants was introduced and in 1957 a host of specimens was donated from New Zealand.

Accommodation: Crown Hotel, Harrogate (tel: 01423 706600 ££–£££); **Local pub:** *Old Bell Tavern; Auctioneer.*

SOUTH & WEST YORKSHIRE

The French-style gardens at Bramham Park, Harewood House grounds landscaped by Capability Brown and Wentworth Castle's 18th-century gardens are all Grade I listed. The Grade II gardens at Brodsworth Hall are a traditional Victorian mixture of formal and informal, and incorporate a rare fern collection.

Map: pages 248–9

Bramham Park

Formal landscape garden in the 18th-century French style. English Heritage Grade I. Map reference ㉘

Bramham, Wetherby LS23 6ND, W. Yorks; tel: 01937 846002/846000; fax: 01937 846001. <www.bramhampark.co.uk>
Opening times: *garden: Apr–Sep daily*

History: The house was built by Robert Benson, whose ideas of garden design were greatly influenced by the French designers of the 18th century, such as Le Nôtre. The layout was masterminded by Benson himself, and his daughter, Harriet, added many of the follies and temples in the woodland.

Accommodation: *Wood Hall Hotel, Linton (tel: 01937 587272; £££).* ***Local pubs:*** *The Red Lion, Bramham; the Bridge Inn, Walshford, Wetherby*

Brodsworth Hall

Victorian garden with water features, woodland and fern dell. English Heritage Grade II*. Map reference ㉙

Brodsworth, Doncaster DN5 7XJ, S. Yorks; tel: 01302 722598; fax: 01302 337165.
Opening times: *gardens: Apr–Oct Tues–Sun noon–6pm, Mon 11am–4pm; Nov–Mar weekends only. House: Apr–Oct Tues–Sun 1–6pm, closed Mon except*

LEFT:
French formal gardens, Bramham Park.

BELOW:
immaculate floral beds, Brodsworth Hall.

11am–4.30pm (last admission 4pm). Parties/coaches accepted by prior arrangement only. House closed except by appointment.
Admission prices: *adults £4, children £2, over-60s £2, season £30.*
Facilities: *parking, disabled access, refreshments. Dogs allowed on leads, but not in formal gardens.*

E arly 18th-century French-style formal gardens with grand vistas and unexpected views, hedges and trees, temples, ornamental ponds and cascades set in over 150 acres (60 hectares) of grounds. There is a significant rose garden and herbaceous borders provide summer colour.

BHs. National Garden Scheme days. Parties/coaches accepted (15 percent discount on groups of 10 +). Viewing by appointment. Pre-booked guided tours of house Apr–Oct mornings.

Admission prices: house & garden: adults £5.50, children £2.80, over-60s £4.10; garden: adults £3.50, children £1, over-60s £2.60.
Facilities: parking, disabled access, shop, refreshments. Picnics permitted. No dogs.

The grounds at Brodsworth are a traditional mixture of formal and informal. Floral displays, water features, statuary, shrubberies, rose gardens and an immaculate croquet lawn contrast with a rambling woodland incorporating charming features such as the Target House, a perfect sun-trap, and a rocky fern dell. A rare collection of 350 ferns from all over the world has recently been planted in the dell in a "specimen" display typical of those that took pride of place in important Victorian landscaped gardens.

The Rose Garden, at the end of the quarry garden, is remarkable for its rose pergola and its 19th-century rose varieties which are at their most fragrant at the end of June and in early July. The waters in the ornamental cascade complete the enchantment.

History: The gardens, like the house, are an essay from the 1860s and are being restored to their original design by David Avery and his team.

Accommodation: Mount Pleasant Hotel (tel: 01302 868696; £££)

Harewood House

Grand garden landscaped by Capability Brown. English Heritage Grade I. Map reference ③⓪

Moorhouse, Harewood, Leeds LS17 9LQ, W. Yorks; tel: 0113 2181010; fax: 0113 2181002. < www.harewood.org >
Opening times: house & gardens: mid-Mar–Oct daily 11am–4.30pm, Nov–mid Dec (gardens only) weekends only. National Garden Scheme days. Parties/coaches accepted. Viewing by appointment preferable for groups.
Admission prices: house & gardens: Mon–Sat adults £9.50, children/students £5.25, over-60s £7.75; Sun & BHs adults £10.50, children/students £5.75, over-60s £8.75; gardens: Mon–Sat adults £6.75, children/students £4.25, over-60s £5.75; Sun & BHs adults £7.75, children/students £4.75, over-60s £6.75. Reductions for groups.
Facilities: parking, disabled access, shop, plants for sale, refreshments. Picnics permitted. Dogs allowed on leads.

Covering 140 acres (56 hectares) and situated within 1,000 acres (400 hectares) of ornamental parkland, the gardens at Harewood are among the most impressive in the country. Set out in the 18th century by

BELOW: the sweeping vistas and Italianate parterre of Harewood House.

Map:
pages
248–9

Capability Brown, the parkland is a stunning example of the traditional English Landscape style, with arrangements of native trees and gently sweeping hillsides surrounding an extensive serpentine lake. The Terrace is an elaborate, Italianate garden, with statuesque fountains and intricate flower beds edged by over a mile of box hedging and planted with seasonal displays of bulbs and bedding plants. In contrast, below the Terrace, is the Archery Border, an exotic mixture of richly coloured flowers and architectural foliage creating a sumptuous sub-tropical display.

An enjoyable walk leads around the Capability Brown lake, which is surrounded by woodlands, where in early summer rhododendrons provide a stunning display of colour. At the head of the lake is a cascade which tumbles into a sunken glade full of Himalayan plants, ferns and bamboos, creating a rich, botanic environment.

History: The first Lord Harewood commissioned Capability Brown to landscape the estate in the 1770s. He dammed a stream to create the great lake. The walled garden has provided fruits and vegetables for the house for over 200 years. Sir Charles Barry created the Italianate parterre in the 1840s.

Accommodation: 42 The Calls, Leeds (tel: 0113 2440099; £££). Local pub: Harewood Arms Hotel.

Wentworth Castle

18th-century mock castle with fine landscaped gardens. English Heritage Grade I. Map reference ③

Lowe Lane, Stainborough, Barnsley S75 3ET, S. Yorks; tel: 01226 731269.
Opening times: *open days in May & June (telephone for details); guided tours mid-Apr–Aug Tues & Thur 2pm.*
National Collection: *species rhododendrons, species magnolias and Williamsii hybrid camellias.*
Admission prices: *adults £2.50, children (up to 16) free, overs-60s & concession £2. No facilities. Dogs allowed on leads.*

Wentworth is situated within South Yorkshire Forest. It features an azalea garden, a "secret" Victorian flower garden, a woodland wilderness and Stainborough Castle, a Gothic folly. The National Collections of rhododendrons, magnolias and camellias are at their best in spring.

History: The park lies on the site of an Iron Age hill fort. The current building was completed in 1734, and the grounds laid out between 1739 and 1791.

Local pub: Strines Inn, Bradfield.

Scotland

*Like Ireland and the West
Country, the west coast of
Scotland benefits from the
warming effect of the Gulf
Stream, allowing tender plants
to thrive. But the gardens of
the east coast are also lushly
planted, and almost every
Scottish garden is set off by
magnificent scenery.*

**Map:
page 280**

SCOTLAND'S HIGHLIGHTS

For many people, Scottish horticulture conjures up thoughts of traditional woodland gardens with banks of gloriously coloured rhododendrons and azaleas, such as Benmore, Dawyck or Glenarn, or lush subtropical gardens such as Logan Botanic. But there are innovative gardens to be found, in particular Little Sparta, the acclaimed moorland garden created by the sculptor Ian Hamilton Finlay.

Arduaine Garden

A woodland garden specialising in rhododendrons and azaleas. National Trust for Scotland. Map reference ❶

Oban PA34 4XQ, Argyll & Bute; tel/fax: 01852 200366. < www.nts.org.uk >
Opening times: all year, daily 9.30am–sunset. National Garden Scheme days. Parties/coaches accepted. House closed.
Admission prices: adults £3.50, children £2.60; over-60s £2.60, family £9.50.
Facilities: parking, disabled access. Picnics permitted. No refreshments. No dogs.

Arduaine is a mild, coastal garden 20 miles (32km) south of Oban in Argyll. It has a wonderful rhododendrons, azaleas, magnolias, camellias and other trees and shrubs. There is also an extensive range of perennials, ferns and water plants.

History: The gardens were begun in 1898 and developed by three generations of Campbells. The property was bought in 1971 by the brothers Edmund and Harry Wright, who presented it to the National Trust for Scotland in 1992

Accommodation: The Manor House, Oban (tel: 01631 562087; £); Loch Melfort Hotel, Lerags by Oban (tel: 01852 200233; ££–£££).
Local pub: Tigh-an-Truish, Clachan-Seil.

Benmore Botanic Garden

A scientific collection, best known for giant redwoods and rhododendrons. Map reference ❷

Benmore, Dunoon PA23 8QU, Argyll and Bute; tel: 01369 706261;

PRECEDING PAGES: wet weather at Greenbank.

OPPOSITE: Logan Botanic Gardens in summer.

ABOVE: water plants at Arduaine.

garden's role in conservation is also demonstrated by its ecological plantings, such as the Bhutanese Glade and a new Chilean Glade.

History: The garden is named after the mountain Beinn Mhor. The first conifers were planted in about 1820 but the magnificent Redwood Avenue, for which the garden is famous, was planted in 1863. Ten years later James Duncan, a local entrepreneur and benefactor, planted 6.5 million conifers. In 1889 the Younger family took over the garden and introduced numerous ornamental trees and shrubs. After the garden was given to the nation by Harry Younger in 1925 it was decided that it should become part of the Royal Botanic Garden, Edinburgh.

Accommodation: The Enmore, Dunoon (tel: 01369 702230; £££).

fax: 01369 706369. < www.rbge.org.uk >
Opening times: Mar–Oct daily 10am–6pm. Parties/coaches accepted. House closed.
Admission prices: adults £3, concessions £2.50, children £1, over-60s £2.50, family £7.
Facilities: parking, disabled access, shop, plants for sale, refreshments. No picnics. Dogs allowed on leads.

On arrival at Benmore, follow the paths from the formal garden, through the hillside woodlands to a spectacular view across the garden and the Holy Loch to the Firth of Clyde and beyond. Among the garden's many highlights are the stately conifers, the avenue of giant redwoods and an extensive magnolia collection.

Reflecting the two collections that dominate the garden, Benmore has been rightly described as both a living textbook of the genus rhododendron, and, with its unrivalled diversity of coniferous trees, as a national pinetum. Both collections serve as standards for the scientific research work of the Royal Botanic Garden, Edinburgh. More than 350 species and subspecies of rhododendron, and 300 hybrids and cultivars can be seen here.

The historic plantings of previous owners provide the backbone of the garden's collection of hardy temperate conifers. These have now been supplemented, particularly with endangered species, as part of the Conifer Conservation Programme. The

ABOVE:
Benmore
Botanic
Garden.

Biggar Park

A working, walled garden, with rolling lawns and woodland.
Map reference ❸

Biggar ML12 6JS, South Lanarkshire, tel: 01899 220185.
Opening times: May–Aug daily 10am–6pm by appointment for groups only. National Garden Scheme day. House closed.
Admission prices: adults £2, children 50p.
Facilities: parking, partial disabled access. No refreshments. Picnics permitted. Dogs allowed on leads.

Biggar Park has a garden of approximately 10 acres (4 hectares). At 700 ft (215 metres) above sea level, it is susceptible to early and late frosts. There is a good collection of hardy hybrid rhododendrons and azaleas in a woodland setting and several species of meconopsis.

The season starts with a carpet of fritilarias and then banks of daffodils. By June the walled garden begins to show its potential with early herbaceous plants in large borders designed in a Saltire cross, with vegetables and soft fruit behind a typical working walled garden with greenhouse and parterre.

By July the shrub roses, mainly old varieties, are in flower at strategic places throughout the garden. Other features include an Italian garden, rolling lawns and an ornamental pond.

History: David and Sue Barnes came to live at Biggar Park in 1974. They have gradually developed the garden around the many old, indigenous trees. The early plans were to restore the walled garden in the Scottish traditional style, then to link the house to this garden by planted areas. This was followed by the construction of woodland walks and a Japanese style garden.

Accommodation: The Glenholm Centre, Broughton, Biggar (tel: 01899 830408; £).

Branklyn Garden

Map: page 280

Intensively cultivated garden with peat walls and rock garden. National Trust for Scotland. Map reference ❹

116 Dundee Road, Perth PH2 7BB, Perth and Kinross; tel: 01738 625535.

< www.nts.org.uk/gardens/ >
National Collection: *Cassiope, Preliminary Lily Collection.*
Opening times: *all year, daily 9.30am–6pm. National Garden Scheme day. Parties/coaches accepted by appointment. House closed.*
Admission prices: *adults £5, children & over-60s £3.75, family £13.50.*
Facilities: *parking (limited for coaches), disabled access but limited facilities, shop, plants for sale, refreshments. No picnics. No dogs.*

There were three major influences that helped Dorothy and John Renton, the designers of Branklyn Garden, produce a garden of international acclaim. First, there was their clear interest in the Sino-Himalayan flora: for example, the receipt of 200 packets of seed from the Ludlow and Sherriff expeditions, collected in the wilds of southeast Tibet and Bhutan. Second, their

ABOVE: Branklyn Garden.

LEFT: oriental influences, Biggar Park.

Scotland

0 ———— 40 km
0 ———— 40 miles

N

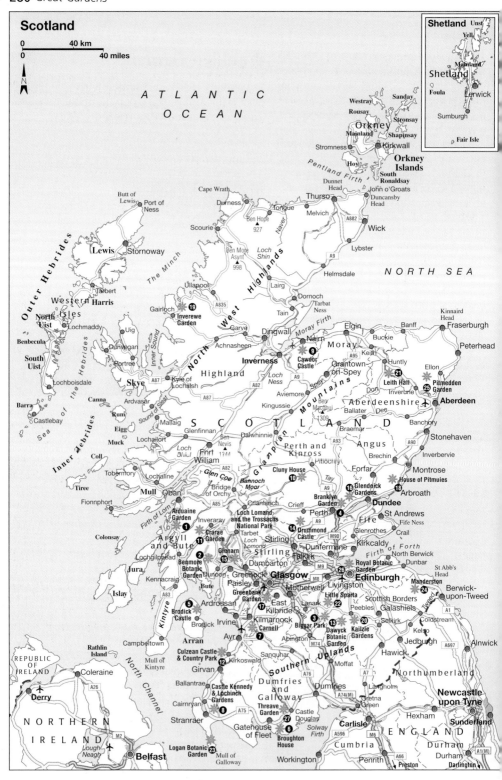

ATLANTIC
OCEAN

Shetland Unst
Yell
Mainland
Shetland
Foula   Lerwick
ₒ Fair Isle

Westray Sanday
Rousay Stronsay
Orkney Shapinsay Sumburgh
Mainland
Stromness Kirkwall
**Orkney
Islands**
Pentland Firth Hoy South
Ronaldsay
Dunnet John o'Groats

Butt of
Lewis Port of
Ness
Cape Wrath Thurso Duncansby
Durness Dunnet Head
Tongue Head
Melvich
Ben Hope A882
Scourie 927 Wick

Lewis Stornoway Ben More
Asynt Loch
Shin Lybster
998 A9
Helmsdale

NORTH SEA

Tarbert
Western Harris Ullapool Lairg
Gairloch 19 Inverewe
Garden Dornoch
Tarbat
North
Uist Lochmaddy Uig Garve Dingwall Moray Firth Elgin Banff Fraserburgh
Benbecula Dunvegan Achnasheen Nairn Buckie Peterhead
South
Uist Portree Inverness MORAY Keith A95 Huntly Ellon
Skye Kyle of
Lochalsh Highland Loch
Ness A9 Grantown-
on-Spey 21 Leith Hall 25 Pitmedden
Garden
Lochboisdale A87 A82 Aviemore Spey Don Inverurie
Barra Canna Ardvasar Kingussie Ben
Macdhui Aberdeenshire Aberdeen
Castlebay Rum Mallaig Ballater Dee
Eigg Glenfinnan Dalwhinnie 1300 Braemar Banchory
Muck Lochailort Ben
Nevis S C O T L A N D Stonehaven
Coll 1344 A93 Angus A90
Fort
William Dalwhinnie Perth and
Kinross Brechin Inverbervie
Tobermory Lochaline Glen Coe Rannoch
Moor Cluny House Pitlochry Forfar Montrose
Tiree 10 Tay House of Pitmuies
Mull Oban Bridge
of Orchy A9 16 Glendoick 18
Fionnphort Arduaine Crianlarich Crieff Gardens Arbroath
Garden Loch Lomond
and the Trossachs
National Park Branklyn
Garden Dundee
Colonsay 1 Inveraray 4 Perth St Andrews
Argyll Crarae
Garden Tarbet Loch Drummond Fife Fife Ness
and Bute 11 14 Castle Glenrothes Crail
Lochgilphead Glenarn Lomond Stirling Dunfermline M90 Kirkcaldy
Jura 2 15 Stirling Falkirk Firth of Forth
Benmore
Botanic Dunoon Dumbarton M9 North Berwick
Garden Greenock Glasgow 26 Royal Botanic Dunbar
Kennacraig Paisley M8 Garden St Abb's
Islay Bute Greenbank Motherwell Livingston Edinburgh Head
A83 Garden East Little Sparta Manderston
5 Ardrossan 17 Kilbride Lanark Scottish Borders Berwick-
Brodick Kilmarnock 22 Peebles Galashiels upon-Tweed
Castle Irvine 3 Biggar Park 13 20 A1
Brodick Carnell Dawyck Kailzie Selkirk Coldstream
Arran Ayr 7 Botanic Gardens Kelso
Campbeltown Abington Garden Jedburgh A697 Alnwick
Rathlin
Island Culzean Castle Sanquhar Southern Uplands Hawick
REPUBLIC Mull of & Country Park 12 Kilkoswald Moffat A7 Northumberland
OF Kintyre Girvan A76 Langholm
IRELAND Coleraine Dumfries Dumfries Gretna Newcastle
Ballantrae Castle Kennedy and A74(M) Green upon Tyne
A26 & Lochinch Galloway Hexham
Derry Gardens Threave Castle Carlisle Sunderland
Cairnryan A75 Garden Douglas A596 ENGLAND
NORTHERN Stranraer 8 6 Solway M6 Cumbria Durham A1(M)
Gatehouse 27 Firth Durham
IRELAND M2 of Fleet Broughton
Lough Logan Botanic 23 House Workington Penrith A66 Darlington
Neagh Belfast Garden Mull of Preston
Galloway

North Channel
North Sound
Inner Sound
Sound of Sleet
Sea of the Hebrides
Inner Hebrides
Firth of Lorn
Sound of Mull
Kintyre
Outer Hebrides
The Minch
North West Highlands
Grampian Mountains

enthusiasm for complementary plant associations, perhaps influenced by the ideas of Gertrude Jekyll. The third influence, which transformed much of the later development at the south end of the garden, was the concept of peat-wall gardening, conceived at Logan House in the 1920s by building mini-terraces with turfs. The idea was taken up by the Royal Botanic Garden in Edinburgh in the 1930s, but peat blocks were used instead of turf and this new method of gardening developed in parallel at Branklyn. The peat-wall areas remain a feature, displaying many unusual, acid-loving plants.

Branklyn contains a spectacular rock garden and scree beds, narrow winding paths and stunning groups of rhododendrons, birches, maples and dwarf conifers, giving the feel of a Himalayan hillside. The peat walls with rhododendrons, Nomocharis, Notholirion and Cassiope (of which Branklyn holds the national collection), Meconopsis, primula, Trillium, Phyllodoce, Kalmia, Vaccinium and Gaultheria.

History: Branklyn Garden was the creation of Dorothy and John Renton, who bought a small area of orchard in Perth in 1922 and built the house in which they were to live for the rest of their lives. At first the garden was very small but within a few years the site was enlarged to its present size of just under 2 acres (0.8 hectares). The beginnings of the rock garden were arduous, involving bringing the largest stones from the now disused Kinnoull Hill Quarry.

During the late 1940s the scree beds were made on the recommendation of the great rock gardener Reginald Farrer and consisted of five parts Tay River gravel to one part of loam, with a surface of pure gravel chips.

Dorothy Renton died in 1966 and John the following year. He bequeathed Branklyn to the National Trust for Scotland.

Accommodation: Isle of Skye Hotel, Perth (tel: 01738 624471; £££); Kinnaird House, Perth (tel: 01796 472843; £). Local Pubs: The Bein Inn, Glenfarg (4 miles/7km south of Perth).

Brodick Castle

A major plant collection in a woodland setting with two walled gardens. National Trust for Scotland. Map reference ❺

Isle of Arran KA27 8HY, North Ayrshire; tel: 01770 302202; fax: 01770 302312. < www.nts.org.uk/gardens/ >.
National Collections: *rhododendron subsection Grandia, Falconeri, Maddenia.*
Opening times: *park: all year daily 9.30am–sunset; castle: late Apr–Oct 11am–4.30pm (till 3.30pm Oct). National Garden Scheme days. Parties/coaches accepted by appointment. House open.*
Admission prices: *castle and garden: adults £7, children & over-60s £5.30, family £19; garden and country park: adults £3.50, children & over-60s £2.60, family £9.50.*
Facilities: *parking, disabled access but limited facilities, shop, plants for sale, refreshments. Picnics permitted. Dogs allowed on leads. Ranger service and adventure playground.*

Map: page 280

BELOW: the garden at Brodick Castle.

Brodick Castle and Country Park lie within an historic designed landscape, influenced by W.A. Nesfield. The gardens cover about 80 acres (32 hectares) and contain one of the major plant collections within the National Trust's care. Some 75 acres (30 hectares) are woodland garden, planted since the 1920s with a notable collection of rhododendron species and specimen exotic trees, including a reserve collection of plants propagated from the Horlick Collection at Achamore House, Isle of Gigha. There are also two walled gardens; the

ABOVE:
Digitalis
purpurea
(foxgloves).

one near the castle (of around 2 acres/0.8 hectares) dates from 1710 and is now a reconstruction of an Edwardian flower garden; the other (of around 3 acres/1.2 hectares) was formerly a kitchen garden and is now a propagation facility and nursery.

History: The key phases in the development of the garden and designed landscape were the introduction of the castle parks in the late 1700s, the laying out of the

Romantic Walks in the mid-1800s, the involvement of W.A. Nesfield in the 1850s, the development of the woodland gardens in the 1920s and of the plant collection since the acquisition by the National Trust. The Brodick estate came to the Treasury in lieu of death duties.

Accommodation: Kilmichael Country House Hotel, Glen Coy, by Brodick (tel: 01770 302219; £).
Local pub: Wineport Bistro, Claddach.

Broughton House

A town garden mixing Japanese and Scots influences. National Trust for Scotland. Map reference ❻

12 High Street, Kirkcudbright DG6 4JX, Dumfries & Galloway; tel: 01557 330437. fax: 01557 330437; < www.nts.org.uk >
Opening times: *Feb–Mar daily 11am–4pm; Apr–Sep Mon–Sat 11am–5pm, Sun 1–5pm; Jul–Aug daily 10am–6pm; Oct Mon–Sat 10am–6pm, Sun 1–5pm. Parties/coaches accepted but must view by appointment. House closed until 2004.*
Admission prices: *garden: adults £2, children and over-60s £1.*
Facilities: *No parking. No refreshments. No picnics. No disabled access. No dogs.*

Set on the banks of the River Dee, Broughton comprises two parts. The Japanese Garden with a curious sundial, a pool filled with waterlilies and spanned by a bridge, and dwarf Japanese stone pines planted in stone troughs, occupies about a third of the garden. The remaining part is an informal Scots garden containing bulbs, early hellebores, primulas and an interesting collection of ferns. The walls are festooned with climbers. Mature arched trees are complemented by ground cover, and the recently restored glasshouse is used as a display house for plants that add extra summer interest.

History: The house was built in the early

Map:
page 280

18th century by the Murrays of Broughton and Cally. The artist E.A. Hornel (1864–1933) bought the property and turned part of it into his studio. It is reputed that he wanted the garden to resemble a Japanese sanctuary. The Trust has been developing the garden in sympathy with Hornel's ideas.

Accommodation: *Anchor Hotel, Kippford (tel: 01156 620205; £); Selkirk Arms, Kirkcudbright (tel: 01557 330402; ££).*

Carnell

A formal garden with a Chinese gazebo. Map reference ❼

Hurlford, Kilmarnock KA1 5JS, Ayrshire; tel: 01563 884236; fax: 01563 884407. < www.carnellestates.com >
Opening times: *National Garden Scheme day one Sunday in late July (2–5pm) or by appointment. Parties/coaches accepted. House closed to visitors.*
Admission prices: *adults £3, children under 12 free.*
Facilities: *parking, plants for sale, refreshments. No picnics. No disabled access. Dogs allowed.*

The park at Carnell includes two squares of lime trees, to represent the Scottish squares at the Battle of Dettingen, 1743, complete with two "officers" on either side, all planted soon after the actual battle. There is also a fine cut-leaf beech and a copper beech. A wild garden, the formal garden of yew hedges and the rock and pond gardens, the latter originally a small limestone quarry, were all laid out by Mrs Findlay-Hamilton in the early 20th century.

One of the main features of the garden is the long herbaceous border stuffed with delphiniums and many unusual plants. Burmese dragons and a Chinese gazebo recall Commander James Findlay's travels.

History: Carnell belonged to the Wallace family, for whom the original 16th-century towerhouse was built. Many alterations to the estate, with landscaping of the gardens, were carried out in the 1840s and a new house, designed by William Burn, was built in 1843. Further alterations to the house and the ornamental development of the gardens were carried out in the early years of the 20th century.

Local pub: Cochrane Inn, Gatehead.

ABOVE: border at Carnell.

RIGHT: Cawdor Castle.

Castle Kennedy & Lochinch Gardens

Famous garden with landscaped terraces and rhododendrons.
Map reference ❽

Stranraer, Wigtownshire DG9 8BX, Dumfries & Galloway; tel: 01776 702024; fax: 01776 706248.
< www.castlekennedygardens. co.uk >
Opening times: *Apr–Sep 10am–5pm. Parties/coaches accepted. Viewing by appointment. House closed.*
Admission prices: *adults £3, children £1, over-60s £2, groups of 20 + 10 percent discount.*
Facilities: *parking, disabled access, shop, plants for sale, refreshments. No dogs.*

The 19th-century castle, now a ruined, is set in 75 acres (30 hectares) of landscaped terraces and avenues. It stands on a peninsula between two large lochs, the Black Loch and the White Loch. The gardens are famous not only for the collections of rhododendrons, azaleas and embothriums, but also for the Monkey Puzzle Avenue planted in about 1890 from the first imported seed. The garden is a Scots interpretation of the style of the early 18th-century designer Charles Bridgeman.

History: The garden was laid out by the second Earl of Stair, with the work carried out by the Royal Scots Greys and the Inniskilling Fusiliers. Stair was a Field Marshal and the garden has "military" grass terraces and a 2-acre (0.8-hectare) circular lily pond.

Accommodation: Creebridge House Hotel, Minnigaff, Newton Stewart (tel: 01671 402121; £££).

Cawdor Castle

A 14th-century castle overlooking beautifully kept gardens and extensive woodland. Map reference ❾

Cawdor, Nairn IV12 5RD, Highland; tel: 01667 404615; fax: 01667 404 674.
< www.cawdorcastle.com >
Opening times: *May–mid-Oct daily 10am–5.30pm. Parties/coaches accepted, preferably by appointment. House open.*
Admission prices: *castle & gardens: adults £6.30, children £3.50, over-60s £5.30, family £18.60; gardens & grounds: adults £3.50.*
Facilities: *parking, disabled access, shop, refreshments, nature walks. 9-hole golf course and putting green. Picnics permitted. No dogs.*

In 1981 Lord Cawdor decided to remodel the kitchen garden at Cawdor Castle and plant a holly maze. The pattern was taken from a design in the mosaic floor of the ruined Roman villa of Conimbriga in Portugal, which depicts the Minotaur's labyrinth at Knossos in Crete, a conundrum devised by Daedelus. In the other half of the garden there is the Paradise Garden, a knot garden and a thistle garden, as well as an orchard planted with old Scottish fruit trees. The flower garden was originally designed for enjoyment in late summer and autumn, but the season has been extended to give pleasure from early spring, with bulbs, bedding plants, herbaceous borders, ornamental trees and shrubs.

The wild garden on the banks of Cawdor Burn gives another contrast; beyond, conveniently marked paths lead to Cawdor Wood, a mixed forest that is one of the finest and most beautiful in Europe.

History: The castle dates from the 14th century and has been lived in by the family in a direct line ever since. The Cawdors have been keen gardeners over many gener-

ations. The oldest part of the garden northeast of the castle was enclosed with walls and bastions in 1620, and cultivated in the old-fashioned manner in which soft fruit, flowers, vegetables and orchards were closely intermingled. The flower garden, south of the castle, was laid out a full century later, again in the old style. Later still, in 1850, Lady Cawdor added the oval rose beds, edged with lavender, thus changing the framework towards formality.

Map: page 280

Accommodation: Royal Hotel, Cromarty (tel: 01381 600217; ££). ***Local pub:*** *Cawdor Tavern, Nairn.*

Cluny House

A wild woodland garden with a fine plantsman's collection.
Map reference ⑩

Aberfeldy PH15 2JT, Perth and Kinross; tel: 01887 820795.
National Collection: *Asiatic primulas.*
Opening times: *Mar–Oct daily 10am–6pm. Parties/coaches accepted. House closed.*
Admission prices: *adults £3, children under 16 free.*
Facilities: *parking, no lavatories, plants for sale, no refreshments. Picnics permitted. No disabled access. No dogs.*

Cluny is a wild woodland garden set in the scenic Strathtay Valley in the heart of Scotland, where it benefits from a climate, altitude and aspect that favour many Himalayan and North American plants. Beneath a canopy of mature specimen trees, rhododendrons and two massive sequoias, drifts of Asiatic primulas adorn the shaded damp positions growing in home-produced leaf mould. Accompanying them are brilliant blue, yellow and red Himalayan poppies, white, pink and red American wood lilies, exotic green arisaemas and huge Himalayan lilies with wonderful scents.

LEFT: blue Himalayan poppies at Cluny House

No chemicals are used within the garden, allowing many plants to naturalise with native wild flowers such as primroses and bluebells. Cluny is also the habitat of red squirrels and woodland birds.

History: Bobby and Betty Masterton bought Cluny House and the surrounding sloping 10 acres (4 hectares) in 1950. A woodland garden was developed with a strong emphasis on Himalayan and North American plants. After the deaths of the Mastertons in the mid-1980s, the garden was taken over by their daughter, Wendy, and her husband, John Mattingley.

Accommodation: Weem Hotel, Weem, near Aberfeldy (tel: 01887 820381; ££–£££).
Local pub: Ailean Chragger, Weem.

Crarae Garden

A hillside garden, with an extensive collection of rhododendrons.
National Trust for Scotland.
Map reference ⓫

Minard, Inveraray PA32 8YA, Argyll and Bute; tel: 01546 886614/886388.
< www.crarae-gardens.org.uk >
National Collection: *part of Nothofagus.*

BELOW: skunk cabbage *(Lysichiton americanus)* at Crarae Garden.

Opening times: year-round 9.30am–dusk. Parties/coaches accepted. House closed.
Admission prices: adults £3, children & over-60s £2.60, family £9.50.
Facilities: parking, disabled access, shop, refreshments. Picnics permitted. Dogs allowed on leads.

Crarae Gardens are situated on the north side of Loch Fyne some 10 miles (16 km) southwest of Inveraray. The property extends to around 124 acres (50 hectares) and is divided into Crarae Gardens (approximately 62 acres/25 hectares) and the forest garden, waterfall and the hill ground of Barr Mor and Droversland.

The main garden, set on a hillside down which tumbles the Crarae Burn, is reminiscent of a Himalayan gorge. The surrounding tree and shrub collections are rich and diverse, planted for artistic and naturalistic effect. The garden contains one of Scotland's best collections of rhododendrons, unusually rich in cultivars, as well as part of the national collection of nothofagus and good representations of acer, eucalyptus, eucryphia and sorbus. An extensive network of paths takes visitors to all corners of the garden, criss-crossing the burn via a series of bridges.

History: Lady Campbell began the development of the gardens from woodland in 1912, although the land had been owned by the Campbell family since 1825. Her son, Sir George, was given the estate in 1925 and lived there for over 40 years, greatly extending the plant collection.

After Sir George's death, the Crarae Gardens Charitable Trust was established, but following financial difficulties the National Trust for Scotland conducted a successful £1.5 million fund-raising appeal to take it into Trust ownership.

Accommodation: George Hotel, Inverary (tel: 01499 302111; ££); Local pubs: Creggans Inn, Clachan Strachur.

Map:
page 280

Culzean Castle and Country Park

A designed landscape with plants that reflect the mild Gulf Stream-influenced climate. National Trust for Scotland. Map reference ⑫

Maybole KA19 8LE, South Ayrshire; tel: 01655 884400; fax: 01655 884522. < www.nts.org.uk >
Opening times: castle & country park: late Apr–Oct daily 10.30am–5pm; country park: all year daily 9.am–sunset. National Garden Scheme days. Parties/coaches accepted (tel: 01655 884455 for information). House open.
Admission prices: castle and country park: adults £9, children £6.50, over-60s £6.50, family £22; country park only: adults £4.50, children £3.50, over-60s £3.50, family £12.50.
Facilities: parking, disabled access, shop, plants for sale, refreshments. Picnics permitted. No dogs.

Culzean Castle and Country Park are situated on the Ayrshire coast and lie within an extensive landscape of around 705 acres (286 hectares). The gardens cover an area of approximately 30 acres (12 hectares) stretching from the castle and its dramatic cliff-top setting, to the Swan Pond at the southern extent of the property. In the more formal areas around the castle are the Fountain Court and terraces, where the plant collection reflects a mild climate, influenced by the Gulf Stream. The key feature of the north walled garden is the double herbaceous border, complemented by traditional fruit and vegetables. The south walled garden is laid out to a contemporary design, within which sit a newly restored Victorian vinery and a grotto. Informal woodland walks link the main areas of interest.

Significant garden buildings include the orangery and the camellia house.

History: The main landscape around the castle was laid out around 1800 in the picturesque style. Culzean Castle Estate was acquired by the National Trust in 1945 and the Country Park, including the garden, was designated in 1969, the first in Scotland.

Accommodation: Kirroughtree House, Newton Stewart (01671 402142; ££); Creebridge House Hotel, Minnigaff, Newton Stewart (tel: 01671 402121; £–££); Fairways Private Hotel, Prestwick (tel: 01292 470396; ££–£££).

ABOVE:
Culzean
Castle and
Country
Park.

special collections, such as the David Douglas trail and the Scottish name plant trail. Seasonal highlights include snowdrops, daffodils, rhododendrons, azaleas, stream-side herbaceous plantings and spectacular autumn colours and berries. The visitor can find out more about fungi, mosses and lichens in the world's first ever reserve for non-flowering plants. The wonderful mature specimen trees include the Dawyck beech.

History: The oldest surviving tree at Dawyck dates from 1690, but many were introduced in the 19th century. There is also a fine collection of Italian stonework created in the 1820s. Dawyck is owned by the Royal Botanic Garden, Edinburgh.

Accommodation: Castle Venlaw Hotel, Peebles (tel: 01721 720384; ££). **Local pubs:** *Traquair Arms, Inverleithen.*

Dawyck Botanic Garden

A splendid woodland garden with North American trees introduced by 19th-century plant hunters.
Map reference ⑬

Stobo EH45 9JU, Peeblesshire; tel: 01721 760254; fax: 01721 760214.
< www.rbge.org.uk >
Opening times: mid-Feb–mid-Nov daily; Feb and Nov 10am–4pm; Mar and Oct 10am–5pm; Apr–Sept 10am–6pm. Parties/coaches accepted. House closed.
Admission prices: adults £3, children £1, over-60s £2.50, family £7; membership available.
Facilities: parking, shop, plants for sale, refreshments. Picnics permitted. No disabled access. No dogs.

ABOVE: autumn foliage at Dawyck.

Dawyck is a spectacular woodland garden with a history of tree planting extending over 300 years. There are waymarked trails which highlight the

Drummond Castle

Italianate formal garden. English Heritage Grade I. Map reference ⑭

Muthill, Crieff PH5 2AA, Perth & Kinross; tel: 01764 681257; fax: 01764 681550.
Opening times: Easter weekend & May–Oct 2–6pm. Parties/coaches accepted. Viewing by appointment. House closed.
Admission prices: adults £3.50, children £1.50, over-60s £2.50.
Facilities: limited facilities for the disabled. Dogs allowed on leads in grounds only.

Drummond Castle Gardens provide a perfect example of Italianate formal landscaping but have an added appeal for their contrast to the Scottish countryside in which they lie. The dramatic entrance, up a mile-long beech-lined avenue, is an eye-opening prelude to the early 17th-century gardens. Designed by John Drummond, second Earl of Perth, they were later terraced by Phyllis Astor,

Countess of Ancaster, and replanted in the 1950s. The magnificent parterre is the main reason for Drummond's reputation for being the most important formal gardens in Scotland.

The garden also boasts several copper beech trees that were planted by Queen Victoria in 1842.

Accommodation/pub: Ailean Chraggan, Weem, North of Aberfeldy (tel: 01887 820346; £–££).

Glenarn

Set in a steep-sided glen, Glenarn has a Himalayan character.
Map reference ⑮

Rhu, Helensburgh G84 8LL, Dunbartonshire; tel: 01436 820493; fax: 0141 221 6834.
Opening times: late Mar–late Sep dawn–dusk. National Garden Scheme day. Special open day on first Sunday in May under Scotland's Garden Scheme. Parties/coaches accepted. Specialist viewing by appointment. House also open.
Admission prices: adults £3, children & over-60s £1.50, season £20 (by arrangement).
Facilities: parking, plants for sale, refreshments on special open days only. Picnics permitted. No disabled access. Dogs allowed on leads.

The sheltered woodland garden of Glenarn overlooks the Gareloch and is well-known for its collection of rhododendrons, many of them rare and difficult to grow in less well-protected locations. Its trees, shrubs and beautiful magnolias, with a carpet of snowdrops, daffodils, crocus and primulas below, make for a delightful walk in spring.

In May, the Magnolia wilsonii with its upside-down flowers and lily-of-the-valley scent, and the Magnolia globosa, are highlights. Other magnolias, such as hypoleuca, flower in June.

History: The house at Glenarn was built in the late 1830s and soon afterwards the garden received plants from Joseph Hooker's 1849–50 expedition to Sikkim, notably the *Rhododendron falconeri* to the side of the house. The garden was extended by the Gibson family over half a century following their acquisition of the property in 1927. The plant-hunting expeditions of Kingdon Ward and Ludlow and Sherriff provided a good many of the plants while others came from other major gardens in Scotland.

When the Thornley family arrived at Glenarn in 1983 they restored the gardens to their former glory and extended their scope still further.

Accommodation: Ardencaple Hotel, Rhu (tel: 01436 620200; ££); Rosslee Hotel, Rhu (tel: 01436 439955; ££). Local pub: Clachan Inn, Drymen (20 miles/32 km west of Stirling).

BELOW: Glenarn, a garden with a Himalayan character.

Glendoick is divided into three sections, with informal walks between them. First, there is the Georgian House, a south-facing garden much replanted since the late 1990s, with a large grass area and interesting trees; then the walled garden, which is mostly taken over by nursery growing, with fine trained fruit trees and ceanothus.

Lastly, the woodland garden, on the slope above, which has meandering paths through the collection of rhododendrons, meconopsis, magnolias and other shrubs and trees. The latter are complemented by many naturalised herbaceous and wild flowers which make it an enchanting walk.

History: The beautiful Georgian mansion is believed to have been visited by Bonnie Prince Charlie during the 1745 Jacobite Rebellion. The garden has developed since 1919 when the late Euan Cox returned from a trip to Burma. Since then two further generations of the family have contributed both plants and experience gained from expeditions to the east.

Accommodation: Glencarse Hotel, Glencarse (tel: 01738 860206; £–££). Local pub: Fisherman's Tavern, Broughty Ferry, Dundee.

Glendoick Gardens

Woodland garden with one of the largest collections of rhododendrons and azaleas in the British Isles. Nursery and garden centre attached. Map reference ⑯

Glendoick, Glencarse PH2 7NS, Perth and Kinross; tel: 01738 860205 (nursery), 01738 860260 (garden centre); fax: 01738 860630.
< www.glendoick.com >
Opening times: *usually first and third Sun in May 2–5pm. National Garden Scheme day & Scottish Garden Scheme day. Parties/coaches may view by appointment during May and first week of June. House closed.*
Garden centre: spring–autumn 9am–6pm.
Admission prices: *adults £2.50, school-age children free.*
Facilities: *general facilities such as parking, lavatories, refreshments, etc are available at the garden centre.*
Limited disabled access (wheelchair access to woodland possible in parts). No picnics. No dogs.

Greenbank Garden

Developed as a gardening advice centre, Greenbank has a walled garden and vast collection of plants. National Trust for Scotland. Map reference ⑰

Flenders Road, Clarkston, Glasgow G76 8RB; tel: 0141 6393281.
< www.nts.org.uk >
Opening times: *garden: all year daily 10am–sunset. House: Apr–Oct Sun 2–4pm. Parties/coaches accepted.*
Admission prices: *adults £3.50, children & over-60s £2.60, family £9.50.*
Facilities: *parking, limited disabled access, shop, plants for sale, refreshments in summer only. No picnics. No dogs.*

Above: the woodland garden at Glendoick.

reenbank lies to the south of Glasgow and extends to around 16 acres (6.5 hectares). The key features are the house (currently used by the National Trust for Scotland as their West Regional Office) and the 2.5 acres (1 hectare) of walled garden, surrounded by the remnants of the 18th-century designed landscape, part of which is in NTS ownership. The walled garden is divided by hedges into sections, each with its own theme or style. These are linked by grass paths to form a unified whole. The Trust has redeveloped different areas of the garden each year to widen the range of interest to gardeners.

The main emphasis of these changes is to increase the educational/demonstration content and thus the garden has a surprising range of features for its size, including glasshouses, ponds and a great variety of plants. A collection of over 3,400 different plant varieties is now established, and many annuals are planted each year. Daffodils and other bulbs, ferns, shrub and climbing roses, flowers for drying and floral art, fuchsias and pelargoniums all figure strongly. The surrounding shelter of trees has also been developed to form a woodland garden and woodland walk.

Map: page 280

History: Greenbank House was built in 1764–65. The property was presented to the Trust in 1976 by Mr and Mrs William P. Blyth who had owned it since 1961.

Accommodation: The Town House, Glasgow (tel: 0141 357 0862: £££); Malmaison, Glasgow (tel: 0141 572 1000; £££).

House of Pitmuies

Gardens featuring interesting 18th-century buildings, plus woodland and river and lochside walks. Map reference ⓲

Guthrie, Angus, By Forfar, DD8 2SN, Scotland; tel: 01241 828245. Opening times: Apr–Oct daily 10am–5pm. Parties/coaches should

BELOW: a quiet corner at Greenbank.

preferably view by appointment. House open by appointment.
Admission prices: adults £2.50, children under 14 free.
Facilities: parking, refreshments available for groups by prior arrangement.

Two walled gardens adjoin an old white-harled house which was much enlarged in the 18th century. The garden walls are still as shown on an estate map of 1780 and shelter a traditional fruit and cut-flower kitchen garden leading to the semi-formal gardens beyond. These gardens have a mix of roses, herbaceous borders and a celebrated summer display of delphiniums.

Old plant varieties are treasured and there are shrubs and shrub-roses, paved areas for dianthus and violas and a lily pond with fountain is central to the rose gardens. Trellises for climbers and a conservatory housing rampant passion flowers all combine to provide varied habitats for a wide collection of plants.

In spring there are massed spring bulb displays and outside the two gardens an "alpine meadow" leading to woodland, river and loch-side walks with some magnificent trees. Intriguing buildings, which include a Gothick-style washhouse, a turreted dovecote, some 18th-century farm buildings and former stabling. These have stone slate roofs and one, the potting shed, is festooned with ferns and bears the date 1775.

History: The gardens seem to have evolved over time. Their present appearance took shape in the 20th century, with much additional planting and alteration by the present owners over the past 30–40 years. This was only possible because they are domestic rather than grand, in scale and ambience. Extensive restoration of the house and ancillary buildings is on-going with support from Historic Scotland.

Accommodation: Wemyss Farm (Tel: 01307 462887; £). **Local pubs:** Fisherman's Tavern, Broughty Ferry, Dundee.

BELOW: **House of Pitmuies.**

Inverewe Garden

Woodland and walled garden, with a diverse plant collection. National Trust for Scotland. Map reference ⓳

Poolewe IV22 2LG, Ross and Cromarty, Highland; tel: 01445 781200. fax: 01445 811497. < www.nts.org.uk >
National Collections: Brachyglottis; Olearia; rhododendron subsections Barbata, Glischra and Maculifera; Ourisisia.
Opening times: all year daily 9.30am–9pm (or sunset if earlier). National Garden Scheme/SGS days. Parties/coaches accepted. Viewing by appointment. House closed.
Admission prices: adults £7, children & over-60s £5.25. Discount for pre-booked groups.
Facilities: parking, disabled access, shop, plants for sale, refreshments. Picnics permitted. No dogs.

Map: page 280

nverewe Garden is among the finest gardens in Europe and is one of the best-known and most visited gardens in Scotland. Set on the slopes – mainly south-facing – of a peninsula of torridonian sandstone jutting out into Loch Ewe, it has a superb position. Its more formal areas consists of an idiosyncratic walled garden, a a lawn, and herbaceous borders and a rockery in front of the mansion house. Otherwise it is principally a woodland garden, with a wide array of trees, shrubs and herbaceous plants set within a mixed canopy of sheltering trees. There are ponds, glades and viewpoints out to the magnificent coastal and mountain scenery that surround the garden.

History: The site was a barren headland, sheep-grazed, until bought for Osgood Mackenzie by his mother in 1862. They first built a house, with a driveway to it, below which was set a curving walled garden created from a former raised beach. There was some initial planting in the early 1860s, but it was not until a few years later that widespread planting of a woodland shelter-belt began.

From around 1890 onwards, major planting of exotic plants – rhododendron species then being newly introduced from China and the Himalayas, for example – started in clearings created within the developing woodland. The garden and 2,000 acres (810 hectares) of surrounding estate were acquired by the National Trust for Scotland in the 1950s.

Accommodation: Poole House, Poolewe (tel: 01445 781 272; £££–££££); Bruach Ard Guest House, Inverasdale, Poolewe (tel: 01445 781214; £).

Kailzie Gardens

A semi-formal walled garden with roses and fine old trees, and a fine display of massed bulbs in spring.
Map reference ⓴

Peebles EH45 9HT, Peeblesshire; tel: 01721 720007; fax: 01721 720007.
Opening times: *Easter–mid-Oct 11am–5.30pm, late Oct–Mar daylight hours. Parties/coaches accepted. House closed.*
Admission prices: *adults £2.50, children 85p, groups £2.20 pp.*
Facilities: *parking, disabled access, shop, plants for sale, refreshments. Picnics permitted. Dogs allowed on leads.*

ABOVE: Inverewe has a superb setting.

Garden Scheme/SGS days. Parties/coaches accepted. House also open.
Admission prices: house & gardens: adults £7; children £5.25; over-60s £5.25, family £19; garden: adults £2.50, children & over-60s £1.90, family £7.
Facilities: parking, refreshments. Picnics permitted. No disabled access but pond walk suitable for wheelchair-users (and disabled toilet). Dogs allowed on leads.

K ailzie is a semi-formal walled garden with rose garden, herbaceous borders, old-fashioned roses and extensive greenhouses. Woodland and burnside walks meander among massed bulbs in spring and, later, rhododendrons and azaleas. The garden has many fine old trees including Scotland's oldest larch, planted in 1725. Set in the beautiful Tweed Valley, it also offers wonderful views across to the Leilheh Hills.

History: Kailzie was first mentioned in 1926 when it was called West Kelloch, which means wooded glen. The old stable block – which now comprises the tea room and shop, plus three houses and an art gallery – were built in 1794, but parts of the earlier building still remain. The walled garden was created by the present owner, Lady Angela Buchan-Hepburn.

Accommodation: Cringletie House, Peebles (tel: 01721 730233; £££); Castle Venlaw Hotel, Peebles (tel: 01721 720384; ££).

Leith Hall and Gardens

A series of small, sheltered gardens, plus parkland, woodland and nature trails. National Trust for Scotland. Map reference ㉑

Huntly, Aberdeenshire, AB54 4NQ; tel: <small>ABOVE:</small> *01464 831216; fax: 01464 831594.*
Kailzie offers *< www.nts.org.uk >*
lovely walks **Opening times:** *garden: all year daily*
with fine *9.30am–sunset; house: Easter weekend &*
views. *May–Sep Fri–Tues noon–5pm. National*

T he garden at Leith Hall is, in fact, a series of smaller gardens, each sheltered by a wall or hedge and each with its own special character, rising on a gentle slope from the West Drive. Particularly eye-catching is the solid carpet of blue catmint filling one entire border, and providing an attractive foil to the colourful palette of the more traditional herbaceous and rose beds.

Redesigned by the Trust is the rock garden with a little stream running through winding gravel paths and stone crevices to which heather and alpine plants cling. At the top of the garden, near the curved stables, is the circular Moon Gate leading to the old turnpike road. Close by is a collection of historic stones. Two of the most interesting – the Salmon Stone and the Wolf – are Pictish in origin.

In contrast to the walled gardens is the open vista to the front of the house where a careful choice of trees and shrubs creates a parkland effect. The estate is fairly modest in size (236 acres/95 hectares) but its interest lies in variety – pasture and glade, woodland and moorland. There are two nature trails and a new pond walk (suitable for wheel- and push-chairs).

History: The lairds at Leith Hall have made improvements over the generations, but the present garden owes most to the penultimate laird, C.E.N. Leith-Hay and his wife Henrietta who extended and designed it on its present lines in the early part of the 20th century.

Accommodation: Gordon Arms, Huntly (tel: 01466 792288; £); Castle Hotel, Huntly (tel: 01466 792696; ££). Local pubs: nearest facilities 6 miles/10 km away at Insch and Huntly.

Little Sparta

A post-modern moorland garden created by the sculptor and poet Ian Hamilton Finlay. ㉒

Dunsyre, nr Lanark ML11 8NG, Lanarkshire. No telephone.

Opening times: mid-Jun–Sep Fri & Sun 2–5pm. Parties/coaches by appointment only. House closed
Admission prices: by donation to Little Sparta Foundation.

Map: page 280

The moorland garden of Little Sparta, created by the sculptor, poet and gardener Ian Hamilton Finlay, is a garden as art form, recalling the role of the garden in the 18th century. Sometimes described as post-modern, it has been designed to challenge the intellect as well as appeal to the senses, combining sensual planting with classical symbols and allusions, in the form of sculptures and enigmatic inscriptions on signs, tools and buildings.

Some critics have described Finlay's

work as impenetrable; most have found it exciting and challenging.

History: Finlay purchased his farmstead in 1996. He said of the garden's design, "The secret of gardening is composition."

Accommodation: Castle Venlaw, Peebles (tel: 01721 720384; ££).

Logan Botanic Garden

Scotland's most exotic garden, with southern hemisphere plants.
Map reference ㉓

Port Logan, Stranraer, Wigtownshire DG9 9ND, Dumfries and Galloway;

ABOVE: detail at Little Sparta.

LEFT: view of the gardens at Leith Hall.

tel: 01776 860231; fax: 01776 860333.
< www.rbge.org.uk >
Opening times: *Mar–Oct daily 10am–6pm (till 5pm Mar & Oct). Parties/coaches accepted. House closed.*
Admission prices: *adults £3, children £1, over-60s £2.50, family £7.*
Facilities: *parking, disabled access, shop, plants for sale, refreshments. No picnics. No dogs.*

Logan's sheltered aspect and mild climate allows a colourful array of exotic, tender plants to thrive out of doors. Among the many highlights are tree ferns in the walled garden, tall cabbage palms around the lily pond in the water garden, and unusual shrubs, climbers and brightly coloured tender perennials elsewhere in the gardens. The woodland garden has many southern hemisphere specimens, from Southern Africa, South and Central America and Australasia, and there is an impressive bog area where gunnera flourishes.

History: Initiated by the McDouall family in the 19th century, the garden flourished in the age of the great plant-collecting expeditions. It was here that the concept of

BELOW: exotics thrive at Logan Botanic Garden.

peat-wall gardening was conceived in the 1920s (though turf was originally used to form the terraces), an idea that was developed by Branklyn *(see page 279)* and the Royal Botanic Garden, Edinburgh. Logan is now a regional garden of the latter.

Accommodation: *Blinkbonnie Guest House, Portpatrick (01776 81082; £).*

Manderston

A combination of formal and informal gardens with rhododendrons and mature trees. Map reference ㉔

Duns TD11 3PP, Scottish Borders ; tel: 01361 883450; fax: 01361 882010.
< www.manderston.co.uk >
Opening times: *mid-May–Sep Thur & Sun 2–5pm. Parties/coaches accepted. Viewing by appointment. House open.*
Admission prices: *house and garden: adults £6.50, children & over-60s £3.50; garden: adults £3.50, children & over-60s £1.50.*
Facilities: *parking, shop, refreshments. Picnics permitted. No disabled access. Dogs allowed on leads.*

At Manderston there are 56 acres (23 hectares) of gardens, a combination of the formal and informal that is typical of many Scottish estates. There are formal terraces at the south front which look over the south lawn and the lake, where there is an ornamental boat house and Chinese-style bridge, and across to the woodland garden, which has a notable collection of rhododendrons.

On the north side there is lawn with mature trees, on the other side of which stands a magnificent gilded gateway leading to the formal garden and herbaceous borders. Sadly the walled garden is no longer open to the public.

History: Manderston house is Edwardian and its four formal terrace gardens,

Map:
page 280

designed by Kinross, are planted in Edwardian style. However, the serpentine lake, the style of the landscaping and the Chinese bridge probably date from the 18th century when the original house was built. The estate is currently owned by Lord Palmer.

Accommodation: One Green Hope Guest House, Duns (tel: 01361 890242; £–££). **Local pubs:** *Wheatsheaf, Swinton*

Pitmedden Garden

A restored 17th-century walled garden with four geometric parterres. National Trust for Scotland. Map reference ㉕

Pitmedden Village, Ellon AB41 7PD, Aberdeenshire ; tel: 01651 842352; fax: 01651 843188. < www.nts.org.uk >
Opening times: *May–Sep daily 10am–5pm. National Garden Scheme/Scotland Garden Scheme day. Parties/coaches accepted. House open.*
Admission prices: *adults £5, children £1, over-60s £4, family £14.*
Facilities: *parking, disabled access, shop, plants for sale, refreshments. Picnics permitted. No dogs.*

Pitmedden is only 15 miles (24 km) north of the "granite city" of Aberdeen so it is no coincidence that this magnificent Grade A listed walled garden was created from the finest granite. Upon acquisition of the estate in the 1950s the Trust embarked on a remarkable pioneering project to return what had become a post-war market garden to its 17th-century origin. Four geometric parterres were set out. Three contained elements from the garden at the Palace of Holyrood House in Edinburgh; the fourth is based on the coat of arms of the Seton family, the original owners. The four parterres were painstakingly measured and marked out in sand, then planted up using over 3 miles (5 km) of box-wood hedging.

In order to provide interest throughout an extended season, densely planted annual bedding plants were used within the main parterres and the existing herbaceous borders retained to add extra summer interest. Neither of these features could be considered 17th-century, but the riot of organised colour made an impact. Over 80 varieties of trained apple trees adorn the walls, providing blossom in spring and producing a healthy crop of fruit in late summer. Yew obelisks and buttresses punctuate the lawn and three fountains provide the

ABOVE:
Manderston
Garden
mixes the
formal and
the informal.

constant presence of water. A herb garden and rose border give interest and colour to the upper garden and two rows of pleached limes provide the framework for the two newly created parterres.

History: Sir Alexander Seton is credited with founding the garden in 1675. The house was badly damaged by fire in 1818 but rebuilt during the 1860s. Today, only the north wing contains visible fragments of the 17th-century grand dwelling.

The Keith family bought the Pitmedden Estate at auction in 1894. Major James

Keith (1879–1953) was one of the country's most influential agricultural improvers of his time, with a desire to combine traditional farming methods with the benefits of mechanical engineering. In 1952, he presented the Pitmedden Estate to the National Trust for Scotland. The Trust inherited a magnificent, working market garden producing fruit and vegetables in abundance.

ABOVE: 17th-century geometry at Pitmeddan.

Accommodation: Buchan Hotel, Ellon (tel: 0870 240 7060; £); Sunnybrae Farm, Ellon (tel: 01651 806456; £); Ardoe House, Blairs, Aberdeen (tel: 01224 860600; £££–££££).
Local pub: Lairhillock Inn, Netherley.

Royal Botanic Garden, Edinburgh

Ten glasshouses, woodland, an arboretum and a rock garden.
Map reference ㉖

Inverleith Row, Edinburgh EH3 5LR; tel: 0131 5527171; fax: 0131 2482901. < www.rbge.org.uk >
Opening times: *all year daily except 1 Jan and 25 Dec; Apr–Aug 10am–7pm, Mar and Sep 10am–6pm, Feb & Oct 10am–5pm, Nov–Jan 10am–4pm. Facilities close 30 mins before garden. National Garden Scheme days. Parties/coaches accepted. House open.*
Admission prices: *free; donations welcome.*
Facilities: *on-street parking, shop, plants for sale, refreshments. No picnics. Disabled access. No dogs.*

The Royal Botanic Garden Edinburgh consists of over 70 acres (28 hectares) of beautifully landscaped grounds on a hillside overlooking the city. Its 10 glasshouse – presented to the public on a tour known as the Glasshouse Experience – comprises 10 glasshouses, including Britain's tallest palm house, the elegant Temperate Palm House, and its neighbour, the Tropical Palm House. There is also an Alpine House and an astonishingly long herbaceous border of 180 yds (165 metres) which contrasts with the Winter Garden displaying plants that are at their best at the end of the year.

The magnificent Woodland Gardens and arboretum hold nearly 2,000 specimens, generally grouped into major genera and including groves of oak, limes, maples and rowans as well as a conifer collection and major groupings of rhododendrons, magnolias and eucryphias.

Other interesting areas include the Demonstration Garden, a heath garden, a peat garden, azalea and pond lawns, the Pringle Chinese collection and, not least,

the acclaimed Rock Garden, whose diverse habitats and clever cultivation supports more than 5,000 high mountain, Arctic and Mediterranean species.

History: The Edinburgh Botanic Garden was established in 1670 on an area the size of a tennis court. The Tropical Palm House was opened in 1834 and the Temperate Palm House in 1858.

Accommodation: Abercromby House, Edinburgh EH3 6LB (tel: 0131 557 8036; ££–£££); Seven Danube Street, Edinburgh EH4 1NN (tel: 0131 332 2755; ££–£££).

Threave Garden

A series of individual display gardens, including a rock garden, peat garden and rose garden. National Trust of Scotland. Map reference ㉗

*Stewartry, Castle Douglas DG7 1RX, Dumfries and Galloway; tel: 01556 502575; fax: 01556) 502683.
< www.nts.org.uk >*
Opening times: *estate & garden: all year daily 9.30am–sunset; walled garden and glasshouse: all year daily 9.30am–5pm; house: Mar–Oct Wed, Thur, Fri and Sun 11am–4pm, guided tours only, max. 10 people, two-hour admission by timed ticket. Parties/coaches accepted (tel: 01556 502575).*
Admission prices: *house & garden: adults £9, children & over-60s £6.50, family £23; garden: adults £5, children & over-60s £3.75, family £13.50.*
Facilities: *parking, disabled access, shop, plants for sale, refreshments. Picnics permitted. No dogs.*

Threave is best known for its spectacular springtime daffodils (nearly 200 varieties), some of which are unique. The garden, spanning some 60 acres (24 hectares), is made up of a series of individual display gardens set in a wooded area with views over the surrounding countryside. They include the rock garden, peat garden, a walled fruit, flower and vegetable garden, a secret garden, a rose garden, a heather garden and a wooded garden. There are also herbaceous borders, annual bedding displays and display glasshouses. A dwarf conifer collection, an orchard, a number of water features and waterfalls and a fine collection of trees and shrubs complete the scene. The garden is used as a training ground for the National Trust of Scotland's School of Practical Gardening.

History: Threave Castle and its lands were originally a country sporting estate which the Trust took over in 1959. At that time the gardens were very limited, comprising shelter-belts, daffodil banks and a walled fruit and vegetable garden. Since 1960 the Trust has continued to develop the garden one sees today.

Accommodation: Anchor Hotel, Kippford (tel: 01556 620205; ££–£££); Longacre Manor, Castle Douglas (tel: 01556 503576; ££).
Local pubs: Anchor Hotel, Kippford.

Above Left: glasshouse, Royal Botanic Garden, Edinburgh.
Below: Threave, a school of horticulture.

Wales

Famously well watered, Wales has many lovely gardens, ranging from prolific cottage gardens to dramatic castle gardens such as Powis and Chirk. Whether grand or simple, almost all of them are enhanced by the beauty of the surrounding Welsh hills

WALES'S HIGHLIGHTS

With one or two notable exceptions such as the remarkable Powis Castle with its hanging terraces, and Erdigg, a rare 18th-century Dutch-style garden, most of Wales's great gardens are located near the coast, where the soil is most fertile and the temperatures mild. The Welsh landscape, with its tumbling streams and lush river valleys, also lends itself to wild gardens, such as Cae Hir and Dolwen.

Bodnant Garden

Historic garden with superb stands of fir, hemlock, cedar and redwood. National Trust. Map reference ❶

Tal-y-Cafn, Colwyn Bay, Conwy LL28 5RE; tel: 01492 650460; fax: 01492 650448. < www.bodnantgarden.co.uk >
Opening times: *mid-Mar–Oct daily 10am–5pm. Parties/coaches accepted. House closed.*
Admission prices: *adults £5.20, children £2.60, groups of 20+ £4.70 pp.*
Facilities: *parking, disabled access, shop, plants for sale.*

Stephen Lacey, the garden writer, lecturer and presenter, once wrote of Bodnant that "the scale, grandeur and scenic beauty of this garden are nothing short of stupendous...this garden is a masterpiece."

Bodnant is worth making a special expedition to see, particularly at the beginning of June when the glorious Laburnum Arch is in full bloom. The surprises start with the walk down the five spectacular terraces with their expanses of lawn, huge mature cedar trees, architectural ornament, water and plants.

On the Canal Terrace is the Pin Mill, an 18th-century mill brought here from

PRECEDING PAGES: Dolwen blends in with the Welsh hills.

OPPOSITE: garden and farmhouse at Dolwen.

ABOVE: Bodnant Garden.

Wales

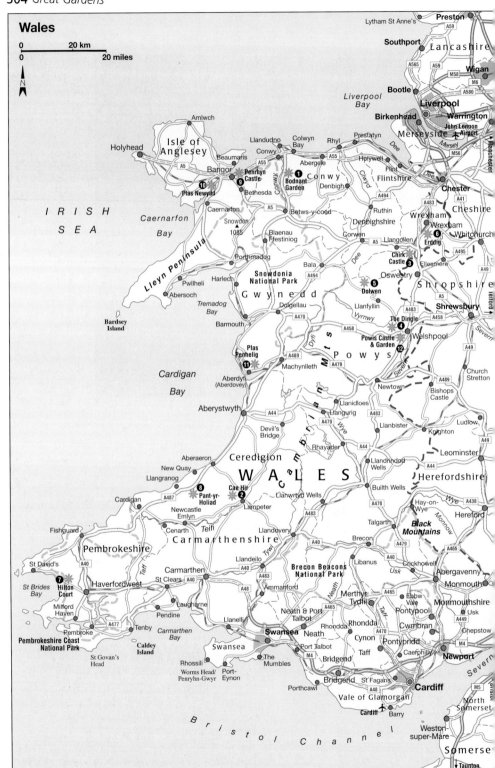

0   20 km
0   20 miles

N

Preston
Lytham St Anne's
A59
Southport
Lancashire
A565 A59
Wigan
M58
M6
Bootle
A580
Liverpool
Liverpool
Bay
Birkenhead
Warrington
John Lennon
Airport
Merseyside
Mersey
M56
Manchester
Amlwch
Holyhead
Isle of
Anglesey
Llandudno
Colwyn
Bay
Rhyl
Prestatyn
Dee
Beaumaris
Conwy
A55
Abergele
Holywell
Flint
Dee
Chester
Bangor
A5
Penrhyn
Castle
Conwy
Bodnant
Garden
Denbigh
Flintshire
A483
A41
Plas Newydd
Bethesda
A55
Conwy
Ruthin
A494
Cheshire
Caernarfon
A5
Betws-y-coed
Denbighshire
Wrexham
IRISH
Caernarfon
Snowdon
Blaenau
Ffestiniog
Corwen
A5
Llangollen
Wrexham
Whitchurch
SEA
Bay
1085
Chirk
Castle
A495
A49
Porthmadog
Bala
Dee
Ellesmere
Pwllheli
Harlech
Snowdonia
National Park
A494
Oswestry
Shropshire
Abersoch
Dolwen
A5
Gwynedd
Tremadog
Bay
Dolgellau
Llanfyllin
A483
Shrewsbury
Bardsey
Island
Barmouth
A470
Vyrnwy
A458
The Dingle
A49
Plas
Penhelig
A489
Powis Castle
& Garden
Welshpool
A49
Machynlleth
A470
Powys
Severn
Cardigan
Aberdyfi
(Aberdovey)
Church
Stretton
Bay
Newtown
A489
Bishops
Castle
Aberystwyth
Llanidloes
A44
Llangurig
A470
A483
Llanbister
Ludlow
A49
Devil's
Bridge
Wye
Rhayader
A44
Knighton
Leominster
Aberaeron
Ceredigion
Llandrindod
Wells
A44
Herefordshire
New Quay
WALES
Llangranog
Builth Wells
Cambrian Mts
Cae Hir
Pant-yr-
Holiad
Llanwrtyd Wells
Cardigan
A487
Newcastle
Emlyn
Lampeter
A483
Hay-on-
Wye
A438
Hereford
Fishguard
Cenarth
Teifi
Llandovery
Talgarth
A465
St David's
A40
Carmarthenshire
A40
Wye
St Brides
Hilton
Court
Haverfordwest
Carmarthen
St Clears
A40
Llandeilo
A483
Brecon Beacons
National Park
Libanus
Usk
Crickhowell
Brecon
A479
Abergavenny
Bay
Milford
Haven
Laugharne
A48
Ammanford
Neath
Merthyr
Tydfil
A465
Monmouth
Pembroke
A477
Pendine
Llanelli
Port Talbot
Rhondda
Ebbw
Vale
Pontypool
Monmouthshire
Usk
A449
Tenby
Carmarthen
Bay
Swansea
Neath
Rhondda
Cwmbran
Chepstow
Pembrokeshire Coast
National Park
Caldey
Island
Swansea
Port Talbot
M4
Cynon
Taff
Pontypridd
Caerphilly
Newport
M4
St Govan's
Head
Rhossili
Port-
Eynon
The
Mumbles
Bridgend
St Fagans
Cardiff
M5
Worms Head/
Penrhyn-Gwyr
Porthcawl
Bridgend
A48
Vale of Glamorgan
Cardiff
North
Somerset
Bristol Channel
Cardiff
Barry
Weston-
super-Mare
Somerse
Taunton

Gloucestershire and re-built in 1939. Further down, the path follows the valley of the river Hiraethlyn among banks of rhododendrons, azaleas, camellias and tree magnolias to the viewpoint over the river far below. There are spectacular stands of fir, hemlock, cedar and redwood, one of the latter, at 150 ft (45 metres) the tallest in the British Isles. In autumn the colours of the Japanese maples, rowans, liquidambar and birches are superb.

History: The massive granite house, 170 ft (52 metres above the River Conway, was built in 1792 and a large number of sheltering trees, such as beech, oak and chestnut were subsequently planted. The estate was bought in 1874 by Henry Pochin, the father of the first Lord Aberconway. With the assistance of the landscape architect Edward Milner, Pochin began laying out a "reposeful" garden with a terrace, grass banks and numerous trees, especially the conifers along the valley floor. A few years later he built the mausoleum and Laburnum Arch.

Henry Duncan, the second Lord Aberconway created the five huge terraces and introduced Chinese rhododendrons. He also subscribed to many plant-hunting expeditions, in particular that by Harold Comber in the 1920s, which resulted in the introduction to Britain of the spectacular Chilean fire bush.

In 1920 Frederick Puddle became the head gardener and was in due course succeeded by his son, Charles, in 1947, and then by his grandson, Martin, in 1982. Both the third Lord Aberconway, who now runs the estate, and his father, have won the Victoria Medal of Honour, the highest award of the RHS (and were both, at times, its president).

Accommodation/pub: Groes Inn, Tyn-y-Groes, near Conwy (tel: 01492 650545; ££).

Map: opposite

Cae Hir

A harmonious mixture of the cultivated and the wild. Map reference ❷

Cribyn, Lampeter, Ceredigion, SA48 7NG; tel: 01570 470839.
Opening times: Apr–Nov Tues–Sun (but open BHs) 1–6pm. National Garden Scheme day. Parties/coaches accepted. Viewing by appointment. House closed. Charity openings, call above number for details.
Admission prices: adults £2.50, children 50p, over-60s £2.
Facilities: parking, limited disabled access, plants for sale, refreshments. Picnics permitted. Dogs allowed on leads.

The 6-acre (2.5-hectare) garden at Cae Hir was created by the present owner, Wil Akkermans. His objective has been to find the right balance between the wild and the cultivated to achieve a truly natural look in keeping with the beautiful setting of this garden. Apart from the extensive informal herbaceous beds there are plenty of semi-hardy shrubs, such as Chilean fire bush and cordylines and good

ABOVE: a sea of irises.

ornamental trees, including prunus, sorbus and eucalyptus. Glorious rhododendrons set the garden ablaze in spring. Hedging, from a variety of species including yew, rose, beech and lonicera, frames the lawns which slope down to ponds and natural lakes.

Accommodation: Falcondale Mansion Hotel, Lampeter (tel: 01570 422910; £££); Black Lion, Lampeter (tel: 01570 422172; ££).
Local pubs: Blue Lion, Lampeter; Crown, Llwyndafydd.

Chirk Castle

A garden specialising in roses and distinctive topiary. National Trust. Map reference ❸

Chirk, Wrexham, Clwyd LL14 5AF; tel: 01691 777701.
< www.nationaltrust.org.uk >
***Opening times:** Apr–Oct Wed–Sun and BH Mons 11am–6pm (Oct–Nov till 5pm; last admission 1 hour before closing); castle noon–5pm (Oct–Nov till 4pm). Parties/coaches accepted. Viewing by appointment.*
***Admission prices:** castle & garden: adults £5.80, children £2.90, family £14.60, pre-booked parties of 15 + £4.80 pp; garden only: adults £3.80, children £1.80.*

ABOVE: castellated topiary at Chirk Castle.

Facilities: parking, disabled access. shop, plants for sale, refreshments. No picnics. Dogs allowed on leads in car park.

The views from Chirk Castle compensate for its exposed location. Belts of oaks provide protection as does the topiary, which shields beautifully planted borders and shrubberies. Masses of roses shelter in a sunken garden. Other trees, such as a weeping silver lime, purple-leaved beech, larch and cedar dot the lawns. There is a well-planted rock bank, a thatched hawk house, a shrub garden and banks of rhododendrons and azaleas among the magnolias, handkerchief tree, dogwoods and pieris.

History: Chirk Castle was built in 1310 as one in a string of defensive fortresses against the defeated Welsh. It is located on a natural strong point with the river on two sides and a view across some 14 counties. It was converted to a home that was lived in by the Myddleton family for generations since 1595. William Emes landscaped the park in 1764 and built a pavilion on the terrace. The castellated topiary, which takes two gardeners 2½ months to prune, was planted in the late 19th century.

Accommodation: Hand Hotel, Chirk (tel: 01691 773472; ££–£££). Local pub: Bridge Inn, Chirk; Bull Inn, Shocklach, east of Wrexham.

The Dingle

A plantsman's garden on a steep, sheltered site, plus an excellent nursery. Map reference ❹

Weslshpool, Powys, SY21 9JD; tel: 01938 555145; fax: 01938 555778.
< www.dinglenurseries.co.uk >
Opening times: *all year except Christmas week Wed–Mon 9am–5pm. Parties/coaches accepted. House closed.*
Admission prices: *adults £2, children free.*
Facilities: *parking, plants for sale, refreshments. No picnics. Limited disabled access. Dogs allowed on leads.*

This 4-acre (1.6-hectare) garden is on a south slope and planted for shape and colour throughout the year. There is a large lawn with shrubs, mixed herbaceous borders and one or two specimen trees. Beyond, there are more mixed borders, then a steep drop to a pool, criss-crossed with paths and planted with sun-loving shrubs such as cistus, lavender, elaeagnus, pittosporum, abutilon, hoheria and piptanthus. Trees include several cercidiphyllum, a wide selection of sorbus, catalpa (flowering and foliage), birches and tulip trees. There

are also magnolias and cornus and numerous Japanese maples. Foliage, especially evergreens, provide winter interest. The beds are attractively colour themed and coordinated.

Map: page 304

History: The garden was begun in about 1955 as a tidying project and then became an addiction. The soil is neutral, medium loam, but much mulched over the years. A pool was excavated so that the family's children could learn to swim, and was later incorporated into the garden and landscaped. The nursery, started in 1960, specialises in rare shrubs, trees and plants.

Accommodation: *The Royal Oak, Welshpool (tel: 01938 552217; ££–£££).* ***Local pub:*** *The Stumble Inn, Bwlch-y-Cibau.*

Dolwen

One of the finest natural gardens in the region with stream and ponds. Map reference ❺

Cefn Coch, Llanrhaedr-ym-Mochnant, Powys, SY10 0BU; tel/fax: 01691 780411.
Opening times: *May–Aug Fri and last Sun in month 2–4.30pm. Parties/coaches accepted. Viewing by appointment. House closed.*
Admission prices: *adults £2, child under 16 free.*
Facilities: *parking, limited disabled access, shop, plants for sale, refreshments, lunches by arrangement. Picnics permitted. Dogs allowed on leads.*

The character and design of this 4- acre (1.6-hectare) garden allows it to blend in perfectly with its natural surroundings of rolling hills. A fast-flowing stream tumbles through the garden beneath a series of imaginatively designed bridges, contrasting with the tranquillity of three large ponds, unconventionally set in the hillside. Irises, gunnera, lady's mantle, willows, acers and viburnums planted around the ponds add colour and structure, while

LEFT: Dingle, a plantsman's garden.

large granite boulders, unearthed during the creation of the ponds, are creatively used to provide unusual natural features.

In addition to cottage garden favourites, the planting includes a good number of rare and distinctive species, many collected abroad. The exotic *Arisaema griffithii* can be found by the web of paths and around the ponds. Seldom seen ornamental willows include the black willow, and among unusual oriental poppies are Patty's Plum, Cedric Morris, Helen Elizabeth and Beauty of Livermere. Acers, hebes and the tree peony thrive.

History: Dolwen garden lies in the beautiful Tanat valley in the shadow of Berwyn mountains at 800 ft (245

metres) above sea level. The potential of this old Welsh farmhouse and an adjacent alder copse was first realised by Frances Denby in the 1970s. Her ideas were brought to fruition with the assistance of David Cotterill over a period of some 20 years and today Dolwen is one of the finest natural gardens in Britain.

Above: natural profusion at Dolwen. ABOVE RIGHT: a Clematis jackmanii' runs riot at Erdigg.

Accommodation/pub: West Arms, Llanarmon Dyffryn Ceiriog (tel: 01691 600665; £££).

Erddig

A relatively unaltered example of a Dutch formal garden with fine fruit trees, including many 18th-century varieties. National Trust.
Map reference ❻

Wrexham, Clwyd, LL13 0YT; tel: 01978 355314. < www.nationaltrust.org.uk >
Opening times: garden: Sat–Wed (and Good Fri); Apr–Jun & Sep 11am–6pm; Jul–Aug 10am–6pm; Oct 11am–5pm; house: Mar–Sep noon–5pm; Oct noon–4pm (last admission 1hour before closing). National Garden Scheme day. Parties/coaches accepted. Viewing by appointment for garden tours (groups of 15 +).
Admission prices: house and garden: adults £6.60, children £3.30, family £16.50, parties of 15 + £5.30 pp; garden and outbuildings only: adults £3.40, children £1.70, family £8.50, parties of 15 + £2.70 pp.
Facilities: parking, disabled access, shop, plants for sale, refreshments. Picnics permitted. Dogs allowed on leads in car park and country park only.

garden in Victorian times. William Emes, who also worked at Chirk and Powis castles nearby, modelled the landscape on the naturalistic style in the late 18th century and built the unique circular weir, known as the Cup and Saucer. The National Trust took over the property in 1973.

Accommodation: Wynnstay Arms, Wrexham (tel: 01978 291010; £–££). ***Local pubs:*** *Pant-yr-Ochain, Gresford, north of Wrexham; Bull Inn, Shocklach.*

Hilton Court

A recently created garden, with lakes, ponds and woodlands, plus a nursery. Map reference ❼

Roch, Haverfordwest, Pembrokeshire, SA62 6AE; tel: 01437-710262.
Opening times: *Mar–Nov daily 10.30am–5pm. No parties/coaches.*
Admission prices: *adults £1, children 50p, over-60s £1, season £5 pp, family season £12.*
Facilities: *parking, refreshments in the garden centre. No disabled access.*

Erddig's neat pattern of paths, lawn, pleached limes, fruit trees, yews, hollies and lines of Portugal laurels is complemented by a wide canal lined with lilies on the east side of the hall. The fruit trees are particularly important, both for decoration and produce, and include many old varieties corresponding to a list of Erddig's wall fruits in 1718. Bulbs, especially daffodil varieties which date from the early 20th century, are planted beneath the fruit trees and in the borders. There are some wonderful specimen trees, including a swamp cypress and an avenue of wellingtonias that was planted in the middle of the 19th century.

History: Owned by the Yorke family since 1718, the garden represents one of the few relatively unaltered examples of a Dutch formal garden. A bird's-eye-view drawing of 1739 shows it very much as it is today, although the Yorkes had introduced embellishments such as fountains in the parterre and a small flower

This 9-acre (3.6-hectare) site contains a wonderful showcase for the owners' nursery, featuring beautifully landscaped woodlands, lawns, lakes and ponds.

The garden has a series of themed gardens, including the Cottage Garden, Japanese Garden and Seaside Garden. The carefully planted shrubberies and walks create a relaxing environment.

History: The site of Hilton Court was originally fields and woodland before being transformed by Cheryl and Peter Lynch, the owners, The garden

LEFT: striking a pose at Hilton Court.

itself is complemented by a first-class garden centre.

Accommodation: Erw-Lon Farm, Pontfaen, south-east of Fishguard; Poyerston Farm, Cosheston, Pembroke. Local pubs: Swan Inn, Little Haven; Cambrian Inn, Solva.

Pant-yr-Holiad

A collection of rhododendrons in natural woodland and a secret rose garden. Map reference ❽

Rhydlewis, Llandysul, Ceredigion SA44 5ST; tel: 01239 851493.
Opening times: two National Garden Scheme days in May 2–5pm. Viewing by appointment at other times for parties of 10 + . House closed.
Admission prices: adults £2.50, children £1.
Facilities: parking, shop, plants for sale, refreshments (teas). No picnics. Limited disabled access. No dogs.

A line of balsam poplars leads into Pant-yr-Holiad, a modern garden featuring massed hydrangeas and some interesting trees, including an unusual *Nothofagus antarctica*. However, the pride of the garden is its superb collection of rhododendrons, some collected from expeditions to China and elsewhere, and others hybrids, produced in this garden, and prefixed with the name Holiad. Scenic walks, a secret rose garden, a mill pond, a walled garden and a potager complete the picture.

History: From an earlier garden in his native Worcestershire, Geoff Taylor was a regular contributor to national gardening publications. In 1971, he and his wife gave up their scientific careers and moved to Pant-yr-Holiad, where they ran a dairy farm until retirement. In their spare time they began to create a garden, which now extends to 20 acres (8 hectares).

Accommodation: Hotel Penrallt, Aberporth (tel: 01239 810227; ££–£££). Local pubs: New Inn on Coast Road; Crown, Llwyndafydd.

Penrhyn Castle

A collection of rare and tender plants grown on the slopes beneath the castle. National Trust. Map reference ❾

Bangor, Gwynedd LL57 4HN; tel: 01248 353084; fax: 01248 371281.
< www.nationaltrust.org.uk >
Opening times: late Mar–Jun & Sep–Oct Nov Wed–Mon 11am–5pm, Jul & Aug 10am–5.30pm (last admission 4.30pm); castle: late Mar–Jun and Sep–Oct noon–5pm, Jul & Aug 11am–5pm (last audio tour 4pm). Parties/coaches accepted and may also view by appointment.
Admission prices: castle and garden:

ABOVE: Penrhyn Castle.

adults £6, children £3, family £15, pre-booked parties of 15+ £5 pp; garden and stable block exhibitions only: adults £4, children £2.
Facilities: parking, shop, plants for sale, refreshments. Picnics permitted. Disabled access. three-seater staff-driven buggy can be booked in advance. Dogs allowed on leads.

The extraordinary Penrhyn Castle, built on an heroic scale, acts as a backdrop to the large and varied collection of trees – Douglas firs, redwoods, pines, holm oaks and native varieties – and a large collection of rare and tender plants that can be grown here courtesy of the mild climate generated by the Gulf Stream.

In the walled garden, situated on the lower slopes below the castle, is an astonishing variety of tender species, such as lobster claw, pot jasmine, Lapageria and Decumaria, even the *Cordyline indivisa* and *Magnolia macrophylla*. At the foot of the slopes are architectural plants such as huge clumps of giant rhubarb, gunnera, ferns, flax and bamboo, standing in front of eucalyptus and purple maples.

History: The castle was built for G.H. Dawkins between 1822 and 1838. It was visited by Queen Victoria, who planted a (still surviving) Wellingtonia in 1859. Many choice trees were planted by Dawkins but when the Scottish forester and botanist Angus Duncan Webster took over the care of the woodlands in 1880 he experimented with numerous new and untested varieties.

The Victorian parterre, supervised by the head gardener, Walter Speed, one of the first recipients in 1897 of the RHS's Victoria Medal of Honour, was replaced in the 1930s by a more flamboyant composition, including a loggia and fountains .

Accommodation: *Country Bumpkin, Llandegai, Bangor (tel: 01248 370477; £).*
Local pubs: *Ye Olde Bulls Head, Beaumaris; Queen's Head, Glanwydden, southwest of Llandudno.*

Map:
page 304

Plas Newydd

A Repton-designed landscape supporting southern hemisphere plants and trees. National Trust. Map reference ⓾

Llanfairpwll, Anglesey, Gwynedd, LL61 6DQ; tel: 01248 714795; fax: 01248 713673. < www.nationaltrust.org.uk >
Opening times: *garden: Apr–Oct Sat–Wed (& Good Fri) 11am–5.30pm; house: noon–5pm; rhododendron garden: Apr–early Jun. Parties/coaches accepted and may also view by appointment. Connoisseurs and garden tours by arrangement.*
Admission prices: *house and garden: adults £4.60, children £2.30, family £11.50, pre-booked parties of 15+ £3.70 pp; garden only: adults £2.60, children £1.30.*
Facilities: *parking, disabled access (including minibus between car-park and house), shop, plants for sale, refreshments. Picnics permitted. No dogs.*

BELOW: deep colours at Plas Newydd.

Set in a spectacular position above the Menai Straits with Robert Stephenson's railway bridge on one side and the mountains of Snowdonia lining the southern horizon, Plas Newydd has a superb scenic backdrop. The garden enjoys a very mild climate due to the proximity of the Gulf Stream and therefore supports a wealth of plants and trees rarely found in the British Isles. To the west of the house, in the area known as the West Indies, lawns are bordered and broken by azaleas, hydrangeas, magnolia and scarlet embothrium, with hoherias and eucryphias flowering just after midsummer.

A dell, created from a small quarry, holds camellias, cherries, pieris and some rare trees. There is an arboretum known as Australasia containing fast-growing trees and shrubs from the southern hemisphere. In May, the rhododendron wood full of wild and exotic varieties, is well worth exploring.

History: The house was built in the late 18th century to a design by James Wyatt for Henry, Earl of Uxbridge, who engaged Humphry Repton to produce one of his famous "Red Books" containing his proposals; dated 1798–99, this book survives. Lord Uxbridge's son, the first Marquess of Anglesey, who commanded the cavalry at Waterloo, began an extensive programme of tree planting in the years following the victory and this was continued by the sixth Marquess in the 1920s and 1930s and by the present Marquess in the 1950s. He received lorry-loads of "thinnings" of rhododendron species from Bodnant as a wedding present in 1948 from the second Lord Aberconway. The National Trust has continued the programme of planting and embellishment.

Accommodation: Henllys Hall Hotel and Country Club (tel: 01248 810412; ££–£££). Local pubs: Ye Olde Bulls Head, Beaumaris; Ship Inn, Red Wharf Bay.

Plas Penhelig

Seven acres (2.8 hectares) of garden specialising in nectarines, peaches and mimosa. Map reference ⓫

Aberdyfi, Gwynedd LL35 0NA; tel: 01654 767676; fax: 01654 767783;
< www.plaspenhelig.co.uk >
Opening times: all year, daily dawn–dusk. Parties/coaches accepted (up to 40-seater). House (hotel) also open.
Admission prices: adults £2, children £1.
Facilities: parking, disabled access, refreshments. Picnics permitted. Dogs allowed on leads.

Seven acres (2.8 hectares) of garden surround Plas Penhelig hotel and the grounds are double that size. Set above the village and overlooking the estuary and Cardigan Bay, the gardens have a micro-climate which enables them to support good examples of exotic and unusual plants. There is a walled garden with greenhouses, containing peaches and nectarines. A large mimosa takes up a considerable area in one of the houses.

Flowers and herbs, together with fruit, are grown for use in the hotel kitchen and there is a wonderful collection of rhododendrons, azaleas and magnolias.

BELOW: camellias at Plas Penhelig.

Powis Castle displays some of the most stylish herbaceous planting in the British Isles. The site is marvellous, high above Welshpool, with views over the River Severn and the border countryside. The terraces, sheltered by high walls have astonishing topiary, especially the 14 enormous yew tumps which overflow down the walls to the terrace below.

Map: page 304

The garden is famous for its tender perennials, particularly a silver artemisia named Powis Castle, brought on in the glasshouses during winter and brought out in April. There is sophisticated thematic planting on the terraces. One terrace has plants from the Mediterranean, California and the southern hemisphere, another has tender scented rhododendrons and chain ferns, a third, luscious herbaceous planting. In the lower formal garden, old varieties of apple trees in pyramidical form stand out from the ground cover and are accompanied by roses, delphiniums, phlox, campanulas and hollyhocks. The walk winds past some lovely trees including a paperbark maple, a gingko biloba, an acer and rhododendrons.

History: The garden was laid out when the house was built in 1909.

Accommodation: Plas Penhelig Hotel (tel: 01654 767676; £££).

Powis Castle and Garden

An historic garden overhung with yew topiary, flamboyant herbaceous planting plus outstanding rhododendrons. National Trust. Map reference ⓬

Welshpool, Powys, SY21 8RF; tel: 01938 554338; fax: 01938 554336; < www.nationaltrust.org.uk >.
Opening times: *gardens: Apr–Jun & Sep –Oct Wed–Sun 11am–6pm, Jul–Aug Tues–Sun (and BH Mons) 11am–6pm; castle and museum (same days): 1–5pm. Parties/coaches accepted by written appointment only; coaches limited to four per day.*
Admission prices: *castle & garden: adults £8, children £4, family £20, parties £7 pp; garden: adults £5.50, children £2.75, family £13.75, parties £4 pp (no discounts Sun and BHs).*
Facilities: *parking, very limited disabled access due to terraces, shop, plants for sale, refreshments. Picnics permitted. No dogs.*

History: The castle was built in about 1200 as the medieval seat of the Welsh princes. It was badly damaged during the Civil War, necessitating reconstruction after the Restoration in 1660. In 1680 construction began on the terraces, probably to a design of William Winde but was not completed until 1703, under the direction of Adrian Duval. The yew tumps and the hedge at the northern end were planted in the 1720s. The castle was renovated in 1815–18 and again in 1902, when the garden benefited from the attentions of Violet, the wife of the fourth Earl of Powis, who determined to transform it into "one of the most beautiful, if not the most beautiful, in England and Wales."

Accommodation: The Dragon Hotel, Montgomery (tel: 01686 668359; ££). **Local pub:** *The Stumble Inn, Bwlch-y-cibau.*

ABOVE LEFT: the terraces of Powis Castle

Ireland

Gardens flourish in Ireland's mild, damp climate, which is influenced by the Gulf Stream. Exotics and frost-tender plants feature strongly, as do woody shrubs such as rhododendrons and azaleas, which thrive in the acid, peaty soil that predominates

Map:
page 320

NORTHERN IRELAND

Though Northern Ireland has fewer great gardens than the Republic, it includes two of the finest, Mount Stewart, considered to be one of the great gardens of Europe, and Rowallene, a top garden for rhododendrons. The other horticultural highlight is the National Arboretum at Castlewellan, set below the spectacular Mountains of Mourne and centring on a delightful walled garden.

Castlewellan and National Arboretum

Outstanding arboretum with walled garden. Map reference ❶

Castlewellan, Down, BT31 9BU, Northern Ireland; tel: 028 4377 8664; fax: 028 4377 1762. < www.forestserviceni. gov.uk/arboretum >
Opening times: *daily 9am–6pm.*
Admission prices: car £4, minibus £10, bus £25, motorcycle £2.
Facilities: *parking, refreshments.*

Located in the Castlewellan Forest Park, the arboretum extends to 100 acres (40 hectares). The core of the collection is in the original 12-acre (5-hectare) walled garden (known as the Annesley Garden) with its formal layout of intersecting paths and two fountains providing focal points.

Apart from the trees and underplantings of bulbs, interest is provided by herbaceous borders, topiary "bottles" of Irish Yew, and one of the largest displays of Tropaeolum in horticulture.

History: In the 1850s the area next to the 18th-century kitchen garden was transformed into a pleasure ground for the Annesley family. It included terracing, flights of steps and pools with stone dolphins supporting water basins.

Many exotics were planted, including 10 wellingtonias, monkey puzzle trees and rhododendrons. In the next decade the fourth Earl Annesley enlarged the area and built vineries and conservatories. When his brother Hugh succeeded in 1874 the pleasure ground was made into an arboretum of international importance.

In 1967 the Forestry Service of the Department of Agriculture purchased the estate from Gerald Annesley and opened it to the public in 1969.

Accommodation/pub: Slieve Croob Inn, Castlewellan (tel: 028 437 71412; £–££).

PRECEDING
PAGES: the
kitchen
garden at
Glenveagh.

LEFT: the
triton
fountain at
Powerscourt,
Wicklow.

Above:
Castlewellan
and National
Arboretum,
Northern
Ireland.

Mount Stewart House and Garden

One of the great gardens of Europe, with sunken parterres and a huge variety of plants. National Trust. Map reference ❷

Greyabbey, Newtonwards, BT22 2AD, Northern Ireland; tel: 028 42788387/487; fax: 028 42788569.

Opening times: formal garden: weekends in Mar & Oct–Dec 10am–4pm, Apr daily 11am–6pm, May–Sep 10am–8pm; lakeside gardens & walks: May–Sep daily 10am–8pm, Oct–Apr 10am–4pm. House: noon–6pm (mid-Mar–Apr & Oct weekends only; May & Sep Wed–Mon; Jun, Jul–Aug daily). Parties/coaches accepted.

Admission prices: house, gardens & Temple of the Winds: adults £4.95, children £2.35, family £10.15, parties £4.15 pp, £2.35 per child; gardens: adults £3.90, children £2.10, family £8.85, parties £3.65 pp, £2.10 per child.

Facilities: parking, disabled access, shop, plants for sale, refreshments. Picnics permitted. Dogs allowed on leads.

ABOVE: Mount Stewart House and Garden.

This is one of the great gardens of Europe. From the extravagantly planted Italian Garden near the house, where visitors begin their tour, to the 15 acres (6 hectares) of rhododendrons through which the return path leads, there is a vast variety of plants, shrubs and trees sheltered to the south by woods and benefiting from proximity to the Irish Sea and the Gulf Stream. Its designer in the 1920s, Edith, Marchioness of Londonderry, took advice from Sir John Ross of Rosstrevor, Co. Down and from Sir Herbert Maxwell of Montreith, Scotland, but she imbued the place with her own character and sense of humour, as illustrated by the sculptures in animal form on the Dodo Terrace, some of which were of politicians, members of her family and members of the armed forces.

Among the garden's highlights are a grand sunken Italian parterre, a Spanish parterre, a tiled garden house, a further sunken garden to the west of the house, based on a design sent to the marchioness by Gertrude Jekyll, a famous garden of Irish symbolism and the wooded walks, lawns and extraordinary burial ground with a statue of a white stag to bear souls up to heaven.

History: The third Marquess dug out the lake in the 1840s and planted around it but it was Lady Londonderry, in the 1920s, who began transforming this garden from "the darkest, dampest, saddest place" she had ever stayed in, to its present splendour.

Accommodation: Mervue, Greyabbey (tel: 028 4278 8619; £).

Rowallane Garden

A great plantsman's garden with numerous Himalayan specimens. National Trust. Map reference ❸

Saintfield, Ballynahinch, County Down, BT24 7LH, Northern Ireland; tel: 0289 751 0131; fax: 0289 751 1242. < www.nationaltrust.org.uk >
Opening times: *May–Sep daily 10am–8pm, Oct–Apr daily 10am–4pm. Parties/coaches accepted. House closed.*
Admission prices: *adults £3, children £1.25, family £7.*
Facilities: *parking, disabled access, refreshments. Picnics permitted. Dogs allowed on leads.*

The 52-acre (21-hectare) Rowallane Garden is famous for its collection of rhododendrons but it is also a plantsman's garden of great beauty and character. The modest farmhouse stands beside the lawns and the arboretum, containing the stone dais from which the Rev. Moore *(see below)* is believed to have addressed his parishioners. This is now the base of a bandstand, surrounded by many fine specimen trees planted by Moore. There are drifts of Himalayan poppies, hostas, astilbes, rodgersias and belts of giant Himalayan lilies, all of which thrive in the damp climate; and spectacular banks of rhododendrons and azaleas set against a background of woodland. The compact form of Viburnum plicatum Rowallane, grows in the centre of a paved area laid out in the form of a Celtic cross. In the outer walled garden stands a handkerchief tree and the original plant of the popular japonica Rowallane.

History: The garden was originally planted by the Rev. John Moore, who bought the property in 1860. His nephew, Hugh Armytage Moore, began his planting in 1903, in spite of being told that the land there was "not fit to graze a goat." Rather than level and plough the area, he made a feature of the dry-stone walls, rocks and spongy turf and his planting follows the undulating line of the country. The tradition has been maintained by his successors and the garden, being largely organic, is home to a profusion of wildlife.

Accommodation: The Hill, Saintfield (tel: 028 9751 1330; £). Local pubs: The Rowallane; The White Horse, Saintfield.

BELOW: summer visitors to Rowallane.

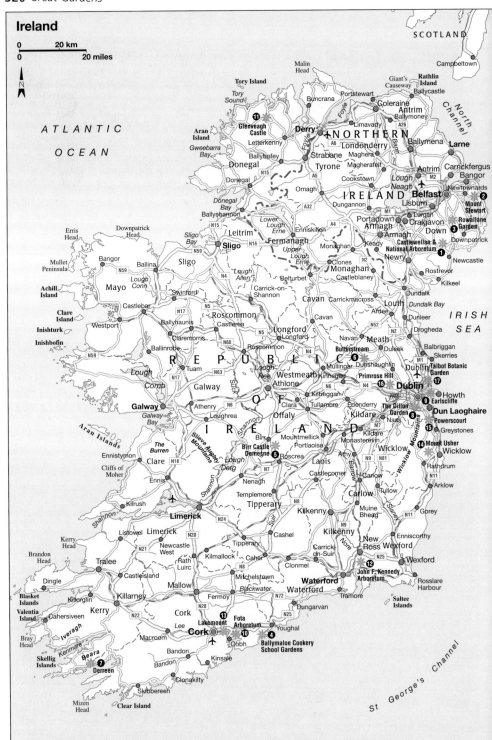

Ireland

REPUBLIC OF IRELAND

Some of Ireland's grandest gardens – Powerscourt, Glenveagh – belong to the great country estates that developed in the 18th and 19th centuries, but there are also innovative modern gardens, such as Ballymaloe, attached to the well-known cookery school; the Dillon Garden, a remarkable plantsman's garden in the heart of Dublin; and Butterstream, created by one man over the course of 20 years.

Map:
page 320

Ballymaloe Cookery School Gardens

A splendid potager, orchard and herb garden, plus a Celtic maze and a Shell House. Map reference ❹

Shanagarry, Co. Cork; tel: 21 646785; fax: 21 4646909;
< www.ballymaloe-cookery-school.ie >
***Opening times:** early Apr–Sep daily 10am–6pm. Parties/coaches accepted. House closed.*
***Admission prices:** adults, € 5; children 50 cents, over-65s € 3.*
***Facilities:** parking, shop. No picnics. No disabled access. No dogs.*

A mong the tall trees and beech hedges of an old garden a series of new organic gardens is being created at Ballymaloe on an ambitious scale by the renowned cook Darina Allen. Several of these are, appropriately, on a culinary theme. There is an elegant potager (vegetable garden) laid out on a strict geometric pattern and made colourful by many exotic vegetables. A formal fruit garden has apples, pears, plums, peaches, almonds, figs and cherries, many trained on arches, as well as soft fruit.

The herb garden is a delightful surprise, a great parterre of gravel and precisely shaped box-edged beds enclosing a fascinating array of culinary and medicinal plants. Beyond, a wide lawn with specimen trees and shrubs leads to a small lake. In the old orchard extensive herbaceous borders have been planted, leading up to the Shell House. A Celtic maze in yew has recently been planted.

History: There have been gardens here since the early 1800s when the house belonged to the Strangman family. However, after the death of Lydia Strangman in 1952, the gardens deteriorated. In the 1970s the Allen family moved in and took over a garden that had become a wilderness. Restoration work began in 1983 and the herbaceous borders were designed by Rachel Lamb in the early 1990s.

The fabulously decorated Shell House was designed by Best Kerr Wilson, and the fruit gardens, which are clothed in blossom in spring, by Jim Reynolds of Butterstream Garden *(see page 322).*

Accommodation: Ballymaloe House (tel: 21 4652531; €€€–€€€€). Local pubs: Spanish Point, Ballycotton; Rath Coursey House, East Ferry.

BELOW: inside the Shell House at Ballymaloe.

Birr Castle Demesne

Trees, shrubs and the tallest box hedges in the British Isles, plus two rivers and a walled garden. Map reference ❺

Birr, Co. Offaly; tel: 21 50920336; fax: 21 50921583.
< www.birrcastle.com >
***Opening times:** all year daily summer 9am–6pm, winter 10am–5pm. Parties/coaches accepted. Guided tours by arrangement. House closed.*
***Admission prices:** adults €7, children €3.50, over-65s €5.*
***Facilities:** parking, disabled access, shop, plants for sale, refreshments. Picnics permitted. Dogs allowed on leads.*

With over 125 acres (50 hectares) of gardens and grounds, Birr Castle Demesne has a huge collection of trees and shrubs. It has a walled garden with a tunnel running through the centre, a fernery, and the tallest box hedges in the British Isles, at over 40 ft (12 metres) high and over 200 years old. The Gothicised castle (closed to visitors) presides over the

ABOVE: Birr Castle Demesne.

RIGHT: the carefully coordinated beds at Butterstream.

demense, which includes two rivers, the Camcor and the Little Brosna, the former crossed by an extraordinary suspension bridge. There has been much recent restoration of key elements of the garden by the Great Gardens of Ireland Restoration programme.

In addition to its grounds, the castle is famous for a huge telescope, "Leviathan", once the largest in the world, which is now restored and operating throughout the day. It testifies to the range of interests of the owner's ancestors.

History: Many of the plants here were grown from original seeds collected on expeditions to Asia and the Americas before World War II, while others were collected from the wild by the parents of the present owner, the Earl of Rosse.

***Accommodation:** Spinner's Town House, Birr (tel: 509 21673; €).*

Butterstream

A plantsman's garden with streams, temple, follies, pools and canals. Renowned for its superb use of colour. Map reference ❻

Trim, Co. Meath, Republic of Ireland; tel: 46 36017; fax: 46 31702.
***Opening times**: May–Sep daily 11am–6pm. Parties/coaches may also view by appointment. House closed.*

Admission prices: adults, €6, children €3.
Facilities: limited disabled access, refreshment, plants for sale.

Butterstream has been described as the most imaginative garden in Ireland. It consists of a series of carefully designed rooms in which hedges of yew, beech and thorn frame the different areas. Beautifully co-ordinated planting schemes integrated with architectural features or garden ornaments ensure visitors a constantly satisfying and surprising progression through the garden.

This is also a plantsman's garden with

Derreen

Tree ferns and rhododendrons in a garden with a subtropical feel.
Map reference **❼**

Lauragh, Killarney, Co. Kerry; tel: 64 83588.
Opening times: *Apr–Oct daily 10am–6pm. Parties/coaches accepted. House closed.*
Admission prices: *adults €5; children €2.*
Facilities: *parking, refreshments. Picnics permitted. No disabled access. Dogs allowed on leads.*

Map: page 320

herbaceous borders in strictly controlled colour tones. Cool understatement is the key. Viewing between June and August is particularly recommended for the herbaceous borders and the old and shrub rose borders.

History: Butterstream is considered to be one of the finest gardens in Ireland. It has been created single-handedly by Jim Reynolds since 1970. What began as a single buttercup meadow now extends to 8 acres (3 hectares). Its development continues.

Accommodation: Wellington Court, Trim (tel: 46 31108; €€). Local pub: Brogans, High Street, Trim.

The most famous feature of Derreen is the large number of *Dicksonia antarctica* tree ferns from South Eastern Australia and Tasmania. They seem completely at home here and self-seed freely. *Myrtus luma*, from Chile, also self-seeds everywhere. There are huge Arboreum rhododendrons and *Cryptomeria japonica elegans*. The Boathouse Walk features superb camellias and acacias. Throughout the garden a rich patina of moss, lichens, ferns and saxifrages cover rocks, paths and tree trunks, giving a subtropical feel to Dereen.

History: The garden was first planted by

ABOVE: Derreen is surrounded by a magnificent mountain landscape.

Lord Lansdowne, the fifth Marquess, after he succeeded to the title in 1866. It was completed by his granddaughter, Lady Mersey, in the 1950s.

Accommodation: *Hawthorn House, Kenmare (tel: 64 41035; €); Park Hotel (tel: 64 41200; €€€€); Shelburne Lodge (tel: 64 41013; €€).*
Local pub: *O'Sullivans Bar, Kilmakillage.*

The Dillon Garden

This beautifully designed plantsman's garden is in the middle of Dublin and incorporates part of a canal. Map reference ❽

45 Sandford Road, Ranelagh, Dublin 6, Republic of Ireland; tel/fax: 1 4971308.
< www.dillongarden.com >
Opening times: *Mar, Jul–Aug daily 2–6pm; Apr, May, Jun and Sep Sun only 2–6pm. Parties/coaches accepted. Viewing by appointment. House also open to groups.*
Admission prices: *adults €5.*
Facilities: *partial disabled access, plants for sale, refreshments (teas) may be ordered for groups only. No parking. No picnics. No dogs.*

This is a plantsman's garden with strong design elements and many choice plants. Never static, it is forever being reworked to reflect changing tastes. Surrounding a Georgian Dublin house, it is remarkable for its canal, pools and spectacular borders. A series of secret rooms, a sunken terrace, an alpine house and a conservatory contain many rare species.

History: The garden was begun 30 years ago by Helen and Val Dillon who still own it today.

Accommodation: *Anglesea Town House, Ballsbridge, Dublin 4 (tel: 1 6683877; €€); The Hibernian, Ballsbridge, Dublin 4 (tel: 1 6687666; €€€–€€€€).*

Earlscliffe Garden Baily

An excellent collection of southern hemisphere woody plants. Map reference ❾

Baron's Brae, Ceanchor Road, Baily, Co. Dublin, Republic of Ireland; tel: 1 8322556; fax: 1 8323021.
< www.earlscliffe.com >
Opening times: *all year for groups/parties by appointment only. House closed.*

Below: a sphinx looks on in the Dillon Garden.

Map: page 320

Admission prices: *on application, as they vary with group size.*
Facilities: *Parking on roadside, coaches stop about 200 yds/metres from garden. No refreshments. No picnics. No disabled access. No dogs.*

Earlscliffe's pride is its fantastic collection of southern hemisphere plants. Tender plants, usually found in South America, South Africa, Asia and Australasia, thrive here. In just under 6 acres (2.5 hectares), one can find Cyathea and Dicksonia tree ferns, Protea, Banksia, banana, Schefflera and Juania, among others. The owner and designer David Robinson jokes, "Some Chilean and Argentinean plants, such as *Luma apiculata* and *Escallonia macrantha* are so much at home that they have acquired weed status."

Earlscliffe's position by the sea on a south-facing slope and the sheltering presence of the Hill of Howth to the north provide the garden with a unique micro-climate, and no artificial protection from the elements is necessary.

There are spectacular views, southwards to Dublin Bay and eastwards towards Baily Lighthouse.

History: The present owners bought the house and grounds in 1969 and began to develop the garden as a low maintenance project, favouring woody plants. The emphasis was laid on rare and frost-sensitive species after the unusual climatic properties of the garden were recognised.

Accommodation: Deer Park Hotel, Howth (tel: 1 8322624; €€). **Local pubs:** *The Abbey Tavern, Howth.*

Fota Arboretum

A fine collections of rare and tender trees and shrubs and numerous species of conifers. Map reference ❿

Dúchas, Fota Estate, Carrigtohill, Co. Cork, Republic of Ireland; tel/fax: 21 4812728.
Opening times: *all year except Christmas Day Apr–Oct Mon–Sat 9am–6pm, Sun 11am–6pm; Nov–Mar Mon–Sat 9am–5pm, Sun 11am–5pm.*
Parties/coaches accepted. Guided tours by prior arrangement. House open.
Admission prices: *free; charge for guided tours.*

Above: coastal views at Earlscliffe.

Facilities: parking, refreshments are provided independently by Fota House. Picnics permitted. No disabled access. Dogs allowed on leads.

Located in the sheltered harbour of Cork, Fota Arboretum and Gardens contain one of the finest collections of rare and tender trees and shrubs grown outdoors in Ireland or Britain. In addition, it contains many hardy specimens. James Hugh Smith-Barry laid out the arboretum with gen-

erous spacing to allow the trees to reach their full potential. An exceptional collection of 130 species of conifers from 26 genera contains some of the finest specimens of pine, cypress and sequoia to be found in Europe. There is also a good collection of broad-leaf trees including acers, nothofagus, ilex, eucalyptus, magnolia and acacia; and shrubs such as pieris, enkianthus, rhododendron, camellia, myrtus and viburnum which thrive in the mild climate.

The Victorian Fernery contains many fine specimens, especially the Tasmanian tree ferns planted in the late 1800s. The walled garden holds an exceptional rose collection and the walls display a large variety of climbers collected with the assistance of the National Botanic Gardens Glasnevin from

ABOVE:
Magnolia
Quinquepeta
at Fota
Arboretum.

the warm temperate regions of the world. The walled pleasure gardens near Fota House contain formal features such as yew hedges, sunken Italian gardens, a classical summer house, herbaceous borders and a rose garden.

About 150 metres/yards from the house is the fully restored 19th-century orangery, and beside it an exceptional specimen of the Canary Islands date palm.

History: Fota Island, about 7 miles (12 km) east of Cork City and 782 acres (316 hectares) in area was originally owned by the Smith-Barry family, the first records of whom date from soon after the Norman Conquest when Philip de Barri was granted lands in South Cork by Henry II. A manor was established at Barryscourt and the family seat became Barryscourt Castle, a 15th-century fortified house 2 miles (3km) from Fota.

The Smith-Barry family enlarged the hunting lodge on Fota Island in the early 19th century and Sir Richard Morrison, one of Ireland's foremost architects, transformed it into a splendid example of Regency architecture.

Accommodation: Anngrove Lodge, Carrigtwohill (tel: 021 488 3834; €).

Glenveagh Castle

**A great variety of rhododendrons and many herbaceous plants.
Map reference ⓫**

*Glenveagh National Park, Churchill, Letterkenny, Co. Donegal;
tel: 74 37088/37090; fax: 74 37072;
Opening times: mid-Mar–early Nov daily 10am–6.30pm. Parties/coaches accepted. House also open.
Admission prices: adults €2.75, children €1.25, over-60s €2, family €7, groups €2 pp.
Facilities: parking, disabled access, refreshments. Picnics permitted. Dogs allowed on leads.*

**Map:
page 320**

History: A hundred years ago the site of Glenveagh Gardens was a barren, boggy hillside, sloping down to the newly-built castle on the windswept shore of Lough Veagh. Much of the general layout of the gardens and some of the earlier plantings date from the early 19th century, but the transformation of Glenveagh into one of Ireland's foremost gardens is the work of the late Henry McIlhenny, who owned Glenveagh for over 40 years from 1937. His own artistic sense and knowledge of plants were augmented by the expert advice of Jim Russell and later Lanning Roper.

A tour of Glenveagh Gardens starts at the entrance to the Pleasure Grounds. The centrepiece is a long irregular lawn, the encircling herbaceous plants backed by colourful shrubs and trees. *Corokia cotoneaster* (wire netting bush) and *Cornus alba Elegantissima* (variegated dogwood) grow beside the stream.

Glenveagh, like a number of other Irish gardens with acid, peaty soils, is notable for its great variety of rhododendrons, both species and hybrids. The fine specimens of the large-leaved species *Rhododendron falconeri* and *Rhododendron sinogrande* were transplanted from the gardens at Mulroy House in about 1950. Beneath these *Rhododendron maddenii* is growing successfully.

Since most rhododendrons and magnolias flower in late spring or early summer great care has been taken to provide a range of plants that create interest through the season. The large palm-like leaves of *Dicksonia antarctica* (tree fern), *Trachycarpus fortunei* (chusan palm) as well as the apple-green leaves of *Trochodendron aralioides*, give striking examples of different foliage types.

Accommodation: Gleneany House, Letterkenny (tel: 00 353 074 26088); Castlegrove Country House Hotel, Letterkenny (tel: 74 51118).

John F. Kennedy Arboretum

The Arboretum has 4,500 types of trees and shrubs, an ericaceous garden and a lake with wildfowl. Dúchas (Heritage Service). Map reference ⑫

New Ross, Co. Wexford, Republic of Ireland; tel: 51 388171.
< www.heritageireland.ie >

ABOVE LEFT:
Dicksonia antarctica
(tree fern) at
Glenveagh.

BELOW: John
F. Kennedy
Arboretum.

Opening times: all year daily except Christmas Day and Good Friday; May–Aug 10am–8pm, Apr–Sep 10am–6.30pm, Oct–Mar 10am–5pm. Parties/coaches accepted. Booking advisable if guided tour required (at no extra charge). House open.
Admission prices: *adults, € 2.75, children €1.25, over-60s €2, family €7, season €28.*
Facilities: *parking, shop, refreshments. Picnics permitted. Disabled access. Dogs allowed on leads. Visitor centre with play area (7–14 years), maze, miniature railway on summer afternoon, nature trail and signposted walks.*

The John F. Kennedy Arboretum is over 620 acres (250 hectares) in extent and rises from 120 ft (36 metres) at its southern boundary to 888 ft (271 metres) at the summit of Slieve Coillte, the "Mountain of the Woods". Half of the total area is devoted to the plant collection, which contains over 4,500 types of trees and shrubs, planted in botanical sequence. Two hundred forest plots of different species, with a separate area allocated to each continent, spread across the higher slopes. The summit, accessible by road, provides panoramic views over six counties. Special features include an ericaceous garden, with 500 different rhododendrons, azaleas, and heathers, dwarf conifers, hedges, ground covers and climbing plants. The lake is is a haven for water fowl.

History: The arboretum was established in 1968 on the initiative of Irish-Americans who wished to create a living memorial to President Kennedy. The Irish government undertook to meet additional costs of establishment and maintenance.

Accommodation: *Creacon Lodge Hotel & Restaurant (tel: 51 421897; €€€; Brandon House Hotel (tel: 51 421703; €€€.* ***Local pubs:*** *The Horse & Hound, Ballinaboola.*

Lakemount

A modern yet mature garden with many southern hemisphere trees and plants. Map reference ⑬

Barnavara Hill, Glanmire, Co. Cork, Republic of Ireland; tel: 21 4821052.

BELOW: Lakemount.

Opening times: *Apr–Sep daily 2.30–5pm. Parties/coaches accepted. House closed.*
Admission prices: *adults €5.50.*
Facilities: *parking, disabled access, plants for sale, no refreshments. No picnics. No dogs.*

Overlooking the River Lee, the beautifully kept garden at Lakemount hosts a variety of plants that ensure interest at all times of year. Australian, South African, and South American plants flourish in the mild climate, among them resio, Dick Souces and tender rhododendrons. This modern Irish garden has contemporary pots and sculptures, as well as sloping lawns, a rock garden and a pond.

History: The garden at Lakemount was originally a chicken and fruit farm on 7 acres (2.8 hectares) of land. It was first planted in 1953, and designed by the owner, Brian Cross.

Accommodation: Vienna Woods, Glamine *(tel: 21 821146 €€–€€€).* **Local pubs:** *The Brook, Riverstown.*

Mount Usher

A sheltered valley garden with rare plants and shrubs, a grove of eucalyptus and a kiwi fruit vine.
Map reference ⑭

Map: page 320

Ashford, Co Wicklow, Republic of Ireland; tel: 404 40116/205; fax: 404 40205.
< www.mount-usher-gardens.com >
Opening times: *mid-Mar–Oct daily 10.30am–6pm. Parties/coaches accepted. Guided tours must be booked in advance. House closed.*
Admission prices: *adults €6, children €5, over-60s €5.*
Facilities: *parking, disabled access, shop, refreshments. Picnics permitted. No dogs.*

Mount Usher is a privately owned garden of some 20 acres (8 hectares), standing in the sheltered valley of the River Vartry as it flows down from the Devil's Glen. The house, around which the garden was created, was attached to a water mill, which used the power of the River Killiskey (a tributary of the Vartry) to turn its wheel. Spectacular *Pinus montezumae*, bluebells, rhododendrons and rare plants and shrubs thrive here thanks to the climate. Among the highlights are a grove of eucalyptus, a kiwi-fruit vine, a huge euchryphia and, among the many trees, the tallest *Cornus capitata* in the British Isles (60 ft/18 metres).

History: The garden dates back to around 1860 and the design was inspired by William Robinson. Five generations of the Walpole family were passionate garden lovers and the gardens were developed by members of each generation. They were fortunate in having the advice of several great horticulturalists, such as Sir Frederick Moore, Sir John Ross of Bladensburg, E. A. Bowles, Augustine Henry and others.

Accommodation: Grand Hotel, Wicklow *(tel: 404 67337; €€€€).*

ABOVE LEFT: the River Killiskey tumbles through Mount Usher's garden.

Powerscourt

A splendid woodland garden with record trees, plus a walled garden and a Japanese garden.
Map reference ⑮

Enniskerry, Co. Wicklow, Republic of Ireland; tel: 1 2046000; fax: 1 2046900.
< www.powerscourt.ie >
Opening times: *all year daily 9.30am–5.30pm (or dusk if earlier). Parties/coaches accepted by appointment. House open.*
Admission prices: *house & garden: adults €8, children €4; garden: adults €6, children €3; waterfall: adults €3.50, children €2.50; under-5s free; garden, house & waterfall: season ticket individual €70, family €120.*
Facilities: *parking, disabled access, shop, plants for sale, refreshments. Picnics permitted. Dogs allowed on leads in waterfall area only.*

ABOVE:
the Italianate
gardens of
Powerscourt
with the
Sugarloaf
in the
background.

Framed by the Wicklow Mountains and with formal tree plantations to the north, the extraordinary series of Italianate terraces on the south side of Powerscourt lead down to a lake and are flanked by a walled garden. On the other side, the Tower Valley, named after the Pepper Pot Tower, features many fine specimen conifers from North America in the surrounding woodland. The Dolphin Pond is bordered by a line of Japanese red cedars. The Japanese Garden leads visitors around its formal pattern on a series of concentric paths and over brightly painted bridges.

Some 3 miles (5 km) away, the highest waterfall in Ireland at 398 ft (121 metres) is set in a deer park with magnificent specimen trees and woodlands.

History: Based on a 13th-century castle, the house and grounds were remodelled under Sir Richard Wingfield in the 1730s. Further alterations were undertaken a century later by Daniel Robertson for the sixth Viscount Powerscourt. The seventh Viscount completed the work in the 1850s. The estate is now owned by the Slazenger family; the current design is by Richard Castle.

Accommodation: Powerscourt Arms Hotel (tel: 1 2828903; €€€); Summerhill House, Enniskerry (tel: 1 2867228; €€–€€€).

Primrose Hill

One of the best plantsman's gardens in Ireland, with an excellent snowdrop collection. Map reference ⑯

Fucan, Co Dublin, Republic of Ireland; tel: 1 6280373.
***Opening times:** Jun–Jul daily 2–6pm. Also for 1 week in Feb for snowdrops and other early bulbs. No parties/coaches. Viewing by appointment. House closed.*
***Admission prices:** adults €4, children €2.*
***Facilities:** parking, plants for sale, no refreshments. Picnics permitted. No disabled access. No dogs.*

A true plantsman's garden, Primrose Hill has been nurtured since 1950 by its owners. Surrounding a period house, it is reached through a beech avenue with an arboretum on one side, which, although only about 1 acre (0.4 hectares) in area, has a good collection of snowdrops, including its own variety. In summer, visitors can enjoy herbaceous borders in which irises, lilies and lobelias feature strongly.

Accommodation: Finnstown Country House, Lucan (tel: 00353 01 628 0644; €€); Lucan Spa Hotel, Lucan (tel: 00353 01 628 0495; €€–€€€).
***Local pubs:** O'Neills, Courtney.*

Map: page 320

Talbot Botanic Garden

A superb collection of southern hemisphere plants just outside Dublin. Map reference ⑰

Fingal County Council, Malahide Castle. Malahide, Co. Dublin, Republic of Ireland; tel: 1 8462456; fax: 1 8169910.
***Opening times:** May–Sep daily 2–5pm; guided tour of walled garden Wed 2pm. Parties/coaches must view by appointment. House open.*
***National Collection:** olearia.*
***Admission prices:** adults €3, children under-12 & over-60s free, groups €2.50 pp. Guided tour of walled garden €3.*

Talbot is devoted to tender and rare plants, with an emphasis on those from the Southern Hemisphere, olearia, hebe, escallonia, nothofagus, syringa, hypericum, clematis species, euphorbia, eryngium, hosta and *Crocosmia spp* thrive.

Accommodation: Belcamp Hutchinson, Malahide Road, Dublin (tel: 1 846 0843: €)

BELOW LEFT: Gallanthus (snowdrops) are a feature at Primrose Hill during February.

ABOVE: Talbot Botanic Garden.

Accommodation & Inns

We have included ideas on places to stay, as well as local pubs serving good food, at the end of each garden listed in this guide. In most cases these have been recommended by garden owners.

In the case of accommodation we have provided telephone numbers and price bands. The latter (based on a double room) are as follows:

UK: £ = under £60; ££ = £60–100; £££ = £100–150; ££££ = over £150.

Republic of Ireland: € = under €100; €€ = €100–150; €€€ = €150–225; €€€€ = over €225.

Additional ideas on accommodation (including descriptions, and information on rates and getting there) can be found on Insight Guides' website:
<www.insightguides.com/insight/hotelguides>

Admission Prices

Although admission charges are subject to change, we consider it worthwhile to give current charges (for adults, children and over-60s), as admission fees vary widely from 50p, or even free in some instances, up to £10 for somewhere such as the Eden Project. Up-to-the-minute information on admission charges can be checked on <www.gardens-guide.com>.

Membership of bodies such as the National Trust, the National Trust for Scotland, English Heritage and Duchas, the heritage organisation for the Republic of Ireland, permit free admission to gardens run by the organisation concerned. Members of the Royal Horticultural Society gain free access to its gardens. For details of these organisations see page 335)

Gardens Website

Insight Guide: Gardens of Great Britain and Ireland was put together in conjunction with the Armchair Travel Company. To confirm information that is subject to change, such as opening hours, admission fees and National Garden Scheme days, consult its website <www.gardens-guide.com>, which is constantly updated.

National Collections

In the early 1980s, in response to a decline in the variety of plants available in many of Britain's nurseries, the National Council for the Conservation of Plants and Gardens (NCCPG) was formed to preserve Britain and Ireland's great diversity of plants. One of its main aims was to set up National Collections of rare and endangered plants.

Based at the RHS's gardens at Wisley in Surrey the NCCPG liaises with the country's top botanical gardens and horticulturalists. But any gardener can become the holder of a National Collection providing they meet the extremely strict criteria laid down by the Council, which monitors the scheme rigorously. Collection holders are expected to care for, propagate, document and research their plant group, developing strategies to combat pests and disease and keeping back-ups.

National Collections held in any of the gardens listed in this guide are mentioned in the italic text at the start of each listing. However, many are held in gardens not open to the public or in nurseries or colleges. To find out where a National Collection is located you can contact the excellent website of the NCCPG,

National Garden Scheme Days

Many gardens included in this guide hold National Garden Scheme days in addition to their usual opening times. On these days the gardens open for charity. The Scheme includes numerous interesting gardens that are not normally open to the public, among them many small, private gardens that are considered to be of exceptional quality. Most of the gardens also offer teas and plant sales on these days.

In February the Scheme publishes its annual *Gardens of England and Wales Open for Charity*, also known as the *Yellow Book*, detailing, county by county, all the gardens, now numbering some

3,500, that will open during the coming year, giving dates and opening times. For further information or to obtain a copy of the book (also available from major booksellers), contact: **The National Gardens Scheme**, Hatchlands Park, East Clandon, Guildford, Surrey GU4 7RT, tel: 01483 211535; <www.ngs.org.uk>.

Scotland runs a similar scheme. For further information or to obtain a copy of their *Yellow Book*, listing around 350 gardens, contact: **Scotland's Garden Scheme**, 31 Rutland Square, Edinburgh, Scotland EH1 2BB, tel: 0131 229 1870; <www.ngs.org.uk>.

<*www.nccpg.com*>. It also lists plant groups still in need of a National Collection.

Opening Hours

Though a few gardens are open year-round, most are open only during their prime season, usually spring to autumn. Rather than state exact dates, which will vary from year to year depending on which day of the week they fall, we provide approximate dates (for example, mid-Mar–Oct). For precise dates at the beginning and end of the season, and also for the dates of special events such as snowdrop weeks, phone the garden in advance.

Special Events

RHS Flower Shows

The Royal Horticultural Society runs a number of highly recommended shows throughout the summer, including the famous Chelsea Flower Show and Hampton Court Palace Flower Show in London. It is essential to book tickets for these in advance. Members of the RHS are entitled to priority booking for such events.

As well as the flower shows listed here, look out for RHS road shows and special talks, demonstrations and garden tours. Contact the RHS (*see Useful Contacts, page 335)* for exact dates for upcoming shows and information on obtaining tickets.

May:

- The Spring Gardening Show, Malvern
- Chelsea Flower Show

July:

- Hampton Court Palace Flower Show
- RHS Flower Show at Tatton Park

September:

- Malvern Autumn Garden & Country Show
- Wisley Shows

Tourist Boards

British Tourist Authority

There are over 800 Tourist Information Centres (TICs) throughout Britain, which provide free information and advice to visitors on local sights, activities and accommodation. Most are open during office hours, which are extended to include weekends and evenings in high season or in areas where there is a high volume of visitors all year round. Some close between October and March. TICs are generally well-signposted.

For general information about the whole of the country, contact (by phone or fax only): **The English Tourist Board/British Tourist Authority**, Thames Tower, Black's Road, London W6 9EL. Tel: 020 8846 9000; Fax: 020 8563 0302; <*www.visitbritain.com*>.

Alternatively, the following are information offices for the different regions of Britain to which you can write or telephone for information. They are administrative offices only and cannot be visited in person.

East of England Tourist Board
Toppesfield Hall
Hadleigh
Suffolk IP7 5DN
Tel: 01473 822922
Fax: 01473 823063

Heart of England Tourist Board
Larkhill Road
Worcester WR5 2EZ
Tel: 01905 761100
Fax: 01905 763450

London Tourist Board and Convention Bureau
6th Floor, Glen House
Stag Place
London SW1E 5LT
Tel: 020 7932 2000

South East England Tourist Board
The Old Brew House
Warwick Park
Tunbridge Wells TN2 5TU
Tel: 01892 540766
Fax: 01892 511008

Southern Tourist Board
40 Chamberlayne Road
Eastleigh SO50 5JH
Tel: 02380 625400
Fax: 02380 620010

South West Tourism
Woodwater Road
Exeter EX2 5WT
Tel: 0870 4420830
Fax: 0870 4430840

Yorkshire Tourist Board
312 Tadcaster Road
York YO24 1GS
Tel: 01904 707961
Fax: 01904 701414

Northumbria Tourist Board
Aykley Heads
Durham DH1 5UX
Tel: 0191 375 3000
Fax: 0191 386 0899

North West Tourist Board
Swan House
Swan Meadow Road
Wigan Pier
Wigan WN3 5BB
Tel: 01942 821222
Fax: 01942 820002

Scottish Tourist Board
23 Ravelston Terrace
Edinburgh EH4 3EU
Tel: 0131 332 2433
Fax: 0131 343 1513.
<*www.holiday.scotland.net*>

Wales Tourist Board
Brunel House
2 Fitzalan Road
Cardiff CF2 1UY
Tel: 02920 499909
Fax: 02920 485031
<*www.tourism.wales.gov.uk*>

Bord Fáilte (Irish Tourist Board)
Baggot Street Bridge
Dublin 2
Tel: 602 4000
<*www.ireland.travel.ie*>

Tourist Boards in the US

British Tourist Authority
551 5th Avenue
45th Street, 7th Floor
New York
NY 10176
Tel: 212 986 2266
Toll free: 1-800 GO 2 Britain
<*www.travelbritain.org*>

Bord Fáilte
345 Park Street
New York
NY 10154, USA
Tel: 212 414 0800
Fax: 212 371 9052
<*www.irelandvacations.com*>

160 Bloor St, E., Suite 1150
Toronto
Ontario M4W
Canada
Tel: 416 929 2777

Tour Companies

A number of British tour companies either specialise in garden tours or include them in their programmes. They include:

Boxwood Tours
Rhiw
Llanbedr
Gwynned
LL45 2NT
Tel: 01341 241717
Fax: 01341 241712
<*www.boxwoodtours.co.uk*>

Compass Holidays
PO Box 463
Cheltenham
Gloucestershire
Tel: 01242 250642
Fax: 01242 529730
<*www.compass holidays.com*>

Destinations Europe
3 Orwell View Road
Shotley
Ipswich
Suffolk
1P9 1NW
Tel/fax: 01473 787160
<*www.europeangarden tours.com*>

Flora Garden Tours
23 Portugal Place
Cambridge
CB5 8AF
Tel: 01223 740444
Fax: 01223 337610

Omega Holidays
White Cross
Lancaster
LA1 4XQ
Tel: 01524 37500
Fax: 01524 843101
<*omega-holidays.com*>

Rowan Tree Ltd
24 Ballifeary Lane
Inverness
Scotland
IV3 5PH
Tel/fax: 01463 715225
Operates tours to Scottish gardens only.

English Heritage Grades

Gardens and parks of special historic interest are listed as worthy of preservation in the English Heritage Register of Parks and Gardens of Special Historic Interest. Inclusion on the register normally depends upon the historic rarity, quality or interest of a garden's layout or its special features.

Listed gardens are graded as follows:
Grade 1 gardens of exceptional interest.
Grade 2* particularly important gardens of more than special interest.
Grade 2 gardens of special interest, warranting every effort to preserve them.

Tour Operators in the US

Europe Vacations
944 Market Street
Suite 821
San Francisco
CA 94102
Tel: 800 498 3726
Fax: 414 837 0153

Lucas and Randall
225 30th Street
Suite 300
Sacremento
CA 95816
Tel: 916 414 4040
<*www.lucasandrandall.com*>

Useful Addresses

Many of Britain's great gardens are owned by the National Trust, the National Trust of Scotland or English Heritage (the National Trust alone runs over 200 gardens and parks open to the public). Their members are entitled to free admission to any of their properties.

Membership of the Royal Horticultural Society (RHS) allows free admission to around 90 of Britain's gardens, including their own gardens at Wisley, Rosemoor and Harlow Carr.

English Heritage
Membership Department
PO Box 569
Swindon SN2 2YP
Tel: 0870 333 1182
<*www.english-heritage.org.uk*>

National Trust
Head Office:
36 Queen Anne's Gate
London SW1H 9AS
Tel: (0870) 609 5380
Fax: 020 7222 5097
<*www.nationaltrust.org.uk*>

Membership Department:
PO Box 39
Bromley
Kent BR1 3XL
Tel: 0970 458 4000
Fax: 020 8466 6824
email:
enquiries@thenationaltrust.org.uk

National Trust for Scotland
Wemyss House
28 Charlotte Square
Edinburgh EH2 4ET
Tel: 0131 243 9300
Fax: 0131243 9301
<*www.nts.org.uk*>

National Trust Office for Wales
Trinity Square
Llandudno LL30 2DE
Tel: 01492 860123
Fax: 01492 860233

National Trust Office for Northern Ireland
Rowallene House
Saintfield
Ballynahinch
County Down
BT24 7LH
Tel: 028 9751 1072
Fax: 028 9751 1242

The Welsh Historic Gardens Trust
Ymddiriedolaeth Hanesyddol Cymru
Ty Leri
Talybont
Ceredigion
SY24 5ER
Tel/fax: 01970 832268

Duchas
The Heritage Service
Education and Visitor Service
51 St Stephens Green
Dublin 2
Republic of Ireland
Tel: 00 353 1 661 3111
<*www.duchas.ie*>

Royal Horticultural Society, RHS
80 Vincent Square
London SW1P 2PE
Tel: 020 7834 4333
e-mail: info@rhs.org.uk
<*www.rhs.org.uk*>

Other Specialist Societies

Association of Gardens Trusts
70 Cowcross Street
London EC1M 6EJ
Tel: 020 7251 2610
<*www.gardenstrusts.org.uk*>

The Garden History Society
70 Cowcross Street
London EC1M 6EJ
Tel: 020 7608 2409
<*www.gardenhistorysociety.org*>

National Council for the Conservation of Plants and Gardens
The Stable Courtyard
Wisley Garden
Woking
Surrey GU23 6QP
Tel: 01483 211465
<*www.nccpg.org.uk*>

The Historic Gardens Foundation
34 River Court
Upper Ground
London SE1 9PE
Tel: 020 7633 9165
e-mail:office@historicgardens.freeserve.co.uk

The Museum of Garden History
Lambeth Palace Road
London SE1 7LB
Tel: 020 7401-8865
e-mail: info@museumgardenhistory.org
<*www.museumgardenhistory.org*>

Further Reading

Guides

Insight Guides publishes several titles on the British Isles. Each one includes full coverage of the main attractions and places of interest, plus in-depth background essays, great maps and photography and a comprehensive listings section: *Insight Guide: Great Britain* (Apa Publications, 2003); *Insight Guide: Ireland* (Apa Publications, 2003); *Insight Guide: England* (Apa Publications, 2000); *Insight Guide: Scotland* (Apa Publications, 2003); and *Insight Guide Wales* (Apa Publications, 2002).

In addition to the country guides, there are city guides to London, Edinburgh, Glasgow and Dublin.

Gardens/gardening

The Royal Horticultural Society: A–Z Encyclopedia of Garden Plants. Editor-in-Chief Christopher Brickell. The standard bible for gardeners and plant lovers.
The Origin of Plants. Maggie Campbell-Culver. Engaging history of plants in the British Isles, ranging from the role of the Romans to modern hybridisation. Packed with fascinating digressions and lavish archive illustrations.
The Gardener's Year. Karel Capek. This entertaining and very personal diary of creating a garden in Prague was first published in 1929. It has been republished by the Modern Library Gardening Series, USA.
Botany for Gardeners. Brian Capon. An interesting practical guide to understanding plants and their requirements.
Beth Chatto's Woodland Garden. Beth Chatto. Study of how the author created a superb woodland garden out of an unpromising site in Essex.
Dear Friend & Gardener. Beth Chatto and Christopher Lloyd. Two-year correspondence between two of England's most respected gardeners. Plenty on gardens, and more besides.
The Garden: an English Love Affair. One Thousand Years of Gardening. Jane Fearnley-Whittingstall. A very readable history of English gardening, placing it in the context of social history and the other arts.
The Glory of the English Garden. Mary Keen, with photographs by Clay Perry. Rich history of garden design. Illustrated by large colour photographs and botanical paintings.

We Made a Garden. Margery Fish. Classic account (first published in 1956) of the author's creation of the cottage garden at East Lambrook Manor in Somerset.
The Story of Gardening. Penelope Hobhouse. A readable and entertaining history of gardening. Ranges from 3,000 BC to the 21st century. Beautifully illustrated.
Gertrude Jekyll on Gardening. Penelope Hobhouse.
Plants in Garden History. Penelope Hobhouse. Sumptuously illustrated history from ancient Egypt to the present day.
Garden Style. Penelope Hobhouse.
The Making of a Garden. Gertrude Jekyll and Cherry Lewis. Anthology of Jekyll's writings with photographs and drawings.
The Landscape of Man. Geoffrey Jellicoe. A look at man-made landscapes throughout world history, showing how they have been shaped by culture and religion as much as climate and environment.
The Virago Book of Women Gardeners. Edited by Deborah Kelloway. Anthology of articles written by women gardeners from the 18th century onwards. Plenty on Gertrude Jekyll and Vita Sackville-West but also scores of interesting observations by less familiar female gardeners.
English Cottage Gardens. Andrew Lawson and Jane Taylor. *Great English Gardens.* Andrew Lawson and Jane Taylor. Both sumptuously photographed by Andrew Lawson, who provided some of the best photographs in this guide.
Gardening at Sissinghurst. Tony Lord. Analysis of the design and planting of Vita Sackville-West's garden in Kent.
The Garden at Highgrove. HRH Prince Charles, Candida Lycett-Green, Andrew Lawson and Christopher Simon Sykes. The story of the creation of Prince Charles's famous garden in Gloucestershire related by the Prince and Candida Lycett-Green, a contributor to this guide.
Magical Paths – Labyrinths & Mazes in the 21st Century. Jeff Saward. Not just about gardens, this lavishly illustrated book studies the maze in relation to myth, philosophy and spirituality.
The Complete Landscape Designs and Gardens of Geoffrey Jellicoe. Michael Spens. Description of some 50 projects by Jellicoe, some realised, some not.

Glossary

allée a straight path between high hedges or strictly alligned trees, often leading to a focal point.

auricula theatre an open-sided tiered out-building on which auriculas (alpine primroses) are displayed in pots.

baroque style popular from the late 16th century. Characterised by heavy and elaborate ornament.

belvedere ornamental building occupying a viewpoint.

clair-voyée a gap in the enclosing wall or hedge that permits a view of the surrounding countryside.

Classical popular in the 18th century, this serene style of landscape garden looked back to the art and philosophy of ancient Greece and Rome. Typical features include temples, Palladian bridges, lakes and grottos.

cottage orné rural retreat. Often a fairly large building with rustic decorative features, such as scalloped gables.

cultivar cultivated variety.

ericaceous plant belonging to the Ericadae family, such as heathers, azaleas and rhododendrons.

espalier fruit trees trained to grow flat along a wall or trellis.

exedra a semi-circular hedge or other feature often enclosing a semi-circular seat.

fernery often dells planted with all manner of ferns. Particularly popular Victorian feature.

game larder out-building in which game was hung and kept cool.

gazebo a summerhouse, often situated so as to allow views of the rest of the garden.

Gothick 18th-century revival of Gothic architecture. Characterised by ornate pinnacles, decorative eaves, etc.

grotto an artificially created cave, sometimes encrusted with shells. Popular in the landscape gardens of the 18th-century.

ha-ha a sunken fence, often used for separating a garden from parkland, giving the impression of a seamless landscape.

hard landscaping modern term describing the paths, patios, walls, rocks, etc in a garden. Soft landscaping refers to the plants.

ice house an out-building of a great house, usually subterranean, in which ice was stored. Common in the 18th and 19th centuries.

knot garden elaborate, interlacing arrangement of low hedges (often box), usually separating small beds of flowers or herbs. Popular feature in Tudor and Elizabethan times.

loggia roofed gallery.

orangery building with large and elaborate windows, sometimes adjoining the house, in which potted orange trees are kept in winter.

parterre formal flower beds cut into a flat lawn.

patte d'oie ("goose's foot") three straight paths radiating from a single focal point.

Pele tower 14th-century defensive structure designed to withstand small sieges. Common in the Lake District where they were built to withstand the armies of Robert the Bruce.

pergola frame covered in climbing plants to form a walkway or arch.

picturesque late 18th-century–mid-19th century style of landscaping which tried to capture the wild beauty of nature. Often incorporating sham ruins. Exemplified by Scotney Castle in Kent.

pleaching the formation of a hedge by interlacing the branches of adjoining trees but leaving the trunks singular. Limes and hornbeams are commonly used.

potager a French-style vegetable garden which is decorative as well as formal.

Pulhamite synthetically manufactured stone often used for garden architecture and ornaments. Similar in appearance to terracotta.

quincunx a five-point pattern with one point at each corner of a square and the fifth in the middle.

rill a narrow artificially created watercourse sometimes stepped.

rococo highly decorative but graceful style popular in the mid-18th century.

stew pond pond stocked with fish for the table.

stumpery dell of exposed tree root stumps in which the crevices are planted with ferns and shade-loving plants.

wilderness an apparently uncultivated area, usually woodland, criss-crossed by paths.

Art & Photo Credits

Credits

Many of the pictures which are not credited below were supplied by the Garden owners and administrators and we would like to express our appreciation for their help with this project. We apologise in advance for any unintentional omissions.

Antiquarian Images 18, 26, 28
David Beatty back flap bottom, 119, 120, 251
Adrian Bloom 191
Ian Browne 157
Clive Boursnell/Garden Picture Library 56B, 236
C. Bowe 265
Penny Coatsworth Productions 118
Collections/Lawrence Englesberg 215T
Collections/Graeme Peacock 257
Collections/Robert Pilgrim 57T
Vera Collinswood 47
Country Life 235
Doug Corrance 58/59, 71, 274/275, 276, 279T, 284, 288, 293, 294C, 295, 296, 297, 298
Eric Crichton/Garden Picture Library 72
Mary Evans Picture Library 20, 21, 23, 24, 25, 27, 29
Glyn Genin back cover left & bottom, 1, 4/5, 46, 81, 125, 129B, 130, 132, 133T
Hilary Genin 37B
John Glover 86, 105B
John Glover/Garden Picture Library 105T, 195
Richard Greenly 103C
Tony Halliday spine, 129T, 242B, 260, 262
John Heseltine 173T
John Heseltine/Corbis 313
Jerry Harpur 6, 8BL, 56T, 78T, 78B, 79, 92, 96, 99, 131, 135, 138, 155C, 182, 183, 199, 201, 224T, 244/245 (designer Arabella Lennox-Boyd), 246, 250, 261, 266, 300/301, 302, 308B
Marcus Harpur 14/15, 30, 50B, 52, 75T, 112, 180/181, 190, 202, 328 (designer Brian Cross)

Jarrold Publishing 239
Neil Jinkerson/Jarrold Publishing 215B
Andrew Lawson 2, 3, 10/11, 12/13, 32/33 (designer Penelope Hobhouse), 34/35, 40, 41, 42, 44, 45, 50T, 51, 60 (designer Christopher Lloyd), 65, 75B, 83B, 85B, 87, 88, 90/91, 101T, 101B, 108, 122/123, 127T, 127B, 139, 140, 142/143. 144, 147T, 147B, 149, 156, 163, 165, 166, 168, 169, 170, 193, 206, 225, 228, 233, 241, 253B, 255 (designer Arabella Lennox-Boyd), 256, 282, 312, 331B
M. Lear 317
David Markson 69B
Tania Midgley/Corbis 174
National Trust Photographic Library 4B, 159, 160, 161B, 162, 164, 167, 216
National Trust Photo Library/Andrew Besley 148B, 150
National Trust Photo Library/Andrew Butler 229, 269
National Trust Photo Library/Neil Campbell-Sharp 171B
National Trust Photo Library/Eric Crichton 185
National Trust Photo Library/Dennis Davis 154
National Trust Photo Library/Rod J. Edwards 197
National Trust Photo Library/Fay Godwin 128
National Trust Photo Library/Jerry Harpur 151B, 234, 259
National Trust Photo Library/Andrea Jones 268T
National Trust Photo Library/Tony Kent 155B
National Trust Photo Library/Tymn Lintell 156
National Trust Photo Library/Marianne Majerus 194
National Trust Photo Library/Rob Matheson 74, 196
National Trust Photo Library/Nick Meers 39T, 177, 188, 189, 213, 217, 311
National Trust Photo Library/Geoff Morgan 212
National Trust Photo Library/Stephan Robson 77, 106, 114/115, 134, 145, 242T, 263, 306, 308/309, 310, 318
National Trust Photo Library/Stephen Rodgers 70

National Trust Photo Library/Ian Shaw 200, 238, 303
National Trust Photo Library/Robert Thrift 253T
National Trust Photo Library/Rupert Truman 226
National Trust for Scotland 287, 291, 299B
National Trust for Scotland/John Boak 277
National Trust for Scotland/Brian Chapple 281
National Trust for Scotland/David Robertson 286
National Trust for Scotland/Harvey Wood 294/295
Clive Nichols 176B
Richard Nowitz 316
Graeme Peacock/English Heritage 258
Dave Penman 97
Clay Perry/Garden Picture Library 37T, 49, 94, 95
Photos Horticultural 110, 220, 232, 237, 290
Gary Rodgers back flap top, 204/205, 218
Royal Horticultural Society/Lindley Library 17, 22
J.S. Sira/Garden Picture Library 55
Harry Smith Collection 64T, 158, 221T, 264, 322T
B.M. Taylor 48C
Brigitte Thomas/Garden Picture Library 66T
Bill Wassman back cover right, 36
Andy Williams Photo Library 107
Raymond Woodham 89, 109
Steven Wooster 9TR, 243, 314/315, 321. 326, 327T

Maps based upon OS data, Crown Copyright PU10003556

Map Production:
Mapping Ideas Ltd

©2003 Apa Publications GmbH & Co Verlag (Singapore branch)

Index

● Gardens reviewed are
shown in bold

A

Abbots Ripton Hall 183
Abbotsbury Subtropical Gardens
  93
acacias 171, 214, 247, 323, 326
acers 30, 88, 135, 148, 183, 286,
  307–8, 326, *see also* maples
aconites 43, 102, 153
Adam, Robert 113, 220
aeoniums 154
agapanthus 154, 167, 235, 260, 262
alchemilla 186
Aldby Park 262
alliums 125, 176
Alnwick Castle 257–8
aloes 25, 154
Amberden Hall 50
anemones 24, 43, 67, 84, 87, 97,
  102, 147, 153, 167, 188
  Japanese 27, 105
Anglesey Abbey 184–5
Antony House 145–7
Araucaria araucana (monkey puzzle tree) 153, 284, 317
arbutus 172
Arduaine Garden 277
arisaemas 285, 308
Arley Hall & Gardens 211–12
Arlington Court 159
artemisia 313
Arts & Crafts Movement 20, 109,
  125, 131, 132–3, 193, 210–11
Ascott 45
asters 25, 177, 195, 242
astilbes 99, 108, 136, 166, 237, 249,
  266, 319
Athelhampton House Gardens
  94–5
Audley End 18, 50–51
auriculas 186, 189, 217
  national collection 81
  azaras 171

B

Badminton House 19
**Ballymaloe Cookery School
  Gardens** 321
bamboos 41, 84, 114, 162, 231, 236,
  273
Banks, Sir Joseph 25, 41
Barnsley House 125
baroque style 264–5

Barrington Court Garden 171–2
Barry, Sir Charles 20, 273
Bateman's 77
Batsford Arboretum 122–3, 126–7
Belmont 61
Belsay Hall 258–9
Belton House 226–7
Beningbrough Hall 263
Benington Lordship 54
Benmore Botanic Garden 277–8
berberis 30, 177, 260
bergamot (Monarda) 67
Berkshire 43–4
Beth Chatto Garden 51–2
betulas (birches) 57, 88, 224, 281,
  305, 307
Biddulph Grange Garden 238–9
Bide-a-Wee-Cottage 259
Biggar Park 278–9
Birmingham Botanical Gardens
  207–8
**Birmingham University Botanic
  Garden** 210–11
Birr Castle Demesne 322
Blickling Hall 189–90
Bloom, Alan 141, 192
bluebells 113, 114, 117, 135, 198,
  215, 230, 252, 255, 286
Bodnant Garden 303–5
bonsai 85, 207
Borde Hill Garden 82
Bosvigo 147
Bourton House 127
Bowood House & Gardens 22, 113
brachyglottis 292
Bradenham Hall 180–81, 190
Bramdean House 101–2
Bramham Park 271
Branklyn Garden 279–81
Bressingham, The Dell Garden
  191–2
Bridgeman, Charles 19, 39, 41, 47,
  72, 188, 265, 284
Brighton, Royal Pavilion Gardens
  80–81
Brodick Castle 281–2
Brodsworth Hall 271–2
Brook Cottage 135–6
Broughton Castle 136–7
Broughton House 282–3
Brown, Capability 19, 40, 41, 42,
  43, 47, 51, 72, 81, 87, 113, 114,
  119, 179, 188, 200, 218, 258,
  262, 272–3
Buckinghamshire 21, 33, 45–9
Buckland Abbey 160
buddleias 108, 189
Burford House Gardens 222–3
Burrow Farm Gardens 160–61

Buscot Park 136, 137
Butterstream 322–3

C

Cae Hir 305–6
Caerhays Castle Garden 147–8
Calke Abbey 217
callistemons 154, 247
**Cambridge University Botanic
  Garden** 186–7
Cambridgeshire 183–8
camellias 76, 93, 103, 135, 145,
  148, 150, 153, 156, 158, 166,
  186, 197, 213, 287
  national collections 152, 273
Canons Ashby House 229
Cape fuchsia (phygelius) 98
Carnell 283
Carpinus (hornbeam) 110
cassiope 281
Castle Bromwich Hall Gardens
  208–10
Castle Drogo 161–2
Castle Howard 263–4
**Castle Kennedy & Lochinch
  Gardens** 284
**Castlewellan & National
  Arboretum** 317
catalpa 46, 128, 222, 307
Cawdor Castle 284–5
ceanothus 98, 189, 290
cedars 39, 44, 61, 74, 97, 153, 196,
  229, 230–31, 303
celmisias 153
ceratostigma 83
cercidiphyllum 307
cestrums 154, 159
Charney Well 247
Chartwell 61–3
Chatsworth 20, 204–5, 217–18
Chatto, Beth 51–2
Chelsea Physic Garden 16, 27, 29,
  37
Chenies Manor House 45–6
Cheshire 211–16
Chirk Castle 306
Chiswick House 39
Church Hill Cottage Gardens 63
Churchill, Sir Winston 61–3
Chyverton 148
cistus 37, 173, 307
Claremont Landscape Garden 72
clematis 65, 86, 89, 95, 108, 166,
  223, 243, 258
Clinton Lodge 78
Cliveden 46–7
Clumber Park 234–5
Cluny House 285–6

Codrington, John 69, 239
colchicum 74
Coleton Fishacre Garden 162–3
convallaria (lily-of-the-valley) 97,
199, 215
cordylines 217, 305, 311
cornus (dogwoods) 30, 65, 110, 168,
267, 306, 307, 327, 329
Cornwall 145–58
Corokia cotoneaster 327
Corsham Court 114
Corylus (hazels) 43, 110, 262
Cotehele 148–9
Cothay Manor 172
Coton Manor Gardens 230
cotoneaster 110
Cotswold school 124, 131
Cottesbrooke Hall 230–31
The Courts 114–15
Courtyard Farm 191
Cragside House 259–60
Cranborne Manor Gardens 95–6
Crarae Garden 286
crocosmias 77, 151, 331
crocuses 26, 66, 74, 84, 102, 289
Crossing House Garden 185–6
Croxteth Hall & Country Park
256
Cryptomeria 69, 323
Culpeper Garden 67, 68
Culpeper, Nicholas 29, 88
cultivar and hybrid 24
Culzean Castle & Country Park
287
Cumbria 247–53
Cydonia oblonga (tree quinces) 215

D

daboecia 74
daffodils 40, 57, 106, 212, 234, 237,
267, 278, 288, 289, 291
Dam Farm House 218–19
daphnes 74, 102, 154, 159
Dartington Hall 163–4
Davidia involucrata (pocket hand-
kerchief tree) 100, 222, 306, 319
Dawyck Botanic Garden 288
day lilies 136, 145, 173, 262
Decumaria 311
The Dell Garden, Bressingham
191–2
delphiniums 65, 129, 185, 241, 283,
292, 313
Denmans 82–3
Derbyshire 20, 217–22
Derreen 323–4
Devon 159–71
dianthus (pinks) 63, 67, 223, 292

digitalis 235, 282
The Dillon Garden 324
The Dingle 307
Dolwen 300–301, 302, 307–8
The Dorothy Clive Garden 239
Dorset 93–101
Douglas, David 27–28
Drimys winterii 260
Drummond Castle 288–9
Duncombe Park 264–5
Dunham Massey 254
Dunster Castle 172–3
Durham 253
Dyrham Park 128

E

Earlscliffe Garden, Baily 324–5
East Lambrook Manor Gardens
173–4
East Ruston Old Vicarage 192–3
Eastgrove Cottage Garden 223
echiums 67, 167, 214
Eden Project 142–3, 149
**Edinburgh, Royal Botanic
Gardens** 27, 29, 278, 281, 296,
298–9
Eggleston Hall Gardens 253
elaeagnus 307
elders 262
Elvaston Castle Country Park 219
embothriums 260, 284, 312
Emmetts Garden 64
English Landscape Movement
18–19, 39, 42, 97–8, 119, 194,
268–70, 272–3.
enkianthus 149, 326
epimedium national collection 74
Erddig 308–9
erythroniums 117, 147, 174
escallonias 154, 325, 331
Essex 18, 50–53
eucalyptus 286, 306, 326, 328
eucryphias 160, 212, 260, 286, 298,
328
Euston Hall 198
Evelyn, John 26, 197
Exbury Gardens 21, 103
Exeter University Gardens 170–71

F

Fairfield House 103–4
**Fairhaven Woodland & Water
Garden** 193
Farnborough Hall 241
Farrer, Reginald 28, 281
Felbrigg Hall 194
Felley Priory 235

Finlay, Ian Hamilton 295
firs 88, 219, 311
Fish, Margery 173–4
Forde Abbey 92, 96
Forrest, George 28, 99, 129, 158,
214, 252
Fortune, Robert 27, 239
Fota Arboretum 325–6
Fountains Abbey & Studley Royal
269–70
Fraxinus angustifolia Raywood 183
French gardens 18, 57, 152, 221,
251, 271
fritillaria 87, 115, 186, 278
fuchsias 67, 115, 154, 159, 188, 261,
262, 265, 291
Furzey Gardens 104

G

Gardens of the Rose 54–5
Gaulden Manor 174
gaultheria 174, 281
gentians 28, 84
Georgian gardens 47, 148, 158,
175–6
Gerard, John 24
Gibberd Garden 52
Gilbert White's House & Garden
104–5
ginkgo 114, 132, 313
Glen Chantry 52–3
Glenarn 289
Glendoick Gardens 290
Glendurgan Garden 150
Glenveagh Castle 314–15, 326–7
Gloucestershire 19, 125–35
Godinton House 64–5
Goodnestone Park 65
**Goodwood (Sculpture at
Goodwood)** 87
Great Comp 66
Great Dixter 60, 78–9
Greenbank Garden 274–5, 290–91
Greencombe 174–5
Gresgarth Hall 244–5, 255
grevilleas 25, 153
Greys Court 137–8
Grimsthorpe Castle 227–8
Gunby Hall 228
gunnera 52, 115, 117, 149, 159, 174,
231, 307

H

Haddon Hall 219–20
Hadspen Garden & Nursery 175
Halesia (snowdrop tree) 57, 225,
250

Ham House 39–40
Hamamelis (witch hazels) 110
Hamilton, Charles 74, 113
Hampshire 21, 101–12
Hampton Court Palace 36, 40
handkerchief tree (*Davidia involucrata*) 100, 222, 306, 319
Hare Hill Gardens 212
Harewood House 272–3
Harlow Carr (RHS Garden) 265–6
Harrogate, Valley Gardens 270
Hatfield House 55–6
Haughley Park 198–9
Hawksmoor, Nicholas 264
hazels (Corylus) 43, 110, 262
Heale Gardens 116–17
heathers 74, 76, 85, 104, 214, 259, 265, 294, 298, 328
Heathlands 105–6
hebes 93, 154, 173, 308, 331
hedychium 67
Heligan 150–51
hellebores 65, 83, 84, 141, 147, 165, 215, 235, 282
Helmingham Hall 182, 199–200
hemerocallis 145
herbalists 23–4, 29, 88, 177
Hereford & Worcester 222–5
Hergest Croft Gardens 224
Hertfordshire 54–7
Hestercombe Gardens 20, 175–6
Hever Castle 66–7
Hidcote Manor Garden 128–9
High Beeches 83–4
Highdown 84
Hillier Gardens & Arboretum 110–11
Hilton Court 309–10
Himalayan plants 84, 88, 99, 214, 239, 273, 279, 285, 289, 319
Hinton Ampner 106
Hobhouse, Penelope 21, 75, 175
Hodnet Hall 237–8
hoheria 169, 307
Holdenby House Gardens 231–2
Holehird 249
Holker Hall 246, 250
holly (ilex) 75, 168, 210, 212, 284, 326
hollyhocks 24, 313
Home Covert 117
honeysuckles (lonicera) 28, 89, 159, 186, 223, 258, 306
Hooker, Sir Joseph 25, 42, 239, 252, 289
hostas 63, 74, 96, 262, 266, 331
Houghall College Gardens 253
Houghton Hall 194–5

Houghton Lodge Garden & Hydroponicum 107
House of Pitmuies 291–2
Howick Hall 260–61
Hussey, Christopher 70, 177, 265
hybrid and cultivar 24
hydrangeas 76, 93, 111, 120, 155, 249
hydroponics 107
hypericums 88, 262, 331

I

Ickworth 200
Iford Manor 118
ilex (holly) 75, 168, 210, 212, 284, 326
Indian Bean tree 222
Ingram, Collingwood "Cherry" 129, 168
Inverewe Garden 292–3
Ireland 317–31
irises 42, 83, 166, 172

J

Jacobean gardens 55–6, 95
Japan, plant hunting 26–7, 126
japonica Rowallane 319
jasmines 128, 159, 311
Jekyll, Gertrude 20, 21, 57, 108–9, 137, 171–2, 175, 177, 281, 318
Jellicoe, Sir Geoffrey 23, 47, 75, 109, 231, 233
John F. Kennedy Arboretum 327–8
Johnston, Lawrence 129, 130, 172, 267
judas tree 111
junipers 84

K

Kailzie Gardens 293–4
kalmias 149
Kedleston Hall 220
Keen, Mary 113, 170
Kelmarsh Hall 232–3
Kennedy, John F. 327–8
Kent 61–71
Kent, William 18, 19, 39, 47, 72, 139, 197
Kew, Royal Botanic Gardens 21, 27, 28, 41–2, 88
Kiftsgate Court 129–30
Killerton 164–5
Kingdon Ward, Frank 28, 99, 156, 214, 252, 267, 289
Kingston Lacy 97

Kingston Maurwood Gardens 97–8
Knebworth House 56–7
Knightshayes Court 165
kniphofias 154, 237
Knoll Gardens & Nursery 98

L

laburnums 89, 121, 125, 195, 237, 303
Lady Farm 176
Lake District 247–53
Lakemount 328–9
Lancashire 255
Langley, Batty 19, 210
Lanhydrock 151
Lapageria 311
Latin plant names 24
lavender 39, 115, 212, 223, 240, 285, 307
Leeds Castle 67–8
Leicestershire 225–6
Leith Hall & Gardens 294–5
Lennox-Boyd, Arabella 45, 61, 203, 255
Leonardslee 84–5
leptospermums 25, 111
Levens Hall 250–51
lewisias 186
lichens 288, 323
Ligustrum (privets) 110
lilacs (Syringa) 84, 237, 255
lilies 25, 30, 95, 108, 112, 172, 173, 175, 254, 259, 285, 319, *see also* day lilies; water-lilies
lily-of-the-valley (convallaria) 97, 199, 215
Lincolnshire 226–8
Lindsay, Norah 109, 129, 190, 233
Linnaeus, Carl 24, 25
liquidambar (sweet gum) 76, 79, 88, 305
liriope 159
Lithocarpus 110
Little Sparta 295
Liverpool 256
Lloyd, Christopher 78–9
Lochinch Gardens, Castle Kennedy 284
Logan Botanic Garden 276, 295–6
London, George 87, 210, 227
London and Middlesex 37–43
Long Close 225
Longleat 118–19
Longstock Park Water Gardens 108
Loudon, John Claudius 19–20, 89, 208

lupins 67, 101
Lutyens, Sir Edwin 20, 56, 79, 162, 172, 175
Lyme Park 213
Lytes Cary Manor 177

M

magnolias 57, 66, 76, 93, 95, 103, 114, 130, 135, 148, 150, 151, 156, 167, 197, 198, 214, 264, 298, 311
mahonia 76
Manchester 254
Manderston 296–7
Mannington Hall 195–6
Manor House 108–9
maples 76, 77, 84, 111, 151, 224, 281, 305, 307, 313
Mapperton 98–9
Marwood Hill 166
Masson, Francis 25, 41–2
medicinal plants 29, 37
Melbourne Hall Gardens 220–21
Merseyside 256
Middlesex and London 37–43
Midgley, Kenneth 239
Millennium Seed Bank 88
Miller, Philip 25
Milton Lodge 177–8
mimosa 67, 162, 312
Minterne 99–100
Monarda (bergamot) 67
monkey puzzle tree 153, 284, 317
Monk's House 79
Montacute House 178–9
Morina longifolia 77
Morris, William 20
mosses 50, 171, 288, 323
Mottisfont Abbey 109–10
Mount Edgcumbe 152
Mount Ephraim Gardens 68
Mount Stewart House & Garden 318
Mount Usher 329
Muncaster Castle 251–2
Myddelton House Gardens 42
Myosotidium hortensia 153

N

narcissi 69, 102, 114, 193
Nash, John 80
National Collections
  alchemilla 186
  Anemone nemorosa 97
  arbutus 172
  asters 242
  astilbe 166, 249

azaras 171
bearded iris 42
betulas 88
bonsai 207
brachyglottis 292
buddleia 108
Calluna vulgaris (heather) 265
camellias 145, 152, 273
Carpinus (hornbeams) 110
cassiope 281
catalpa 46
ceanothus 98
Centaurea 259
Cistus 37
clematis 108, 166, 222
colchicum 74
conifers (dwarf) 76
convallaria 97
Cornus (dogwoods) 110, 168, 267
Corylus (hazels) 110
cotoneaster 110
crocosmias 151
crocuses 74
Cydonia oblonga (tree quinces) 215
daboecia 74
daphnes 74, 102
elders 262
epimedium 74
erica 74
erythronium 174
ferns 76, 174, 249, 265
fritillaria 186
fuchsia 265
gaultheria 174
geraniums (hardy) 173, 186
Ghent azaleas 81
grevilleas 153
Hamamelis (witch hazels) 110
hebes 93
hemerocallis 145
Hillier plants 110
holly (ilex) 75, 168
honeysuckle (shrubby) 186
hosta 74
hyacinths 269
hydrangeas 249
hypericums 88
Iris ensata 166
Japanese acers 135
Japanese anemones 105
Juglans (walnut trees) 188
Ligustrum (privets) 110
Lithocarpus 110
magnolias 75, 147, 273
mahonia 76
Monarda (bergamot) 67
nothofagus 88, 286
olearia 292

ourisisia 292
penstemons 97
pernettya 76
phormiums 247
Photinia 110
phygelius (cape fuchsia) 98
pieris 76
Pinus (pines) 110
porophyllum group 141
primulas (Asiatic) 285
pulmonaria 74
Quercus (oaks) 110
rhododendrons 76, 273, 281, 292
rhubarb 265
roses 55, 109–10, 211
salvias 97
saxifrages 141, 186
skimmias 88
snowdrops 74, 102
stewartias 83
Styracaceae 250
trilliums 111
tulbaghia 166
tulipa 186
vaccinium 174
willows 135, 214
National Museum of Gardening 157–8
Nesfield, William A. 20, 41, 190, 203, 216, 282
Ness Botanic Gardens 214
Nettlestead Place 68–9
Newby Hall & Gardens 266–7
Newstead Abbey 235–6
Nicolson, Harold 71, 172
Norfolk 189–97
North Cove Hall 201
Northamptonshire 229–34
Northumberland 257–62
Norton Priory Museum & Gardens 214–15
nothofagus 88, 286, 310, 326, 331
Nottinghamshire 234–6

O

oaks 110, 128, 134, 154, 188, 189, 196, 228
olearias 25, 292, 331
olives 37, 67
Orchards (Leicestershire) 226
orchids 84, 107, 186, 214, 268
osmanthus 86
ourisisia 292
Overbecks Museum & Gardens 167
Oxburgh Hall 196–7
Oxford Botanic Garden 18, 19
Oxfordshire 20, 21, 135–41

P

Packwood House 242
Page, Russell 21, 67, 68
Painshill Landscape Garden 73–4
Painswick Rococo Garden 130
palms 67, 155, 156, 167, 173, 193,
   217, 247, 296, 326, 327
Pant-yr-Holiad 310
Parcevall Hall Gardens 267
Parham House 86
Parkinson, John 24–5
Pashley Manor 79–80
passion-flowers 128, 292
paulownias 105, 225
Paxton, Joseph 20, 216, 218
pelargoniums 43, 67, 154, 291
Pencarrow 152–3
Penrhyn Castle 310–11
Penshurst Place 69
penstemons 97, 206, 213, 225
peonies 65, 84, 102, 114, 138, 195,
   221, 237, 308
pernettya 76
Peto, Harold 89, 116, 118, 136, 137
Pettifers 138
Petworth House 87
phormiums 154, 247
Photinia 110
phygelius (Cape fuchsia) 98
Picturesque style 258–9, 270
pieris 76, 100, 154, 214, 264, 306,
   326
Pine Lodge & Nursery 153–4
pines 44, 110, 128, 282
pinetums 61, 85, 113, 154, 158, 170,
   218, 219, 278
pinks (dianthus) 63, 67, 223, 292
Pitmedden Garden 297–8
pittosporum 25, 307
plane trees 110, 189
plant collecting 20, 24–29, 214
plant history 16–29
Plas Newydd 311–12
Plas Penhelig 312–13
Polesden Lacey 74
poppies 28, 153, 254, 278, 281, 285,
   290, 308, 319
porophyllum 141
Powerscourt 316, 330–31
Powis Castle & Garden 313
Pridheum 178–9
Primrose Hill 331
primroses 44, 114, 167, 193, 268,
   286
primulas 96, 102, 108, 117, 126,
   136, 149, 161, 166, 237, 266, 267
   Scotland 281, 282, 285, 289
Prior Park Landscape Garden 179

Proteas 25, 325
prunus 306
pulmonaria 29, 74, 165

Q–R

quinces 24, 215
quincunx 57, 105
redwoods 44, 57, 188, 278, 305, 311
Regency gardens 80–81
Renishaw Hall 221–2
Repton, Humphry 19, 113, 114, 119,
   132, 145, 188, 189, 194, 197,
   215, 265, 312
Rievaulx Terrace & Temples 268
Ripley Castle 268–9
Robinson, William 20, 202, 212,
   224, 260
rococo style 49, 130
Rode Hall 215–16
rodgersias 111, 117, 132, 319
Rodmarton Manor 131
Romans 17, 21
Roper, Lanning 49, 63, 69, 75, 104,
   133, 137, 183, 327
Rosemoor (RHS Garden) 168–9
roses 95, 103–4, 162, 195, 198,
   199–200, 220, 221–2, 236, 242,
   264
   bush and shrub roses 52, 56, 104,
   136, 211, 241, 258, 279, 291, 292
   climbing roses 89, 104, 108, 116,
   176, 199, 220, 230, 258, 272, 291
   Gardens of the Rose 54–5
   history of the rose 210–11
   national collections 55, 109–10,
   210–11
   old-fashioned roses 43, 78,
   109–10, 117, 121, 129, 138, 183,
   190, 195, 220, 221, 233, 235,
   264, 272, 291, 292, 326
Rothschild family 20, 45, 48–9, 103,
   252
Rousham House 19, 139
Rowallane Garden 319
Royal Botanic Gardens,
   Edinburgh 27, 29, 278, 281, 296,
   298–9
Royal Botanic Gardens, Kew 21,
   25, 26, 41–2, 88
Royal Horticultural Society 25, 27,
   74–5, 168–9, 265–6
Ruskin, John 20, 28, 252

S

Sackville-West, Vita 21, 71, 160
St Michael's Mount 154
St Paul's Walden Bury 57

Saling Hall 53
Saltram 169
salvias 66, 97
Savill Garden 21, 75–6
saxifrages 102, 141, 186, 323
Scotland 276–99
Scotney Castle 70
Sculpture at Goodwood 87
seeds 23, 88, 214, 252, 279, 321
Sezincote 19, 131–2
Sheffield Park Garden 81
Sheringham Park 197
Shropshire 237–8
Shrubland Park 201–2
Shugborough 19, 240
Sissinghurst Castle 70–71
Sizergh Castle 252–3
skimmias 88
The Skippet 139–40
Smit, Tim 149, 151
snowdrop tree (Halesia) 57, 225,
   250
snowdrops (galanthus) 54, 74, 102,
   130, 147, 185, 215, 288, 289,
   331, *see also* spring bulbs
Somerleyton Hall & Gardens
   202–3
Somerset 2o, 171–9
sorbus 178, 214, 286, 306, 307
Spinners 111
Staffordshire 19, 22, 238–40
Stancombe Park 133
Stansfield 140–41
stewartias 83
Sticky Wicket 100–101
Stone House Cottage Garden &
   Nursery 224–5
Stourhead 119–20
Stourton House Flower Garden
   120
Stowe Landscape Gardens 19, 47
Stroud, Horace 175
Studley Royal & Fountains Abbey
   269–70
Styracaceae 250
Suffolk 198–203
Sugrave Manor 233–4
Surrey 72–6
Sussex 77–89
Syon Park 42–3

T

Talbot Botanic Garden 331
Tapeley Park 170
Tatton Park 216
Taxodium distichum Nutans 153
taxonomy 24
Threave Garden 299

Thuja plicata 170
Tradescant family 18, 24–5, 55, 96
Trebah 144, 155
tree of heaven 149
Trelissick 155–6
Trengwainton Garden 156
Tresco Abbey Gardens 157
**Trevarno Estate & National
  Museum of Gardening** 157–8
Trewithen 158
trilliums 111, 165, 174, 281
Trochodendron aralioides 327
tulbaghia 166
tulip trees 44, 61, 65, 68, 70, 117,
  128, 134, 149
tulips 20, 42, 45, 80, 95, 186
tupelos 76
Turn End 47–8

U–V

Upton House 242–3
vaccinium 174, 281
Valley Gardens (Harrogate) 270
**Valley Gardens (Windsor Great
  Park)** 76

Vanbrugh, Sir John 47, 72, 264
Veitch family 27, 165, 171, 239
Verey, Rosemary 21, 125, 231–2
viburnums 115, 264, 307, 319, 326
violas 63, 223, 292
violets 117, 147, 174, 196

W

Waddesdon Manor 48–9
Wakehurst Place Garden 88
Wales 302–13
Wallington 261–2
walnut trees (Juglans) 68, 109, 114,
  115, 128, 188
Waltham Place 44
Wardian Case 26, 27
Warwickshire 241–3
Washington, George 234
water-lilies 56, 99, 108, 115, 141,
  201, 282, 292
Waterfield, Humphrey 138, 183
Waterperry Gardens 141
Wellingtonias 88, 196, 238, 309,
  311, 31.
Wentworth Castle 273

West Dean Gardens 89
West Green House Garden 112
West Wycombe Park 37, 49
Westbury Court Garden 134
Westonbirt Arboretum 135
White, Gilbert 104–5
willows 88, 135, 214, 307, 308
Wilton House 18, 121
Wiltshire 18, 20, 113–21
Wimpole Hall & Home Farm
  187–8
Windsor Great Park 21, 75–6
Wise, Henry 210, 227
Wisley (RHS Garden) 74–5
wisteria 61, 125, 138, 166, 223
Woodpeckers 243
Woolf, Virginia 79
Worcestershire 222–5
Wyatt, Lewis 189, 213, 216
Wyatville, Sir Jeffrey 226, 227

Y–Z

Yorkshire 262–75
yuccas 154, 169, 221, 262
zelkova 224